D1034800

Ambassador Dodd's Diary

1933-1938

Ambassador Dodd's

1933   *Diary*   1938

Edited by William E. Dodd, Jr, *1869–1940*
and Martha Dodd

WITH AN INTRODUCTION BY
Charles A. Beard

NEW YORK
HARCOURT, BRACE AND COMPANY

41-51521

327. D30943

COPYRIGHT, 1941, BY

HARCOURT, BRACE AND COMPANY, INC.

*All rights reserved, including
the right to reproduce this book
or portions thereof in any form.*

Third printing, March, 1941

~~3000~~

2100

PRINTED IN THE UNITED STATES OF AMERICA

BY QUINN & BODEN COMPANY, INC., RAHWAY, N. J.

To the Memory of Our Beloved Father,

Teacher and Friend,

Who Kept the Democratic Faith

in an Age of Betrayal

40700

BIOGRAPHICAL NOTES CONCERNING
THE PRINCIPAL PERSONS OF THE DI-
ARY WILL BE FOUND ON PAGE 448.

Retrospect and Recollection

Among all the diplomatic missions at the disposal of President Roosevelt in the spring of 1933 none had more immediate significance for the United States than the Embassy in Berlin. None presented more thorny problems of policy, conduct, negotiation, and spirit. Ever since the outburst of commercial rivalry between Germany and the United States in the closing years of the nineteenth century, the management of their diplomatic relations had been disturbed by frictions and disputes. The participation of America in the World War against Germany had accentuated ancient grudges. The economic crisis which broke in 1929 had disrupted efforts at reconstruction in German-American relationships, especially as German governments, banks, and corporations found it difficult, if not impossible, to meet the charges on the huge debts recently incurred in the United States. To all these stresses were added the strains due to the banking and industrial crash in both countries and the spectacular accession of Adolf Hitler to power in Berlin, with grave consequences, then dimly discernible, likely to flow from this "revolution of nihilism."

Although, after the lapse of seven years, it is impossible to recover the state of mind existing in 1933, certain facts stand out in the record and in memory. In January, Mr. Hitler had become Chancellor, the head of a government of concentration, in a nation divided and bewildered. For many months his fate was uncertain. Surrounded by powerful associates bent on curbing and using him, confronted by a bureaucracy trained in the old traditions and bitterly opposed to his progress and methods, the new Chancellor's fortunes were, at the moment, hidden from all vision, even his own. He might be subdued to a conservative reaction. He might become the complete master of Germany, using either the right or left wing of his party in the process. That he was a dangerous and ruthless personality was well known everywhere in the spring of 1933, but, as the veil could not be lifted on the future, several varieties of policy in relationship with his government were recognized as available in all diplomatic circles, including the Department of State in Washington.

In this confused and deteriorating situation, fraught with high tensions, President Roosevelt faced the necessity of choosing the American Ambassador to Germany. He could select a representative from among the rich men who had made heavy contributions to the Democratic campaign fund of 1932. But a selection from this class meant taking a financier, a rich lawyer, or a soldier of great fortune—a man little versed in the history of European politics and likely to use the Embassy as a debt collection or salvaging agency for American creditors, or in selling raw materials for German rearmament, while making lavish displays at dinners and entertainments.

A second class of potential candidates for the post embraced "career" men in the diplomatic and consular service of the United States—permanent civil servants more or less "trained" in the conduct of foreign relations. They were "correct" in matters of protocol—precedence, propriety, formalities, and traditions; yet they were not all mere bureaucrats. In fact, the careerists most "available" for the Embassy in Berlin were either rich themselves or had married fortunes; they were ambitious, or had ambitious wives. Only innocence regarded them as purely objective agents of the national interest.

If mighty contributors to campaign funds and career diplomats were to be passed over, President Roosevelt had another range of choice before him. Bearing in mind the difficulties of the mission, he was morally bound to select for the post an American citizen acquainted with the German language, with German history, literature, politics, policies, traditions, and life.

This meant choosing someone of scholarly attainments, for knowledge of German history, traditions, policies, and life could only be acquired by years of study and experience in Germany.

Here, too, President Roosevelt had precedents. George Bancroft, the historian, a doctor of philosophy from Göttingen, had served as American Minister in Berlin during the crisis of the Franco-Prussian War and the establishment of the German Empire. Andrew D. White, for a season a student in Germany, author of the *History of the Warfare of Science with Theology,* first President of the American Historical Association, had represented the United States in the Empire throughout the period of high tension over the Spanish-American War.

With these examples before him, amid the crisis at home and the dissolution in international relations, President Roosevelt, advised, it seems, by Daniel C. Roper, his Secretary of Commerce, chose another scholar to serve the United States in Germany—William E. Dodd, professor of history in the University of Chicago. Although Mr. Dodd had not been as active in politics as Bancroft or White, he was widely recognized, by those competent to pass upon such matters, as one of America's ablest historians, a writer and teacher of distinction. He had already been designated to serve as President of the American Historical Association in 1934. If his record as scholar was little appreciated by casual readers of the news announcing Mr. Dodd's appointment as Ambassador to Germany, the choice certainly indicated that President Roosevelt had decided to take a particular line in opening relations with the new German government.

The line, destined to prove hopeless, was an appeal to the best in old German culture. Mr. Dodd was eminently fitted to make that appeal and at the same time represent the best in the American democratic tradition. He was of old English stock, born in Clayton, North Carolina, in 1869, a graduate of the Virginia Polytechnic Institute, the holder of a doctor's degree from the University of Leipzig, won in 1900 by three years of hard work, crowned by a dissertation on Thomas Jefferson's return to politics in 1796 (*Jefferson's Rückkehr zur Politik*). After teaching for eight years in Randolph Macon College, he was called to the University of Chicago in 1908 and there dedicated himself to research, instruction, and writing in the field of American history, while retaining his early interest in European affairs.

Brought up in the Baptist Church, Mr. Dodd belonged to the wing of the Roger Williams tradition—separation of Church and State, religious liberty, and freedom of conscience. His bent in this direction was strengthened by his marriage in 1901 to Martha Johns, of Auburn, North Carolina, a woman of similar spirit, idealistic, buoyant, courteous, and intelligent. The love of freedom which he acquired in his youth and fortified by drawing upon the kindred sympathies and tenacious loyalties of his wife, Mr. Dodd continually refreshed by affectionate, yet critical, studies of the life and writings of Thomas Jefferson (after whom, incidentally, his wife's father was named). Thus by disposition and training he belonged to a specific school of American politics; but, as a scholar disciplined in historiography, he did not mistake his predilections for the whole of history. Nor did he imagine that the democratic dispensation had been closed by Thomas Jefferson, Andrew Jackson, Woodrow Wilson or Franklin D. Roosevelt. About all this he was singularly "objective," to employ a term of his guild.

That Mr. Dodd possessed a talent for viewing history, himself, and his work calmly and in perspective, I can myself testify out of an acquaintance with him extending over more than thirty years. It was one of our favorite pastimes at meetings here and there to descant on our respective "biases." When I twitted him mildly about his Jeffersonian leanings he replied by asking whether anyone brought up, like myself, in the Federalist-Whig-Republican school, could be competent to render an impartial judgment in the case. After he had spoken in a quizzical tone, with a dry ironical humor typically his, about the "plutocratic" affiliations of my ancestral party, he could take in good spirit a sardonic inquiry about the "slavocracy" that long ruled the Democracy of Jefferson. With preliminaries disposed of in this manner, Mr. Dodd could discourse out of wide knowledge and with an even temper, on the parties and interests which had divided the Republic since the days of Hamilton and Jefferson. Doubtless his tranquillity of mind in historical research was due in a large measure to his belief that democracy was in process, not finished, and had its greatest work yet ahead. His favorite saying in this respect was "Democracy has never really been tried."

Amid the diversity of his articles, essays, reviews, and works dealing with historical problems and personalities, embracing a wide range of historical interests, Mr. Dodd's greatest contribution to historical research was on the Old South. Selections from his major titles reveal this stress in his thought: *Life of Nathaniel Macon* (1905); *Life of Jefferson Davis* (1907); *Statesmen of the Old South* (1911); *Expansion and Conflict*, in the Riverside Series on American History (1915); *The Cotton Kingdom* (1919); and *The Old South*, the first volume of which (*Struggles for Democracy*), he completed amid the distractions and distresses of his labors in Berlin and published in 1937. His book on *Woodrow Wilson and His Work* (1920) and his co-operation with Ray Stannard Baker in editing *The Public Papers of Woodrow Wilson* (1924-1926), if they marked a deviation from the Southern interest, were nonetheless in the Southern tradition, now nationalized. That the crowning achievement of his life-long historical labors was to be *The Old South* (in four volumes), left unfinished at his death, is silent testimony to the enduring locus of his affections. This series he had designed as a monumental work of interpretation covering the economic, cultural, and political features of that social order.

During his long academic life even more of Mr. Dodd's energies went into teaching and advising students than into historical writing. In the art of instruction he was singularly effective. Unlike some of the masters in his guild he did not regard students as disturbing elements that interfered with his personal interests and projected works—intolerable, if necessary afflictions. On the contrary his time was generously bestowed upon the brilliant and the dull, it seemed, without reserve or thought of the sacrifice involved. He drew out and sought to amplify the native powers of his students, commanding their affections by the innate gentleness of his character while sharpening their minds by the ingenuity of his methods. He had the inimitable gift, in describing historical events, of making them seem like happenings of the day, full of life, vividness, and immediacy. Unending devotion to work was in his nature and neither determined pressure nor the years ever changed it.

Even so, while he was a great teacher, always remembered affectionately, he did not seek to make disciples, but rather craftsmen free to choose their own interests, work their own way, and criticize the offerings of the old masters. This attitude toward liberty was also deeply rooted in Mr. Dodd's nature. He was not and could not be a dogmatist of the chair, notwithstanding the firmness of his own cherished convictions. While he could be partisan amid the necessities of practice, Mr. Dodd was by nature a man of toleration, aware of human limitations and frailties, ready to grant much of this right to others. Unflinching in the integrity of his spirit, tireless in labors, he must have loved two lines from Goethe:

> *Das wenige verschwindet leicht dem Blicke,*
> *Der vorwärts sieht, wie viel noch übrig bleibt.**

In all personal relations, whether with colleagues, students, family, or high officials, Mr. Dodd was a democrat in the full American sense of the word. He was not born to purple; neither did he aspire to it or join the striving throng engaged in climbing toward it. In his scale, worth, not wealth, was the measure. Associations with riches and power left him entirely unchanged and unimpressed. Displays of conspicuous waste, the sport of the vulgar, offended his sense for the treasures of intelligence and useful living. Great concentrations of wealth, which marked his times, awakened in him fears for the safety of the Republic and led him to seek ways and means for a wider distribution of property—the true basis, as Daniel Webster had said long before, of popular government.

Far more democratic in sympathies and far more flexible in mind than Woodrow Wilson, Mr. Dodd nevertheless attached himself to the ideas and policies of that statesman. With the

---

* "The little that we have done seems as naught when we look forward and behold how much remains for us to do."

shrinking band of the faithful, he held fast to the view that democracy and peace might become a way of life for the world. In no other philosophy could he find a basis for great faith and high action.

Such, in an outline all too brief and fragmentary, was the life of the man whom President Roosevelt selected in the spring of 1933 to serve as the American Ambassador in Berlin during the early years of Adolf Hitler's regime. For pursuing the diplomatic line to be taken at the moment, for weal or woe, Mr. Dodd was peculiarly and adequately fitted by study, training, and temper. His loyalty to the humanistic traditions of American democracy was beyond all question. His esteem for the finest features of old Germany and the affectionate warmth he felt for her people were deeply established in his character.

Being a mortal man, Mr. Dodd might make mistakes, but they would not be the mistakes of appeasement for the sake of a mess of pottage in the form of temporary payments on defaulted debts. An Ambassador more concerned with "practical affairs" might have wrung from German financiers and the German government larger allotments of exchange for discharging obligations in the United States, for a time, although even that is doubtful; but Mr. Dodd's function was to strengthen and rally the moderate elements in German society then bewildered, no doubt, but not yet solidified and *gleichgeschaltet* under the iron regime of Chancellor Hitler and his party. The task may have been hopeless from the beginning. A knowledge of history, or anything else, does not permit an unequivocal verdict on this problem in politics and morals. In any case, William E. Dodd could speak to the leaders of German intellectual life and the doctors of philosophy in the German Foreign Office and the bureaucracy in a language and a spirit which they could understand, if they so desired, even at this late hour in their destiny.

Faithfulness to the record no doubt requires an admission of the fact that Mr. Dodd had critics, with reference to matters in general and in detail. By some members of the diplomatic set, both American and foreign, the simplicity in style of living which he chose, the directness and quiet candor of his speech, the ingrained democracy of his thought and action, the indignation of his spirit in fettered Germany, and his neglect of protocol rigidities were regarded as inappropriate to success in negotiations.

That Mr. Dodd did not prevent, by his steady counsels of moderation, the expansion of Chancellor Hitler's power may be conceded. That he did not put a stop to the persecution of the Jews, though his efforts in this direction were persistent, is self-evident. That he was unable to effect the collection of all debts due to American creditors is demonstrated by events. That he did not, despite his regular and repeated attempts, break the deadlock in German-American commerce and start up an era of relaxing prosperity is admitted. That he did not crash the diplomatic impasse in Europe, restore the concert of powers, and prevent the war which he early foresaw and forecast, requires no documentation. Nor did he satisfy certain Americans who sought his aid and official protection in the prosecution of various activities and interests in Germany which he thought not in keeping with American democratic tradition.

Could any diplomat, professional or otherwise, from the United States have accomplished, in the circumstances of Nazi Germany, desirable ends? For years, beginning long before the outbreak of the first World War, the negotiations of European governments had been conducted by career men, correct in protocol and fortified by expensive establishments. Was their diplomacy a success? The condition of Europe since 1914 offers a reply which seems unequivocal. Rich Americans were serving the United States in other capitals during Mr. Dodd's tenure in Berlin. Do their achievements indicate that they could have done better in his place? History also answers this question.

It is in such a perspective that Mr. Dodd's record and wisdom are vindicated. He saw more clearly than most of his colleagues, American and foreign, in the diplomatic corps, the hard drift of things toward the tragedy of the coming years. He repeatedly predicted, despite the epithets "alarmist" and "sensationalist" applied to him by unfriendly critics, the ruthless course which Germany, Italy, and Japan were destined to take, if unchecked by the concerted action of their neighbors. He divined the frightful crash bound to come from the policy of appeasement, intrigue, and vacillation, and he fought relentlessly, as far as he was able, to stop it. That Russia was to play a decided role in Western affairs, Mr. Dodd understood from the beginning of his mission. In all this, time has certified, in no uncertain terms, to the correctness of his judgment. Furthermore, amid the whirl of events beyond his control, Mr. Dodd awakened no false hopes of American aid in the conduct of power politics in the old style; he made no glittering promises to mislead the thoughtless and unwary.

Above all things, he was guiltless of that crime against Europe and the United States, too often committed by some other representatives of American foreign policy: he avoided loose and irresponsible conversations likely to encourage members of the Berlin diplomatic corps in taking fateful, perhaps ruinous, steps, on the easy assumption that the full military and economic power of the United States would be immediately forthcoming in any hour of trial and crisis. In that respect, too, Mr. Dodd served with fine devotion the great body of the American people whose interests he had at heart and thereby, we hope, the people of Europe, burdened by long history.

As a dossier of evidence bearing on policies, methods, and labors, Mr. Dodd has left this journal covering affairs from the beginning to the end of his mission. But it is more than that. To use a metaphor, it casts a flood of light into the dark passages of the time now past in which Adolf Hitler was solidifying and expanding his dominion in Germany, from July, 1933, to the close of 1937. Unlike many writers who have dealt with this historic crisis, Mr. Dodd was behind the scenes at Berlin, the strategic center of the National Socialist movement. He knew personally the leaders in that upheaval, spoke with them, and had an opportunity to form first-hand judgments of their personalities. He was in constant communication with representatives of the German government, with the agents of other governments in the diplomatic corps, with international leaders who came to Berlin, with American citizens, high and low, engaged in political, economic, and journalistic activities in Germany. As a participant in the scenes described, he had opportunities for analysis and interpretation not always granted even to investigators inside the circle of official and social intimacy.

In all these relations, Mr. Dodd was never a superficial observer caught in the clash of ambitions, animosities, rumors, and intrigues which have characterized diplomatic operations since the beginning of official intercourse among nations. He was a life-long student of great history, European and American, trained in the school of Lamprecht and Ranke to seek the truth of things as they actually had been. Ironical as this may seem, his acquaintance with German history was wider and more profound, by far, than that of the leading figures who were governing the country. This is not to say that Mr. Dodd's accuracy is to be unchallenged in every detail, or that the stress of instant decisions never warped his judgment.

Such infallibility is granted to no mortal. But the training and experience in historical study and writing which Mr. Dodd brought to bear upon his journal are clearly revealed in it and distinguish it from whole libraries of diplomatic memoirs compiled by professional gossips. They give the diary a quality which makes it peculiarly significant for an understanding of our own times.

Moreover, when the history of our troubled age is written, in distant years to come, this journal will be regarded as a priceless source of primary information and a vibrant human document illustrating American character in this period. Although numerous passages will doubtless be supplemented, perhaps modified, by evidence from other quarters, the permanence of this journal seems certain, amid the uncertainties of life.

Of William E. Dodd, scholar, teacher, writer, and servant of the Republic we may say, therefore, to paraphrase a maxim of Chateaubriand, "He will live in the memory of the world by what he has done for the world." And I can vouch for the statement that Mr. Dodd, indomitable foe of the meretricious, would not have it otherwise. Here the argument may rest, for beyond it none can rise.

CHARLES A. BEARD

New Milford, Connecticut
Autumn, 1940.

Ambassador Dodd's Diary

1933-1938

I

June 8, 1933 to October 11, 1933

June 8, 1933. Thursday. At 12 o'clock in my office at the University of Chicago, the phone rang. "This is Franklin Roosevelt; I want to know if you will render the government a distinct service. I want you to go to Germany as Ambassador."

I was greatly surprised, and replied I would like a little time to think it over. He said: "Two hours; can you decide in that time?" I said: Perhaps, but I must confer with the university authorities. I hope you will ascertain whether the German Government takes exception to my *Woodrow Wilson.*

He replied: "I am sure they will not. That book, your work as a liberal and as a scholar, and your study at a German university are the main reasons for my wishing to appoint you. It is a difficult post and you have cultural approaches that would help. I want an American liberal in Germany as a standing example." He closed by saying: "I will call the German Embassy and find out their attitude; you call me back at 2:00 o'clock."

I called my wife and gave her the story. I went to President Hutchins' office. He was out. I then went to see Dean Woodward, who was vice president of the university. He said he would call Hutchins, then at Lake Geneva, Wisconsin, I believe. He added, however, "You must accept even if the position is most difficult, and the university must find a substitute for this summer's and next winter's work." Roosevelt had said: "You may return in the winter of 1934, if the university insists."

3

I then went home to luncheon and talked things over. My wife and I decided to try the task; and at 2:30 I was connected with the White House. The Cabinet was in session. The President's secretary, whose name was not known to me, carried my affirmative answer to the President and he at once reported it to the Cabinet. A friend of mine, Daniel C. Roper, later reported that no member objected, that Harold Ickes of Chicago and Claude Swanson of Virginia were enthusiastic supporters.

The nomination was delayed until the German Ambassador in Washington, Dr. Hans Luther, ascertained the German attitude. The result was favorable and when the nomination went to the Senate on June 12, it passed without opposition. The German Ambassador gave out the story of my having taken my doctorate in Leipzig and published a book on Thomas Jefferson in German and added that I spoke German fluently. On June 13 there appeared a careful digest of my doctoral dissertation, "Jefferson's Return to Politics in 1796," in the Berlin newspapers.

From June 13 on, I was pestered every hour of the day by newspaper people and photographers. All kinds of stories and pictures, silly and otherwise, appeared in newspapers all over the country. I never dreamed of such publicity. My friends everywhere were enthusiastic, especially my former students, and at least 500, perhaps 700, letters and telegrams poured into our house or the university office.

June 16. Friday. I went to Washington at the request of the President. Roosevelt sat at his large desk and at one o'clock the servant brought two luncheons and placed them before us.

The talk turned at once to German affairs. He described the arrogant bearing of Dr. Hjalmar Schacht in May when he was threatening, as head of the German Reichsbank, to cease paying interest and principal on debts of more than one billion dollars due American creditors next August. The President said he had told Secretary Cordell Hull to receive Schacht, but to pretend to be deeply engaged in looking for certain papers, leaving Schacht standing and unobserved for three minutes, with Hull's secretary watching the German's nervous reactions. Then Hull was to discover a note from the President which indicated serious opposition to any such defaults of German debtors. He was to turn to Schacht and hand him the document and watch the changing color of the German's face as he, Hull, greeted him. This, the President said, was to take a little of the arrogance out of the German's bearing, and he added that the effect was even more marked, as reported from Hull, than had been expected. It was a repetition of Roosevelt's treatment when Schacht had visited him.

After this description of his method of bringing the great banker to terms, or at least reason, about debt affairs, he said about as follows: I know our bankers made exorbitant profits when in 1926 they loaned huge sums to German corporations and cities and they succeeded in selling bonds to thousands of our citizens with interest at 6 and 7 per cent. But our people are entitled to repayment, and while it is altogether beyond governmental responsibility, I want you to do all you can to prevent a moratorium. It would tend to retard recovery.

The next subject we discussed was the Jewish problem. The President said, "The German authorities are treating the Jews shamefully and the Jews in this country are greatly excited. But this is also not a governmental affair. We can do nothing except for American citizens who happen to be made victims. We must protect them, and whatever we can do to moderate the general persecution by unofficial and personal influence ought to be done."

I had telegraphed the President that I accepted the appointment with the understanding that there was to be no official complaint at my living in Berlin within my salary, $17,500. When I touched upon this problem, a subject of much discussion in Chicago, he promptly said: "You are quite right. Aside from two or three general dinners and entertainments, you need not indulge in any expensive social affairs. Try to give fair attention to Americans in Berlin and occasional dinners to Germans who are interested in American relations. I think you can manage to live within your income and not sacrifice any essential parts of the service."

The talk turned to trade concessions between the two countries and he added: "We ought to be able to make arrangements on certain items and thus increase German exports so as to aid them in their debt payments. But at present the drift in London at the Economic Conference is all toward economic nationalism. What do you think of that tendency with us?" I expressed the opinion that pyramiding of the economic structure in the United States would soon lead us into a new feudalism which would tend to make peasants and day laborers of farmers, and proletarians of all unorganized city workers. He agreed but added that: "If European states refuse to make tariff concessions, we shall make special arrangements with Canada and Latin America and develop a mutual trade policy which will give us markets for our surplus products."

We then talked a little of Colonel Edward M. House and the President's proposal for reduction of offensive armaments in France. "Limitation of armaments is necessary if the world is to avoid war. Norman Davis has been working on this. I can't be sure of his success. He cabled he wished to attend the London Economic Conference. I replied: 'Come home,' and he is coming soon. I wish you to talk with him before you sail."

I bade the President good-by at 2 o'clock and went to the State Department to study dispatches from Germany since the beginning of the Hitler regime. The same day I went to dinner at 8 o'clock with Ambassador Luther where about twenty people sat down to an elaborate dinner, after drinking fashionable cocktails, except for me. There was no good talk though we stayed until 12 o'clock.

June 17. Saturday. In the Department of State I met Professor Raymond Moley who asked me into his office. I talked and heard him talk for half an hour and concluded that he held entirely different views from the President about the American attitude towards the Jews in Germany; also he talked like an "Economic Nationalist" of the first order, entirely different from Roosevelt's view. Talking about tariffs, I found him practically ignorant of the workings of the Walker and Peel Laws of 1846 and of trade conditions which followed them. He was frank enough to say he never studied the subject—a professor of economics as well as economic adviser to the President! I told my friend Roper of this and we agreed that he, Moley, could not long hold his confidential relation with Roosevelt.

Later I went with my son William out to the little farm I own near the Blue Ridge mountains, in Virginia.

June 21. Wednesday. Back in Chicago. The members of the history and other faculties of the university gave my wife, my daughter Martha, and me a dinner at Judson Court, one of the new undergraduate dormitories. About 200 people were present, including Carl Sandburg, Harold McCormick, Mrs. Andrew MacLeish (whose husband, now deceased, endowed the chair I held in Chicago), President Robert M. Hutchins and others. It was a sad occasion because I felt badly, saying farewell to colleagues of twenty-five years' standing like A. C. McLaughlin and C. E. Merriam, foremost men in their fields. Home at 11, after shaking hands with most of those present.

June 23. Friday. A public dinner was given under the auspices of German-Americans, Democrats, Republicans and progressive groups in the so-called Gold Room of the Congress Hotel.

Charles E. Merriam closed the evening about 11:30. My good-by address was printed in part the next day in the daily papers. Carl Sandburg and his wife were again present and a few days later he sent me a poem on the distressful occasion, for he knew how much I dreaded to leave.

June 30. Friday. I spent from Tuesday to Friday afternoon in the State Department going over dispatches from Berlin up to June 15.

On Wednesday, my son William and I had dinner with Daniel C. Roper and his family. After dinner Mr. Roper and I drove to the railroad station to see President Roosevelt off for his vacation. It rained rather briskly but we went into the private car where Mr. Roosevelt asked me to sit down by him and advised me to sail on the *Washington* for Hamburg from New York on July 5. He particularly asked me to talk with

Norman Davis who was just then returning from Geneva to report on the Disarmament Conference.

July 1. Saturday. My wife and I took a sleeper for Raleigh, North Carolina, where we arrived early today. I drove to Fuquay Springs to visit my eighty-six-year-old father. Returning, I called on Governor Ehringhaus whom I had never met. Unaware of my work and identity, he suddenly, on a remark of mine about Germany and in the presence of newspaper men, said: "Are you Professor Dodd?" Whereupon there was a little stir and the newspeople at once made a story. The afternoon sheets showed how such an incident can be converted into a story.

In the afternoon I visited the family burying ground and saw some of the signs of the Civil War tragedy. A great-uncle killed in the Valley of Virginia campaign of 1862 was buried there as well as two others who surrendered with Lee at Appomattox later. My mother was buried there in 1909. It was a solemn visit, with signs of family misfortune.

I also visited my uncle Louis Creech, owner of the Creech lands on Neuse River where I was born, though the house has been torn down. It was a reminder of the earliest scenes of my life. The lay of the land was quite the same; the old hilltop where my grandfather's house and barn used to stand was marked by two or three half-dead oaks; and the old Horne burying ground was covered with trees about a foot in diameter.

A rather sorrowful day, though our kinsfolk did all they could to give us a pleasant sojourn.

July 3. Monday. We reached New York at about 9. I went at 10 to a conference at the National City Bank where State Department people had asked me to review the financial problems of German-American banks, involving payment of $1,-200,000,000 to American creditors who had been hoodwinked by bankers into making loans to German corporations. Vice president Floyd Blair presided over the gathering. About ten other bankers attended.

All were concerned about the so-called "standstill" agreement with the Reichsbank president, Schacht, whereby American obligations were being paid in cheap marks rather than no marks at all and American bondholders were in the doubtful position of having to sell their securities at thirty cents on the dollar. There was much talk but no agreement other than that I should do all I possibly could to prevent Germany's defaulting openly, as that would upset financial interests in the United States. The National City Bank and the Chase National Bank hold more than a hundred millions of German bonds! If they could be sure of 4 per cent interest, instead of the original 7 per cent, they would be satisfied.

Then came a prearranged conference with Judge Julian W. Mack, Felix Warburg, Judge Irving Lehman, N. Y. Court of Appeals, brother of Governor Lehman, Rabbi Stephen S. Wise and Max Kohler, who is writing a biography of the Seligman family of New York. This conference had been arranged by George Gordon Battle, a liberal lawyer.

For an hour and a half the discussion went on: The Germans are killing Jews all the time; they are being persecuted to the point where suicide is common (the Warburg family is reported to have had cases of this kind); and all Jewish property is being confiscated. These were the subjects, in brief, of the conversation, and I was urged, as a liberal and humane person, to press for governmental intervention. I insisted that the government could not intervene officially but assured the members of the conference that I would exert all possible personal influence against unjust treatment of German Jews and of course protest against maltreatment of American Jews. We adjourned at 10 o'clock and I took the train at 11 o'clock for Boston on a visit to Colonel House at Beverly Farms, thirty miles up the coast from the hub of the universe.

July 4. Tuesday. Colonel House's car met me as I walked out of the railway station. An hour later I had breakfast with him, and found him rather vigorous physically, though seventy-five years old, and mentally very alert. We talked two hours about my "difficult mission."

He frankly said: "I sent two nominations to the President, yours and Nicholas Murray Butler's, but I felt that you ought to be given precedence. However, the relations I had had with the Butler family led to my giving his case strong pressure in case yours was not preferred." I did not complain, because late in May, in Washington, when asked about my possible acceptance of a diplomatic appointment, I had declared positively that I did not wish to go to Berlin where the whole Hitler movement was most disagreeable to me and where I would be under constant pressure, too much for my temperament. Furthermore, I had said, in case any diplomatic position were offered, I would prefer Holland where I could write my history. This was stated to Daniel C. Roper and also to a close fellow-worker of his, Dr. Walter Splawn.

Hence, House in no way peeved me by his statement. Besides, Butler had peculiar claims, though I do not think he would have been a suitable man for any European place, except perhaps London. He is arbitrary and dictatorial and his expenditure of huge sums of money is not always justified by the results. Aside from House's story, I had heard from Roper that Butler's name had been urged upon Roosevelt. In addition, House said Newton Baker had declined the appointment to Berlin. So I was not over-egotistical with the Colonel.

As far as my task in Berlin was discussed he said: "You have the most difficult post in Europe and I think you have a better approach to the problem of the Germans than any man I know." That was based on my university contacts and he seemed to think a Wilson liberal would be welcome in Berlin in spite of the hatred of the War President. He said: "You should try to ameliorate Jewish sufferings. They are clearly wrong and even terrible; but the Jews should not be allowed to dominate economic or intellectual life in Berlin as they have done for a long time."

After discussing Roosevelt's Cabinet, the Recovery Act, and reading some interesting letters from eminent men, he called his chauffeur and we drove to Boston where I took the New York train at 12 o'clock. I was sure I had been wise in going to see him.

I was again in New York at 5 and my whole family were guests at the home of Charles R. Crane on Park Avenue. His apartment contained a marvelous display of Russian and Asiatic works of art. Mr. Crane endowed the chair Samuel Harper of the History Department at Chicago has held for the last seven or eight years: Russian History and Institutions. He has also given a million dollars to support the Institute of Current World Affairs with Walter Rogers as its manager—an organization which conducts surveys of conditions in all parts of the world and furnishes reports to the government. Crane is seventy-five years old, quite delicate in health, a traveler these last twenty years in all parts of the world.

He was quite enthusiastic about his work, still bitter against the Soviet revolutionists in Russia and enthusiastic about the Hitler regime in Germany. Jews are anathema to him and he hopes to see them put into their place. His advice to me was, of course: "Let Hitler have his way."

July 5. Wednesday. George Sylvester Viereck, author of the *Strangest Friendship in History* (Wilson and House), came to see me at 9 in the hotel. He talked about Germany and the debt problem. He impressed me as a curious sort of journalist with whom one would best not be too free.

The German Consul General in New York, Dr. Otto Kiep, a handsome Prussian type, came after Viereck, for a word about Germany. I then went out with my wife to buy a dictionary or two for family use.

The taxi took us to the wharf at 11 o'clock where we met Mrs. Roosevelt who had just bid her son, Franklin D., Jr., good-by for a trip to Europe on the *Washington.* A dozen newspaper men, whom I had eluded until that moment, crowded about us. I talked in general terms and gave no interview. Then they begged us for photos, to be taken on the front deck. My wife, son and I yielded reluctantly and, unaware of the similarity of the Hitler salute, then unknown to us, we raised our hands.

July 6. Thursday. I noticed Rabbi Wise on board as I walked the deck. At luncheon we became acquainted with Mrs. Breck-inridge Long, wife of Ambassador Long in Rome, a descendant of the famous Blair family of Kentucky, Washington and St.

Louis, and very conscious of the fact. Norman Davis, whom I had managed to see an hour in New York, had engaged for us a two-room apartment with a salon. The ship managers offered these rooms as suitable to ambassadorial dignity. We declined because we preferred simpler quarters and because there was not room for the two children.

July 13. Thursday. In the early afternoon the *Washington* anchored at Hamburg. The newspaper people tried in vain to get an interview, the representative of the Jewish *Hamburger Israelitisches Familienblatt* pressing the hardest. We did allow family photos by the ship's photographer. George Gordon, Counselor of the Embassy in Berlin, and the American Consul General in Hamburg met us as we left the boat. After some lingering in the city, we took our places on the Berlin train— an old-fashioned German train. Gordon talked an hour about the state of things in Germany and the personnel in the State Department.

In Berlin a protocol officer, some other officials of the government and the American Consul General, George S. Messersmith, met us. We were duly lodged at the Hotel Esplanade where I had wired: "Reserve us three bedrooms and a sitting room." We were put in the so-called "royal suite," six embarrassingly elegant rooms with beautiful furniture. But the price was 40 marks per day and one could not complain. We went into the dining room where we talked a little German and ate an excellent dinner. We were at the beginning of our task. The Germans seemed very friendly.

July 14. Friday. At the Embassy at 11 o'clock where I spoke briefly to the American correspondents about my mission, indicating in very general terms the idea of making contacts with the older cultural elements of Germany. There were questions about the President's Recovery Act and some hints as to possible difficulties. My replies were merely formal. At the end, Edgar A. Mowrer came up to shake hands and I remarked that I had read his *Germany Puts the Clock Back* with interest; but I did not comment on the fact that his book had been forbidden in Germany and that the government had demanded his resignation from the presidency of the Foreign Press Association in Berlin. Sigrid Schultz, who represents the *Chicago Tribune*, introduced herself, saying she had a letter from Colonel R. R. McCormick, owner of the *Tribune*, about Martha.

I next met representatives of the German press, about twenty people. I read them a brief statement in German which was printed the next day in all the leading German papers. It so happened I had just read the Minister of Economics Kurt Schmitt's careful statement about economic recovery, which appealed to me as most statesmanlike, and when questions were asked, I referred to his work as very similar to the Recovery program in the United States. When asked whether I had seen the statement of the *Familienblatt* of Hamburg to the effect that I had come to Germany to rectify the wrongs to the Jews, I read a brief disavowal which was likewise printed verbatim.

July 15. Saturday. I was presented today at the Foreign Office where I talked with Freiherr Konstantin von Neurath, the Minister for Foreign Affairs, and found him most agreeable. President Paul von Hindenburg, reported unwell, was at his estate near Neudeck in East Prussia and is not expected to appear in Berlin until September 1. The introduction to the Foreign Office was to enable me to act officially and to sign papers and reports for Washington. I rather preferred this to an immediate reception because the work in Berlin was of course new to me and the situation tense.

A Mr. Rowe, attorney for the Irving Trust Company of New York, called to ask, almost demand, my intervention with the German Reichsbank against possible or probable discrimination in repaying a $100,000,000 loan which the International Match Company had made to German business concerns. The Germans were proposing to discharge their obligations with something less than full payment to American creditors, who were being paid perhaps a third of the amounts borrowed.

I simply said: The government of the United States is in no way connected with these loans and all we can do here is to suggest unofficially to the authorities that it will injure German economic standing to violate Reichsbank agreements. He was very disgruntled, saying he would fly to London that afternoon. We had dinner with the Gordons, about twenty people present. Very dull.

July 17. Monday. Louis P. Lochner, of the Associated Press, called to pay his respects. He said that a friend of Chancellor Adolf Hitler wished Lochner to bring me to a quiet, secret luncheon where I might talk with the "Fuehrer," as everyone calls the dictator.

July 18. Tuesday. Lieutenant Colonel Jacob Wuest, Captain Hugh Rowan, Captain Chester Keppler and Commodore Howard Bode, all of the Army and Navy staffs, came to pay their respects, very correct in cutaways and top hats. At 5 Von Neurath and the protocol chief returned my official call and we discussed at some length the unsuccessful efforts of the German Government to relieve unemployment. Von Neurath said the various settlements of city people on the land had failed. He was about to leave for Bavaria to visit the Fuehrer. The rumor in the Embassy was that the Minister for Foreign Affairs would be removed.

July 22. Saturday. German Ambassador Hans Luther, who was supposed to be recalled from Washington, came in at 11 o'clock to say good-by. He informed me he was returning to Washington and wished visas for two guests who are planning to spend a year in America.

He talked at length about Hitler's recovery work; it could not succeed without free land; he thought the plains of East Africa or the highlands of Brazil ought to be opened to all German unemployed who are willing to emigrate (he thought there would be a considerable number), those who are restless and ambitious. Also he held the opinion that lower tariffs between Germany and the United States would aid recovery of industrial prosperity. He showed no belligerent spirit toward France and did not mention the Polish Corridor.

The William A. Nitzes, colleagues of mine in Chicago, asked us by letter particularly to meet their friends, Mrs. Henry

Wood and her family, in Potsdam. Mrs. Wood was the wife
of a famous professor at Johns Hopkins when the Nitzes lived
in Baltimore. Consequently we all drove out to Potsdam this
afternoon to call on the Wood family. They lived in a beautiful mansion. We arrived a little after 4. There was a tea.
Everybody stood up in good Hohenzollern style until they
were led into a large dining room, with tapestries on the walls.
About twenty people sat down. We had sandwiches and so
forth, and talked English and German all intermingled; a
number of representatives of old baronial families were present.
The conversation was good but not very clever or learned, and
the tone was quite Hitlerite.

July 24. Monday. Representative Sam McReynolds of Tennessee, a member of the American delegation to the Economic
Conference in London, led a party including George Messersmith, George A. Gordon and others of the Embassy staff to
the so-called Blücher Palace—an enormous, antiquated structure purchased by the State Department on the recommendation of a committee of Congress headed by Representative
Porter at a cost of $1,700,000. It was intended for a great offi-
cial and residential home of the diplomatic and consular services here, like that in Paris. My predecessor, Frederic M.
Sackett, Jr., supported by Senator Swanson, a year ago refused
an offer of the original owners to cancel the purchase contract
if they were allowed to receive the insurance money then pay-
able for damages due to a fire which caused a large part of the
roof to fall in. Although Sackett and Swanson were urged by
all the Embassy staff to give up the palace and save the government a vast sum of money, they insisted on completing the
deal.

It was this building that McReynolds and the rest of us now
visited with a view to a possible investigation by the next session
of Congress. We spent an hour going through the dilapidated
structure and concluded that the government would do well to
sell at $500,000, losing $1,200,000. This was the unanimous
vote of all concerned.

In the afternoon Mr. Messersmith asked me to his office

to talk with McReynolds, himself and Mr. Gordon. When I had been in the office a few minutes, Gordon called on the phone to say he could not attend. It was clear from what was said that he was indignant that Messersmith should have an official conference in his office. Later it was made plain by Gordon that he thought I had degraded myself by participating in discussion anywhere but in the Embassy office. He is an industrious career man with punctilio developed to the *n*th degree.

July 26. Wednesday. This morning Frederick Oechsner, United Press correspondent, revealed the usual intense feeling of most American newspaper folk toward the new German government. A little later two Chase National Bank officials called to discuss German financial contracts for paying American debts. They acknowledged the foolishness of loans in 1926 based on the Dawes plan expectations, billions loaned on doubtful security.

Edgar Mowrer called at 12 and asked me to a luncheon, quite private, at his house, where I met a young Von Moltke, grandson of the famous general, and Rosenstock, a Jewish professor in the University of Breslau, now in the German Foreign Office. Since they showed extraordinary understanding of history, I directed the conversation along scholarly lines rather than those of sharp governmental criticism, conscious of the danger of being quoted.

In the afternoon Professor Otto Hoetzsch of the University of Berlin, former member of the Reichstag and well-known internationalist, called. He talked of his visit to Williamstown in 1928 or 1929, of his visit to Mr. Hoover in the White House, and of his comparative satisfaction with the Hitler regime. So far nearly all university men seem to acquiesce in their own intimidation, but one sees that it is fear of unemployed status rather than a willing surrender.

One of the many social worker folk who can never see two sides of any problem came in to recount her experiences studying German "siedlungen" (settlements) for unemployed around industrial centers. She thought them almost ideal solutions of the unemployment problem.

July 28. Friday. Dr. Fritz Haber, perhaps the foremost chemist in Germany, brought a letter from Henry Morgenthau, Jr., of New York and told the saddest story of Jewish persecution I have yet heard. He is sixty-five years old, has serious heart trouble, and has been dismissed from his position without the pension to which he was entitled under the law prior to the Nazi regime. He wished to know the possibilities in America for emigrants with distinguished records here in science. I could only say that the law allowed none now, the quota being filled. I promised to write the Department of Labor to know if any favorable ruling might be made for such people. As he said good-by, he insisted that I be careful in mentioning his case, as consequences might be bad. Poor old man, thought I, though he is only one year older than myself. He was going to Spain to see if there was any possibility there. Such treatment can only bring evil to the government which practices such terrible cruelty.

July 31. Monday. I wrote a letter to Daniel C. Roper describing in some detail the characters of some of the men in the diplomatic service, their false notion of their real functions, the effects of several rich men here as ambassadors and the sharp rivalries of counselors and consul generals.

August 1. Tuesday. Joseph E. Ridder, son of the man of the same name who owned and edited the New York *Staatszeitung* during the Wilson era, called at 11. The *Staatszeitung* is now his property. He explained the difficult position of this paper in 1914 when German-Americans demanded it support the Hohenzollern policy while New Yorkers were swinging more and more toward the Allied side. In the end, the *Staatszeitung* gave its allegiance to Wilson and his administration. I asked him about George Sylvester Viereck and his connections with German propagandists. He said "the German Government gave Viereck $100,000 to push their cause," adding that the recipient did not really render Germany any important service. The Ridders do not fancy Viereck. They are now enthusiastic supporters of President Roosevelt.

Walter S. Rogers was the next visitor. His principal wish is to have the Embassy accept one of the Fellows of the Institute of Current World Affairs, of which he is the director, to study the strange emotional life of Germany and submit a report which is to be kept confidential in his New York office, a copy to be sent to the State Department for the information of government officials. I was too new in my position to make any promises, nor could I see how such a student could do more than a mere historian, for the German authorities will not think of giving free access to their documents, or even to their labor and other camps, to their political opponents. The newspapers tell nothing except by indirect suggestion. They are all under government control. I told him I would think the matter over and write him later.

August 2. Wednesday. In bed with a cold. But the Consul General came to report on another case: A young New York student in one of the German universities who had avowed himself a Communist had been arrested about July 1 and kept *incommunicado* in spite of all of the efforts of the Consul General. About July 24, Messersmith sent his assistant to visit him and ascertain the facts. The newspaper men had learned most of the facts and wished to feature the matter in the American press.

A little later in the day Edgar Mowrer and young H. R. Knickerbocker came to me and wished permission to publish the story in the *Chicago Daily News* and the *New York Post.* They did not tell me what I learned later, that they had already cabled the story to their papers. Nor did Messersmith tell me that he had given them permission.

The next day he was brought to Berlin for examination and it soon developed that he was guilty of the German charges and an indiscreet sort of fellow. He was released and hastened off secretly to New York. The facts now reported, the newspapers so much concerned declined to feature the story and he disappeared entirely from the scene. It was a characteristic incident.

August 3. Thursday. Mr. Gustav Oberlaender, founder of the Oberlaender Trust which sends a group of young scholars to Germany each year to study life and institutions, came to call. He said he was about to abandon his venture on the advice of his directors. The reason was the cruelties inflicted by the government on Jews. He asked my advice.

I said: Do not cease your work; it's a good time to study Germany; besides the Jewish troubles may not continue. He went out doubting still. He was on his way to see Adolf Hitler, and would then decide. He is one of the many wealthy Jews who were more German than the Germans during the World War and who gave huge sums to all kinds of undertakings. Now he is naturally embarrassed that his race is so ruthlessly treated. But, I feel, why not give the proceeds of millions of invested dollars to young Americans to study German life and institutions?

At 11:30 Karl von Wiegand, for twenty-five years Hearst correspondent in Germany and now with the whole of Europe for his terrain, called. I had received a letter from Colonel House about him. He impressed me most favorably. He is a rather close friend of the exiled Kaiser; he was also intimate with the leaders of the German Republic; later sympathetic with the Hitler group, he is quite well acquainted with Von Hindenburg. He told me that in April, 1918, when the Germans were so near Paris, and a little later when French workingmen, 400,000 strong, were on strike, he had a visa from the American Government and was authorized by Colonel House to go to Sweden, whence he was to go to Germany to prepare preliminary terms for a separate peace. He said Colonel House had cabled for permission and that House awaited events before authorizing his departure. The turn of the tide prevented Von Wiegand's mission. Clemenceau settled the strike and restored the morale of the French army.

No mention of anything like this has ever been made in any history of the war I have seen; nor is there reference to it in House's *Diary*. I doubt the accuracy of the story. But Von Wiegand impressed me as the sort of man well enough informed to consult on occasion.

August 5. Saturday. Professor R. G. Harrison of Yale University called. He seemed to be about seventy years old. He reported that a distinguished woman professor of Berlin University, who had been under strict United States Government surveillance at Yale during the war as a possible German spy, was in jail as a Jewess and dismissed from her position. Harrison thought so well of her that he asked whether I could intervene. As she was a German citizen I could make no move. He said there was a great conference of scientists (biological, I believe) to be held at Oxford in two weeks. This woman was the executive secretary and there would be world-wide criticism of Germany if she were detained. "Can you put me in contact with any German official so that I can lay the facts before him?" I sent him to Consul General Messersmith. That afternoon the Consul General introduced Harrison over the phone to the Secret Police Chief, Rolf Diels. Messersmith said: "It is not our affair. I simply wish you to know the circumstances and possible consequences." Diels said: "Tell the Herr Professor to come to dine tomorrow; we will see what can be done."

A stranger figure came at 11:30: Professor John F. Coar, according to "Who's Who" a distinguished professor of German Literature and Philosophy in Canada, but born seventy-two years before, of American parents, in Berlin. He is retired on a pension and lives near Boston. He is lame in one leg, dignified and agreeable.

He wished to speak in all confidence. He told me he had been a personal friend of Adolf Hitler and he had advised Hitler against the putsch in Bavaria in 1923. Hitler still granted him interviews and he wished to go to the Reichskanzler's summer place in Bavaria in a few days. He offered to bring back an accurate report on the Hitler conversation if I would give him a note to President Roosevelt to whom he wished to make a final report.

August 9. Wednesday. Professor Coar came again, saying he was going away on the 11th or 12th, Friday or Saturday, to visit Hitler. The chief Nazi Party adviser, Rudolf Hess, was taking him by airplane. He presented a brief letter to President Roosevelt which he wished me to read and then put into the next pouch to Washington. I agreed and he departed quite anxious about Germany's foreign policy and somewhat hopeful that he could influence the Chancellor. I told him the Jewish problem must be solved in a different way; that German exports would continue to fall if the ruthlessness were not abandoned; and that the belligerent tone of German conduct would almost certainly lead to international boycott. I concluded: The Nazis do not seem to me to know what are the natural consequences of ruthless procedure. Coar agreed entirely.

August 10. Thursday. David Levinson, Jewish lawyer from Philadelphia who looks definitely Jewish and who has played a role in civil liberties cases in the United States, came to call. He had power of attorney for the defense in the Reichstag fire case which is to be tried in Leipzig on September 21. He wished a letter to some German authority which he might use in his application for a place on the defense side of the trial. I could not give him the letter but suggested that he call on Louis P. Lochner, Associated Press correspondent.

August 11. Friday. The brother of a former German official came to talk over the problem of the Carnegie Foundation plan for a new chair in the University of Berlin and for better international understanding. He at once revealed anxiety for his own safety, talked of possible contacts with eminent German scholars who are not a little distressed over Nazi coercion of university life, and said that when the opportunity offers, these men will reveal themselves as champions of submerged cultural Germany. I was sorry indeed to see such an able and competent young scholar under such duress.

Winthrop W. Aldrich, President of the Chase National Bank, New York, came at 11:30 to express satisfaction with the German financial plan under which repudiation of German bonds sold to Americans would not be announced. He was not completely satisfied, but measurably so. He said: "How unfortunate for us were those loans!" But he was on his way to Hitler's quarters with Reichsbank president Schacht and the

Minister of Economics Schmitt. He would let me know what the Reichskanzler's policy was.

Late in the afternoon Messersmith and directors of the United States Lines came to report the foolish order of German-American lines, supported by the government, to the effect that nobody leaving Germany might buy tickets for any transportation costing more than 200 marks, *i.e.*, on any but German ships. This would compel all travelers to take ship on German lines. The order would promptly put American and British companies out of competition. I sent a cable at once to Washington. The State Department moved slowly, but American shipping interests gave notice in New York that all American travelers would be advised to avoid German lines. In a few days the German Government announced abandonment of their policy and gave a lame excuse. It is another illustration of Nazi clumsiness in international affairs.

August 13. Sunday. We drove southward today to Wittenberg and Leipzig over the Potsdam road, arriving at the Luther church at 11 o'clock. We could not enter because the doors were barred against travelers, unlike my experience of 1898 or 1899 when I visited this ancient Reformation town. In those days I participated in or sat through the service.

Not much of the Luther spirit remains now. The town is four times as large as in 1899—an industrial center. Noticing a Nazi parade, I happened to catch the expression of an onlooking policeman. It was not approving. After an hour, loitering about the older parts of the town, we drove on toward Leipzig. We arrived at one o'clock and drove to the old Market Place and then went to Auerbach's Keller for dinner—an excellent meal for 3 marks without wine, which I do not drink save on formal occasions and then only a small amount.

William and Martha drove on later toward Munich, a young journalist, Quentin Reynolds, of the Hearst service, being with them. Mattie, my wife, and I rested in the hotel some hours and went to the old Market House restaurant for supper where we got a good meal for 2 marks. Afterwards we took a walk about the old, narrow streets to Das Alte Theater, where

I used to see in my student days Lessing, Schiller and Goethe adapted to children's needs. It had been my way of trying to learn German. We strolled through the famous Brühlstrasse, headquarters for centuries of Jewish merchants and fur auctioneers, and back to our hotel where we retired unrecognized by anybody and so most comfortable.

August 14. Monday. We joined a party of sightseers and were driven over the city until 12:30. We saw the different divisions of the university and the abandoned palaces of the wealthy who lost their fortunes in the World War or immediately thereafter. It was a dreary section of the city. One great mansion after another was a solemn reminder of the follies the great men of 1914 allowed to be perpetrated.

The most imposing structure in the city is the massive monument to the German victory of Leipzig over Napoleon I in October, 1813, when 80,000 men were killed and buried or their bodies thrown into the Plisse river. The huge stone tower was built in 1913-14 by the Imperial Government. One climbs the immense stairs to a resting place, then enters the tower and climbs about fifty feet more to a corridor around the inside of the building and under the dome. There our party paused to hear Nazi as well as Imperial propaganda about the power and heroism of the German people. Four huge stone figures are supposed to tell the story. One of them represents a mother nursing twin children at her huge breasts; another shows a philosopher-teacher with a German youth sitting at his feet; another represents the God of War; and the fourth is a generous soul lending aid to the poor and helpless. It was all most interesting to one who could keep in mind the ambitions and the blunders of the German folk. The suggestive explanations of the guide were distinctly Nazi in character.

When the tour was over we paid our bill at the hotel, after a little visit to the main hall of the university, and took a train for Berlin where we arrived about 5 o'clock.

August 16. Wednesday. Professor Coar came again to describe his visit with Hitler. He had spent two hours with the Chancellor, with Hess as a witness. Coar reported that Hitler talked wildly about destroying all Jews, insisting that no other nation had any right to protest and that Germany was showing the world how to rid itself of its greatest curse. He considered himself a sort of Messiah. He would re-arm Germany, absorb Austria and finally move the capital to Munich. There were other and equally important points, but Coar was not at liberty to mention them. He thought Hitler had no comprehension of foreign attitudes or the significance of the economic effects of his Jewish program.

At dinner James McDonald and his wife talked well. With them were the Messersmiths and the Mowrers. There was some discussion of Mowrer's trouble on account of his stories of Nazi behavior toward all foreigners who do not salute or who look like Jews. Mowrer is under instructions to leave Germany on September 6. I felt at the end that Mowrer was almost as vehement, in his way, as the Nazis, but I could understand his point of view.

August 18. Friday. Forty representatives of the American Women's Club of Berlin came to pay their respects and to listen to Mr. Gordon talk a little about the situation in Germany under Nazi rule.

At 9 o'clock Fritz, the butler in our new mansion—rather the old one where we live in a manner which requires a butler— reported that a Professor Langbeine wished to speak to me over the telephone. When I took up the receiver I recognized the voice of Professor Coar, who is long-legged! He reported that a friend of his and Hess had returned from a visit to the Fuehrer, but he called the Fuehrer No. 1, Hess No. 2 and his friend No. 3. There was no change in Hitler's attitude. He spoke without in any way allowing a possible eavesdropper to grasp his meaning or anybody's name. I wonder what game he is playing. Such is the German situation, and I am learning.

August 19. Saturday. I received an invitation today from the Foreign Office asking me, as well as all other members of the diplomatic corps, to attend a great demonstration meeting of the Nazi Party and its Fuehrer in Nürnberg, September 2 and 3. Elaborate train and hotel service was offered at the expense of the government. It was plain that the invitation came by order of the Hitler chiefs and the word "Partei" (Party) was used three times in the first paragraph of the letter. I saw at once that attendance would be embarrassing and concluded that I would not attend unless all other ambassadors did. I suggested that Mr. Gordon ascertain the French attitude, and continued debating in my own mind whether I would refuse to attend even if all the other diplomats went.

August 21. Monday. I lunched with Dr. Hans Dieckhoff at the Adlon Hotel on Unter den Linden. President Rufus von Kleinsmid of the University of Southern California was the guest of honor. There were about twenty members of the government circle present at an elaborate luncheon with three kinds of wine. I took only a sip or two.

After the luncheon some Foreign Office men gathered about me to determine, if possible, my attitudes. The Minister of Education, Bernhard Rust, who spoke no English, seemed most concerned. I talked of German historians: Mommsen, Von Ranke and the rest. Rust said the Jews had forced Mommsen to omit certain passages from his *Roman History* because it reflected on the "chosen people." I listened. He said the publishers compelled him to do it. I listened. Aside from historical discussion I said little that could be reported, but I did allow my general agreement with the cultural Germany of 1900 to be obvious. I bade the party farewell at 4 o'clock. As I walked out the door of the hotel, the chief butler followed me to help me into my car. He was astonished, perhaps disgusted, when he saw me *walk* off briskly toward the Embassy.

At 4:30 the Spanish Ambassador called (very pleasantly unconventional because neither of us had been officially received) to talk over possible attendance at the Nürnberg show. I implied that I would not go and added that precedents in American history were all against it, referring to Lord Sackville's and Jackson's cases (the first under Cleveland in 1888, the second under Madison in 1811). The Spanish Ambassador spoke German about as well or as badly as I did. We went over the matter thoroughly and agreed, though I did not say positively what I would do, as it was my first meeting with him.

August 22. Tuesday. I asked for instructions from the State Department and I received a non-committal reply insofar as the American Government was concerned, but they added they would support anything I decided to be the right thing to do. I at once made up my mind not to go, even if all other ambassadors went.

At 10:45 Edgar Mowrer called to talk over his case, the State Department having advised his withdrawal. At 11:15, Dr. Dieckhoff of the Foreign Office came in to ask for Mowrer's immediate departure. Dieckhoff talked about a number of subjects before he came to the real one: the danger of Mowrer's being physically attacked, especially if he went to Nürnberg to report the Party demonstration. The government already had guards about Mowrer's house and office. In view of the intensity of feeling and the danger of another "atrocity," I agreed to advise Mowrer to go by September 1. Dieckhoff said he would give him all possible protection.

When Dieckhoff went out, Group Leader Karl Ernst of the Berlin S.A. (Storm Troops) came in to apologize for violence done to Dr. Mulvihill, a medical specialist here working on lung problems. Mulvihill, standing on the curb of Unter den Linden and not saluting when S.A. troops marched by, was knocked down and taken away unconscious. Messersmith demanded immediate punishment of the offender, who was promptly put into prison. The Secret Police Chief, Rolf Diels, had ordered Ernst to apologize.

As the young officer clicked his boots together and gave the Hitler gesture, I arose, returning the greeting as best I saw fit and listened to his German confessions of regret and his promise that such a thing would not happen again. When he was done, I asked him to be seated and then read him a lecture on the dangers of such behavior on the part of his followers. He protested to me that he was sincere and resolute in his promise to put a stop to violence toward foreigners. He arose, stood at attention, saluted, made a Prussian bow and went out.

I was not a little amused. At one o'clock, I explained to Messer-smith that the amends were properly made. He said: "The incidents will go on."

August 23. Wednesday. After a busy morning, I called on Under-Secretary of State von Bülow in his office on the Wil-helmstrasse. Mr. Gordon accompanied me, and being *persona non grata* in the Foreign Office, he said to me: "I expect to be left standing outside half an hour." But Von Bülow came into the reception room in two minutes. We sat around a table and talked agreeably for fifteen minutes about unemployment re-lief and international relations. I made the move to go but talked a moment about Von Bülow's uncle who left a remark-able autobiography, though I spoke only of Von Bülow's *German Politics* published in 1916, an excellent critique of German foreign relations before 1914 as well as of German ineptitude in foreign affairs.

At 4:30 the same day Von Bülow returned my call and he remained nearly an hour. We agreed on most subjects dis-cussed. I spoke of Ernst's apology and he promised to do all he could with the Police Department to stop further offenses. He said German foreign relations were very acute, and that "the hostility of Jews in the United States did much harm."

I asked if there would be any reason given for aggression on the French or Austrian border. He said: "Not a single aggressive move will be made; but we must have air-defense and anti-tank guns regardless of the Versailles Treaty, if con-tinued offensive armament goes on in France. Germany has the right to arm if other nations violate the treaty and arm. On this point we are all united in Germany, but you must not think all this marching in the streets is simply war-like. It is the needful discipline of our unemployed!" I made no com-ment. We then talked of other less pressing themes, though he did come back to the subject to say: "The Chancellor will make a pacifist speech at Nürnberg." I replied that I was glad, but did not refer to my doubts or my decision not to attend the meeting. We parted very agreeably.

August 25. Friday. Dr. Karl Wehner of the *Berliner Tageblatt*, who recently published in his paper a very comprehensive review of my *Cotton Kingdom*, came to talk about possible reviews of other books of mine. I gave him a copy of my *Woodrow Wilson*, not for review but for a study of my ideas of economic and international problems during the Wilson era. He said he would come again when he had finished the book. I wonder.

At 12 o'clock George Sylvester Viereck came with a letter from Colonel House. Viereck impressed me as unstable, a real pro-Nazi, here to see officials of the government. We had him to lunch and I still felt it a little unsafe to talk frankly with him. His manner makes me uneasy. I think Colonel House has been imposed upon. He should know better. Viereck said he was going to Nürnberg and would return and then bring the young Hohenzollern Prince Friedrich to see the family, if we were willing.

August 26. Saturday. I sent a reply to the German invitation to Nürnberg. I declined it on the grounds of pressure of work, though the main reason was my disapproval of a government invitation to a Party convention. I was also sure the behavior of the dominant group would be embarrassing.

August 28. Monday. H. C. MacLean, chief of American Commercial Attachés in Europe, with headquarters in Paris, called. We conferred with our Commercial Attaché here, Douglas Miller, who speaks German fluently and is married to a German wife. My first acquaintance with his work came only a day or two ago when his admirable survey of German conditions under the Hitler regime came to my desk, exceedingly well done.

More interesting for the moment was the visit of H. V. Kaltenborn, European news analyst for the Columbia Broadcasting System. His work has been to assess Hitler and the Nazi movement and prepare informal radio addresses in the United States about present-day Germany.

August 29. Tuesday. Karl von Wiegand called again. He is just back from a journey to Vienna, Geneva, Paris and London. His story was amazing. Chancellor Engelbert Dollfuss of Vienna had given him a six hour interview, driving through the mountains of Austria. Dollfuss has defeated the planned Hitler putsch over the Austrian border, which had been set for September 6. The abandonment of the scheme was due to the growing Austrian dislike of the Nazis and to Mussolini's intervention on the side of Dollfuss. Von Wiegand reported Dollfuss as saying: "There will not be a putsch after the great Nürnberg Party Congress in September." I was convinced, and was also inclined to think the failure of France, England, the United States and Spain to participate in the Nazi Party Day has been influential in the same direction.

He then told me that France was completing her treaty with Russia (Edouard Herriot was then on the way to Moscow), according to which Russia would support any French move against Germany. Also it would soon be shown that Germany had bought a vast amount of airship materials in Russia and that France had seized this material because the Treaty of Versailles had been violated. France and England were in accord and would show a solid front in the event of any war-like attitude on the part of Germany. However, a boycott would be tried first, then a blockade.

Finally Von Wiegand reported that the night before he had cabled—rather long-distance telephoned—to the Hearst news service in London the contents of President von Hindenburg's will: (1) A Hohenzollern would be urged upon the German people; (2) Hitler was to be Chancellor with limited powers; and (3) there was to be a restoration of popular participation in the government.

I asked him if it were not dangerous to transmit the contents of a man's will that way. He said: "I am sure of the facts; my information comes from one of Von Hindenburg's intimate friends, and I think the world ought to know the facts. Of course the Secret Police here know what I have done. I have intimations that I am soon to be cited to appear before Diels, Secret Police Chief." I told him he should not allow himself to be ordered out of the country. Mowrer is a lesson in this. Von Wiegand impressed me as half ready to be made a martyr. I was, however, a little astounded to hear his story.

In the afternoon Whiting Williams, *Saturday Evening Post* writer, came to give me a strange tale of Russian woe, a ten-thousand-word story, soon to appear in print, of starving millions of peasants. He asked for a letter to President Roosevelt which I said I might give him, but I am not sure. I could hardly believe 20,000,000 were starving in Soviet Russia!

August 30. Wednesday. I went with the Embassy staff, each of us in dress suit, top hat and all that, to present my credentials to President von Hindenburg. My three-page statement was conventional except for the inclusion of "German people" as the object of my mission, and also the statement of German intellectual life as of great interest and importance to the people of the United States. The President responded in vigorous language and laid particular emphasis upon what I said about the German people and culture. The President and I sat on the "preferred sofa" while Von Neurath, Von Bülow and Hans Otto Meissner, Foreign Office chiefs, the last-named being the President's secretary, sat about the table in front of the President and myself.

The conversation turned upon President Roosevelt and economic problems in the United States and Germany. I said there have been strong differences of opinion about the President in Washington but that his decision had been against economic nationalism, recently urged upon him. Von Hindenburg asserted vigorously his doubts of economic nationalism as a solution for a distressed and unemployed people. He stressed the subject of international relations so pointedly that I thought he meant indirect criticism of the Nazi extremists.

After fifteen minutes of agreeable exchange of conversation in which I was asked about my German university life and history teachers, I moved a little as a sort of gesture. I thought it was time to go and in a minute I arose and went into an adjoining room where I introduced the members of the Embassy staff to the President. That over, I retired to the entrance hall and marched sedately out of the building with the uniformed Von Bassewitz on my left, my staff trailing behind. When we drove away, several companies of the Reichswehr stood at attention on both sides of the street. It was all over and I was at last a duly accepted representative of the United States in Berlin.

At 5 o'clock I called upon the Papal Nuncio who lives in a marvelous palace not a little unbecoming to the priestly garb and ascetic look of its master. We spoke German fairly well for fifteen minutes. He could not go to Nürnberg—the Catholic Conference at Trier compelled his attendance. I asked if he .thought there were any Christians left in the world. He shrugged his shoulders but said "Yes." I asked about the Papal-Hitler concordat and he approved the idea. He finished the conversation with enthusiastic support of absolute religious freedom and separation of church and state! That from an orthodox Catholic!

August 31. Thursday. We lunched with a delightful party of German scholars. The conversation was in German and English and of a very high character. There were some Nazi officials present. I showed the Germans how President Roosevelt has managed public opinion thus far and how his opponents are brought into line without ruthless treatment. One of the Nazis said: "He is wise not to ask for his powers for too long a period." There was general indirect acknowledgment that Hitler has undertaken too much and for too long a period. If I had known at the beginning that there were several Nazi leaders present, I might have given my part of the talk a somewhat different direction.

September 1. Friday. Henry Mann of the National City Bank spoke of the conversation he and Mr. Aldrich had had some ten days before with the Chancellor at his summer place. The ideas advocated by Hitler were the same as those he had advanced to Professor Coar. He is a fanatic on the Jewish problem. He has no conception of international relationships. He considers himself a German Messiah. But despite Hitler's attitude these bankers feel they can work with him.

September 5. Tuesday. The stately Papal Nuncio called and we talked agreeably in German, our only means of communication. At 5 in the afternoon I made my second formal call, on the French Ambassador, André François-Poncet, in his beautiful palace on Unter den Linden, by the Brandenburger Tor (a monument to commemorate French defeat!). We talked English for a while but rather conventionally. I stayed just twelve minutes by my watch.

September 6. Wednesday. Von Prittwitz, a former German Ambassador to Washington, called at 11 and talked rather cautiously about the problems before the Hitler government. I understood from Representative Robert Bacon of New York that Von Prittwitz stood in some danger of imprisonment, but he told me that the Reichskanzler had recently received him and showed a conciliatory spirit. The former Ambassador will now open a business office in Berlin with a view to using his American contacts to advantage. He impressed me as a good deal of a diplomat but in a somewhat precarious situation with reference to his own government.

We went to lunch formally with Dr. Dieckhoff in Dahlem. My wife and Martha were with me. The Reichsbank president, Dr. Schacht, Mayor Sahm of Berlin—seven feet tall with a wife six feet tall and a little broad, too—and other members of the government circle were present. After retiring from the table, Schacht told a story of a conversation last May with President Roosevelt, whom he professed to admire, in which he asked why there was no ambassador on his way to Berlin. The President replied that he was having a hard time finding a man who knew German life, who sympathized with the German people in their dilemma, and who could speak German.

A little later Schacht expressed regret that I had not been able to go to Nürnberg. I quickly replied that the invitation had been to a purely Party gathering and that it was generally regarded in the United States as highly improper for an ambassador or minister to attend. I cited Lord Sackville's case in 1888 and other similar incidents in support of my decision. He seemed not to have thought of that as others also had not, according to their part in the conversation. It was an agreeable party, the conversation mostly in German. We ate duck and sauerkraut.

September 7. Thursday. I had been told by the etiquette authorities of my staff that I must give a reception to all the diplomatic corps soon after the formal acknowledgment, by the President of Germany, of my status. They said there would be some forty or fifty people. But before the day arrived and after invitations had gone out I was informed that each diplomat would bring members of his staff.

So today the show began at 5 o'clock. The Embassy rooms had been prepared; flowers abounded everywhere; a great punch bowl was filled with the accustomed liquors. Mr. Gordon and myself, with Count von Bassewitz, protocol official, introduced the ambassadors and ministers as they came. Many distinguished people came, including Von Neurath, Schacht and the French Ambassador. There was a little talk, a little commingling of the officials of various countries, and over two hundred names in our guest book. It was not a bad affair, and cost 700 marks.

September 8. Friday. The Spanish Ambassador, Luis Zulueta, called and we had a half hour's talk in German. He impressed me as most reasonable and wise. He was formerly a professor of philosophy in the University of Madrid—thus a little my own kind of man.

September 11. Monday. I returned formal calls of the Irish and Hungarian Ministers, the latter very poorly housed on the third floor of an ancient apartment. But he was very agreeable and intelligent, as most of them *seem* to be. He spoke of having Hungary re-annexed to Austria and both economically annexed to Germany. He was quite undiplomatic in placing his cards all on the table.

I then returned the call of the Spanish Ambassador, elegantly housed in a palace built and furnished during the heyday of German imperialism, far too elaborate for the present modest and intellectual representative of modern Spain, if there is such a thing as modern Spain. It was plain that we are far more akin than a Spaniard and an American are supposed to be.

In the evening we all went to dine with Professor Erich Marcks, under whom I studied for my German degree. There was a delightful company: two young sons, officers in the Reichswehr, a Herr Drexler of the Foreign Office and his wife, a Dutch woman with a sense of humor and bushy hair, Mrs. Marcks and other members of the family. Conversation was historical, political and very lively as Marcks is gifted with a high sense of humor. The talk was half German, half English.

September 12. Tuesday. At 12 o'clock Monsieur François-Poncet came, a half hour ahead of the appointed time, and remained forty minutes. The conversation began in English. It soon shifted to German which the Ambassador speaks admirably, having been a student in Berlin before the World War. It was clear from the beginning that he was excited. He repeated a very disagreeable conversation he had had the day before with Baron von Neurath. It was plain that they had disagreed sharply and he wished me to know how tense are the relations between the French and the Germans.

He said: "They gave a play last Sunday before a large audience in which Germany was represented as a great area with two dissevered sections begging to be returned. The German people were represented by a group of Brown Shirt men, bedraggled prisoners, disarmed and helpless. French soldiers armed to the teeth, Englishmen and Americans stood by approvingly. The whole scene was designed to stir the deepest hostility against France, as also against the rest of the world. I made strong protest to the Foreign Minister who simply shrugged his shoulders. He made a promise to stop such insults. And it was plain to me that he had no power to effect any change, even if he wished."

Monsieur François-Poncet, a handsome, imposing-looking person, was much excited. He insisted that war is almost certain to come. In my opinion, economic conditions are better than at any time since I have been here. The Nazis have the press and their chiefs under such discipline and control that I feel there will be no outbreak for some time, perhaps a year. As for international relations, the situation is too problematical to estimate the future.

I asked him if he had read Lloyd George's translated article in last Sunday's *Vossische Zeitung*. He said he had not. I then repeated its main points, with its conclusion about the last war: "If it were all to do over again, I should decide exactly as I did then." The Ambassador said "Yes," and continued: "The English are coming again to recognize the German menace to European peace," and he returned to his former warning that unless America and England lend assistance again we are going to have another great war. He added: "The Germans are playing with fire now as in 1914, and I said as much to Von Neurath yesterday."

I then asked whether he had heard what Von Hindenburg's attitude is. He repeated exactly the story that Karl von Wiegand had given me a week or two before: the President's will provided for a Hohenzollern to come to the throne, for Hitler to be Chancellor, and for some sort of national assembly. M. François-Poncet added: "But it won't be a Hohenzollern. Nobody in that family is fit. The Crown Prince is idle and dissolute and has no will of his own, and the sons are not old or promising enough. Nor would Goebbels allow Von Hindenburg's will to prevail. He wishes to put the Duke of Hesse on the throne and make himself the real master." I thought the people of Germany were inclined to give the Reich President more attention, and that one of the Hohenzollerns is more likely to be chosen than the Duke of Hesse, a violent Jewbaiter.

September 14. Thursday. Count de Kherchove, Belgian Minister, spent a half hour presenting his view of the dangers of German rearmament. He said Belgium must rely always upon Britain's support, rather than that of France.

I went at 12:15 to talk things over with Baron von Neurath, and remained until 1 o'clock. Von Neurath agreed that our move toward Latin America, as indicated in the Montevideo Conference, would be serious for Germany, if it meant abandonment of another economic conference to do what was planned at the London Conference. I illustrated the German ineptitude in foreign economic affairs by repeating the story of the North German Lloyd attempt early in August to prevent Germans or other travelers from taking passage on any but German ships. I showed him how fatal that order would have been if Americans had applied a similar rule in New York, taking 80 per cent of the traffic from German vessels. He seemed surprised at the folly and frankly acknowledged that German authorities are naive in such matters.

I spoke of the beatings of Americans on German streets when they failed to give the Hitler salute during parades. I cited the cases of Mulvihill, Brossard and the young son of H. V. Kaltenborn, and said that no punishment of offenders had been reported. Although Group Leader Ernst had made public apology in the Mulvihill case, the authorities seemed to pay no attention. I acknowledged that Americans were negligent but said that was their privilege, and that they never or rarely saluted their own flag when they met a column of soldiers. It simply is not their habit. He replied that he appreciated the gravity of the matter, especially if the State Department contemplated an announcement that it was unsafe for Americans to visit Germany. I explained the newspaper attitude at home, said that I had kept two or three cases out of the press reports and otherwise tried to prevent unfriendly demonstrations. He assured me he had recently gone over the matter with Goering, President of Prussia and Police Chief, and also with the Chancellor, both agreeing that stricter enforcement of the law would be made thereafter. He referred to a notice in the papers two days before which referred to the Communist elements in the S.A. (Storm Troops) as the unruly ones. He thought it was all over; I hoped so.

Then we talked at length about the Jewish outrages. Here was a problem which seemed to give him much more trouble. Hitler means to put all Jews out of responsible positions in Germany, even to expel them from the country. Von Neurath said he sat on the platform a few days before in the Baden-

Baden sport field and no sort of affronts were given to three prominent Jews on the same platform. I reviewed events in the United States since July 5 and showed how the boycott in America and England was operating and how newspapers were exciting liberal opinion everywhere. I intimated that many liberal people of eminence had come to me to report their complaints. But I did not need to repeat some stories of brutalities and murders that had come to me. The case was too clear.

He asked whether we did not have a Jewish problem in the United States. I acknowledged that some people thought so, and again repeated my dislike of German brutality methods. I continued: You cannot expect world opinion of your conduct to moderate so long as eminent leaders like Hitler and Goebbels announce from platforms, as in Nürnberg, that all Jews must be wiped off the earth. He was embarrassed as on one or two previous occasions. He did not promise any reform, much as he seemed to lament the facts.

As I arose to go, I said: Is there to be war? He replied: "No, absolutely no." I said: You must realize that Germany would be ruined by another war. He agreed and said: "I am leaving Wednesday for Geneva where I shall support American demands for decreasing armaments and hope Norman Davis may succeed." I left, a little concerned that I had been so frank and critical. The Minister seemed to be in good humor nevertheless.

September 15. Friday. One of the amusing days! The Prussian authorities had invited the diplomatic corps to attend the formal opening of the new Council of State, substitute for the former German Upper House. As the thing was purely official, I decided to go. On the way, vast masses of Brown Shirt soldiers lined the streets on both sides from the Victoriastrasse to the university, about a mile—perhaps 100,000 uniformed men.

Entering the Brandenburger Tor, the Prussian and Hitler flags stood on the right and the soldiers were at attention. I gave a half-humorous, if not sarcastic, salute, which was taken by newspaper men to mean a surrender to Party authorities. It was incorrect to do so since my top hat was off and no salute at home would be expected. But Nazi people do not understand this. It is embarrassing not to wave to cheering people, but any wave can be interpreted as a Hitler salute. However, I waved, thus becoming to some newspeople a Nazi partisan. I decided my words could speak for themselves.

When I found my place it was on the right of the speakers' stand. The Papal Nuncio sat next to me. It was a beautiful hall. Slowly the officials of the new Nazi state filed in to their seats in the middle of the room. Hermann Goering, a fat ridiculous-looking man according to my taste, came toward his centrally located chair with a score of men behind him. He stopped and gave the Hitler salute, a click of shoe-heels, a raise of the right hand and a sharp Prussian bow. The diplomatic corps, following the suggestion of the Nuncio, bowed in the usual English-American easy style.

The Prussian Minister, Goering, in Hitler uniform, began a long harangue which, not being in front of him, I could understand only in broken snatches here and there. It was a passionate oration on the meaning of the new state, the Third Reich, in which three or four times I discerned contemptuous remarks about the discarded parliamentary system. It is curious: next week they are trying three or four men in Leipzig on a charge of treason for burning the old Reichstag building, and yet this man, next in authority to Hitler himself, denounces parliamentarianism as a betrayal of Germanism.

The meeting adjourned about 12:30 and the diplomatic corps took its place on the terrace in front of the university to witness the marching of thousands of Prussian police, Brown Shirt and Stahlhelm troops. Some of them indulged in the absurd parade step in which the soldiers march without bending the knee— the goose step—perfectly executed. When a division of cavalry followed, I nudged and whispered to the Nuncio: You notice the horses do not keep step and they walk naturally. What's the reason they are not so obedient? The Papal dignitary seemed not to catch the point, or he hesitated to show that he did. I admired the horses.

September 16. Saturday. Von Wiegand called, after a five-day visit to England, and reported what he considered semi-war-like plans of the British. He said: "The British Cabinet have made a formal study of a plan to blockade Germany in the event of an outbreak of war. The idea is for France, England, Poland, Russia, Czechoslovakia and Austria to unite to bar all exit and entrance of military or other goods to Germany. Belgium would also co-operate. The plan has been submitted to the Cabinet, but tabled for the present."

September 18. Monday. A young Reimer Koch-Weser, the son of a former Prussian Minister of Justice, who has studied in New England and has a position in a New York law firm, came to beg me to use what influence I could to procure restoration of his father to his former rights as a practicing lawyer in Berlin. The father's grandfather was a Jew. Hence the father is denied a means of livelihood in Germany. He left me two books to prove his father's claim to some attention as a conservative-liberal writer. I repeated what I had said a hundred times since July 14: I have no authority at all to approach any German official about such a matter. He hoped I could find occasion, unofficially, to mention the subject and bring a little pressure to bear. I saw no immediate prospect, harsh as the ruling against the family seemed.

September 21. Thursday. Young Herbert von Bismarck called at 12 o'clock. He seemed favorable in appearance, about twenty-eight years old as I judged. I said: You live under the great disadvantage of being the grandson of the greatest statesman Germany has ever had. The handsome young man flushed a little and said: "Yes, that's so." I then asked him Bismarck's attitude in 1871 about the annexation of Alsace-Lorraine, suggesting that my interpretation of the correspondence of his grandfather was to the effect that the great blunder would not have been made if the then Prime Minister had had his way. He agreed at once that Bismarck had opposed Kaiser William I and Von Moltke and proposed to give the long-disputed area to Switzerland. We then talked of the folly of victors in most wars. After a bit of conversation about Germany in which he acknowledged friendly relations to the Nazi regime, we parted company, my secretary making the polite blunder of coming in too soon.

September 22. Friday. At 5 o'clock, Minister Francis White, long-time Under-Secretary of State with Latin America for his realm, came in to talk about the situation in Germany. He had been at Prague a month where he had been putting in order, at much expense to the government, the famous palace (once belonging to Charles R. Crane) of fourteen rooms, for himself, his wife and one child. He made the impression of a loyal, industrious official, not well-informed about Europe in any way.

Mr. White and his wife, Prince Friedrich Hohenzollern, son of the Crown Prince, now living at Potsdam, and Ernst Hanfstaengl, a curious, well-to-do Hitler enthusiast since 1921, came to dinner. It was an interesting evening. The prince showed himself very modest, gentle-mannered and appreciative. Hanfstaengl was a boisterous Harvard graduate of young Theodore Roosevelt's day. When "Teddy Jr." was mentioned, he flew into a rage. After dinner, he played on the piano. The party broke up at 10:30, the proper hour according to my taste.

September 25. Monday. At 8 o'clock, Dr. Schacht, the Reichsbank president, came to dine with Senator McAdoo, two very clever, stubborn-willed men. The latter is seventy years old and hardly looks to be fifty-five; the former is around fifty, I believe, but looks older. Conversation was the keenest and most interesting I have ever heard on financial subjects. The two men went away together. This was one of the real dinners of our stay here thus far.

September 27. Wednesday. Lord Astor of the New York-London family, called this morning and reported that Boston leaders of the Mother Church (Christian Science) had called him to come to Germany to protest against dissolving Christian Science organizations in south Germany, one of the societies having been ruthlessly treated in Weimar. I had already learned of the matter and had a cable from the State Department asking for information. I told Lord Astor that I thought the matter had been corrected by the German authorities, thinking of Von Neurath's promises of September 14, and that he might perhaps rest easy. It is the same troublesome story: inexperienced Nazi local authorities acting hastily, and evil results with difficulty corrected.

I then suggested to Lord Astor that he remain in Berlin, study the general situation and try to see Chancellor Hitler in the hope of influencing him to support Von Neurath in Geneva as against Goebbels who was publicizing Germany as more belligerent and reckless. He agreed and I arranged with Louis P. Lochner, the Associated Press correspondent, to get an interview with Hitler. Astor was a much more interesting and alert person than I had expected from the impressions I received of him when he was in Chicago ten years ago and I talked with him at Hull House.

September 29. Friday. At lunch, tall, dark Lord Astor sat down with Von Bülow, one of the German Secretaries of State. We had an interesting interchange of views on recovery problems but no real talk about the critical matter of world peace which his Lordship came here to promote if possible, after his Christian Science fellows are relieved.

When the other guests had gone, Lord Astor sat down in the library and said: "I am to see Hitler at 6. Is there anything you think I might discuss with him to advantage?" I replied: If you can impress upon him the importance of improving his British and American relationships, and the need for Germany of an agreement as to disarmament at Geneva, you will only be re-emphasizing what I have been urging upon officials at the Foreign Office. After a few minutes he went away, not very hopeful.

At 6:30 I went with Counselor Gordon, who was most anxious to go, to see Von Bülow. Gordon doesn't get on with Von Bülow and Von Bülow has not shown any cordial feeling for Gordon when we have been together before. I suggested because of this that the First Secretary of the Embassy, Joseph Flack, should also go. He had prepared the data we were to use in the discussion of the so-called "quota system" now being

applied all over Europe against the United States because of
debts and high tariffs.

So we took seats by a table in the Foreign Office exactly on
time. Von Bülow and an assistant sat opposite us. We protested
against a quota for Yugoslavia on imports of prunes at low
tariff rates and the failure to grant the same privilege to American prune growers. The volume of trade involved was much
larger than I had any idea of. Von Bülow said the arrangement
was already fixed for eight months and it could not be modified.
Yugoslavia allowed similar concessions to German imports.
There was nearly an hour of earnest talk but no compromise,
except Von Bülow's remark toward the end: "The time for us
all to agree on easier trade relations was last summer in London," with which I concurred. We came away at 7:30, just as
wise or not wise as to German policy as before. But the State
Department request had been met in full.

October 4. Wednesday. Charles R. Crane came to talk beforehand about his interview with Adolf Hitler. I asked him to
stress, if the opportunity arose, two factors which influence
Germans and foreigners against the present regime: (1) The
mass of educated and professional Germans who resent the
arbitrary and violent behavior of many of Hitler's under-officers
and some of his colleagues (Goebbels and Goering) require
more consideration. There is a silent resistance to arbitrary
measures like the recent dismissal of Mendelssohn-Bartholdy,
grandson of the great musician and eminent professor of international relations at Hamburg. (2) The ruthlessness with which
Jews are treated should be abandoned. Goebbels' talks, though
I said not to name him, cause great injury all over the world.

At 5 o'clock, Mr. Crane was again at the house, tea-drinking.
He has been some months at Carlsbad where he thinks one's
health is better restored than anywhere else. He talked of his
coming interview with the Pope about a sort of pact with the
Islam world whereby the followers of Mohammed may be
protected against the Jews who are taking Palestine. He makes
the impression of being a little in his dotage. He is seventy-five
years old. Long years of strange experiences in American poli-

tics, in Russia where he did much to bring on the Kerensky revolution which gave way to Communism and drove Crane out of the country, and in China as Wilson's Minister there, have upset his equilibrium somewhat.

October 5. Thursday. Mr. Crane came tea-drinking again today. He was enthusiastic about his Hitler interview. In his opinion, the Chancellor was not learned like Mr. Houston of the Wilson Cabinet, who was so often wrong because of lack of imagination. Crane found Hitler simple, enthusiastic, bent on stirring the German people to passionate self-confidence and wanting in knowledge of foreign problems. This is the same story I have heard again and again.

Mr. Crane was so friendly that he offered to furnish me a trustworthy private secretary. Of course I could not accept; it is contrary to the rules of the Department. Much as I need such a person, I have no means of engaging one myself, nor of accepting one paid by another. The reason is that such arrangements would surely tend to demoralize the service. So many wealthy men would endeavor to serve their own interests by lending aid to public officials, especially in the Foreign Service. Crane was disappointed.

At 8:30 we went to the Esplanade Hotel where Frederick Wirth, President of the American Club in Berlin, met us. We were most ceremoniously escorted into a waiting-room. Mr. Gordon insisted that I must precede my wife, which I was not inclined to do, and all others as we marched with a party of Embassy folk to the beautiful dining room where some 150 people were ready to participate in a grand dinner, costing 8 marks a plate, wine extra. It was a fine demonstration in full evening dress of the interest of the American colony here in the "new Ambassador."

In due course, Mr. Wirth introduced me and I spoke on the *Dilemma in the United States* which seemed to hold the audience's attention closely. At the end, a Dr. Fuehr of the German Foreign Office spoke on behalf of the government and dwelt on the fact of my having taken my doctorate in Leipzig and published my dissertation in German. There was no hint of my failure to fall in with the Nürnberg Party show of September, though I had heard there was a good deal of criticism. When the speaking was over we had half an hour of personal talk and hand-shaking and then we came home. Both the Americans and the Germans present were most cordial in every way.

October 11. Wednesday. The Dutch Minister called. He had been acquainted with the Kaiser when still on the German throne and he indicated a sympathetic feeling for the old regime. I did not respond to this in any way. The subject of atrocities came up and I told him of the shameful case of a Woolworth store man in Düsseldorf being attacked on the streets there last Sunday in a most disgraceful way. The last such case occurred on September 1. After ample time and promises over the telephone by the police authorities, I had gone to Von Neurath, Foreign Minister, and had an hour or nearly that with him. He regretted every one of the eight or ten cases that were listed to him and promised everything one could ask, but said, "The S.A. men are so uncontrollable that I am afraid we cannot stop them," repeating, "I will do all possible." On Thursday, October 5, I had sent a request to the Foreign Office urging a report on what officials had done. No reply came, which I think means that the police have taken no measures against the guilty men.

I gave the friendly Dutch Minister an idea of my difficulty. He said: "I have had some trouble myself since last spring, and a recent case compels me to see Von Neurath tomorrow. I expect nothing. The Foreign Office has no authority and Hitler gives no orders to the Nazis in such matters, not knowing what such behavior means to his own cause." It has been my experience, too, that Von Neurath has been strangely evasive on this and even more important international discussions.

I told him the Spanish Ambassador had sent word that he was in the same plight. He wanted to know what I was contemplating. I said: We may advise the government in Washington to announce to the world that Americans are not safe in Germany and that travelers had best not go there. He said he was considering the same action, that Dutchmen would never give the Hitler greeting—the main cause of attacks—and that he would not give it either.

The Minister is very angry but says the present regime is here to stay. He said, "Even the death of the Old Man, Hindenburg, would bring no real change." He then added: "The European world is half crazy or worse. We quarrel and wrangle and perhaps go to war. That will finish us, and Japan, after annexing China, will sail into the Baltic. It is terrible to contemplate the folly of the free peoples of the United States, England and Holland."

II

October 12, 1933 to March 4, 1934

October 12. Thursday. I went today to the Adlon Hotel to lunch with the American Chamber of Commerce where it had been announced two weeks ago that I was to speak. I had my paper, eleven pages, in hand. Mr. Gordon, the Counselor, had read it carefully and approved of every sentence. Among the guests were Dr. Schacht, Dr. Keppler from the Economics Ministry, Dr. Fuehr and Dr. Davidson, both of the Foreign Office, two representatives of Dr. Goebbels, and many American and English correspondents. There were about 200 people present; the newspapers said 300. I felt very keenly the tension of the situation.

I was introduced with rather fulsome praise as an historian and diplomat. I began to read the address after disallowing some of the praise. As I started to read the audience was at once tense. My points were that half-educated statesmen of our day misunderstood the Caesar regime; that England, France and the United States had all tried economic nationalism and failed; and finally that the world is confronted with alternatives of economic co-operation or chaos—war and its aftermath. There was extraordinary applause considering the implied criticism of statecraft here, in Italy, France and England. Dr. Schacht said he had never known there was so much proof of his contentions today. Dr. Davidson said: "You are another Philipp Melancthon, Mentor Germaniae." I was not taken in by irony. The two Goebbels men said to the *New York Times* representative that they were going to print the whole speech.

Though I did not know it then, they were forbidden to do so that afternoon. The *Berliner Tageblatt*, the *Boersen Zeitung* and the *Vossische Zeitung* all carried good excerpts next day, I think against the suggestion, not the command, of the Propaganda Ministry.

October 13. Friday. I was due to protest today to Von Neurath over the failure to punish those Nazis who had assaulted Americans and the ignoring of my request, ten days before, for information on this. My engagement was postponed twice during the day, but in the evening I was finally received.

Von Neurath apologized for the delays and listened patiently to my case and the protest from Washington. He said General Goering had promised him a report on the punishment of all offenders, but had not kept his promise.

We then talked of dangers to Germany and of the growing hostility abroad. He repeated as usual how fully he agreed with me, but I'm afraid the lesson of economic nationalism has not been learned by him or, more important, by Hitler himself. If they really believe a country can be economically independent and discard international codes of behavior, as I suspect they do, real trouble will come. I came away fairly, not completely, satisfied, having a lingering suspicion that Hitler had compelled Von Neurath to postpone the interview as a sort of rebuke for my speech of yesterday.

October 14. Saturday. We gave a dinner party to military and naval attachés. At 9:30 a special messenger brought the long-awaited formal report—of one lone man in a concentration camp for striking Mr. Mulvihill on August 12 or 13. The Düsseldorf offenders were on the way to trial in Berlin, as if the regular authorities on the Rhine were not equal to the task!

But before this episode reached its lame conclusion, Hitler spoke over the radio to Germany, the rest of Europe and the United States, announcing the German withdrawal from the League and from the Disarmament Conference and proclaiming a Reich election for November 14. The speech was moderate for him. He demanded equal rights with other nations as to armaments, defended his "revolution" as simply an anti-Communist move, and assured the world of peaceful intentions. We listened attentively. It was not the address of a thinker, but of an emotionalist claiming that Germany had in no way been responsible for the World War and that she was the victim of wicked enemies.

After our company had gone, I went to bed a little troubled, the more so as Norman Davis, the President's roving ambassador to Europe, called on the long distance from Geneva to ask for what information I could give. As I knew my telephone wire was tapped by the German Propaganda Ministry, I spoke only in general terms and promised to call him in a few days if any real information came to me. The Germans have made another huge blunder for want of statesmen.

October 15. Sunday. This was a day of tense feeling though no new information has come to me. A young member of the old German nobility came to lunch. He revealed a touch of German hostility in his conversation, mainly in his defense of Japanese aggression against China. He is deeply patriotic but, like so many educated Germans, does not know what real patriotism is. It is evident some dislike of me is arising here now in official circles. I believe it is simply Nazi opposition. My refusal to go to Nürnberg was the beginning. But as the English, French and Spanish Ambassadors declined, I cannot be singled out. The pressure for ceasing street beatings and fair commercial treatment and now my speech of October 12 begin to look critical to them.

We went to a movie this afternoon. Hitler was shown as making a brief speech in Leipzig. There was no applause. Later, Hitler was shown marching with a division of troops; there was very moderate applause. Then the unpopular Crown Prince was put on the screen; he drew quite as much applause as the Chancellor. Hitler is surely not so powerful with the people as Mussolini, the Italian despot, has been.

October 17. Tuesday. I went today at 12 o'clock sharp to see Chancellor Hitler in the palace where Bismarck once lived and

worked. I went up broad stairways guarded at every turn by
Nazi soldiers with hands raised in the Caesar style, making the
usual bows as I made various turns along the route. In the
waiting room I met a young Mr. Hans Thomsen with whom
I talked five minutes about persons I knew in Germany. Then
Von Neurath opened the door to the Chancellor's office, a great
room some fifty feet square with tables and chairs placed all
around for group conferences. The decorations on the ceiling
and walls were beautiful but not so elaborate as in the great
ballroom adjoining. Adolf Hitler appeared in simple work-a-
day suit, neat and erect. He looks somewhat better than the
pictures that appear in the papers.

We rehearsed two subjects, the assaults upon Americans and
the discriminations against American creditors. Everything I
asked was agreed to and the Chancellor assured me personally
that he would see that any future attack was punished to the
limit and that publicity would be given to decrees warning
everyone that foreigners were not to be expected to give the
Hitler salute.

On financial discriminations, Von Neurath made the reply:
"We have a falling export market and hence must make deals
with any nation that will take our goods. That's the reason for
our paying Swiss creditors full interest on their bonds and
Americans only half the guaranteed rate of interest." These
were not his exact words. We were talking German.

I could not fail to recognize the dilemma, for failure to export increasing amounts of goods would mean a default pure
and simple, far more serious than partial payment. One benefit
the Germans do not mention is the fact that German bonds fall
on the New York market to one-third or one-fourth their face
value, and German cities and companies thus buy back their
bonds at low prices, saving sixty to seventy-five cents out of
every dollar which they borrowed in 1926-28. German financiers are not unequal to their New York fellows who made
enormous profits at the expense of American buyers of German
securities.

But the conversation turned quickly to the all-pervasive question of the German thunderbolt of last Saturday. The Chan-

cellor was clearly excited. I asked him why he had withdrawn from the League. He ranted about the Treaty of Versailles, the failure of the powers to keep their promises about disarmament and the indignity of keeping Germany in a defenseless status. I replied: There is evident injustice in the French attitude; but defeat in war is always followed by injustice. Witness the terrible treatment of our southern states after the Civil War. He remained silent on this score.

After an exchange of niceties, I asked the Chancellor whether an incident on the Polish, Austrian or French border which drew an enemy into the Reich would be allowed to be a *casus belli*. Of course he said, "No, no." I then said in case such a thing were to occur in the Ruhr valley would you hold off and call a conference of the European powers? He said: "That would be my purpose, but we might not be able to restrain the German people." (I saw that he meant the violent Nazis whom he has trained to violence.) I continued: If you would wait and call a conference, Germany would regain her popularity outside. A few more remarks and we parted, after a forty-five minute interview. Many other subjects were touched upon. My final impression was of his belligerence and self-confidence.

October 18. Wednesday. Bank Director Solmssen of the great Disconto Gesellschaft spent a half hour with me. He reviewed the Nazi uprising of last spring with approval. It was necessary, he indicated. He thought the abolition of parties had been warranted, and also that Jewish repressions were justified, in a measure. Then he said: "But these repressions have gone too far. Some Jews ought not to be dismissed; Professor Mendelssohn-Bartholdy of Hamburg, for example; and the universities should be left free and also the schools and the press." I felt he was saying this for my benefit.

He concluded, "I heard your address before the American Chamber of Commerce and have come here specially to thank you in the name of liberal Germany which is overwhelmingly grateful. You have said what we can or dare not say. It is a great help to us. We wish you to continue to speak on occasion." He seemed to be very sincere, and also a very able, though a self-contradictory business man, more liberal than some American business men have been in my day.

October 20. Friday. To make sure of Hitler's attitude about the possibility of war, I saw Von Neurath this morning and he repeated what was said on October 17. When the last of the reports were in the pouch and another cable was off in the afternoon I went home with a headache and the threat of a cold.

I dressed for a dinner at the Herren Klub on Hermann Göringstrasse. I ate only a boiled egg and rolls. Minister Curtius, of the Bruening regime, greeted me in a half hour's speech at 9:30. He came pretty close to the Nazi attitude about war. I responded for fifteen minutes, without notes, giving a brief story of the incidents of my life in Germany as a student and of the accidental appointment to my present dangerous position, and closed with a brief statement that wars are no longer rational solutions of any problem. Man's inventive genius has made war utterly destructive and a resort to war is but a reversal to medievalism, a defeat of all nations. The Herren, many nobles and Stahlhelms present, seemed to accept this philosophical criticism. At least they couldn't politely berate me. Home at 11:00.

October 25. Wednesday. I received this morning a letter from Senator Robert J. Bulkley, now in England, quoting a friend in Holland who had just had dinner with Fritz Thyssen, the great steel and munitions manufacturer in the Ruhr valley. Thyssen said: *"We* compelled the German Government to withdraw from the League." Bulkley was absolutely certain of the reliability of his informant.

October 26. Thursday. An eminent German of a former regime came to let me know he is departing for New York to lecture in the New School for Social Research instead of remaining here subject to possible ill treatment by the Nazi leaders. He is a most promising and clear-thinking man, who said: "You Americans must teach us Germans how to govern ourselves. I go away for a year with the understanding I can return next spring, or remain another year if I wish. I am announcing that I return next spring."

He had come to me three weeks ago and said he thought he would not accept the offer of my friend, Dr. Alvin Johnson, president of the New School. It then looked like a surrender to him; now he thinks it best to go and return later if things improve. He thinks Hitler is moderating and perhaps the German situation will improve. I fear German authorities will regard the New School as simply a Jewish propaganda institution and so not welcome his return next year.

October 27. Friday. Two German-Americans with prominent business connections, one of them an official of the North German Lloyd steamship company, came to me to know what can be done here or elsewhere to assuage the rising anti-German feeling in the United States. They reported that it was positively embarrassing to be known as a German in New York, partly due to Jewish resentment there and partly due to recent Nazi propaganda. They had joined the Nazi Party to put down Communism and now Nazis were as unpopular as Communists there. Yesterday's Paris papers report Representative Dickstein's investigation into Nazi activities is to be carried on by official committee action on November 14. From appearances the propaganda office here has been engaged in the most dangerous performances imaginable.

These gentlemen had consulted officials in the Foreign Office and they said the officials had been nonplused and suggested a visit with me. They went away depressed—nor is the outlook promising. French politicians have for ten years violated the spirit of the disarmament clauses of the Versailles Treaty. The German Social-Democratic movement was ruined by French policy. Now, after the German Nazi uprising in protest, the Germans are trying to govern themselves by autocratic methods, alienating the world by their indiscretions and forcing unanimous world dislike. Wrong and right are so mixed and confused everywhere.

October 28. Saturday. At 5:30 Sir Eric Phipps and his lady came to tea and remained an hour. The conversation was better than his reputation in Berlin had led us to expect. They were really delightful and quite convinced of the mistaken policy which has permitted the Germans to withdraw from the League. He told me a correspondent of the London *Daily Telegraph* had been in prison two days in Munich for telling his newspaper that S.A. troops had recently marched with arms. His consul was not allowed to see him for two days. He is charged with treason. This is another opportunity for American excitement.

October 29. Sunday. Walking along the Tiergartenstrasse at 12 o'clock I saw a Brown Shirt procession coming. I walked into the park to avoid embarrassment. The procession stopped before the Turkish Embassy and stood at attention for a time. Then they sang songs in honor of the tenth anniversary of the founding of the present Turkish state. A vast crowd of people gathered along the street and gave the Hitler greeting. It was but a warning of what was to come that evening when we were expected there at a Bierabend at 9:30. I went my way through the park to the Esplanade Hotel.

At 10 we drove to the door of the Turkish Ambassador. The whole place was infested with Brown Shirts. Salutes were given at every possible turn. The halls were crowded. A table thirty feet long was loaded with cold meats, vegetables and bread. The people ate ravenously as though they had not had anything all day, then drank beer. I saw Von Papen, of unenviable American record, but I avoided a meeting. We remained only a few minutes.

October 31. Tuesday. In bed with a light cold. Dr. Charles S. MacFarland, former representative of the Federal Council of Churches of Christ in America who has been traveling about the country a week or two, a former pro-German and well acquainted here, pressed for an interview. He came at 6:30. He had had nearly an hour with Hitler and reported to him that 4,000 Protestant preachers had refused to accept the Hitler church creed, that 2,700 were making formal protest after the election, that one of the leading theological schools refused the new creed and that the Catholics were likewise in a similar revolt and the Pope was considering a remedy. MacFarland said

Hitler declared he had not known of the 4,000 recalcitrants and he wished MacFarland would say to the leaders that he wished to see them. Then MacFarland argued that Protestants in the United States would make loud protest if the churches here were denied absolute freedom of conscience. Hitler seemed to sense his dangers in religious matters and saw the likelihood of another incendiary issue.

At 8:15 we departed, full-dress, for a long appointed dinner with the French Ambassador and his wife. There was a great room for the accommodation of men's and women's wraps, with two servants, in livery, to receive them—expecting tips. Up the magnificent stairway there were pages dressed in the gay liveries of Louis XIV's time. At the entrance to the reception hall, there were two other servants to hand out cards indicating dinner companions. In the reception room there was a marvelous rug with a huge letter N in the middle to remind one, especially Germans, of the conquests of Napoleon. Dr. Hjalmar Schacht and Count von Bassewitz were compelled to walk over or around the famous initial. No remarks were made, but they noticed the letter.

The walls were covered with beautiful Gobelin tapestries. The chairs were of Louis XIV style. When the party of thirty went into the dining room, Madame François-Poncet walking on my right, I noticed Gobelins on the walls, also portraits of French generals of the Louis XIV period, a peculiarly good painting of young Louis XV and a lavish table with decorations in the best of form and taste. There were eight or ten servants, in liveries as pages, all standing at attention. It surpassed the Belgian's dining hall outfit.

We ate for an hour. Nothing worth while was said, unless the German conversation on my part with Frau Dr. Schacht was worth while. After we were through, all marched correctly to the reception room where everyone stood gossiping in little groups until 11:45 when the musicians came to open a concert. Although I had said nothing about getting out of bed to attend the dinner, I now felt so uncomfortable that I had to beg to be excused. It was a little embarrassing and I felt our hosts might feel a little affronted. There was nothing else to do, so we went out as the great party moved into the music hall. Such was the show of democratic France to autocratic Germany.

November 5. Sunday. John White, son of the famous Henry White, Republican member of Wilson's mission to the Paris Conference, 1918-19, and Orme Wilson, a relative of Pierrepont Moffat, State Department official, arrived to take up their work. The one will be Counselor of the Embassy here, the other Second Secretary. Both seemed to be good men—White a little too English in bearing and with a distinct Harvard-Oxford accent.

November 16. Thursday. We sat down to dinner tonight with Hjalmar Schacht, the Swiss Minister and the famous nitrate manufacturer, August Diehn, whom I had met at luncheon a few days before. The conversation was not very good though we had to leave too early to get a good test of it. Dr. Schacht said in a rather conspicuous way that the addresses I had been delivering in Germany were worth a great deal to the country. I could not be sure of his meaning unless it was to say indirectly that such discussions as I engaged in aided his side of the Cabinet situation. He swears openly by Hitler but convinces me that he believes in a liberal, even free trade, policy, which is anathema to the Reichskanzler, if judged by his speeches and writings. Diehn talked only a little but I know his attitude is that of a great trust chief, counting always on government aid yet refusing to pay taxes commensurate with the advantages enjoyed.

November 18. Saturday. Dr. Mendelssohn-Bartholdy, great international lawyer and professor at Hamburg University, recently dismissed because his grandfather was a Jew, although he was himself baptized as a Christian, came to see me this morning. He told me of his visit last summer to the World's Fair and the University of Chicago where he lectured, as I knew from other sources, with great success. He is to leave his position January 1, 1934. Since he is so well known in the United States and England, I could not see how the Hitler Government could afford to dismiss him. He made the impression of a very competent and dignified man. When he left, I dictated a letter to the Carnegie Institution in New York asking for an appropriation of the amount of his salary for two years, in the hope that the German Minister of Education, Bernhard Rust, would find a way to reinstate him.

November 19. Sunday. Two months ago I agreed to lecture before the German-American Church Forum on Martin Luther. I did not then know that the government had set aside a Luther Day in November when high officials were to speak on the great reformer. I indicated the 19th as the most convenient date for me. When the government decided in October, about the 15th, to run a campaign for approval of German withdrawal from the League of Nations, they chose November 19th, the Sunday after the election, as Luther Day. This gave my appearance a somewhat embarrassing aspect, as it seemed semi-official. There was nothing to be done.

I appeared at the church in due time. The house was crowded to the last seat, some standing. My address had been carefully prepared and was in the hands of both German and American press people. A Nazi leader introduced me and said Hitler was another Luther. The audience did not applaud this strange remark. Although two-thirds of the audience were German, attention was given to every word I said—a fact which seemed significant. I spoke for an hour and treated Luther's career just as I would have done before an American audience. At the end there was extraordinary applause and many correspondents, German as well as American, wished copies of the speech. It was clear to me that Germans wished me to say in public what they are not allowed to say in private, especially about religious and personal freedom.

November 20. Monday. I went today to Von Neurath's office to complain about a letter I had written to Leo Wormser, Jewish leader of Chicago, which had been opened here by German authorities. It was peculiarly offensive because the letter bore the stamp and seals of the United States and because the Jewish problem has been acute ever since I came to Berlin. The Foreign Secretary seemed to be quite nonplused; but I was sure he would, or could, do nothing to prevent a recurrence. I wrote to Wormser for the original to see what the German Government had learned about me.

November 21. Tuesday. My wife and I had dinner with Dr. von Bülow tonight. Dr. Schacht was the one guest who interested me; there were others, including one or two princes from the old regime who wore on their arms the Hakenkreuz, symbol of extreme attachment to the Fuehrer. A former naval commander who had played a role in the World War was present and talked of his experiences as though he hoped to have repetitions soon. Von Bülow and his sister, our hostess, were quite modest but still willing to talk of their family as dating back to the 13th century and composing 1,500 members, scattered all over Germany and meeting occasionally to celebrate their fame. Many were lost in the World War. There was no hint that any of them thought the Germans had been wrong in that struggle.

November 23. Thursday. A young social worker from Baltimore who had been in Germany two years came at noon. She reviewed for a second time her experiences as a student of existing German conditions. She was first in sympathy with the republican regime here and lived in a German family until she learned the language almost perfectly. She was roughly treated by the Nazi regime, but continued her studies of labor and concentration camps. Existing authorities then reversed their attitude and escorted her all about the country. She reported the existence of huge ammunition plants, the arbitrary behavior of Dr. Robert Ley, head of the Labor Front, and the sometimes stubborn refusal of workers in a great factory in Bavaria to give him the demanded Hitler greeting. She wishes to lecture in the United States and Charles R. Crane wishes to support her in this. I warned her that whatever she said for or against the Nazi system, and no one can be exactly neutral, she must not quote me.

Since the United States Government has recognized Soviet

Russia, I called today at the request of the State Department on the Soviet Ambassador. He said he had been a student here about 1888-90 and had taken his doctorate in Berlin. He spoke German a little more fluently than I do. He impressed me in no way as an extreme Communist. The talk turned almost exclusively to the Russo-Japanese conflict in Manchuria. Help in that area seemed one possible result of American recognition, with trade important only in a secondary degree.

The Associated Press had a photographer waiting as I came from the office. The Russian had indicated his willingness to have a photo made of us standing together. I demurred a little, telling him that certain reactionary papers in America would exaggerate the fact of my call and repeat their attacks upon Roosevelt for his recognition. He assented quite readily. The newspaper man was not a little peeved, from appearances. Perhaps I was wrong.

At 8:30 we sat down to a great table at Von Neurath's house on Hermann Göringstrasse, near the Brandenburger Tor. The dinner was elaborate. The Turkish Ambassador was the guest of honor; we were second in the great procession of thirty people from the reception room into the dining room. A countess of the old regime walked in with me. She was so enthusiastic a Nazi that conversation on any other subject always, strangely enough, turned itself to Hitler. She thought the Chancellor would soon see that the Hohenzollerns came back to the throne. My wife and I left at 10:30, a little to the disgust of the wife of the Turkish Ambassador who seemed to think nobody could possibly leave before she made the first move.

I had an exchange of words with the Foreign Minister, learned that his family is an ancient Württemburg one and that earlier members of it have played conspicuous roles in German history. His library contains some rare pictures, books and a copy of Prince von Bülow's famous autobiography of which the younger Von Bülow never says anything. It is a book of wonderful egotism, although it contains much truth about the German role in the last half century before his death. I noticed the four thick volumes, but made no comment on their contents.

November 24. Friday. James Hazen Hyde, New Yorker whom Theodore Roosevelt was once pressed to appoint Ambassador to France, now living in Paris and married to an attractive French woman, called this morning to talk over French-German relations. He is well informed and still wealthy, although not half so rich as formerly. He has endowed a chair in the Sorbonne for an American professorship-exchange with Harvard. He remained a full hour and was far more agreeable and better informed than most millionaires I have met.

The Soviet Ambassador, about to leave for Moscow, came to return my call of yesterday. At night we were guests of Louis Lochner and Miss Sigrid Schultz at the annual press ball, a dinner-dance. I sat opposite the famous Franz von Papen whose espionage role in Washington was such that my friend Louis Brownlow, now of the University of Chicago, had to arrest him. He was ordered out of the country a little before the United States entered the World War. He is now Vice-Chancellor of the new Reich but without any real administrative function. Being a Catholic he has been used for papal contact purposes and he is reported to have betrayed his former party leader, Heinrich Bruening, ex-Chancellor, now in hiding, in a way not unbecoming his record in Washington.

His wife sat on my right and seemed in no way uncomfortable in my presence. We did not talk of Von Bernstorff's famous work in America during Wilson's Presidency. She boasted of our university system. Her son had been a student at Georgetown University. The dinner was a bore, though the company present might under other circumstances have been most informing. François-Poncet, Von Neurath, Sir Eric Phipps and other leaders of the diplomatic corps were near us. The photographers never tired of making snaps.

November 27. Monday. Mr. Kittridge of the Rockefeller Foundation called to talk over possible withdrawal of support here. I advised against that policy but urged greater care in applying funds so that real men with free minds now under terrible pressure might not be silenced for good and all. He named Professor Hermann Oncken as one of the Rockefeller advisers. I know Oncken is in an embarrassing position and dares not write history frankly as we may do at home, if we try, though our history has never yet been written correctly.

November 29. Wednesday. We started in our little car at 10:30 for Dresden where I am speaking at a Thanksgiving dinner tomorrow night at the famous Bellevue Hotel. It was a cold, dreary day, the roads very crooked, and only one town on the way, Jüterbog, was of any historic interest. We stopped there and had a plain country dinner at two marks each. The hotel was of ancient build and the service was such as Martin Luther and Johan Tetzel might have had when the latter was selling Papal indulgences in the town in 1507-1517. It is a 14th century town with its old walls still standing, three great gates and one famous church. But neither royalist tradition nor Lutheran creed prevents Nazi flags and uniforms from being flaunted on every possible occasion.

November 30. Thursday. I read President Roosevelt's Thanksgiving Proclamation before about fifty people in the American Church at Dresden. At 8:30 a company of 150 Americans and Germans gathered in the Bellevue for dinner. I spoke fifteen or twenty minutes about Roosevelt and his talk, but not for press comment.

A young German, Herbert von Gütschow, who had lived ten years in the United States and become closely connected with James B. Duke, North Carolina's greatest buccaneer, and then set up branches of the American Tobacco Company in Germany, came after my speech to our table and talked half an hour. It was plain that one effect of the war had been to make him chief owner of the Duke tobacco interests in Germany, with Dresden as headquarters. He is a very rich man, entirely reconciled to the Hitler system, even though he has been compelled to endow some one hundred and fifty couples of his employees under the present marriage law of the Third Reich.

Gütschow is one of the many big business men who expect to govern Germany under the Nazi regime. August Diehn of Berlin, head of a world-wide nitrate trust, and Fritz Thyssen, steel and munitions manufacturer, are among the others. Gütschow is clever though not liberal in social philosophy; but I am convinced that he and all the rest are allowed great tax exemptions for their support. Six or eight of them sit in semi-official Cabinet sessions on occasions when any crisis threatens. Consul General Messersmith has explained to me how great corporations here escape heavy taxation, far more than in America. My Dresden acquaintance talked for an hour about the marvelous success of his tobacco and cigarette business here and urged as his opinion that Adam Smith must again become the economic master of public men.

December 1. Friday. We set out for Prague over the mountainous road to the southeast. A beautiful and fertile country all the way, about 125 miles. There was snow most of the time, though people were still working in the fields. I never saw such magnificent pine forests as those which cover the mountains. We arrived about 4 in the famous old Huss city.

At 6:30 I talked with Eduard Beneš, the Czechoslovak Premier, confidentially. He is to all intents and purposes the President of the ancient Bohemia so hated for hundreds of years in Germany. He is not optimistic, and says the Germans are determined on annexing a part if not all of his country. He sees the Hungarian Foreign Secretary tomorrow, Saturday, and then goes to Paris where Balkan-Italian rivalries are up for discussion. He impressed me as very clever and ready to fight at the drop of a hat.

December 2. Saturday. We started back to Dresden at 11 o'clock, snow everywhere and the weather quite cold. We had a somewhat risky drive over the mountains and arrived in the city about 6 o'clock. Stopping at the Hotel Eden, we remained incognito and had a very delightful dinner at the Kaiserhof. To bed early, the Eden being too cold for comfort except in bed.

December 3. Sunday. The family drove via Jüterbog to Berlin while I took the train, third class, at 8.50 marks. A German commercial salesman was in the same compartment and I learned a good deal from him about public opinion and so-called recovery. He was not a Nazi but hopeful of improvement and willing to wait until fair trial had been granted.

December 4. Monday. John Foster Dulles, legal counsel for associated American banks, called at noon to give an account of claims being urged on behalf of bondholders against German cities and corporations, more than a billion dollars. He seemed very clever and also resolute. He will have a conference with Reichsbank directors tomorrow.

December 5. Tuesday. We arrived in Munich at 8 o'clock this morning and went first to the Hotel Kaiserhof. It seemed too cold. Then we inspected the Regina where more comfortable rooms were found, but they were still rather cold.

I spoke for an hour tonight on "The Beginnings of First Social Order in the United States." Although I cannot believe more than half the audience understood what I said, there was extreme silence, except for applause now and then when I described some early American democratic ideals. This I took as evidence of the audience's disapproval of the restraints put upon men in Germany.

December 6. Wednesday. I received a long-distance message from the Embassy that William Bullitt, new Ambassador to Russia, would lunch with us Saturday. I was told that the Soviet Foreign Commissar, Maxim Litvinov, returning via Rome from Washington, would join Bullitt in Berlin. I decided to return via Nürnberg so as to have them at our house.

December 9. Saturday. Ambassador Bullitt came alone, Litvinov having hurried off to Moscow. Bullitt said Roosevelt sent cordial regards and thanks for my work here and then added that Russian recognition had been too long delayed. He also said Litvinov had agreed to pay the debt of $100,000,000 and to open Russian markets to American industrial goods and leave Germans in the lurch since they were indignant at Hitler attacks upon all Communists. One more thrust at the Third Reich. But Germans owe Americans over a billion dollars. How can these be paid if German markets are closed, *i.e.*, if the United

States monopolizes Russian markets and still further isolates the Germans. Collect one hundred millions from Moscow and lose one billion in Berlin. Bullitt never referred to this.

We walked to our house at 1:30 for luncheon where we had a party of ten, including the Russian Chargé d'Affaires, the German Foreign Office specialist on Russia, Counselor White, Ambassador Cudahy and others. It was an interesting group, though little could be said because of the conflicting attitudes of Germans and Russians.

Sir Eric Phipps, the British Ambassador, called at our house tonight to show me points of Chancellor Hitler's offer to treat with the French on disarmament. About October 15, details were wired to Washington: Germany must have a standing army of 300,000, guns and defensive airplanes. Now, Hitler offers to submit the same scheme again and adds that the Germans wish a ten year pact against war and will agree to an international commission to inspect and supervise armaments, including supervision of the S.A. and S.S. troops, 2,500,000 strong.

These offers had been cabled to London and the reply of Sir John Simon was submitted to me. It looked to me like a real move toward disarmament and I agreed to telegraph a summary to Washington.

December 10. Sunday. I was still meditating Sir Eric Phipps' negotiations. I called him at 10 and said: I shall be walking at 11:30 on the Hermann Göringstrasse alongside the Tiergarten; would you be able to meet me there and talk for a while? He agreed and we spent a half hour going over disarmament problems. My points were these: Japan, according to certain diplomatic information, is apt to attack Vladivostok next April or May; second, if the United States were to support the German-British position on disarmament, would the British lend moral support to American opposition to Japanese aggression in the Far East?; third, did he not think it would be far better for an English-German-French pact to be made on disarmament than to take the chance of an eventual Italian-German-Russian deal which might force France into a dictatorship?

Sir Eric was not disposed to accept the Japanese danger; he wished American moral support but indicated, indirectly, that England had recognized Japanese claims in Manchuria. He seemed ready to acknowledge the danger to world peace if autocracies of Central Europe were allowed to compel French submission. We ended our conversation in agreement on one general point: a ten year peace pact for Europe, initiated and pressed by England, Germany and the United States, would be far more effective if Russia were a party to it and peace in the Far East were also fixed. I thought the English ought to compromise, then President Roosevelt might negotiate and Europe would be out of its impasse. I returned to the Embassy and hurried off a telegram to the State Department with a request that it be discussed with the President.

December 20. Wednesday. The papers carry stories of the week-end visit of Sir Eric Phipps to London, his reception by the King at Windsor, his visit to Sir John Simon, and the proposed visit of the latter to Paris and Rome, all to iron out difficulties between Germany and France. Sir Eric is generous-minded and, in my judgment, frank and open; but Sir John, the Foreign Secretary in London, is everywhere regarded as tricky.

William and Martha attended a birthday party at the house of the Crown Prince at Potsdam, son of Kaiser William II. They reported a delightful evening and hearty cordiality. One of the sons is now in the United States working for Henry Ford. Another is a student of law at the University of Berlin and a most charming young fellow but clearly aware of the greatness of his ancestry.

December 21. Thursday. Sir Eric is again in Berlin and spent an hour with Von Neurath, although the latter was due to leave for Württemberg for the Christmas season. Von Neurath had surprised me a few days ago by his concern about the imminence of war in the Far East and his distinct interest in Soviet Russia. He said Japan would invade Russia in case of war and that the result would be chaos in Russia.

December 22. Friday. A newspaper man, whose information I have found always to be reliable but whose name I dare not mention even in this diary, came to me this morning to say that a high German official—my guess is Secret Police Chief Rolf Diels—had told him that tomorrow the German Supreme Court would declare all the Communists except Van der Lubbe, on trial since September for burning the Reichstag, not guilty. But Georgi Dimitrov, the Bulgarian Communist, disowned by his own country, was to be murdered before he could get out of the country, by order of the Prussian Prime Minister, Goering. My friend's informant went on to say, "I know my life is in danger when I speak to you, but I have had several terrible nights and must let you know in the hope you can do something which will cause the order to be annulled." My newspaper friend was perturbed, refused to give me the name of the official informant but avowed that the murder of Dimitrov was certain unless something were done immediately to inform the world.

It is a curious case. In my judgment the official who gave the information is the one man in Germany who knows exactly who burned the Reichstag. In November he was threatened by Goering with concentration camp for an undisclosed reason, but was merely removed from office early in December. Late in November, Consul General Messersmith reported that he, Diels, felt his life in danger and he wished I might help him in some way. Messersmith could do nothing. I had no approach personally to any high official who had his case in hand, and I could do nothing. Two weeks later, he was reported as restored to his office, after an interim during which it was announced Goering was functioning as Chief of Secret Police. I think it was all a ruse, perhaps to intimidate Diels because he possesses damaging information.

At 11:30, Sir Eric Phipps brought the official British reply to Hitler's statement which had been submitted to me before Sir Eric took it to London. The British agree with the German demands except that they ask further reduction of the German Reichswehr and one or two more specific statements about armaments. It looked reasonable. Sir Eric said Von Neurath had indicated Hitler's approval and hoped England could bring France into the negotiations soon after January 1. I have heard from Washington that government officials there are alarmed at a rumor that Great Britain is contemplating a large loan to Japan which would, in the opinion of our officials, encourage Japan to make war on the Soviet Union.

At 4 my newspaper informant reported that the London afternoon papers had carried the story of the possible killing of Dimitrov which a news agency had got from him. He had then framed a story for the American press which could in no way injure anyone who had given him information but which would react tomorrow in Germany in such a way as to save Dimitrov's life. He said: "I do not regret what I have done. It is more of a service to Germany and to peace negotiations than anything else I could have done. If I had done nothing, the terrible deed would have been perpetrated and the outside world would have been in furore."

I could not say him no, though it was clear he had taken a risky action. He showed me a telegram to the foreign press from Goebbels denying the whole story, but blaming Goering, fellow member of the triumvirate, with indiscreet statements which caused the "lie" to be spread about the world. I am awaiting the arrival of British and American news. Of course the German papers will carry nothing. There may be a sad aftermath to this.

December 25. Christmas Day. German demonstrations are extraordinary: Christmas trees at public squares and in every house I saw. One might think the Germans believed in Jesus or practiced his teachings!

I stopped by this afternoon at the home of my journalist friend. After a moment's admiration of the Christmas decorations, I took him aside and learned that his friend in high office had thanked him for the effective way he had handled the press matter, committing no one and yet producing a reaction in official circles here. Goering being away, his substitute ordered the Saxon police to take the released prisoners in charge and see that they were safely kept and were not allowed to cross over the Prussian border, lest the order to put Dimitrov out of the way be executed. So the matter rests.

I believe there was some order issued by Goering before his departure, that Diels, very hostile to Goering and in danger all the time, ventured to defeat the order to save Germany the terrible reaction which would have come from all over the world. The Secret Police Chief did a most dangerous thing and I shall not be surprised later to hear that he has been sent to prison. The only safety he has is his immense knowledge of the details of the Reichstag burning and the possibility that his proof may be lodged outside of Germany.

January 1, 1934. Monday. All the members of the diplomatic corps made a point to be in town today to pay their respects and good wishes to President von Hindenburg, eighty-six years old on his last birthday. We drove to the Presidential Palace, where we were conducted into a large waiting room on the second floor, being greeted as we entered by servants in uniform giving the Hitler salute. I fell in with Sir Eric Phipps, M. François-Poncet and the Spanish Ambassador. At 12 sharp we took our places, standing all around the large and ornate reception room of the President's Palace.

Soon Von Hindenburg greeted the Papal Nuncio, senior diplomat, and the latter read a rather formal New Year's greeting in French which it was evident the President did not understand and which I also did not follow. The President replied in a formally written speech, mentioning the "rebirth" of Germany and touching delicately upon the meaning of the Hitler regime, a subject for which hardly a member of the corps showed any sympathy.

When these formalities were over Von Hindenburg spoke a few words with the Nuncio and then talked cordially with M. François-Poncet who understands and speaks German very well. After greeting M. Cerruti, the Italian Ambassador, in the same way, he shook hands with me, asked me how my son William's work in the University of Berlin was progressing, went out of his way to flatter me about my German, which is rather ready if inaccurate. We then exchanged remarks about Professor Oncken, the famous historian Mommsen and, at the Reich President's suggestion, "the great Von Treitschke," who was not great in my judgment. He walked a little badly, leaning upon his cane, but talked glibly and intelligently. He seems to know intellectual Germany.

Then came Hitler who, as I had observed all along, seemed very much subdued, almost embarrassed. Hitler greeted me with "Happy New Year" and I returned it. Only the Italian Ambassador answered the Fuehrer's official salute. I asked the Chancellor if he had not spent his Christmas at Munich. I said we spent two days in Munich early in December and that I had greatly enjoyed the visit, that I had met a fine German historian, Professor Meyer, a former fellow student with me at Leipzig whom I think a really good scholar and thinker. Hitler was a little nonplused and indicated that he had never heard of Meyer. I mentioned other Munich University matters only to get no response, and he passed on, leaving the impression that he had never had contacts with the people I knew and respected. He showed no such interest as the President showed; I am afraid he thought I was trying to embarrass him a little. I was not. There was, however, no diplomatic or political subject we could mention these touchy times.

January 3. Wednesday. The foreign press today carries a story that there was a hard fight on the morning of January 1 between Hitler and Goering about the failure to apply the decree of two months ago to the effect that all Germany was to be co-ordinated, *i.e.,* all the ancient states—Prussia, Bavaria, Saxony and the rest—were to be cast into one and then subdivided into some hundred or more equal-sized districts each to be ruled by a district leader appointed by the Chancellor.

The order had been issued and everyone supposed that it was to become effective this year, thus abandoning states and legislatures. But on January 1, Hitler and Goebbels found themselves challenged by Goering, supported by the Governor of Bavaria. There was apparently a sharp conflict for some days because Hitler sent no New Year's greeting to Goering, only to apologize on January 2. It was this struggle, which had been

decided in favor of Goering, on January 1, before the diplomatic reception by Von Hindenburg, which in my judgment
gave Hitler's countenance such a dejected look that morning.

It was really an important issue, for the German people are
clearly opposed to Hitler's position in this matter, as they are
opposed to his plan of putting all Protestants under one State
Bishop and into one solid phalanx. From 3,000 to 4,000 preachers are resisting to the limit. These two issues reveal a good
deal of the spirit of Germany, though no speeches are allowed
and the press never does more than mention the fact that certain decrees have been postponed in their application. In these
cases concentration camp and beatings are not applied, but there
is a powerful silent resistance.

I received a cable advising a protest to German officials against
Schacht's ruling that interest on German bonds held in the
United States must be decreased from previous reduced payments, 50 per cent in real values and 50 per cent in promises
to pay, to 30 per cent in real value and 70 per cent in promises
to pay. I was also to add that the manner of doing it was
highly objectionable, that is, without consulting creditors and
then buying back German bonds when their values fell to low
points on the New York market.

As Von Neurath and Von Bülow were away on their vaca-
tions, I saw Dr. Koepke, acting for the Secretary, and made
two points rather strongly: 1. The sudden announcement that
Germany would not pay, without conference, was inconsiderate;
German cities which had borrowed huge sums are not insolvent;
great public buildings constructed out of American funds constantly advertised the nature of the loans; and known buying
of large blocks of bonds on American markets looked bad, like
stock-market manipulation. 2. This sort of conduct was arousing
millions of Americans and causing the government to take an
active role whereas formerly it had been disposed to leave such
private matters to the banks which had originally sold the bonds
and made profits from so doing. I stressed the point that the
German Government could not afford to appear in the actions
of its national bank as a mere stock manipulator.

Koepke agreed with both my points and indicated that the

Foreign Office had not been consulted. He also made plain that such rulings were wrong, that Germany could pay her obligations, at least the great cities could, and that the speculative aspects of Schacht's rulings were unworthy. I came away quite sure that the Foreign Office would try to bring Schacht to a more co-operative way of doing things, but doubting still whether they would succeed. Schacht is the real master and government officials here dare not order him to do anything.

January 5. Friday. Bishop John L. Neilson of the Methodist Episcopal Church in the United States, now a resident of Zurich and supervising Methodists in Central Europe, called to talk over Protestant church problems in Germany. He showed an intimate acquaintance with the recent religious conflict here and thought splendid the Lutheran resistance to Nazi efforts to force all church people into one solid National Church, even worshiping Wotan and adopting the myths of the early German people.

He said American Methodists here had been assured of their independent status, but they must not proselytize Germans. His story was much like that of Dr. Charles MacFarland's in October. I wonder whether the Germans of 1934 have the courage of Luther and will simply say: "We cannot surrender; burn us if you will!" If Lutherans say this, Catholics are apt to support them.

January 6. Saturday. The Swedish Minister, M. C. E. af Wirsen, came in to say that he was going to the German Foreign Office to make the same protest I had made about debts. Germans owe the Swedes large sums.

At noon the Dutch Minister, Limburg-Stirum, an able and experienced diplomat, came to voice his agreement on the debt question, though German discrimination in favor of the Dutch was not discussed. I simply let him know that I knew the Germans were paying his people the full face value of bonds and the regular rate of interest. Schacht argues that this is because the Dutch buy more German goods than they sell of their own to Germany.

Limburg-Stirum dwelt much more upon Japanese aggression in China. He said Japanese generals were organizing independent governments in former portions of China, aimed at setting up a Far Eastern League of Nations under Japanese domination. He added that Holland's possessions in the Far East, also the Philippines, would soon fall into Japanese hands if the United States did not strongly resist, and especially if England continued to give underhand support to Japanese aggression.

January 9. Tuesday. I had luncheon at the Hotel Adlon as the guest of the American Chamber of Commerce. The Russian Ambassador read a very discreet address on Communist commercial policy. He was well received. He went the limit in approval of the United States. I think he is one of the best equipped diplomats in Berlin and personally not much of a Communist.

January 10. Wednesday. Dr. Otto Vollbehr of Washington, the man who sold the Gutenberg Bible to the Library of Congress about 1929, came to see me. He had tried later to propagandize American university professors in Germany. I had protested against this in more than one letter to him, but he did not refer to my rebukes to him. He said he had visited the Propaganda Ministry, that he had talked with Ambassador Luther in Washington, and that he had an appointment with Hitler in a day or two. He was not altogether discreet, but I thought he wished to let me guess that he had come to Berlin on a special mission. I warned him as to the harmfulness of propaganda. He pretended entire agreement and departed in good humor.

January 11. Thursday. My wife gave her first general reception. It was a tiresome affair but it was the only way to renew acquaintance with many people who had left cards. The expense was around $200.

January 16. Tuesday. The American Minister in Vienna, George Earle, called at 11 o'clock. He is one of the rich men appointed to foreign posts who know little history of their own or any other country. He is good-natured and very anti-Nazi. I had seen him before, when he came here to report on Austrian problems sometime in November.

I then thought he had made a good survey of Austrian conditions. Since that time he has shown rather curious attitudes for a Minister in so critical a zone as Vienna. He went once to Prague, out of his diplomatic territory, and denounced the German Nazis in Czechoslovakia in a manner which caused a protest to the American Legation there. A few days before last Christmas, he wired me to dine with him at a public dinner in honor of Dollfuss, the Austrian Chancellor, so hated in Germany that he dares not put his foot on German soil. I wired that I could not accept. It would have made a sensation of the first order if I had gone to Vienna, and Earle would have been even worse off than he is.

He related some of his disagreeable experiences with Nazi chiefs in Vienna, including threats against his life, and told of Dollfuss' dangerous position, with the prospect of devaluation constantly confronting him. When he asked if I wished to send any messages to the President, I declined, as the pouch was leaving anyway the next day. But I asked the poor fellow to lunch.

Sitting with the family at table Earle related his experiences again. One day while hunting in the Austrian Tyrol, he had been shot at and his boot torn half off. He left his boots on the train as he went home so as not to let his wife know what had happened. "That is Nazi Austria," he said, "and any time the leaders of the old army element turn Nazi, Dollfuss will be overthrown and there will be chaos." He added that the Nazis say: "Hitler is Jesus Christ for the whole of Europe and everybody must recognize it. If the Jews keep on resisting in Austria, the greatest pogrom in history will be executed."

Earle's conversation was good. He is intelligent, but he has a rich man's estimate of social values. For instance, servants, valets, butlers were to him a mark of distinction. He thought it terrible that less than 300 families in Vienna had as many as three servants each. I sent him to his train in my car as a means of protection in case the Secret Police were watching.

January 17. Wednesday. A message came from Louis Lochner that the church problem had taken a curious turn yesterday. The new Nazi Reichsbishop Ludwig Mueller was in session with fifteen or more bishops and other church leaders. Chancellor Hitler came to explain to them that he and the President had agreed to the Protestants' claim for freedom from the control of the new pagan state religion called Deutsche Christen, Mueller being the head of this movement.

When Hitler had finished and a compromise seemed about to be worked out, Goering, a Catholic though not in good standing with Rome, walked uninvited into the conference room and made a violent speech: "I have a record of all of your conversations over the telephone for the last month. You Protestant trouble-makers have been most unloyal. You are trying to break up the unity of the State. You have gone so far as to persuade the Chancellor to surrender. I think most of you are on the borderline of treason." The meeting broke up and all agreements were canceled, though another meeting may follow.

January 19. Friday. The Dutch Minister at dinner on the 16th informed me of a long-distance call he had made to the Bank of Holland in Amsterdam, instructing them to call the Westminster Bank in London regarding an official British loan to the Japanese. The London bank assured them that no loan was at all possible.

My wife and family attended a party of Baron Eberhard von Oppenheim who is a Jew still living in style near us. Many Nazi Germans were present. It is reported that Oppenheim has given the Nazi Party 200,000 marks and has been given a special Party dispensation which declared him an Aryan.

January 22. Monday. I went today to see Dr. Schacht in his office at the Reichsbank. He was very conciliatory. He read aloud the protest which I gave him and said he agreed substantially with all that was said. He would confer with the Foreign Office and send me a reply at 5 o'clock. He added that the one thing he wanted and had asked was a delegation from all the bondholders with power to act, *i.e.*, power of attorney to each national delegation authorizing reduction of rates of interest from 7 per cent to 4 or 4½ per cent. He thought all bonds everywhere were on the market at lower rates or were being defaulted and felt the German Government should not be expected to pay so high a rate. I agreed that some such arrangement should be made.

The Belgian Minister came again to my office and talked for half an hour very despondently about the difficulty of maintaining peace. He emphasized the dangers to his country, its close reliance upon England and the atrocities of the German occupation. He expressed no skepticism on the last point. He agreed there is a lot of talk about a "preventive war" in French official circles, fearing this would mean general war.

John Foster Dulles of New York and Laird Bell of Chicago followed the Minister and reported readiness for the debt conference which Schacht had called, the English delegation arriving tomorrow. I had a message from President Roosevelt that the American Government was much concerned and hoped I could render assistance. Dulles and Bell were described as official spokesmen of creditors holding more than a billion dollars. American bankers had loaned this after the Dawes and Young negotiations, at high rates, issued bonds in New York and sold them at $90 to the public, taking enormous profits for themselves. Money was put into city, state and corporation improvements, a vast building scheme like that of 1922-1929 in the United States. Now my job is to save as much of this as possible. The National City and Chase National banks hold $100,000,000 of these securities. Last June Roosevelt said: ". . . the bankers have gotten themselves into this. You must lend what personal, unofficial aid you can, but no more." Now the creditors, the New York bankers, have organized and pressed the government into fighting their battles. I shall do what I can but agree with the Germans that rates of interest ought to be reduced to 4 per cent.

At 1:30 Ivy Lee and his son James came to lunch. Ivy Lee showed himself at once a capitalist and an advocate of Fascism. He told stories of his fight for Russian recognition and was disposed to claim credit for it. His sole aim was to increase American business profits.

January 23. Tuesday. Messrs. Bell, Dulles, Junius Wood of the *Chicago Daily News* and Joseph Flack of the Embassy staff came to lunch. They talked about the conference over debts which has broken up into private discussions between the different delegations. They expect to persuade the Dutch and Swiss to yield their advantages after the present terms have expired, which will be in June of this year.

January 24. Wednesday. Newspaper people showed such increasing interest in the debt conference that I invited them to meet me at 5 o'clock. They came and I went over the problems, explained Schacht's attitude and mentioned the bankers' large measure of responsibility.

January 25. Thursday. I went to a *Bierabend* at the mansion of Ernst Roehm, Chief of Staff of the S.A. He had recently served as a messenger of Hitler to Rome. I was introduced to the host in all his decorations. How the German Nazis love decorations! Von Neurath and the Italian Ambassador were present. I stayed half an hour, then left, politely, I thought, for home.

January 26. Friday. Dr. Wilbur K. Thomas, of Philadelphia, representative of the American branch of the Carl Schurz Foundation, called to report on his month of travel all over Germany. Not one man had spoken to him favorably of the Nazi policies toward the churches, universities and the outside world. He said hundreds of Germans had talked to him. This also is my experience everywhere except in the presence of uniformed people. He said he had stopped the Carl Schurz Foundation from engaging in propaganda work in America. We shall see.

January 29. Monday. Ivy Lee again came with his son James to report on his experiences here during the week of his stay. Lee did nearly all the talking. He had seen Goebbels an hour, had talked freely with Dr. Kurt Schmitt, Minister of Economics, and other key men. He had warned Goebbels to cease propaganda in the United States, urged him to see the foreign press people often and learn how to get along with them.

Lee said that Dr. Schmitt and Dr. Dieckhoff of the Foreign Office had suggested expulsion of foreign press correspondents, which I had suspected was contemplated here. Lee said he warned the Foreign Office that such an act would ruin the Nazi movement.

Lee had not seen Hitler, though I suspect he had hoped to have an interview. I told him something of the delicate situation in Vienna. He replied that he had urged the Party leaders to abandon their propaganda in Austria on the theory that thus they would soon win that nation into the German Nazi orbit! From all I have learned these last eight months, the Austrians have grown so sick of the methods practiced here that they, like the Germans of Czechoslovakia, would be unwilling to join the German Reich. Lee was on his way back home, via Paris, to New York to continue his strange work.

January 30. Tuesday. I went to a *Bierabend* at Alfred Rosenberg's. He is the head of the Foreign Office of the Nazi Party. The Minister of Justice for Bavaria spoke of the new laws enacted to secure the unity of Germany, the subordination of the Jews, and the new spirit of the Nazi state which he thought almost perfect. He subscribed to a Nazi version of the Hegelian philosophy of state: all peasants and workers in the cities are happy to serve the Nazi state, without thought of self. On my right sat a member of the Propaganda Ministry. I asked him if he believed workers and peasants were so happily absorbed in the state. He said: "Yes, absolutely." Rosenberg sat on my left but he did not talk like an educated, trained man, even though he is the author of a famous Nazi classic, *The Myth of the Twentieth Century.*

January 31. Wednesday. I attended a dinner at Dr. Kurt Schmitt's in Dahlem. He is Minister of Economics and lives in a large house fitted out in grand style, though in good taste. The party included some aristocrats of the old days but they were not in the least pretentious. Schmitt is a Bavarian and a big landlord. He seems to be a most loyal Hitlerite though his public speeches show him to be courageous in opposition to some Nazi policies. The day of my arrival in Berlin he deliv-

ered an address on economic recovery which I thought notable
though conservative.

February 1. Thursday. This day illustrates the folly of the
diplomatic world. At 8:30, after a busy morning and afternoon
at the office, my wife and I went to the Italian Ambassador's
palace. At a time when Italy declares herself unable to pay any
part of the billion dollar debt due the United States for preserving her existence in 1918, M. Vittorio Cerruti, the Ambassador, took us into a palace, newly rebuilt and enlarged, where
the most expensive decorations imaginable adorned every wall.
As we went up the broad, winding stairs, servants attired in
18th century livery and with wigs dressed and colored after
the manner of Louis XV's time, stood at attention on both
sides of the approaches.

In the reception room there were some forty guests, the
diplomats in official diplomatic regalia and the Germans in
army or Nazi uniforms. The dining room was the largest we
have yet seen and there was a servant for every fourth guest.
They stood at attention behind the chairs, watching every movement of knife and fork and I know not what else! I would
guess the show cost at least $800, and the palace is almost as
great as the White House in Washington while its halls and
rooms are more expensively fitted out. Yet Italy is unable to
pay a dollar of her debt!

I sat on the left of the clever Madame Cerruti, a Hungarian
Jewess, whom the Germans do not dare to embarrass, and who
is such an ardent Hungarian nationalist that she talks all the
time about her "poor stricken country." She lives hopefully for
the day when it will be restored to mastery of the Balkans. She
hardly spoke of Italy, which her husband represents. There
were masses of expensive flowers on the table, three or four
wine glasses at every place and everything was served on huge
silver platters and in heavy silver dinner plates. There was no
general conversation and nothing of importance mentioned the
whole evening. Diplomatic display and strut and nothing more!

From the Cerrutis' we went to the Hotel Kaiserhof where
we were joined by our children at a grand reception, a stand-up

party given by the Foreign Minister and his wife. The hosts receive their friends, official Germans and the diplomatic corps, like this once a year. There must have been at least 700 or more people. Supper was served on a huge table literally loaded down with food of all kinds, beer, wine and liquors of all sorts, and there were servants by the score to assist. It was a grand show that must have cost more than $1,000, at the expense of poor Germany! There was some opportunity for a little gossip as people gathered in groups to look at one another's decorations or women's exposed backs and breasts. We were duly received, loitered around from 10:30 to 11:15, and then we took our departure. To me it was quite as useless a display as the dinner party of the Italians. I have always acted upon the assumption that people give such entertainments in order that men may learn something from one another. Not this evening. I was delighted to return to our quiet home. I drank a glass of milk and ate a stewed peach before I retired.

February 3. Saturday. Louis Lochner of the Associated Press and a prominent German religious leader who has supplied Lochner with much secret church information on the Nazi religious warfare came to call. It is counted treason in these times for a German to give foreign newsmen information unless it is favorable to the existing regime. This informant told reckless stories of the Lutheran struggle for freedom of conscience and Lochner expressed fear that his friend might be thrown into a concentration camp. I had the idea they wished help in case of trouble. Both spoke of Dr. MacFarland's "surrender" to the Nazis and said that the English Protestants were yielding to the curious, primitive Aryan Christianity of Hitler and Rosenberg. A peculiar religious unity is prevailing here but I believe the Lutherans will surrender; the incomes of their clergy come from the government.

February 7. Wednesday. James G. McDonald came at 3 o'clock to our house. He is the League of Nations High Commissioner for German Refugees. The task of his organization is to help the persecuted to find homes somewhere in the United States or Latin America. His headquarters are to be at

Lausanne, Switzerland, and he is now organizing his staff and collecting funds.

McDonald impressed me again as not very much enamored of his new and difficult position, though his work as planned seems to me very important, for Hitler is never going to cease trying to ban all Jews from the Reich. McDonald told me he had raised 500,000 pounds sterling from English Jews but that the givers were not enthusiastic and did not wish many German Jews to enter England. He said that in the United States ". . . there is much interest in limited circles but no enthusiasm for taking persecuted Jews into the country." These people must have clerical, professional or financial jobs wherever they migrate and there are few such positions available anywhere.

He wishes to arrange with the Germans for a ten-year plan for the removal of Jews and the transfer of German property for their initial support. Von Neurath is not opposed to this plan, but unable to give any promises. To remove over 600,000 people, most of whom are fairly well-to-do, from any country, is no easy task. To expel them, as has been tried the last twelve months, would arouse intense hostility. Perhaps 50,000 have departed from Germany since Hitler became Chancellor in January, 1933. McDonald remained an hour talking over his difficulties.

At 8:30 we went to dinner with the President of the Reich in his palace on the Wilhelmstrasse. There were fifty diplomats in gala attire present, servants as numerous as in the Italian palace. There was a military tone to the evening. I sat between the wives of the Russian and Italian Ambassadors, the Russian very simple and peasant-like, the Italian like a French lady-in-waiting of former times. Von Hindenburg himself was apparently quite vigorous looking.

After dinner we stood in the beautiful reception hall with 18th century paintings of Roman subjects on the walls. Chancellor Hitler moved rather gracefully about speaking somewhat freely. Von Hindenburg retired to a magnificent neighboring room where he received his guests sitting. When I went in and sat down for what was intended to be a brief talk, I noticed Von Neurath came in and sat down near me. I retired promptly.

Perhaps Von Hindenburg would have talked frankly. Von Neurath, in my judgment, intended to prevent that. We came away at 10:30 as suggested on our invitation cards. While the entertainment was good and the attitudes less formal than at other places, I do not think the evening added to anybody's information about anything.

February 10. Saturday. William and Martha gave a ball for 120 people to whom they felt under obligations. It was a gala affair. Prince Friedrich Hohenzollern and the great violinist Kreisler and others were present. I retired at one o'clock.

February 15. Thursday. The Soviet Ambassador called to talk over Far Eastern problems. He is uneasy about Manchoukuo and also the railway controversy with Japan. My feeling is that the situation is not so ominous as when Bullitt passed through.

We had a grand dinner attended by twenty-two diplomats, but nothing to compare with the Belgian or even the Rumanian displays which we have attended. It was an agreeable evening, although there were too many guests for real acquaintanceship or good conversation, except in the corner groups that sat down together after leaving the table. The cost was perhaps $100 or $200, terribly simple for an ambassador.

February 17. Saturday. We had dinner with the Danish Minister, fifty people present, a grand stand-up party. It is dreary to have to repeat the tiresomeness of these affairs, but they seem to be a part of this life.

February 20. Tuesday. Dr. Hjalmar Schacht called at 4:30 to propose a scheme for the U. S. Government to assist American creditors to better faith in German payment of interest and principal by some sort of guarantee until Germans can buy $500,000,000 worth of cotton and then sell cotton to other countries. He says he could convince Roosevelt in fifteen minutes, and then American foreign trade would greatly improve, German credit become good and creditors would be satisfied. I did not quite understand his scheme but sent a report to the State Department. Somehow I came to think that Dr. Schacht could carry his scheme through successfully if given the power. Contrary to public opinion at home, I am amazed and impressed at the great German financier who manipulates German credits and debits so cleverly that, although he has little gold, he keeps his currency value at par and business stable. I wonder if he can get his cotton scheme accepted.

February 21. Wednesday. James Gannon, of the Chase National Bank, New York, called to report a satisfactory conference with the German Reichsbank about the hundreds of millions of dollars in loans known as "standstill" agreement loans. He was quite satisfied and gave Schacht the highest rating for cleverness and honesty.

February 23. Friday. I attended a dinner at Roehm's, Chief of Staff of the S.A., at his new palace on the Matthaikirchestrasse, with about fifty people present. Von Neurath sat on my right and indicated that the League of Nations is essential to world economic recovery and added Germany ought to return if economic questions were taken up in Geneva. I suspected, as once before, that he had not favored German withdrawal last autumn. On the left of the host sat Sir Eric Phipps, British Ambassador, who never said a word the whole evening that could in any way be considered as revealing any kind of attitude of mind. Two or three Nazi chiefs talked with me a half hour about the unfortunate character of German leadership over the last fifty years, except for Bismarck in whose work no error is ever acknowledged here. I went so far as to say Germans do not understand their problem, especially as regards foreign relations. They agreed; even the Nazis are polite.

February 24. Saturday. Our Minister to Vienna, Mr. Earle, who went away from his post a month ago, called at 12 o'clock to report attitudes and opinions of the government and people at home about Austria and its "revolution."

He was quite pleased at Roosevelt's leadership. He said, however, the President looks much older than he did six months ago. This is somewhat disturbing to me in view of the personalities who might become leaders in case of Roosevelt's decease or serious illness.

Earle thinks Dollfuss was right in his ruthless handling of the Socialist rebellion in Austria during the second half of February. I think Dollfuss was very shortsighted, and believe he has given the Nazi group in Austria a fine chance of capturing the government before very long.

February 26. Monday. Another dinner! At 9 o'clock we sat down in the Herren Klub on the Hermann Göringstrasse, as guests of Vice-Chancellor and Frau von Papen. He represents in the Hitler Cabinet the remnant of the Center Party which played a great role from the time of Bismarck to 1932. He is a Catholic and is especially commissioned to rally German opinion for the recovery of the Saar Territory which has been under French mandate from the League since 1920 as a penalty for German destruction of French mines during the war. Von Papen also tries to keep Hitler in contact with the Pope when difficulties threaten the new Reich from a Catholic direction. The opinion here is that he is a futile if intriguing person.

There were more than fifty people present. My wife sat on Von Papen's right, and on both sides of the great semi-quadrilateral table there were counts and countesses, generals, Cabinet officials galore. Of course the conversation could not be general, just the small talk of each man between two women and each woman between two men. When we all marched ceremoniously out of the dining room into the great adjoining reception hall of the military club, we stood in groups and talked a little and looked at the many battle scenes as shown on the broad canvasses of the old Hohenzollern regime. Every picture bore a military stamp.

The one man I talked a little frankly with was the Finance Minister, Count Lutz von Schwerin-Krosigk, a Rhodes Scholar at Oxford before the World War, a soldier on the Western Front for four years, an under official in the Finance Ministry after the Versailles Treaty, and now one of the wisest men in the Hitler Cabinet, I am told. He showed in all he said a decided attitude of distrust toward the present German drift, though he did not mention Hitler. He has been a student of history and a thoughtful observer of events. He is the first eminent German who has agreed with me that Bismarck failed in one large undertaking: he angered eminent and honest leaders when that was entirely unnecessary and he was immensely unpopular in the Foreign Office when he retired. The Count also acknowledged that the Kaiser had made a terrible blunder in 1914 when he allowed the military-financial-industrial groups to drive him into war. No other eminent man here has ever said this much, though several have implied it. We departed at 11, our usual hour, and I wrote a while in my diary when I got home.

February 28. Wednesday. A busy day. I had a long talk with Dr. Ritter of the Foreign Office about a proposed commission to go to Washington to negotiate a new commercial treaty with our government for an increase of imports and exports. It was, like a favored nation treaty, only another way of lowering tariff walls and of course I was sympathetic. The Assistant Secretary of the Economics Ministry, Dr. Posse, was to head the commission.

At 5 o'clock, I went to tea with Propaganda Minister Goebbels who sat down with the Papal Nuncio, the British Ambassador, myself and others of the diplomatic corps. At the appropriate moment he arose and read a somewhat conciliatory speech to the diplomats and all the foreign press people. It was plain he was trying to apply the advice which Ivy Lee urged upon him a month ago and reported very carefully to me. Louis Lochner replied in a clever, humorous manner, assuming there would be frank, weekly conferences thereafter with the press. Goebbels smiled significantly when I happened to catch his eye at this moment. There were no questions asked or answered afterward, which would have been according to British and American habit.

March 2. Friday. We sat down tonight at an informal dinner with Sir Eric Phipps. There were too many guests for any really frank talk, except my favorite way, in a corner. I learned that Anthony Eden, Keeper of the Seals, had been rebuffed in

Paris, perhaps simply put off. French *popular* opinion is reported to be very pacifist, French *official* and *military* opinion to hold that a "preventive war" with Germany should start this spring. The idea is to catch Germany and to seize the Rhineland before it is too late.

March 3. Saturday. At 4 o'clock, I sat down for a frank talk with M. François-Poncet who showed some concern, even anxiety, about the attitude of his government on the Eden negotiations. However, he did not reveal his real attitude as I had half expected, and I came away a little disappointed. If the French were to accept the British scheme of partial disarmament and supervision, the Germans would be put on the defensive and as time passed they would find it impossible to go on arming, as they now are, due to the French attitude since 1920. The French Ambassador indicated that he would communicate with me in the event of any change of policy of his government before my departure for Washington.

March 4. Sunday. Today is the anniversary of President Roosevelt's first day in office. Roosevelt came to office at a moment when all social-economic relations of the so-called western world were undergoing drastic reform. It was a decisive moment in history, like the beginning of the American Revolution in 1774. The individualism which Englishmen and Americans forced into application in their countries between 1774 and 1846 and which the French adopted in their way has everywhere been abused and defeated so that modern society must now act through governments to subordinate individual and corporate aggrandizement, and use social control so that individual independence, equality and initiative may once more prevail, as was planned, except as to religion, by Sam Adams and Thomas Jefferson. Roosevelt sees this in spite of the fact that his training at Groton and Harvard was faulty, even vicious, and the wealth of his family burdensome. The task which he must perform is quite as difficult as Jefferson's effort to abolish slavery.

He has started upon a series of experiments which have already increased the national debt by several billion dollars, and some of the experiments are showing harmful effects. But unlike other Presidents he recognizes errors and shifts his position in order to carry his objective: the reordering of all social and class relations. If he succeeds, the ideal of Adams and Jefferson will be applied in a society where slave-holders (big business chiefs) no longer rule. But it will require modification of his methods and eternal vigilance for decades to come.

In case Roosevelt does not succeed, or if he should die before the greater part of his work is accepted, there will be a dictatorship, which would be ruinous to the United States. My hope is that he carries on until 1941 when he would be able to name his successor and secure prolonged application of his reforms, thus showing Big Business and European autocrats that leadership through democratic processes is still possible in a world of mechanics and invention.

III
March 5, 1934 to July 8, 1934

March 5. Monday. A brief visit to the Dutch Minister revealed evidence of a less belligerent attitude by the Japanese toward Vladivostok than has hitherto appeared to be the case. He keeps in close touch with the Far East and with London and watches the moves in the United States as few other diplomats do.

At 6:30 I went, upon request, to the German Foreign Office. Von Neurath kept me waiting ten minutes which, in view of my experience last October, I noticed and resented. When I entered his office, the old Bismarck room, he was still engaged in reading pages of a memorandum which he held in his hand as we shook hands. He showed a little perturbation and proceeded at once to read me part of a telegram from the German Ambassador in Washington. The telegram gave information about a forthcoming mock trial of Hitler in New York. The Mayor, Fiorello La Guardia, Alfred E. Smith, Judge Samuel Seabury and former American Secretary of State Bainbridge Colby were to indict the German Chancellor for returning Germany to medievalism and for the barbarism of the methods he resorts to. The Jews of New York City, organized labor, and the American Legion, sponsors of the demonstration, had invited the Ambassador, Hans Luther, to defend his chief or send some lawyer to represent him or Hitler!

Von Neurath was nonplused. I had told him more than once

the Jewish policy of Hitler would bring further trouble if not changed. He had pretended agreement. When he asked me to cable Washington in the hope that the President or Secretary Hull would intervene and stop the trial, I said that it could be done only by violating fundamental American principles, that nobody in the United States could suppress a private or public meeting (although I knew the governments of cities and states had suppressed meetings of socialists and pacifists during the World War period) without violating the constitutions of the nation and of the several states.

He agreed that he knew these facts but hoped once more I could do something to influence the New Yorkers. I said that if Luther had cabled the news before publicity of the plan had been given out, it might have been possible for Roosevelt to dissuade the leaders from such a demonstration on the ground of hurting relations between our two countries. Of course Luther was not apt to know of such preparations. After a few minutes more of anxious talk, Von Neurath gave me the memorandum he had been reading. I returned to the Embassy and gave the document to Mr. Orme Wilson, secretary for political matters, for a digest for consideration next morning.

At 9:30 my wife and family and myself went to the Hotel Kaiserhof to see what Von Papen wished to do at his *Bierabend*. There were hundreds of people, including many diplomats, present. It was a demonstration on behalf of the German desire for the restoration of the Saar Territory. A number of reels of film were shown, a lot of Saar wine was given away and some talk indulged in. We came away at 11:30 convinced that all the money spent, perhaps $1,000, had been wasted. It was all such obvious propaganda that even Germans admitted the futility of it. Another wasted evening!

March 6. Tuesday. I called by request on Dr. Ritter to discuss a second time the possibilities of a German commission to Washington to discuss Schacht's scheme along with others designed to increase German exports. Ritter showed anxiety as had Schacht. I urged that a commission of the best economists in Germany be sent and that his people be prepared beforehand for real concessions if they expected results. I know the United States protectionist policy the last twelve years is the greatest cause of trade difficulties. But I saw hope in the plan and promised to advance it all I could.

Then I referred to the disagreeable event discussed with Von Neurath yesterday and gave him a copy of a foolish Nazi propaganda pamphlet sent out for foreign consumption some ten days ago. It was a renewal of the 1913 Imperial idea that all Germans over the whole world owed a double allegiance. I reminded him that such matters injured Germany, not the countries where German emigrants lived. He agreed, but he indicated that the officials of the Foreign Office did not have power under the present regime to control such matters. Von Neurath had said as much the evening before. I am sorry for these clearer-headed Germans who know world affairs fairly well, who must work for their country and yet must submit to the Hitler-Goering-Goebbels ignorance and autocracy.

March 7. Wednesday. At 1 o'clock I called by appointment to see Chancellor Hitler. Hanfstaengl had arranged the interview and no one was supposed to know about it. As I went in, Von Neurath met me, walked a few steps and entered the door of a room adjoining the Chancellor's. He was plainly a little peeved, as he always accompanies those foreigners who see the President or the Chancellor.

Hitler was very cordial. We sat down at a table, I with my back toward the room where Von Neurath was supposed to be. Unless there was some electric device concealed in the walls, no one heard what was said.

For nearly an hour we reviewed problems of German-American relations. I asked Hitler if he had any message he wished me to give the President when I reached Washington. He was a little surprised, looked a moment at me and said: "Let me think it over and see you again."

I then raised the subject of disagreeable and harmful propaganda, as suggested by Secretary Hull, saying that unwise propaganda in 1915-16 had done a great deal to bring the United States into the World War. He pretended astonishment and asked for more details. I did not give names as two of the worst offenders are now officials of the Hitler regime: Von Papen, his second in command, and Dr. Fuehr of the Foreign Office. I then spoke of the pamphlets calling upon all Germans in the United States, as elsewhere, to remember that they are and must always remain Germans, almost like the law of 1913 claiming double allegiance for Germans. He at once said with emotion: "Ach, that is all Jewish lies; if I find out who does that, I will put him out of the country at once."

I then explained the Jewish situation as existing in New York where the mock trial was to be held, but did not mention the subject itself. He broke in frequently with such expressions as "Damn the Jews" and insisted that if agitation continued in the outside world, he would make an end of all Jews in Germany. He spoke of having saved Germany from the Communists and said 59 per cent of the officials of Russia were Jews. I privately questioned his figures but said: Sovietism is no longer a menace. He shook his head. I added that the Communists had polled only a few votes in the United States in 1932. He declared loudly: "Happy country. Your people seem to be so sensible in this respect."

Finally, I raised the question of universities and academic freedom and pressed the point that by university contacts and free discussion of international relations we should solve many of our difficulties. He agreed and in closing our talk he emphasized Roosevelt's plan for better commerce.

As I left the room, I met the Minister of Education, Dr. Rust, who had of late given out drastic orders against academic freedom. We talked a minute or two and I stressed the subject of intellectual freedom as important in relations between the United States and Germany. He seemed never to have thought seriously of that phase of the subject.

At 8:30 we had our second diplomatic dinner. Twenty-two persons, including the Spanish Ambassador and Finance Minister von Schwerin-Krosigk, were present. We had an agreeable evening, but there was little chance for close acquaintanceship. I like the Spaniard very much but got only a few minutes with him. Everybody went away about 11:30.

As I am writing my diary tonight after having seen Hitler, I am inserting the general impressions I have received and written about three of the chief Nazi leaders.

The Hitler regime is composed of three rather inexperienced and very dogmatic persons, all of whom have been more or less connected with murderous undertakings in the last eight or ten years. It is a combination of men who represent different groups of the present German majority, not an actual majority.

Hitler, now about forty-five, was an orphan at thirteen, went through the World War without promotions or decorations, so much worshiped here, and had some very curious experiences in Munich between 1919 and 1923. He is romantic-minded and half-informed about great historical events and men in Germany. He was for a number of years a strict imitator of Mussolini. He rose to power by organizing elements in Germany which were unemployed and indignant because Germany had not won the World War. His devices are the devices which men set up in ancient Rome, namely, the Hakenkreuz and the personal salute.

He has definitely said on a number of occasions that a people survives by fighting and dies as a consequence of peaceful policies. His influence is and has been wholly belligerent. The last six or eight months he has made many announcements of peaceful purposes. I think he is perfectly sincere and is willing to negotiate with France, but only on his own terms. In the back of his mind is the old German idea of dominating Europe through warfare.

Hitler's first lieutenant is Joseph Paul Goebbels, some ten years younger, a miniature figure who was not engaged in the war but who imbibed the bitterness against France and the rest of the world during that long struggle. After the war he engaged in organizing militant gangster groups in western Germany and took every possible occasion to challenge the Social-Democratic regime which submitted to the Treaty of Versailles. He joined Hitler and made constant declarations that the German people, once united, would dominate the world. While Hitler is a fair orator as German oratory goes, Goebbels is a past master. He makes a point of stirring animosities and hatreds whenever there is opportunity, and he has combined all the newspapers, radio, publications and art activities of Germany into one vast propaganda machine. Through this agency he is bent upon forcing all Germans into one solid Nazi phalanx. He is far cleverer than Hitler, is much more belligerent, and, I am told, always refuses to have contacts with foreigners.

The third member of this triumvirate is Hermann Goering, about forty, who comes from southern Germany, and who was involved, as was Goebbels, in the 1923 Munich beer-hall putsch. He was a fugitive from justice for some months while Hitler was in jail at Landsberg, and became intensely violent against all democratic and socialist parties. The republican government issued pardons for Hitler and Goering who rewarded this friendly act by renewing their gangster agitations.

While Goebbels uses something approaching a socialist terminology, he mobilized his Storm Troop units against the official Communist party. Goering represents a more clearly aristocratic and Prussian Germanism. He enjoys great support from the larger business interests. He had a marvelous experience during the war as an aviator and became as intensely warlike as Goebbels and Hitler. He is the President of Prussia, and has mobilized the old Prussian extremists (including the Black Reichswehr) and militarists on behalf of the present regime.

A unique triumvirate! Hitler, less educated, more romantic, with a semi-criminal record; Goebbels and Goering, both Doctors of Philosophy, both animated by intense class and foreign hatreds and both willing to resort to the most ruthless methods. They do not love each other, but in order to maintain their power, they have to sit down together. I do not think there has ever been in modern history such a unique group. There was such a group in ancient Rome.

March 10. Saturday. Poultney Bigelow, son of John Bigelow, an unusual man and friend of the Kaiser, who had just spent three or four days at Doorn, was to dine informally with us. We asked Louis Ferdinand, grandson of the Kaiser who has spent two or three years with Henry Ford in Detroit and who is most spoken of as possible successor to the German throne, to join us. Consul General Messersmith, just appointed Minister to Uruguay—and very happy about it—was also of the party. Since Von Neurath had seemed a little distressed on Tuesday, we also asked him; he was guest of honor. There was more frank and informing conversation than we have had in months. Von Neurath and Bigelow embraced each other more than once. The Prince was very interesting but discreet.

March 12. Monday. I spent today in closing up official matters in the Chancery of the Embassy and seeing a few people who wished to talk over some matters. The most interesting of these was Stephen P. Duggan of the International Institute of Education of New York. He had spent ten days at Geneva and two weeks in Paris. He is very anxious about international relations and lays most of the blame for the critical situation upon Hitler and to less extent upon Mussolini.

When I went up to bed, I found Fritz, our butler, packing my suitcases. This is disagreeable to me, as I do not think it a disgrace for a man to pack his own bags.

March 15. Thursday. All the family drove to Hamburg to see me off for Washington. I had a sneaking feeling that the company was unwilling for the ship to sail on the 13th (Woodrow Wilson's lucky day). So we sailed on March 14th to avoid challenging luck. I went to bed hopeful, but suspecting we should have started on Friday and regretting that I had forgotten to take out an accident insurance policy.

March 22. Thursday. One of our American consuls is on board, a man of fine qualities who wishes to leave Germany as soon as possible and asks me to help his transfer while I am in Washington. He deserves promotion and being a Jew he is unhappy in Germany. His position is certainly difficult and he is convinced the State Department decides promotions and transfers according to favoritism.

This accords with a similar story of another consul in Czechoslovakia who is also returning on leave. The further I go in my study of State Department policies, the more evidence there is that a clique of kinspeople connected with certain rich families are bent upon exploiting the Foreign Service for their set, many of them Harvard graduates who are not even well informed. Snobbery and personal gratification are the main objects with them.

March 23. Friday. At Quarantine, Dr. Karl Werkmeister, acting German Consul General in New York, came to me with a letter from Chancellor Hitler to President Roosevelt. Werkmeister was merely finishing the interview I had with Hitler on March 7th.

March 23. Friday. Colonel House sent his handsome limousine with a friend to meet me when the *Manhattan* docked and take me quietly to his house. It was a lucky thing, for taxi folk were on strike, and if I had gone to a hotel the newspaper folk would have pestered me until my train for Washington departed. House gave me valuable information about unfriendly officials in the State Department with whom I would have to deal.

March 24. Saturday. I went at 11 o'clock to talk with Secretary Hull. We had forty-five minutes together, reviewing recent attitudes in Germany. He was a little puzzled about an answer to be given by the President to Hitler's code message— publicity might follow. Hull repeated his recent conversations with the German Ambassador, Luther, who showed no control over his emotions and seemed to be a complete convert to Hitlerism, which he seemed not to be last summer. Hull said Luther seemed entirely unable to understand freedom of the press, free speech and freedom of religion as practiced in the United States. While I doubt the real freedom of press and speech in my own country, the absolute denial of all these in Germany makes Luther's position understandable: he must be a Hitlerite or be recalled.

March 30. Friday. For a week, I have been working in the State Department. On Sunday, March 25, I had dinner with Daniel Roper and members of his family. Monday I was again busy visiting State Department officials like Walton Moore and Wilbur J. Carr, of the personnel division. Tuesday I had dinner, after a busy day, with Jouett Shouse and his wife and guests: Desha Breckinridge and Lowell Mellett, of the Scripps-Howard press syndicate. Conversation was frank and open.

In the afternoon I attended a conference of personnel officers in the State Department: Moore, Carr, Sumner Welles (of doubtful Cuban fame), Hugh Wilson and others were present. I reported that American diplomacy had a new role to play. The Louis XIV and Victoria style and times had passed. The nations of the world were bankrupt, including our own. It was time to cease grand style performances. I described Belgian, Italian and French dinners of state in Berlin. There was some amusement.

I then talked of American staff officials who shipped furniture enough for twenty-room houses at the cost of $3,000, with only two persons in the family! An assistant to me in Berlin had a chauffeur, a porter, a butler, a valet, two cooks and two maids. All for two persons! While these people paid all these extraordinary expenses, the government paid the $3,000 freight and then found that such a person was not even well qualified for best service. I urged that men should not be allowed to spend more than their salaries: $4,000 to $17,500 a year. Besides, I urged the necessity of having ambassadors and assistants who knew the history and traditions of the countries to which they were sent, men who think of their own country's interests, not so much about a different suit of clothes each day or sitting up at gay but silly dinners and shows every night until 1 o'clock. Sumner Welles winced a little: the owner of a mansion in Washington which outshines the White House in some respects and is about as large.

There was much talk and some embarrassment, but general agreement that the time had come for a new kind of service. I was not fooled, however, after two hours of pretended agreement.

Thursday I had luncheon at the Library of Congress. Librarian Herbert Putnam was in fine humor. After some two hours of work in the stacks, I was called from New York by James

McDonald who was about to leave for Europe in another effort to solve the German Jewish problem.

I drove away today to my farm near Round Hill. Later, I drove three miles south on a sandy-clay road to engage Mason Peyton to help me open some choked water pipes. On my way back, following another road, recently repaired, I was stalled in the mud and the car would not move forward or backward. It was getting dark. Waiting a little and wondering what to do, having no chains, I saw a sturdy-looking farm worker coming down the road. He willingly lent a hand and put some broad boards, which he found nearby, under the rear wheels. But the car could not be started. A few minutes later another farmer came along the road. Both lent willing hands. After fifteen minutes of muddy work, I was able to pull out. Neither of the men would accept any pay for their work. How unlike Europe!

April 19. Thursday. In Chicago I lunched with Leo Wormser and Max Epstein to talk over the Jewish problem in Germany. Wormser and Epstein explained how they and their friends had calmed their fellows and prevented any violent demonstrations in Chicago as planned. James Gerard had not spoken. But the Chicago Jews were indignant and unwilling to ease off their boycott. I told them that a month ago the Chancellor of Germany had ordered the closing of Columbia House, Berlin's worst prison, and the re-establishment of a warrant system in making arrests, and added my own opinion on how the drift seemed to be going.

April 20. Friday. At a library meeting of the University of Chicago, Carl Sandburg, author of a definitive life of Abraham Lincoln, and Lloyd Lewis, author of a popular biography of General William T. Sherman, and I made short speeches tonight about the Barton collection of Lincolniana. It had also been arranged that Governor Henry Horner of Illinois be present—only I knew Horner would not be there because I had more than once rebuked him in 1933 for not using his gubernatorial power to rid Chicago of its terrible racketeering mayoralty. With this in the background, I knew Governor Horner would allow Sandburg and myself to function alone as far as he was concerned.

The audience was large and great interest was shown in the frankest discussion of Lincoln I have ever heard in Chicago, Lincoln interpreted as a great human soul in high position ignorant at times of the intrigues behind his back. All of us gave Lincoln full credit for his one great objective: a union of democratic states such as Jefferson had dreamed of and worked for. All of us raised questions concerning the wisdom of certain crucial decisions: allowing war instead of compromise in 1861; granting economic control to industrialists and financiers, perhaps unavoidably once war was on. Even these points obtained a sympathetic hearing.

April 21. Saturday. I slept late, had lunch with university co-workers and came back in time to speak to the social science faculty and students. This speech was the main object of my visit to the university. For an hour I analyzed the status of the social sciences: history, economics, political science, sociology. My major points were: history should be required of all specialists in these fields and made a real discipline as well as a philosophical background; two languages, besides one's own, must be required of all candidates for the doctorate and these made disciplines too; the faculties must be self-governing and participate in university control. There were some 400 people present and I think there were no dissenting voices. All the older professors as well as the graduate students indicated unity of feeling and some excitement, due, as I thought, to Hutchins' recent interventions in departmental affairs without allowing traditional self-government. Professor A. C. McLaughlin, Schmitt and all my former friends and even opponents indicated their warm support. President Hutchins was absent as he had been on the evening of the 20th.

April 23. Monday. I went to luncheon afoot today to Mrs. Kellogg Fairbank, on North State Street, where I was offered the usual cocktail fashionable folk in the United States must drink or be counted out of style. After the cocktail ceremony, which some of the guests seemed really to enjoy, we sat down to a delightful luncheon where everybody but myself condemned the New Deal, Roosevelt and all his Cabinet, especially Ickes, Wallace and the Brain Trusters. I asked for a counter policy and received this for comment: we must go back to the gold standard, free banking and free industry. This seemed to me no real policy at all, those policies having failed everywhere, nowhere worse than in Chicago. German problems were discussed rather more freely than I felt had been wise, but all agreed the conversation was "off the record."

April 29. Sunday. I drove today to Fuquay Springs where my father, eighty-seven years old next November, lives in a quiet little cottage. We talked for two hours about old family matters and little about Berlin. Later, I drove out to Mr. Daniels' magnificent place, too elaborate for his small fortune and too expensive for his children when he passes away, where I discussed some of the State Department problems and Hull's liberal policy.

May 2. Wednesday. After having set everybody to his task about the farm and getting an early dinner, I drove to Washington again today. I stopped at the Cosmos Club and at 8 o'clock went to the Mayflower Hotel where the Ropers were giving a formal dinner to fifty-two people in the accepted diplomatic style. Many eminent men in the present regime were present, including Mr. and Mrs. Josephus Daniels, guests of honor, Jesse Jones of the Federal Reconstruction Finance Corporation, William Phillips of the State Department and a score of senators and representatives. As usual no informational talk was indulged in, save perhaps what Representative Sol Bloom of New York revealed of his attraction for Mussolini and the pro-Roosevelt attitude of his Republican constituents who condemned him for his vote against the President's bonus bill veto.

May 3. Thursday. I visited Secretary Hull, Secretary Dern and Secretary Swanson during the morning and at 12:30 saw the President for a farewell and also to invite him to speak before the annual meeting of the American Historical Association next December in Washington, D. C., where I am to preside and read the annual address. Roosevelt accepted, saying that he had addressed the Association at its meeting in Charleston some twenty years ago. When we finished this subject there was some talk about a possible American boycott of any nation which crossed its own borders in a warlike move into another sovereign nation and the meaning of the tariff powers then being discussed in the Senate.

The President asked me to give unofficially his greetings to Hitler when I saw him, but to be sure to imply no political approval of his policies. With best wishes for his success I bade the President farewell, and returned to my farm.

May 6. Sunday. This was a beautiful day. The budding trees and the apple blooms were most appealing, especially since I must leave. The herd of cows came in and grazed an hour on the lawn and took off the surplus of blue grass.

May 7. Monday. At 9 o'clock Flave Clark and I drove away over the mountains via Charlestown, West Virginia, to Frederick, Maryland, where I bought a few articles to take to Berlin. We drove on to Gettysburg where I had lunch in a neat restaurant whose manager would not allow Flave, a Negro man of attractive bearing, to think of such a thing as eating in the main room. He must enter the kitchen through the rear door exactly as would be required in Charleston or Atlanta. Flave made no complaint and we drove on toward Philadelphia where I was to have a conference with my old friend Conyers Read.

May 8. Tuesday. I left Philadelphia today for New York, after sending Flave Clark back to Virginia with my car. At 1 o'clock, I went to the Century Club where Herbert S. Houston, who had made the arrangements a month before, gathered together around a huge table about twenty foremost editors and newspaper executives in the city for luncheon. The *Times,* the *Herald Tribune,* the *Forum,* the *Literary Digest* were represented, as well as my former students W. L. Chenery, editor of *Collier's,* and Edwin L. James, the *Times'* European specialist. The discussion ran for an hour and a half. I never met with more open and frank support on all the leading problems which I ventured to touch upon. Even the editor of *Time*, the weekly which has treated me unfairly once or twice, was cordial and sympathetic. Germany seemed profoundly important to them all.

There was unanimous opinion that President Roosevelt still had the overwhelming support of the masses in all sections of the country. The first returns of the *Digest* poll, its editor said, showed overwhelming enthusiasm in spite of all newspaper criticism. The State Department had advised me to accept Houston's invitation a month before, that is, William Phillips had; and I was sure the conference was a good thing from every point of view since I was about to leave. I was disappointed that my friend John Finley of the *Times* could not have been present.

At dinner tonight at Colonel House's, soon after we sat down to the table Mrs. House engaged my attention closely about persons and interests more social than otherwise. When the talk had gone on for a good while, Colonel House broke in: "My dear, you must desist. There are other more important subjects we must discuss!" Mrs. House had forgotten herself a little; but the Colonel also forgot himself a little. I was calm and showed no signs of observing the incident.

Later we went into the sitting room of their very handsome but not elaborate apartment. In fifteen minutes the Colonel asked me into his study where he had pictures of Wilson and Franklin Roosevelt, with other eminent American leaders. We sat together on the sofa and he showed me letters from prominent leaders, including a significant one from the President. We talked intimately about the groups in the Cabinet and a recent visit of Secretary Hull who had reported that Raymond Moley was trying again to worm his way into government circles in Washington which Hull resented and House thought dangerous.

This reminded me of the pressing invitation I had had from Gerard Swope to take luncheon or breakfast with him, Herbert Bayard Swope, Owen D. Young and Raymond Moley while I was in the city. This had been sent to me in Virginia two weeks or more before. Gerard Swope is head of the General Electric Company; Herbert figured in a doubtful capacity at the Lon-

don Economic Conference; and Owen Young I have never regarded with any enthusiasm. I had declined the invitation
mainly because of the feeling that some sort of game was in
mind. I distrust every one of the four. Perhaps I should have
accepted their invitations to learn what was behind their interest, but personal distrust got the better of me. I would not sit
down to lunch with a Morgan—except possibly to learn something of his motives and attitudes.

May 9. Wednesday. This is the day of my departure. Judge
Julian Mack of the Federal Circuit Court in New York came
to see me. He talked half an hour about the Jewish problem in
Germany. I reported to him Hitler's order of March 11 or 12
closing Columbia House, the place where Jews and others had
been tortured, and announcing that warrants must be proved
before anyone could be detained more than twenty-four hours
on any charge. He thought these good omens, as I had reported
them in Chicago.

He asked if I thought the boycott in the United States ought
to be eased up. I said: Yes, if you think Hitler is easing down.
Do it only tentatively, then more positively if the Germans
abandon their extreme ruthlessness. He did not say he would
urge it but did indicate that he would take up the problem.

The *Washington* sailed at 12 o'clock and I went to bed.

May 17. Thursday. I arrived in Berlin at 10:30 P.M. My
family and all of the staff were at the train to meet me. I was
delighted to be home but the tense atmosphere was revealed
at once.

May 18. Friday. I had a plain, confidential talk this morning with Messersmith who is going to Austria as Minister. We
canvassed the subjects of Jews in Austria, the danger of publicity, the wisdom of restraining one's propensity for large social
shows, and especially the value of keeping in close, confidential
relations with our Berlin Embassy. He agreed on all points. He
submitted a copy of his survey of the Paris Embassy made at
the request of Secretary Hull. The report showed a score of
useless employees there and showed how to dispense with them.

While I have felt all along that we have too many on our staff and several only semi-competent ones, I have not been able to bring about more than one transfer, that of a man who had engaged in embarrassing behavior with German women.

May 24. Thursday. I had lunch at a small restaurant on Unter den Linden today with Dieckhoff. He is a liberal German, a university Ph.D. who had lived for several years in Washington and the last few years been what amounts to Assistant Secretary of State. I reminded him of the assurances before I left on March 14 that the German Government was easing up on the Jewish atrocities and cited his personal announcement at the German Press Club luncheon, on March 12, that no man could thereafter be held in restraint more than twenty-four hours without a warrant duly approved by a local judge. I also reminded him of a recent order closing the Columbia House.

He agreed at once that the Chancellor had made these moves in the interest of better relations with the United States. I then told him what I had done in the interest of mutual understanding with the Jews, and what Colonel House had helped me to do. I added that Goebbels' speech of May 12 had upset everything I had done and that Americans would consider me as imposed upon, perhaps naive.

Dieckhoff then revealed his whole attitude of opposition to Goebbels and his expectation that Hitler would be overthrown soon. He gave what he considered good evidence that the Germans would not much longer endure the system under which they were drilled everlastingly and semi-starved. He could hardly have said more if he had been in England or in the United States. It was understood that all we said was to be confidential, except that I might give his explanation to my friends at home: Hull, House and other officials.

He added that a boycott against the Jews had been planned here for the last week in March but that the Foreign Office, Schacht and Schmitt had dissuaded Hitler, so that his consent had not been given. Goebbels' attitude had embarrassed Hitler though the Chancellor had not changed his policy. It was sim-

ply the economic situation in March and April which made him
uneasy. But Dieckhoff added: "I fear if the American Jews
ceased their boycott and agitation, we might not get out of this
situation," *i.e.*, an overthrow might not be possible. I felt the
deep concern of a high official who could thus risk his life in
criticism of the existing regime. We parted rather sadly, walking slowly toward the Wilhelmstrasse where I was sure he
would relate what I had said of Roosevelt's attitude and my
embarrassed position at home. After two hours of routine work
in the office, I went for a walk around the Tiergarten.

May 28. Monday. The last few days have been occupied with
routine work. At 12:30 I went to the Foreign Office. Von Neurath kept me waiting ten minutes, a delegation coming out of
the private office as I went in. From 12:40 to 1:15 I talked
with Von Neurath who was more cordial and more interested
in understanding my viewpoints than ever before since my arrival in Berlin in July, 1933.

He asked about my vacation at home and about the United
States but I focused conversation on the real topic by asking
what he thought of Mussolini's speech before the so-called
Italian Parliament last Saturday, the great dictator having declared in a formal way that war was as natural and necessary
as child-bearing to women and that the scale of living in Italy
must be lowered in order to maintain military and naval armaments against Italy's rivals.

Von Neurath said: "That is like Mussolini; there are some
fools in Germany who talk that way also; but there is no substantial element of the German people who want war." This
was repeating what Dieckhoff had said on Thursday.

Von Neurath dwelt some time on the unfortunate attitude of
France. "If they would only meet us part way, we would gladly
resume negotiations at Geneva. I think that it would be one of
the greatest things in the world if France would yield."

I then asked him what he thought of Roosevelt's declaration
about armaments. He congratulated the United States on such
leadership but added: "You cannot control the shipment of
arms even if you enact strict regulations." I described stock de-

clines when Roosevelt's speech was published, particularly the decline of DuPont armaments stocks. He answered: "Good, but even if your Congress goes on with the investigation and European states agree to lay embargoes, there will still be shipments of arms in one form or another."

After a few words more I started to get up. He put his hand on my arm: "Do not go; what do you think of the Jewish problem?" It was a part of my purpose to give him a chance to explain the German change of policy after the promises of March 12 and the speeches made while I was in the United States.

I reviewed my position when I left Germany and the checking of the mock trial planned in Chicago for mid-April, and closed my story with the statement that my position was embarrassing. It might even be said, I told him, that I was naive in assuming Germans to be sincere in their assurances. I told him Roosevelt had thanked me for checking the Chicago agitation. I said Goebbels' speech as reported to me on the *Washington* was immediately printed all over the United States on May 12 and that it had reopened the anti-Nazi agitation.

He was not a little perturbed. He said the German Government had meant what it said when I left, but that Streicher of Nürnberg had broken all bounds and started persecutions on his own authority and that to the astonishment of all, Goebbels had joined Streicher and made the terrible blunder of May 12. He added that he, Schacht and Schmitt had gone to Goebbels and protested. He added that even the Chancellor was uncomfortable.

I repeated part of what I had said to Hitler about the way Americans are trying to control profiteering by great financial interests. He said he was glad to learn that I had informed Hitler, but I added that the Chancellor had not agreed with me. Von Neurath was silent for a moment after my remarks. It was plain that he was entirely of my way of thinking. He begged me to say to Washington that the outbreak was entirely contrary to the German Government's purpose, but he did not commit himself on Hitler. He did say that Goering had become a moderate on the Jewish problem.

Then he turned to commercial relations, the decline of German gold reserves to only 4 per cent of German paper money. "What shall we do?" It is a terrible situation. He added: "It is the Jewish boycott, the tariff barriers of all countries and our inability to purchase cotton and rubber or to sell anything abroad." He was very uneasy but did not say revolution was in waiting.

He said he agreed entirely with the American Transfer Conference delegates, Laird Bell and others, that "Germany ought to pay half the interest due"—a liberal concession by the American bondholders—"but the French won't yield an inch. They must have their 6 per cent and we have no gold or exchange at all." I sympathized with him in this as in most of what he said. There was no sort of boasting or pride in his attitude. He dreaded the effect of asking a six-month moratorium. It would have the same kind of influence in the United States that the boycott has had, to close the markets still more firmly.

He referred to possible negotiations in Washington under Roosevelt's tariff powers. "Can anything be done?" I said: Yes, if Germany is willing to make real trade concessions. The President had not authorized me to make any suggestions on this subject. But I was so sure of the Washington attitude that I added: If you send a first-rate commission, I think a good deal can be done; but do not send persons whose reputations would arouse opposition. You know what the press could do in such cases. My idea was to avoid Dr. Schacht being sent, much as he wishes to go. He would be very unwelcome to Hull and Roosevelt.

June 1. Friday. I had a short interview this morning with Von Neurath about German violations of a treaty with the United States. The Foreign Minister took my written protest with discomfort and promised to give an answer in a day or two. I said that Germany must not violate its treaties if she ever wishes to stand well with public opinion in the United States. He asked me: "What can we do?" Germany had no exports to the United States and only promises of exports to Denmark and other countries. I had proof of serious violations due to heavy imports of lard from Hungary and a great decline of imports from Chicago meat packers. He asked for a document or memorandum from my hand. I said that I could not give this to him. As I came away I felt sorry for the Secretary who always has to defend, before me, the conduct which he wholly disapproves. He and Secretary Hull are of the same school of economic and international thought.

We went to Dr. Schmitt's to lunch. He is a man of the same attitudes as Von Neurath. His speeches, always printed rather freely in German papers, reveal an independence of mind in his field. We sat around a table on his beautiful lawn, White and Flack of our staff with us. After the meal was finished Schmitt pulled me aside, walked round and round his lawn and talked for an hour about Germany's calamitous situation; a great and threatening drought, no exports to the outside world, intense hostility in the United States and England on account of Hitler's treatment of the Jews, Protestants and Catholics. How can the Germans negotiate a new treaty with the United States with such tremendous hostility? I listened and talked as much as I could during pauses. I have never seen a German statesman so much distressed, and I was quite sympathetic when he again and again referred to the folly of Hitler's policy.

I intimated that if a commission were sent to Washington, Schmitt himself might be more successful than other German officials who had become very unpopular in Washington and New York because of their actions in regard to debts due American creditors. He said he could not leave very well, but would go if there were a prospect of success. He showed interest enough to ask me to speak to Von Neurath about his possible appointment—another of those suggestions that liberal German officials have made from time to time.

June 2. Saturday. Germany looks dry for the first time; trees and fields are yellow. The papers are full of accounts of the drought in Bavaria and in the United States as well.

After a busy day we drove to Cecilienhof, the home of the German Crown Prince, a beautiful park-like residence and grounds near Potsdam. We were asked to sit down with the Crown Princess and take tea. She is the sister of the Queen of

Denmark and a most sensible and attractive woman, the unhappy wife of the dissipated eldest son of the Kaiser, now in
exile in Holland.

She was most agreeable. We sat at her table some twenty
minutes and then asked to be excused, in order not to deprive
others of being received at the table. The British Ambassador,
just returned from England, and his wife were with us at the
table for a time. We then walked about a little, met and talked
with the other members of the family and came away. It was
a rather sad reminiscent experience, as I recalled all the time
the great Hohenzollern days of late nineteenth and early twentieth century history.

June 4. Monday. Yesterday I received a letter from Colonel
House saying an agent or friend of Hitler had called on him
about May 20 and asked him to go to Germany and see Hitler
about the solution of the Jewish problem. House declined. A
day later one of the foremost Jews in the United States, Samuel
Untermyer, had visited House and although he agreed to no
definite policy, he suggested to House that I undertake negotiations, entirely personal, looking toward a moderation of Hitler's attitude. If that succeeded, both House and Untermyer
were sure the Jews in the United States would ease up their
boycott. The cause of this move was the growing anti-Semitism
in the United States of which Judge Julian Mack spoke on
May 9 in New York. It has provoked opposition even to Roosevelt because of his few Jewish appointments.

This morning I saw Von Neurath alone in his house and
read him House's letter and suggested that he see Hitler and
sound him out. He said he would do so as soon as the Chancellor was home again, also that Dr. Schacht and Dr. Schmitt
would join him. He suggested that the restraining of Streicher,
the violent Nürnberger who keeps the agitation going, and
Goebbels was the first move. I suggested that some Nazi chief
make a speech calling for moderation. If this could be done, I
would wire House. I drove back to the office; I had taken only
seven minutes of Von Neurath's time.

June 5. Tuesday. The French Ambassador came and reported that he had word from Geneva about my interview with Von Neurath on May 28 to the effect that I thought the Germans might yield to the Geneva demand that they negotiate a disarmament agreement again. I repeated what I thought about world folly at the present moment and my guess that Germany would yield if France made any real concession, even a small one. He was somewhat of my mind. I wonder if Norman Davis repeated the contents of my confidential letter of May 29 to him.

June 6. Wednesday. I drove at noon to the French Ambassador's to ascertain whether he had further news from Geneva. He had not, but was going to see Von Neurath about possible German concessions if France yielded anything. He would inform me if he obtained any real information. About 6 o'clock young Armand Bérard, the Ambassador's confidential secretary, came to report no new moves in the Geneva negotiations. Young Bérard said: "There is great excitement in Paris about the imminence of war." I said: I do not see how Germany can make war, bankrupt as she is.

June 7. Thursday. Three bankers, led by Banta, came to learn what they could from me. They were very uneasy. One criticized Roosevelt rather severely until I intimated that the opposition leaders must have a positive plan. He then charged Roosevelt with loading himself up with Jews, and added: "There is going to be rioting in New York. Sam Untermyer is apt to be attacked."

June 8. Friday. Another nervous, uneasy New York banker came in today. When he drifted into criticism of the President, I spoke strongly in favor of Stock Exchange regulations soon to go into effect. He fell in with that and came slowly to agree that Roosevelt was the only leader with any real promise. He was very troubled lest something happen here.

At Ernst Hanfstaengl's tea, the French Ambassador again raised the Geneva problem. He said the prospect is better there and that I was too pessimistic about the German situation being so critical as to compel Germans to yield considerably on the armament problem.

A German Foreign Office official, Dr. Davidson, urged negotiations in Washington about trade. I frankly said I had hoped to see a commission begin work, that it was time for tariff readjustment. He reported that Von Neurath had said I favored such a move at an early date and that Ambassador Luther had talked an hour with Hull on Wednesday, the day I sent my telegram about the German failure to understand the international incidents they allow to occur almost daily.

June 10. Sunday. We drove out to the former Imperial hunting lodge where Hermann Goering has set up a Prussian state animal park and where he has a sort of week-end retreat. We arrived late on account of some hitch in the car machinery (a new Buick my wife finally bought in place of the wrecked Chevrolet which protocol people thought ridiculously simple for an Ambassador) and found most of the diplomatic folk standing in a forest around a speaker who welcomed us.

Then Goering spoke. He wore a medieval hunter's uniform. He is a big, fat, good-humored man who loves display above everything. While he spoke three photographers with elaborate outfits took pictures which he was particularly pleased to permit. He next led us about the woods and showed us bisons and tiny wild horses. He mounted an old-time carriage drawn by two horses and driven by a peasant. Madame Cerruti, wife of the Ambassador from Italy and very proud of display, took her place on the right of Goering. All the rest of us followed in peasant two-seat carriages driving slowly about the forests where occasionally one saw a deer or an eagle.

When the journey was over, each of us gave his driver a mark or two and then took to our cars which carried us to Goering's hunting lodge on the shore of a beautiful lake. Goering had hurried off ahead of us and when we arrived he met us in a wonderful new white summer garb and showed us through his new log house, an elaborate reproduction of a medieval country gentleman's house, if there were gentlemen in that day. All of us scattered about the place and drank tea, coffee or beer according to our taste. Vice Chancellor von Papen sat at the head of the table on my left. Sir Eric Phipps, British Ambassador, sat across the table; the French Ambassador was on my right two persons away. The conversation had no value, unless perchance a few remarks about Admiral Spindler's new book on the German navy in the World War were worthwhile. I seemed to stop that discussion when I said: If peoples knew the truth of history there would never be another great war. Somehow Sir Eric and François-Poncet laughed a good deal, but said nothing. After a considerable pause, we turned to other and less risky subjects.

At 6 o'clock Goering took us about the premises and displayed his vanity at every turn, often causing his guests to glance amusedly at each other. We were led to another lovely lake shore and shown a tomb, with deep foundations of stone fronting the water, the most elaborate structure of its kind I ever saw. It is the burial place of Goering's former wife whose remains had been brought from Sweden where the people indicated their dislike of Nazi Germany by dishonoring the grave. Goering boasted of this marvelous tomb of his first wife where he said his remains would one day be laid. For half an hour this went on. Sir Eric and I, weary of the curious display and already due in Berlin fifty miles away, went to him to say farewell. Lady Cerruti saw our move and she arose quickly so as not to allow anybody to trespass upon her right to lead on every possible occasion.

June 13. Wednesday. I went to a tea at Goering's beautiful mansion in the city. Most of the diplomatic corps were present. Schmitt, a very able member of the Cabinet whose work forces him to threaten resignation now and then, sided me off for a discussion once more of possible trade negotiations between Germany and the United States. He was excited and distressed by the announcement then just maturing that Germany would pay none of her debt after July 1. He also knew Secretary Hull had informed Ambassador Luther on June 6 that no trade negotiations could be undertaken for some time yet.

I told him Hull had complained of German treaty violations and their failure to treat American creditors justly. He pretended not to know of Germany's conduct. For some time we

talked frankly about the blunders that seemed to have defeated
the one thing Germany had hoped for: freer access to American
markets. We agreed about the dangers of Hitler's fanciful economic autarchy. He said the Chancellor would force his system
upon Germany in defiance of the American attitude. I told him
the attitude was due to three things: the unwise treatment of
Jews here which had caused a vast boycott, the secret violation
by Germans of the treaty which gave Americans certain trade
concessions, and the refusal of Foreign Office officials to explain
such acts or even answer my earnest official requests for explanation of such conduct. I said things like this cause great public
dislike on the other side, and in the face of your announcement
of inability to pay, we have learned recently of the German purchase of a hundred airplanes from American manufacturers per
month. This is so contradictory! The Party people were looking
too much at us and we parted. He showed much anxiety.

June 14. Thursday. There is much talk in the press about a
spectacular meeting of Hitler and Mussolini in Venice today
and tomorrow. I can see no possible objective except the encouragement of German and Italian peoples who are greatly
concerned about the economic failure of their Fascist systems.
Goering laughed a little sarcastically when I said yesterday:
You did not go to Venice, I see. It is commonly said here that
he expects to be the beneficiary of a putsch managed by the
Reichswehr, and it may happen any time. I see no way it could
succeed.

June 15. Friday. Von Ribbentrop, Hitler's contact man for
international problems, came to see me. He talked a little about
the Venice meeting but said nothing. He then broached the subject of disarmament, concluding by saying Hitler would return
to the League if France would only make some small concession. I had talked with François-Poncet to this end before he
went away to Paris on June 13. Now the Chancellor's agent repeated my point: a little concession from France and then a renewal of the disarmament question. Was he sounding me out?
I then repeated what I had said to Schmitt at Goering's tea

party. Von Ribbentrop pretended to be surprised and showed a good deal of concern as he went away.

After a walk in the Tiergarten, I sat down to lunch with a group of American visitors to Berlin: Former Minister to Sweden Morehead and his wife, convinced capitalists who do not know what was the cause of American disaster in 1929; Dr. and Mrs. Mapels of Wilmington, Delaware; and Professor and Mrs. T. V. Smith of the philosophy faculty at the University of Chicago. It was an interesting group of people differing widely on every possible subject, the Moreheads the most complacent and least informed, in spite of their great wealth and in spite of wide experience.

Morehead said: "Ten per cent of any people make the money, lead in every phase of life and should have unmolested control of public affairs." That certainly was Hoover's idea and Morehead boasted of his relations with the discredited ex-President. How different the views of Smith who teaches philosophy in Chicago! He is a near-Socialist, but not oblivious of man's long and cantankerous record in all ages.

June 16. Saturday. I sent a personal telegram yesterday to Secretary Hull asking him to nominate R. D. W. Connor of North Carolina to the President for appointment to a position now open in Washington: National Archivist. Connor has the support of all the executive committee of the American Historical Association. Today I wired the gist of Schmitt's and Ribbentrop's discussions with me, and gave a brief summary of German blunders as they appear to me.

June 17. Sunday. I received a cable from Hull saying I must talk personally with the Foreign Office tomorrow, June 18, as he is giving out a press statement about Germany's declared moratorium and failure to keep treaties. He made it plain that he understands the complex situation and perhaps recognizes American blunders in previous years,—our tariff walls now imitated here, and pretended isolation. So he makes no formal protest.

What more can I say than I have said a score of times? Germany is in a terrible plight and for once she recognizes war is no remedy, yet she talks war all the time. Hitler is back from the Venetian show where he rivaled Mussolini in vain pomp and parade, agreeing to nothing. Tomorrow will be a good day to talk to Von Neurath, if he is available.

June 18. Monday. At 5:30 I saw Von Bülow and read him a striking passage of Hull's telegram. Von Bülow at once declared: "There is no discrimination in the German proclamation of a moratorium on payment of debts, nor is there discrimination in possible arrangements between Germany and Holland, and Germany and Switzerland."

My reply was that the American people did not view the subject as the German Government does. Perhaps there is no discrimination in the payment to France of 6 per cent and to Americans of 4 per cent, on bonds, because American loans were made under different contracts and American representatives had agreed to a reduction of interest rate in the recent Transfer Conference. The French had not agreed to reduction, their government having made the contract with the Germans. But these narrow distinctions are not appreciated by the hundreds of thousands of American creditors.

Moreover, there have been so many other things: persecution of Jews, Nazi propaganda in the United States at such high cost to Germans, and the recent purchase of hundreds of aircraft for war purposes. What Germans call financial prostration seems not to be as actual or imminent as they make out. Americans feel that prior obligations on bonds are being neglected without sufficient justification. Von Bülow was not quite at ease. He understands full well the drift of opinion in the United States and is in reality not satisfied with the policy of his own government, though he did not say so.

On the general commercial dilemma we are agreed. Nations cannot set up hard and fast barriers and then expect payment of international debts. He complained that the United States had not allowed commercial negotiations to begin in April, as I had in fact hoped while in Washington. I said the outbreak of fresh Jewish atrocities in Germany and public addresses of high officials, like the one of Goebbels on May 12, had produced reactions in the United States which had made Congressional consent more difficult. He assented. I reminded him that since June 1, I had been asking for explanations and promises which I might wire to Washington in the hope of easing off the excitement. He said Dr. Schacht and Dr. Darre, of the Agriculture Ministry, always delayed such explanations and the Foreign Office could do nothing.

As I was about to go, I asked about the Venice conference. He said promptly: "We declined the Far East pact with Russia and Poland which Litvinov urged because we are not armed and could not participate on equal and safe terms. It involved Germans in a guarantee of the Baltic states' safety, and also Czechoslovakia's, against aggression of any kind." It was plain that Hitler is not willing to allow these states with German minorities to maintain their independence.

Von Bülow added, "We wish to get a conference of the greater powers which signed the Kellogg pact to meet and agree to a peace pact including Germany, France, England, Italy and the United States." I agree that such a substitute for the Litvinov "eastern Locarno pact" might be advisable. This supported the idea Von Ribbentrop had suggested on Friday. Perhaps the Germans recognize the terrible risks of their position and are sincere in their representations to Italy and France. François-Poncet is still in Paris and perhaps is doing more there than he could do here. I left Von Bülow after forty minutes talk, not wholly convinced of any single thing.

June 19. Tuesday. Goering today carried his wife's remains to the tomb he had shown us a week before. I had thought that the poor woman's remains were already under the pile of Swedish marble he had shown me. Not so; there was a second display with Hitler present, also many high officials of the Foreign Office and others. There was an attack upon the car of Goering's chief lieutenant, according to press stories, but no one was seriously injured. About the same time Goering's bodyguard refused to obey orders and was dismissed, the Prussian police being assigned this vital task.

June 20. Wednesday. A copy of an address delivered at Marburg by Vice Chancellor von Papen last Sunday was sent me by Junius Wood of the *Chicago Daily News*. The address was a moderate and entirely reasonable criticism of the Hitler autocracy. It was made before the university which has been known for its opposition to Hitler's religious coercions. President von Hindenburg had read the address before its delivery; he had telegraphed hearty approval. But Goebbels, learning of its content, had suppressed the speech after the *Frankfurter Zeitung* and one Berlin paper had published parts of it.

There is now great excitement all over Germany. All old and intellectual Germans are highly pleased. We made copies of the address in English and mailed it to Washington. Hitler's emotional speech near Munich on Monday is now better understood. His visit to Von Hindenburg, as reported for tomorrow, is a part of the excitement. All guards of the leaders are said to be showing signs of revolt. At the same time, aircraft practice and military drills and maneuvers are reported to be increasingly common sights by those who drive about the country.

June 21. Thursday. I learned this afternoon that the *New York Times* asked that the whole of Von Papen's speech be cabled over. London and Paris papers are featuring the Von Papen episode.

At a press conference given by Goebbels at 5 o'clock, Dr. Schacht made another defense of the German moratorium and demanded a freer world trade if German debts are to be paid. The audience showed intense interest. I thought Schacht's points were, in general, well taken; but his digs at England and America seemed to me rather unwise in view of the helpless condition of Germany as compared to those countries. Everybody noted Von Papen's presence and, at the close, as many people crowded around him as about Schacht, or even more. He sat down at Goebbels' table to take a cup of tea when the address was over, and shook hands with Goebbels who after the Marburg speech would have ordered his prompt execution if Hitler and Von Hindenburg had not intervened.

June 23. Saturday. We had a luncheon where Sir Eric Phipps, Dr. Schmitt, and the widow of Gustav Stresemann were present. There was no useful discussion except a long confidential talk between Schmitt and Sir Eric when the other guests were taking their coffee on the glassed-in terrace which fronts the beautiful garden in the rear of our house. Lochner of the Associated Press and Miss Schultz of the Chicago *Tribune* talked about all the rumors, true and untrue, but no new decisions were reported to have been made by the government.

The week closes quietly but with great uneasiness. At 6:30 Ambassador Long called long distance from Rome, very anxious to know the state of things here. I was surprised at his indiscretion, but talked as freely as the eavesdropping of the German Secret Police would allow. I said: All is quiet here; there is a good deal of discussion of Von Papen's speech. He asked about the reaction to it and I said perhaps two-thirds of the people I am in contact with endorse it; there was a conference Sunday at the President's house at Neudeck; there is no great disturbance in Germany that I know of as yet but a considerable tension in the atmosphere and some anxiety about Austria where there has been no improvement since the Venice conference.

This was perhaps too much to say but Long pressed questions. I hung up the receiver a little annoyed and uneasy. I would not think of calling the American Ambassador in Rome in the midst of impending events of great importance when the existence of the Mussolini regime was in question. No wires in Europe, England excepted, are ever free of eavesdroppers when such talk is indulged in. I hope no ill results of this may come.

June 24. Sunday. A quiet day. I spent one hour and a half in my office. I received a long, interesting letter from Norman Davis now in London. He thinks Germany must return to the League or be ruined, also that England and the United States must unite in their attitudes on the Far East before the coming naval conference.

June 28. Thursday. During the last five days, stories of many kinds have tended to make the Berlin atmosphere more tense than at any time since I have been in Germany. I cabled

Washington that the situation was much as it was in Paris in
1792 when the Girondins and Jacobins were struggling for su-
premacy. The Von Papen speech was discussed every day. Hitler and Goering and Goebbels spoke almost every day attacking those who objected in any manner to the existing regime.
Goering and Hitler were together at the Krupp plant in Essen
today, and there was some comment on their apparent agreement against Von Papen.

June 29. Friday. We gave a luncheon at the usual hour. The
first arrival was Madame Cerruti, the wife of the Italian Ambassador. She showed considerable nervousness. She sat on my
right at the table and quickly indicated that her husband worked
to the limit, that we were all on a volcano. "The Germans are
again in the position of July, 1914; we may be plunged into
war again; these people are simply crazy." I was not convinced
but felt concerned since it had been only a week since she had
witnessed the conference of Mussolini and Hitler at Venice.
Something was in the atmosphere.

Across the table sat Von Papen on the right of my wife. On
the left was Ambassador Luther, just returned from Washington, where State Department officials had shown no liking for
him when I was there. Secretary Hull had told Assistant Secretary of State R. Walton Moore that he must not have Luther
to dine with me at Moore's house April 15. But Luther was
most charming today, witty, friendly to our President, and humorous on the subject of our Congress. Von Papen, however,
was less talkative, reserved but good-humored.

When we arose Luther and Von Papen edged up to one another in the room adjoining the dining room. There was a
rather tense attitude between the two. I intervened and asked
them to come with me to the sun parlor. There Limburg-
Stirum, Minister from the Netherlands, joined us and the conversation turned to politics. I remarked: Herr von Papen, you
and Dr. Goebbels seemed to be quite friendly at Hamburg the
other day. He laughed and said it was an agreeable occasion,
the people were very enthusiastic in their greetings. I then alluded to the speech Von Papen had made the day before at

some club and noted the fact that Hitler was absent, though expected to be present. Luther and Limburg-Stirum joined in a discussion of the speeches and hinted at differences in their attitudes. There was no favorable comment on Goebbels. Von Papen said just as he was rising to go: "Anyway I shall not be torpedoed." As the party broke up the Vice Chancellor and Luther went away together and in the same car.

June 30. Saturday. This afternoon as we sat down to lunch about 2, William returned from a drive to Unter den Linden and reported that the streets were closed and that arrests had been made, at Chief of Staff Roehm's headquarters, of S.A. officials. There were rumors of violence in Munich.

It is clear some putsch or coup d'état is on. A rather uneasy evening followed. I received today a formal note from Roehm's office declining my invitation to him for a dinner on July 6. In view of the uncertainty of the situation, perhaps it was best he did not accept. On the other hand, it might have meant something more ominous than appeared on the surface. His excuse was that he was to be away on a cure.

July 1. Sunday. Although the papers say but little, I learn from various sources that Hitler and Goebbels journeyed yesterday morning at 2 o'clock from Godesberg in the Rhineland to Munich and there ordered the execution of two officials of the famous S.A. troops. At six, he was at Wiessee, some forty miles away, where he went into Stabschef Roehm's sleeping rooms and ordered his arrest and execution, Roehm's guard failing to defend their chief. He also ordered the death of several other chiefs of the S.A. and returned to Berlin at 1:30 where Goering had already seized Roehm's elaborate house and caused General von Schleicher to be killed in his home. Although the streets of Berlin gave no sign today of disorder, there were constant rumors of summary executions. Vice Chancellor von Papen and his family were imprisoned in their house and his staff were reported to be killed or imprisoned. We drove a little too leisurely, perhaps, by his house this afternoon, but on purpose. It was a strange day, with only ordinary news in the papers.

July 3. Tuesday. For two days, the excitement has been intense. Newspaper men came and went all day. They made sensational reports as the facts, of course, required. Some of them were, however, unsupported except by rumors.

Martha called Tuesday at the house of a German acquaintance where we had dined once. A strange telegram from London had been delivered to me by young Bérard, personal intimate of the French Ambassador, and I learned that this acquaintance, an able German liberal, was in London, that his house had been searched on Saturday at 8 and that the police had taken his son to a prison near the Anhalter Bahnhof where he had been held *incommunicado* since Saturday. I thought Martha might help the family a little by calling and at the same time not compromise the government in Washington.

July 4. Wednesday. After a busy morning in the office, I ate lunch at the usual hour and drove to Dr. Schmitt's to pay him a brief call as he has been ill a few days and was reported to be going away on leave for a month or two. I knew that Hitler had visited him yesterday afternoon under heavy guard and was not sure but that Schmitt was about to resign for good.

He showed that he had been seriously ill—overworked too—and I did not remain with him long. He was greatly troubled about the horrors of the last few days and asked what American opinion was. I said: You can guess when I say that if our President were to arrest a man without a warrant and then put him to death, he would be impeached and removed from office. Schmitt seemed not to understand fully and I simply added: Our people cannot imagine such things happening in their country as have happened here.

We talked a little about German economic distress and the health of my host. He said he was leaving tonight and would be away some five or six weeks and would then come back to his difficult task. He said he would like to resign but felt he must not do so for his country's sake. He did not mention Hitler's visit, but I think the Chancellor practically forbade him to resign now. I came away rather depressed: so good and true a man compelled to serve under a regime which he considers murderous. If he resigned I think he would be in danger of being killed.

I noted that Schmitt did not repeat his invitation to my wife and myself to spend a week with him at his home in Bavaria. It might endanger his life. Since the attitude of the Nazi leaders is so violently anti-foreign, close contact between diplomats and Germans seems really dangerous at the moment. He lives near Berchtesgaden where Hitler spends about a third of his time. If I were at Schmitt's and did not offer to visit Hitler, it would look partisan, and I certainly would not ask to see any man who has committed a score of murders the last few days.

We gave a big reception today, with at least 300 callers, some very interesting people, among them the musician Kreisler who tours the United States each year. There were others of almost equal appeal, many of them showing concern about their position here, but none daring to mention events of the last five days. We were really tired when the entertainment was over. Newspapers went the limit in asking for photos.

July 5. Thursday. An eminent professor at the University of Berlin called at noon to talk with me about an address I was to make before the history faculty and students on the 13th. We agreed that it would be best to call it off. University professors might be embarrassed or even endangered by my appearance among them at this time, and I might be made uncomfortable by some newspaper story that might get into print.

He was greatly perturbed because of recent events. He said the London *Times* editorial on Germany's return to medievalism of July 3 was entirely true. He said: "Poor Germany, she cannot recover in decades to come. If I could go to any other of the greater countries, I would leave the university at once." That is how most professors and students feel. He says Hitler has aroused a savagery and barbarism which he thought had long since disappeared. In my opinion it is a curious quality of the Nazi mass mind here which passed away in England with the Stuart kings in 1688.

July 6. Friday. I received a cable from Secretary Hull this morning asking me to protest to the German Government against payment of British creditors of Germany, under the Dawes-Young plan, and the announced purpose not to pay American creditors under the same plan. I have protested three times before about these discriminations and they have had no effect at any time, for the German exports to the United States are only one-fourth of American exports to Germany. While debts are valid and interest is due, German balances are utterly unequal to the payment of obligations.

At 5:30, I sat down with Von Neurath and handed him Hull's telegram. Both of us were embarrassed. He knew Germany had done wrong to promise the payment of English debts and not pay American; I knew the same; both of us knew Germany could not pay even the English debt. She must promise to do so in the hope of preventing England from joining France in case of war which might come any day, if the wilder elements of Germany get the upper hand. He asked me to say he was sorry and would pay, if any reserves were available, but these are not at all probable. The Reichsbank shows a worse condition every week.

When this disagreeable impasse was over, I asked a question about the recent atrocities. Von Neurath said Hitler, Goering and Goebbels were to have been killed last Saturday and that all the Cabinet members were to have been put in jail. Von Schleicher and Roehm were to have been the chiefs in a new putsch and S.A. men were to have taken over the governing forces. He added this would have meant civil war. I said little, merely asking if Hitler now really listened to him and other wiser men of the regime. He said: "Yes." I returned to the office and wired Secretary Hull at once about this curious conversation.

Charles R. Crane and his son, Richard, came to an informal dinner. Baron von Bülow, Admiral Spindler, retired naval commander and author of a three-volume history of the German navy in the World War, and three or four others were present. I had asked the Crown Prince, General Goering, Minister of Education Rust, Ambassador Nadolny and ex-Minister von Kühlmann, all of whom for curious but unavowed reasons declined. I knew the Crown Prince wished to come, but he has been under government observation since June 30. Goering had directed the killing of opponents for a week, more than seventy-five people in all, and it was a relief that he did not appear. I don't know what I would have done if he had. Ambassador Nadolny, dismissed from his post in Moscow because he had tried to get a commercial treaty adopted between the two countries, was deliberately out of the country. Rust never replied to my invitation and Von Kühlmann was in South Germany. The Cranes understood the absences, though they did not criticize all the ruthless terrorism of recent measures.

The moment I sat down to eat, the telephone rang. I answered and was told that a *New York Times* photographer, who had been taking pictures of our house and all members of the family, was under arrest because the car he drove happened to bear the number of a car which had been seen at General von Schleicher's house before he was killed. I called the Consul General and asked him to make contact with police officials and secure the release of the American employee, although he was a German, unless some crime were proved or charged. Consul Geist went about his task. When we were finishing dinner Geist and Birchall of the *Times* called to announce that the man was released. It is a rather tense atmosphere when such things are happening all the time, even though not to Americans. But the dinner went off well and the elder Crane was very amusing— telling stories all evening.

A curious incident of the week: On July 4, when I learned that Vice Chancellor von Papen had been released from prison, I sent a brief note expressing my good wishes and saying I would call if he thought it would be agreeable. The note was in an Embassy envelope and it was delivered by messenger. By mistake it was left at the office of the Vice Chancellor. On the 5th, the son of Von Papen called and I asked if his father had received my letter. He said: "No." I then sent a messenger to the man who had receipted the letter to ask what he had done with it. He referred to a police officer in the room from which office furniture was being taken. The police official said it had been sent to the Secret Police. This is typical Nazi behavior. This is the second letter of mine that has been opened before delivery.

July 7. Saturday. I was in the office until noon. In the afternoon at 4 o'clock we drove to the home of Professor Erich Marcks, my old Leipzig professor, and there had tea and talked for an hour. He and his son, an officer in the Reichswehr, showed uneasiness and sorrow. Marcks' older son had been private secretary to General von Schleicher some years ago, and all the family were glad to know their older son was thus far safe. They had received a letter on the 6th very carefully worded but showing the safety of the older son, now a higher officer of the Reichswehr in Münster.

July 8. Sunday. I received a telegram from Secretary Hull asking me to see German officials and try once more to correct their attitudes on debt payments. The American public does not understand debt problems and the Secretary feels compelled to keep prodding Berlin foreign officials. I shall go again to the Foreign Office tomorrow and see if any possible satisfaction can be given. I see no way out except a frank moratorium.

I had a curious illustration today of German naïveté in treating foreign problems. The Carl Schurz Foundation, supported by government aid, had arranged a dinner today at the Automobile Club. I had agreed to attend the preliminary reception. But the president of the foundation asked me if I would make a short speech about Von Hindenburg if he opened the talk after dinner with an address on President Roosevelt. At such a moment a German speech by a Nazi leader on Roosevelt would have been most unwelcome, but a reply by me on Von Hindenburg after his approval of the murders of the last few days would have started nation-wide indignation. I refused, and to avoid any possible embarrassment I declined also to attend the dinner.

In such matters even the best of Germans are easily misled. Germany is tense in every section. The outside world is almost entirely hostile. There are fifty American guests at this same dinner this moment. They are all nervous and some of them said to me this afternoon that they had requested that no press announcement be made of the reception and dinner because they are aware of an easy misunderstanding in America. I can think of no country where the psychology is so abnormal as that which prevails here now. Frenchmen seemed to me in 1928 almost as "crazy."

My task here is to work for peace and better relations. I do not see how anything can be done so long as Hitler, Goering and Goebbels are the directing heads of the country. Never have I heard or read of three more unfit men in high place. Ought I to resign?

IV

July 9, 1934 to September 1, 1934

July 9. Monday. I learned this morning that Professor Morsbach, who had invited American professors and students to travel about Germany for a month and who had managed the foreign student exchange fellowships, is in prison and in danger of being killed. He happened to be an acquaintance, perhaps a friend, of Roehm, S.A. Stabschef killed at Wiessee, near Munich, on June 30. A committee of the Carl Schurz Foundation visitors tells me the Americans are amazed that their host is thus persecuted, without proof, at the very moment of their arrival. They ask if I can do anything. Morsbach being a German citizen, I have no authority or rights in the case. But the unusual aspects in the case led me to call acting Consul General Geist and commission him to make inquiries and report to the American travelers.

July 11. Wednesday. Mr. Geist reported that Professor Morsbach is in a concentration camp near Wittenberg. His hair was clipped close to the skin; his clothing was that of a field hand, with the large letter L on his shirt-front (the name of the camp begins with L—Landsberg); he had not been allowed to shave since his incarceration. There were 300 sterilized German workers in the camp. When Geist, in the presence of police officials who had driven him to the lonely camp and the superintendent of the prison, was about to say farewell to Morsbach, the persecuted professor said: "Please give my regards to and thank the American Ambassador." Geist said there were strange, surprised expressions on every face.

July 12. Thursday. We had forty of the Carl Schurz Foundation visitors at our house for a reception. It was an interesting and distinguished company. Reports of courtesies and attentions from the German semi-officials who had shown them around Berlin and ancient Potsdam were many and appreciative, but all said: "Strange, we can hear nothing about the horrible deeds or about public attitudes from anybody. Nobody ventures a remark and no newspaper gives any of the facts."

The party adjourned at 6:30 and we went an hour later to dinner at Fritz Kreisler's marvelous house in Dahlem. Kreisler is forbidden to conduct or give concerts in Germany because he is a Jew. There were German and American guests but no one indulged in any frank discussion about anything but the United States and the subject of art, which I said was about to collapse in Europe.

Strange, is it not, that Germany has had no great literary light since Goethe; England no great writers since the World War; the United States not a great historian since Henry Adams, not a great writer since Mark Twain; and few great artists anywhere of genuine creative character? Kreisler, who enthusiastically showed me a signed portrait of Mussolini, said, "It is all because we have democratic government everywhere, except at present in Germany and Italy, where there has not yet been time to develop masters under dictatorial power." A statement like this is false, because all great writers and historians have been developed in spite of dictatorships and patronage, not because of them.

A good German woman who is a close friend of the Kreislers took pains to show me a portrait of her baby, a sturdy, healthy-looking child of six months, and made a point more than once of the Hohenzollern dogma (even more Hitler's dogma): Woman's business is Kirche, Kinder and Küche (church, children and kitchen). She looked quite equal to the undertaking. I did not argue the matter.

July 13. Friday. A busy day. At 9:30 I gave an interview to an American group who insisted on some explanation of Hitler Germany. I devoted an hour to them as all were teachers or writers at home. Some statements made were confidential and given with the understanding that I was not to be reported to anyone. I shall see perhaps some echoes in the American press later but so far almost all who have come to me and with whom I have talked frankly, have kept faith. I have no complaints to make of anybody, though I have given facts and judgments that would certainly give trouble if they were known to have come from me.

This evening at 8 o'clock, the Chancellor is to proclaim to the world in the old Reichstag building, restored after last year's burning, the reasons for the murders which he has perpetrated since June 29. Everybody looks forward to the meeting with great interest or seems to do so. I decided last Tuesday that I would never again attend an address of the Chancellor or seek an interview for myself except upon official grounds. I have a sense of horror when I look at the man. Consequently on Wednesday afternoon when I visited Sir Eric Phipps, British Ambassador here, and he asked: "Are you going to hear the Chancellor Friday?", I replied: No. He said, rather humorously, he thought it would be "a grand show, all kinds of flash-lights, photographers and pomp." But I replied: He is such a horror to me, I cannot endure his presence.

After discussing British-American debt relations and declaring to him that the English creditors ought not to demand preferential treatment over American creditors to whom the Germans owe twice as much under the Dawes-Young plan as to the English, I asked: Do you not think the British act of Parliament compelling bankrupt Germans to pay was pushed through by interested parties without due consideration? He agreed, though he added: "I have no authority at all to discuss matters officially. Still, I think you are right and it would be better for international relations for England and France to accept the German moratorium in the same spirit as the Americans." He agreed to discuss the matter in Downing Street when he returned next week. I said I would wire the gist of our conversation to the State Department where public opinion presses very hard for equal treatment.

On Friday afternoon, I had a walk with the French Ambassador, François-Poncet, in the Tiergarten, the only really peaceful spot I have access to, outside my home, at the moment. He was incensed at the German charges that he had conspired with Von Schleicher and Roehm, and at the failure of the Foreign Office officials here to force public disavowal on the part of Goering or Goebbels. He gave me his interpretation of the so-called "conspiracy of foreign powers" in the German Reich. He knew Von Schleicher fairly well; he had dined with him and Roehm; and there had been talk of pressure on Hitler and the French Government for a sensible agreement on disarmament. That was all.

I had declined to call on the Ambassador today because I feared the fact of my visiting the British yesterday plus a visit to the French today would be observed by the Germans and interpreted as an effort on my part to persuade the Ambassadors to remain at home when the Chancellor made his speech. That was the reason we walked an hour in the famous park. But François-Poncet told me as we parted: "I shall not attend the address." And he went on to say that conditions are so acute that "I would not be surprised any time to be shot on the streets of Berlin. Because of this my wife remains in Paris. The Germans hate us so and their leadership is so crazy."

I have not felt myself in danger, though I know the leaders here cannot like me: my whole philosophy of life is so different and they must know it. Eminent German professors and leaders of the old order come to me in all confidence and tell me facts and attitudes that would cause their deaths if known. Poor fellows. However, they do not know the real cause of Germany's reign of terror: the failure of the 1848 movement to resolve itself into a democratic parliamentary system and the failure of Bismarck to wean his Prussians away from the military brutalism hallowed by the successes of Frederick the Great. Bismarck had the chance at the end of the 1866 war, again in 1871 when he had all power and could have refused to annex Alsace-Lorraine. Frederick III might have served Germany, but a cancer of the throat took him away within a year after his accession to the throne. No historian has seen this, not even in republican Germany of 1919-1933.

At 8 o'clock we turned on the radio and heard Hitler's heated and emotional story of the conspiracy to take his life and of his necessary killing of the "traitors." Roehm who had been in jail with him for months in 1923 and who fought with him through the long brutal struggle for the overthrow of republican Germany, was the major traitor in all the maneuvers of April, May and June. Von Schleicher was the next criminal, and with them foreign representatives were supposed to have intrigued. There is some doubt in my mind that Roehm planned the overthrow of Hitler and the death of several members of the Cabinet.

Hitler told the world that Roehm had raised 12,000,000 marks and spent them in his wicked cause. Of course Roehm had no chance to deny anything, nor any of his friends. The statement that Germans who sat in conference with foreign representatives in Germany, keeping secret what was said, were traitors and to be killed did not improve troubled relations outside. I was glad I did not go to the meeting where artificial applause was vociferous and where, it was clear even over the radio, all the Germans were frequently rising and giving the Hitler greeting. The Chancellor retired from the building at 10 o'clock, everybody cheering except the diplomats.

July 14. Saturday. I had lunch with Dr. Schacht at the Reichsbank, a famous state dining room. Finance Minister Schwerin-Krosigk was present too. He had been reported to be under arrest some days before. He was present at the Chancellor's meeting last night but he said nothing. I knew what he thought. Schacht said he too was reported to be shot. I walked home with Counselor John C. White, and had a quiet afternoon and evening, writing two hours on my *Old South*.

July 15. Sunday. In the office at noon, Vice Chancellor von Papen called and sat for half an hour describing the terror of the last two weeks. His confidential assistant, Von Bose, was shot for possible contact with Von Schleicher. He was much excited and asked that I should not report anything he said either to the press or to the State Department in Washington.

Hitler had been an hour with him yesterday begging him to remain in the Cabinet and to co-operate. Von Papen said he could not promise anything at the moment. He also indicated his hatred of Goering and Goebbels and said he demanded proof of the guilt of his assistant who had been killed and others who were put into prison, their heads shaved, with no knowledge of what would happen to them from day to day. This was Hitler's treatment of all who are suspected of disloyalty. Von Papen was also very critical of Von Neurath who "never does anything." As Von Papen's car stood at the Chancery nearly an hour, the American press learned the fact and cabled their papers. The German Secret Police probably know more by now.

July 16. Monday. I lunched at home with the Russian Ambassador who is going home for good next Sunday. His name is pronounced Khinchuck, though I do not think it is spelled that way. He is not a Communist though he fights valiantly for the cause.

The British Ambassador, Sir Eric Phipps, was also present as was Mr. Harry Hopkins, confidant, it seems, of President Roosevelt. Sir Eric was as non-communicative as ever. Mr. Hopkins was engaging and rather glad we had not arranged an interview with Hitler according to his telegraphed request. He said he would be ashamed to shake hands with such a murderer.

Another guest, George Harrison, president of the New York Federal Reserve Bank, was more liberal in philosophy than I had expected, but very much concerned about Germany's being commanded by England to pay 6 and 7 per cent interest on the hundred million dollar Dawes-Young loans, while the United States creditors under the same plan to the extent of two hundred millions receive nothing. He journeys home in two days with Montagu Norman, president of the Bank of England. Norman thinks the British Government made a mistake in demanding preferential treatment.

At 5:30 I presented the U. S. Government protest against payment to British creditors if Americans cannot be paid. Von

Neurath was as concerned as I was. I know well Germany cannot pay any of her obligations if conditions continue as now. I stayed with the Minister only ten minutes.

July 17. Tuesday. At François-Poncet's luncheon in honor of Khinchuck, there was Sir Eric Phipps, also the Spanish Ambassador. It was a most correct and protocol affair. The conversation at the table was more about history than present conditions in Europe. When we all stood for a half hour in the grand reception room, Sir Eric called me aside to ask if I did not think the diplomatic corps should send their dean, the Papal Nuncio, to the German Foreign Office in October to know whether we should not all refuse to entertain any German officials at our houses in view of the Chancellor's denunciation of Germans who attended diplomatic entertainments. I agreed we should make such a move and then I added: I think we should all agree too on the limitations of large dinners and receptions. He agreed. We shall see what comes of it. Certainly Germans fear now to be seen at a diplomat's house.

July 19. Thursday. Mattie, my wife, and I sat down to dinner with the bankers at the Mann mansion in Dahlem. To my surprise, Von Ribbentrop, Hitler's confidential negotiator, was present. He was a little nervous, talked of a visit to the United States next October, and also stressed the fact that the U. S. has 8 billions of gold and Germany only 20 millions! "How can your people ever suffer?"

We came home impressed again with the bankers' fear of German collapse. No one has any confidence in Hitler's ability to direct German affairs.

July 22. Sunday. Today I spent two hours in the Embassy office. At 12:30, I took a half hour's walk in the Tiergarten where one saw the agreeable effects of the rain which had fallen the night before, though all the elms, blighted by some strange disease, showed no signs of improvement. At 1:30, we sat down to Sunday dinner with Herr Diehn and several professors and others, including their wives. Although no one liked to talk frankly before Diehn, there was general and bitter criticism of the Hitler regime and its barbarism, unparalleled since the Middle Ages. One professor and his wife lingered a long time and were the most sorrowful of all about the Germany in which they live. I was a little surprised in view of the dangers involved in case anyone should report on them.

July 24. Tuesday. Mattie, William and I all went to dinner at the house of Von Ribbentrop. We arrived at 8:10 at his beautiful home in Dahlem with a marvelous lawn in the rear. The guest of honor was Ambassador Cerruti of Italy, peculiarly silent all evening. Henry Mann and his wife were also guests. Mann, former Nazi enthusiast, showed no patience with the Hitler regime now. He told us that about July 1 a neighbor of his was coaxed out of his house, misled to Mann's house and there murdered. The dead body remained on Mann's front door steps one whole day. Then it was removed and Mann's servants were asked by the police to wash up the blood.

Another strange fact: Count Helldorf, Chief of Police of Potsdam, had been reported as shot to death on June 30. We were amazed to be introduced to "Count Helldorf, Chief of Police of Potsdam." He showed himself a rather silent figure in Nazi uniform, his wife sitting on my left and talking a good deal about the wisdom of Hitler's sterilization law, and the need of sterilizing all Negroes in the United States. "If you do not do this, the Negroes will one day own the country. White people are not increasing since immigration is not allowed." After the party left the table Countess Helldorf talked again about the vicious Jews who never work and who never live in a country where the population cannot be exploited by them. The Count himself joined his wife in this. The Italian Ambassador remained silent.

I was surprised and a little affronted at the presence at the dinner of young James Lee, son of Ivy Lee, the clever big business propagandist who has been trying for a year or more to sell the Nazi regime to the American public. A House of Representatives investigation, organized by Dickstein, revealed that Ivy Lee has been receiving $33,000 a year for this work. Why did Von Ribbentrop invite Helldorf and Lee to meet us?

We returned, quite tired and disgusted, at 11 o'clock. I had a good baked apple and a glass of milk before I went to sleep.

July 25. Wednesday. A busy day preparing, reading, and signing reports for Washington. A fantastic story came to me of an alleged Jewish-Hohenzollern conspiracy last winter and spring to put Hitler out of power, with 12,000,000 marks sent over by Jews. The Crown Prince was mixed up in the affair and talked too much. Goering's Secret Police learned of the intrigues. Roehm and Von Schleicher were involved. Von Papen carried the story to Von Hindenburg who compelled Hitler at last to act, which resulted in the June 30 terror. I think the idea in reporting this fantasy to me was an attempt to deceive me with this sort of history of the terror.

At 5 o'clock while I was talking with a committee of American municipal reformers here studying German city life, Consul Geist called me on the telephone and reported a conversation he had just had with Minister Messersmith in Vienna. A putsch of the German Nazis in Austria had been on for five hours. Dollfuss was overthrown and promised to surrender his powers. A little later the Heimwehr, Dollfuss' supporters, released the Austrian dictator who at once retracted all his promises.

I asked Geist to walk home with me. He came and as we strolled along the canal towards home, I told him how unwise it was for Messersmith to talk over the long distance with the Consulate here. With Messersmith known as very hostile to the Nazis, and both of us watched all the time, such indiscretion might be considered by the Germans as a sort of intrigue of our diplomatic work which would do both of us and our government harm. I had warned Messersmith before he went to Vienna, but I had not sufficiently warned Geist.

July 26. Thursday. A very busy day. I sent two telegrams to Washington explaining the putsch against the Austrian Government by the Nazi conspirators.

The attack upon Austria, from all evidence, was supported if not planned by the German Propaganda Ministry. Last February Ernst Hanfstaengl told me that he brought what was practically an order from Mussolini that Germans must leave Austria alone, and that Theodor Habicht, the German agent in Munich for Austrian annexation, must be dismissed and silenced. In May and June, Mussolini pretended to be in accord with the German anti-French, anti-Russian policy, and June 18, at Venice, Hitler was reported to have promised Mussolini to leave Austria alone. At any rate, great ado was made in the German press about the friendly accord of the two "greatest statesmen" of Europe. On June 30 came the Hitler murder of "traitors" and their assistants.

Mussolini, who had murdered even more Italians than Hitler has thus far murdered Germans, allowed his press to denounce Hitler unmercifully. On Monday, July 23, after repeated bombings in Austria by Nazis, a boat loaded with explosives was seized on Lake Constance by the Swiss police. It was a shipment of German bombs and shells to Austria from some arms plant. That looked ominous to me, but events of the kind had been so common that I did not report it to Washington.

Today evidence came to my desk that last night, as late as eleven o'clock, the government issued formal statements to the newspapers rejoicing at the fall of Dollfuss and proclaiming the Greater Germany that must follow. The German Minister in Vienna had actually helped to form the new Cabinet. He had, as we now know, exacted a promise that the gang of Austrian Nazi murderers should be allowed to go into Germany undisturbed. But it was realized about 12 o'clock that, although Dollfuss was dead, the loyal Austrians had surrounded the government palace and prevented the organization of a new Nazi regime. They held the murderers prisoners. The German Propaganda Ministry therefore forbade publication of the news sent out an hour before and tried to collect all the releases that had been distributed. A copy was brought to me today by a friend.

All the German papers this morning lamented the cruel murder and declared that it was simply an attack of discontented Austrians, not Nazis. News from Bavaria shows that thousands of Austrian Nazis living for a year in Bavaria on German support had been active for ten days before, some getting across the border contrary to law, all drilling and making ready to return to Austria. The German propagandist Habicht was still making radio speeches about the necessity of annexing the ancient realm of the Hapsburgs to the Third Reich, in spite of all the promises of Hitler to silence him. But now that the drive has failed and the assassins are in prison in Vienna, the German Government denounces all who say there was any support from Berlin.

I think it will be clear one day that millions of dollars and many arms have been pouring into Austria since the spring of 1933. Once more the whole world is condemning the Hitler regime. No people in all modern history has been quite so unpopular as Nazi Germany. This stroke completes the picture. I expect to read a series of bitter denunciations in the American papers when they arrive about ten days from now.

July 28. Saturday. I have been requested to visit all consulates in Germany and make reports as to work done and the character and size of the staffs. Consul Geist is now visiting Breslau, Bremen and Hamburg for me. Later I shall go to Leipzig, Dresden, Munich, Stuttgart, Frankfurt and Cologne.

There is great need of drastic change in Hamburg where United States imports and German exports have fallen the last two years by more than half. The consuls at Hamburg are practically useless, at least one-third of them. It's a characteristic attitude of the time for men to live off the government.

A Jewish Rabbi, Morris Lazaron from Baltimore, came to see me this morning. He had letters from Messersmith and others. He is a friend of Felix and Max Warburg and hopes to make contact with the Foreign Office people here and see if a more sensible Jewish policy cannot be adopted. He shows no signs of Jewish characteristics in his ways or countenance, nor is he a self-conscious person, but he handed me about a dozen letters to different people here which seemed to show quite ambitious purposes. I counseled him to go slowly. He might do harm if not careful. Max Warburg is in Hamburg waiting for possible signs from Berlin. I told Lazaron to be sure he gave a correct picture of things here to Warburg so as to avoid any appearance to the Germans of a campaign on my part in co-operation with these men which might embarrass Foreign Office officials who have been wise and considerate ever since I have been here. Hitler has promised me so much and done so little that I could not give anyone very much encouragement.

July 29. Sunday. I spent all day working on the *Old South,* the most difficult chapter of all thus far, VIII, in which I explain the Stuart colonial policy and the troubled era in western Europe as far as commerce and economic exploitation were concerned. I have written this chapter three times. I hope this is the last. There was a most remarkable group of leaders in England contending sharply with Louis XIV and Jean de Witt.

July 30. Monday. At 4 o'clock I made a call on Limburg-Stirum to learn, if I could, whether the Netherlands and England had come to any agreement as to the Far East or on co-operation with Belgium in case of war between France and Germany. We talked freely about the first subject and he said: "No; and I fear we are not going to be able to agree with the Japanese, now in Batavia, as to our commercial proposals. It was a mistake to have the negotiations in Batavia, for it put us at a disadvantage and gave the Japanese a chance, which they are surely using, to stir up trouble with our colonials in Java." He then expressed the fear that Japan would force the Chinese into submission before England and the United States came to a common policy in that vast region.

"England and Holland are on the best of terms," he said, which was no direct answer to my query. I came away, however, fairly well convinced that the Netherlands are included in the recent statement of policy whereby England agrees to regard the Rhine as her eastern frontier in case continental war breaks out. This means, if true, the completest encirclement Germany has ever known.

July 31. Tuesday. Senator Thomas of Utah came in this morning. He was not slow in letting me know that he is interested in Mormon missionary work in Germany and that he is traveling as Oberlaender Fellow with the best wishes of Presi-

dent Roosevelt. He is about sixty years old, was formerly a
college teacher and is now a member of the United States
Senate Foreign Relations Committee. I was favorably impressed, although it has always been hard for me to understand
how a man of intellectual distinction can be interested in Mormon missionary work. There are a number of Mormons in
Germany and Hitler has not dissolved their organizations or
expelled their active preachers. There are other than religious
aspects to Hitler's let-up on the Mormons.

August 1. Wednesday. Paul Block, owner of the *Pittsburgh
Post-Gazette* and the *Toledo Blade* and of seven other influential newspapers in United States industrial regions, including
New York, called and talked for half an hour about his earnest
help of Roosevelt in 1932 and his doubtful support now.

Ambassador Luther called this afternoon. He was a good
deal amused when I showed him copy of our consul's account
of Luther's clever remarks at a Cologne dinner some weeks
before. Although Luther is very unpopular in Washington, he
shows me every time I see him an appealing trait: frank, intelligent mental attitudes which few German officials here venture to show. In order to emphasize this trait in Luther I forwarded the Consul's report to Under-Secretary Phillips.

Although the Ambassador was in most things frank and
interesting, neither he nor I mentioned the high officials in
the regime here. I am sure he has no sympathy with the Hitler
brutality and he knows I am most uncomfortable in an atmosphere so unnatural in a highly civilized country, which all men
have been disposed to consider Germany in spite of the Hitler
regime.

Both Luther and I agreed that payment of American creditors depends entirely upon the revival of German-American
trade which both peoples are not ready to make possible. Why
American bankers induced their hundreds of thousands of
clients to buy two billions of German bonds or why they
granted such huge short-term credits between 1924 and 1930,
I cannot understand on any other grounds than that they were

willing to risk their people's savings in order to make huge profits themselves.

Luther and I parted company in better understanding than ever before, though I could go only half-way with him in his denunciations of the Treaty of Versailles which was not so bad as the United States coercion of the broken South in 1865-69 which resulted in a fifty-year economic oppression of that region worse than anything Germany has suffered.

August 2. Thursday. I went to the office early. A few minutes after I arrived, the news of Von Hindenburg's death was announced. At 10 A.M. Hitler sat down with his Cabinet. They quickly agreed to a "statute" making the Fuehrer President without any change of his status as Chancellor. The President of the Third Reich, Leader of the National Socialist Party, and Chancellor of the Reich are now all united in one person: the adolescent Austrian who started the putsch business in 1923 and who has killed hundreds of opponents in order to consolidate his powers.

All this was done now in one hour, every member of the Cabinet rising and heiling Hitler when he finished his statement of his new position. It was also decreed that the Reichswehr, the old military folk, must take an oath of allegiance to Hitler at once. No time was allowed for any opposition or for the possible putsch in Berlin which so many people had expected and many thousands had, doubtless, prayed for.

At 12 o'clock, I went to the Foreign Office, left my card and signed the usual book of condolence to the German people for the loss of their single distinguished soul, so far as we know present German souls. As I stood in the room the Japanese Ambassador came in, very obsequious in bearing toward me. In a little while he told me of his visit to Von Hindenburg a week or two before and of a long talk. It was astonishing. No member of the German Cabinet except Von Neurath had been allowed to visit Neudeck since July 11, not even his close friend, Von Papen. How strange for the Japanese to have been there! When we had signed the book, I noticed the

Japanese had arranged to see Von Neurath who had returned only the day before. None of the other ambassadors or ministers had appointments to see the Foreign Secretary. This looked to me a little unusual too.

August 3. Friday. I must not omit to mention a luncheon yesterday at home where Senator Thomas, Rabbi Lazaron and President Clifton Gray of Bates College, with Mrs. Thomas and our family, made up the group. There has not been better, freer conversation since we have been here. The Mormon spoke frankly of Mormon minority unreasonableness. Dr. Gray, the Baptist divine, and Rabbi Lazaron were equally frank. Lazaron is here to feel out possibilities for the Warburgs and others who regret Rabbi Wise's extreme attitudes. Not much prospect here, I believe.

Today Dr. Gray brought five or six leading Baptist divines to the office to assess their situation in Berlin at this critical moment. Some fifteen hundred preachers and leaders are here for a week's discussion of the Baptist situation. This conference was set a year before Hitler came to power. Their leading subjects for discussion are: nationalism and race groups; freedom of religious opinion; and self-government in church life. These subjects can hardly be touched upon without challenging Nazi opposition. According to the Nazi view, all religions in Germany must be merged into one state church; no such thing as freedom of conscience is possible; and local government of any sort is close to treason. Free speech in Germany now is an invitation to be shot.

How these Baptist preachers are to function I cannot guess. But Dr. Gray and others discussed their problems frankly and asked my comment, also my assessment of their plan which is to go on as though no change had come over Germany. When they were about to leave they asked me to attend their meeting and take a seat on the platform. Thinking the matter over a little, I declined for the time. It would look too much like a challenge to all German official life to which I am accredited. Yet I was reared a Baptist and am still a non-active member at Hyde Park, Chicago. Perhaps I should go and show once more what sort of man America believes is entitled to live undisturbed. I will decide after the Hindenburg burial.

I called at the Foreign Office to leave President Roosevelt's message to the German Government and nation on this sad occasion. Von Neurath, whom I was to have seen, delegated Von Bülow to receive me. We talked a few minutes about Von Hindenburg's ideas and qualities of mind, especially as they had been revealed when I was presented to him on August 29, 1933. Von Bülow had been present and Von Hindenburg gave me ten or fifteen minutes free conversation, unprecedented I was told. What he said on international relations and cultural contacts with the United States would be a sensation if printed now, and would anger Hitler but delight Germany.

In the afternoon, the British Ambassador called, just returned from his vacation in the Wiltshire hills, and also just returned from a Von Neurath interview. He said Von Neurath had told him that he feared Hitler did not know what the assumption of presidential powers really meant, but according to all reports Von Neurath heiled Hitler yesterday when supreme powers were taken on. I have never seen evidence that the Secretary ever resists the arbitrary conduct of the Fuehrer.

Sir Eric acknowledged that England had declared her eastern border was the Rhine. "What else could we do?" He thinks Hitler would gladly go to war if he had the power and therefore that all Europe must keep united against Germany, which seems to me to be necessary if Europe is not to collapse one day under thousands of airplanes dropping bombs and poison gases. France played a sad game in 1919 and then continued her mistake under the League from 1930 to 1932. That helped to give Germany Hitler, but Hitler, once in power, lost Germany all the growing sympathy of England and America by his barbaric conduct. Now, as Sir Eric says, all Europe must watch Germany day and night, living under an encirclement system which may even bring economic collapse. We parted company, discouraged, at 7 o'clock.

August 4. Saturday. I worked in the office until 12:30 and then I quit for the day. A delegation of American forestry people came and we talked a while about the wonderful German forests which they are studying.

August 5. Sunday. I spent an hour in the office to see if any telegrams had come in and to read some letters from the United States. Then I finished my reading of Pepys's *Diary* to get touches of social habits and graft in Stuart England. Many things reminded me of the habits and methods which prevail in Nazi Germany. But there is one trait here, the love of animals, which reveals a German characteristic I have never noticed in any reading I have previously done.

The Germans love horses and dogs especially. At a time when nearly every German is afraid to speak a word to any but the closest friends, horses and dogs are so happy that one feels they wish to talk. A woman who may report on a neighbor for disloyalty and jeopardize his life, even cause his death, takes her big kindly-looking dog in the Tiergarten for a walk. She talks to him and coddles him as she sits on a bench and he attends to the requirements of nature. The dog is never scolded or kicked, which is so common in the United States. He is never nervous, never shows any fear of any sort and is always fat and clean.

Only horses seem to be equally happy, never the children or the youth. I often stop as I walk to my office and have a word with a pair of beautiful horses waiting while their wagon is being unloaded. They are so clean and fat and happy that one feels that they are on the point of speaking. If I raise my hand as if to hit one of the pair, he does not even dodge his head. He has not the slightest notion that anybody would harm him. The law forbids cruelty to animals here, and any man who maltreats a horse or dog or cow is liable to immediate imprisonment.

In Nürnberg last December I noticed the same kind of "horse happiness" and approached a pair of wonderful grays as I came out of the Lord Mayor's and petted them. They seemed to understand me. It was the same in Dresden. Animals are the only happy beings I see, unless the birds are equally so, but I see few birds.

At a time when hundreds of men have been put to death without trial or any sort of evidence of guilt, and when the population literally trembles with fear, animals have rights guaranteed them which men and women cannot think of expecting. One might easily wish he were a horse!

August 6. Monday. At 12 o'clock, my wife and I took our places in the Reichstag auditorium where a tribute was to be paid to the deceased Field Marshal von Hindenburg. Every member of the diplomatic corps was present. The hall was filled. Goering was on the speakers' stand in gay uniform with medals all over his coat, in the high presiding officer's chair, literally joyful because he was so conspicuous in appearance. Hitler sat a little below on the right of the chairman's desk with Von Papen on his right and Von Neurath next to Von Papen. Other cabinet officials were duly arranged according to rank, nearly all in uniforms and with decorations much in evidence.

Hitler was in his Brown Shirt uniform. He looked contented and complacent: he was to deliver an oration to be radioed all over the world. The main floor was occupied by men who were called members of the Reichstag. They were in no sense legislators, being appointees of Hitler, not one of them at any time ever having voted against a wish of the Chancellor or ventured to offer a bill for the consideration of his fellows. The Reichstag members were in Brown Shirts, showing no signs of grief. The diplomats were in their appropriate places, most of them in official and highly decorated garb, black gloves for the few cutaway members, white gloves for those who had on the costumes of Louis XIV's time.

At the appropriate time, Goering arose and introduced the Chancellor who took his place as speaker, all the house rising and holding their right hands at a 45° angle until he acknowledged the greeting. This was far more important than any evidence of sorrow for the departure of the aged President.

The funeral oration took twenty-five minutes for delivery. It was much better than I had expected, though there was no tribute to the President or his services as a leader of his country.

All the emphasis was upon the military genius and service of the hero of Tannenberg. A significant remark towards the end was the claim that Von Hindenburg had brought the National Socialists to power. When the address was over, Hitler went to the first row of seats on the main floor and kissed the hands of Von Hindenburg's daughters and shook hands with the son, Colonel Oscar von Hindenburg. There followed a solemn strain of music and we all retired. At 10:35 I took the train for Tannenberg, East Prussia, where the first great German victory of the World War was won in the autumn of 1914. I went to bed promptly and so escaped the photographers who came to the train seeking to take pictures.

August 7. Tuesday. Our train reached Hohenstein, a neat little town two miles from the Tannenberg monument, about 11. We were driven promptly to the battlefield where Von Hindenburg was to be buried at noon. The Spanish Ambassador and I sat down in the first row of the diplomatic seats. We were greatly impressed with the scene: eight great brick towers about sixty feet high with fires flaming from the top of each, everlasting signals, I suppose, of the war soldier. The unknown soldier, buried under the Arc de Triomphe in Paris, is also honored by an unceasing flame. So the Germans go the French one better at Tannenberg, where the power of Imperial Russia was broken.

The soldiers marched into place, company by company, keeping marvelous goose-step, until some 3,000 men stood grim in their places, in all kinds of uniforms, black, brown, gray and blue. They were picked men from all the groups of German soldiers. Hitler, Goering and Goebbels were soon in evidence, the first in his Brown Shirt with a sort of butcher knife hanging by his side—the badge of honor for all Nazi soldiers. Goering was in his aircraft uniform with medals all over his front, Goebbels in civilian clothes with no medals or war signs, although he is quite as warlike as any of the rest. He was spared from the front line trenches of the World War by the fact that he is club-footed and so walks like a lame person.

Von Hindenburg's family, two daughters and one son, were

present. So also was Meissner, the President's private secretary, whose status is very doubtful now that his chief is dead, since he is not known to be a Nazi, which he did not dare to be so long as Von Hindenburg was alive. It is said that he has destroyed a copy of his chief's will. No one knows but it is strange that Von Hindenburg's will is not to be found. Common talk is that he decreed his remains be buried beside those of his ancestors, through four generations, on the Neudeck estate. There were several aged generals on the stand, including Von Mackensen who conquered Rumania in the autumn of 1916. The belligerent Ludendorff was not present. He is reported to have hated Von Hindenburg. He joined Hitler in the Munich beer-hall putsch of 1923 which failed. Somehow he and the Fuehrer broke and they hate each other.

At the proper moment a war chaplain read a sermon, war-like in character. Then came Hitler who faced the coffin of the deceased President and made a second address which closed with the statement that Von Hindenburg's remains were being consigned to Valhalla. There was no appraisal of the old leader's character, his devotion to the Imperial cause of his country as it once was. Nor was there any reference to any of the nine years of the Von Hindenburg presidency. It was all military, though there were no challenges to the French or English or Americans who had decided the fate of the Hohenzollern Reich.

At the end of the services, Hitler repeated yesterday's performance and kissed the hands of the President's daughters, the whole audience looking on, many of them conscious of the bitterness between the family of the deceased and the Fuehrer. Hitler quickly mounted a huge flying machine and returned to Berlin. The diplomatic corps found its way again to its train which started for Berlin about 1 o'clock. The weather was beautiful and East Prussia looked very prosperous. The rains had restored things.

As I went back to my berth, a young Dr. Berger, of the German Foreign Office, was at the door. He was appointed to serve me in any way I thought necessary. I needed no service. I asked him to be seated and for an hour he tried to entice me into criticism of the Hitler regime. I talked of history

and its false teaching in all great countries, especially ours
where the Civil War was concerned. He informed me that his
function in the Foreign Office was to study Austrian relations.
I still refused to enter into criticism of the Hitler relations to
Austria, thinking all the while that he had been "planted" on
me. There was an associate of his, young Prince von Wittgen-
stein, who talked less but served the same useless service of
page to the diplomats of our car. I am sure I disappointed them
bitterly.

The train journeyed slowly for six hours across the Polish
Corridor. The idea seemed to be to show us the bedraggled
look of the country, the dirty towns and ragged farmer-folk,
more children than I have ever seen in such a short journey.
Berger made few comments but what was said rested on the
assumption that Poland properly belonged to Germany. He
showed me bridges and great industrial structures that were
built while Germans dominated the country—now all dilapidated. There is no doubt that the Poles are a backward nation
politically and economically, but why should Germany feel that
she must govern them?

The moment the train crossed the Oder into German territory, the speed doubled. The countryside looked neat and
orderly. The towns were clean and the people about the railway
stations moved quickly and were well dressed. There were no
filth and rags anywhere. No one could fail to note the difference. Night soon came on and we halted at the great Fried-
richstrasse station in Berlin at midnight. I was glad to be home
again. It had been a revealing trip.

August 8. Wednesday. A bit of talk at lunch today illustrates
the kind of conversation one may have when not too many
people sit down at once. Von Wiegand said, when the talk
turned to European debts: "I invested my life-long savings in
German bonds. I have not received a dollar in return for years
and never expect a cent more." That was not discussed at the
moment and Von Wiegand a little later added: "There are
two countries of Europe which I admire and associate together
in their payment of debts: England and Finland." The former

had recently announced that she would not bother about paying interest on her four billion dollar debt to the U. S. and the latter about the same time had paid in full an installment on her obligations.

It was a touchy subject for my friend, Sir Eric, and I said at a moment when everybody at the table was quiet: Mr. von Wiegand, do you dare compare so great a power as the British Empire with so little a country as Finland in the presence of the Ambassador? Everybody laughed and Sir Eric joined in a good-humored way. Nobody pressed the comparison further, but there was no ignorance of the real point in anyone's mind: Europe's general disposition not to pay or seriously try to pay the people of the United States who loaned the Allied powers $11,000,000,000 in 1917-1918 in order to help save themselves.

There was a good deal else said of similar trends but I cannot repeat it here and now. Daily life here is full of the strange conduct of civilized people.

August 9. Thursday. At the request of Rabbi Lazaron of Baltimore, Max Warburg, eminent Hamburg banker and brother of Felix Warburg of New York, came to see me in the Embassy. He showed the effects of his troubled life the last year and now stands in danger of losing his life if he ever allows his opinions to become known to authorities here.

He remained an hour. He thinks Rabbi Wise and Samuel Untermyer of New York have done the Jews of both the United States and Germany great harm by their craving for publicity. He said Felix Warburg was of the same opinion. Both these men are fully in sympathy with Colonel House in his efforts to ease off the Jewish boycott and reduce the number of Jews in high position in the United States.

I was glad to speak frankly with such a man. Before leaving he indicated that he doubted the wisdom of James McDonald's activity in his position at Lausanne. That has been my attitude from the beginning. Warburg suggested that Lazaron, living quietly in Berlin, might do more with the German Government than McDonald, and I agree with him. Any man who would take a big salary for such a service, all from people who give the money for the relief of suffering fellows, is not apt to appeal strongly to other givers, and McDonald has shown so much self-esteem on different occasions that I fear these traits have become too well known in Berlin official circles.

How few people really think of the service they can render in high station! Do not most officials think of how great they are or ought to be considered, rather than the realities of life? I have seen so many men and women here, the last twelve months, of mediocre ability and knowledge, strutting day and night and exploiting their countries' meager wealth, that I am strongly inclined to leave such an atmosphere and make my reasons public at home.

At one o'clock an American housing expert, studying conditions in Europe, called. He had been in Rome and was captivated by Mussolini. He was later in Vienna to study housing work done there after the World War, and then in Moscow to study housing in the Soviet Union. Without having made any study of Germany, he had become an enthusiastic sympathizer. What he said about his building work and the general undertaking at home was interesting enough, but he seemed to have lost his balance. His complete acceptance of Hitler as a great statesman revealed his mentality. I did not try to correct him. I merely asked him: What do you think of a "statesman" who murders his opponents? The question puzzled him a little but it did not seep into his mentality.

August 10. Friday. At 11 o'clock the mother of a former student of mine in Chicago, who is becoming an American citizen after my intervention against his forced return to Germany in 1933, came to see me to read a letter from her son which he had dared commit to the open mail. She was glad to know he was well, even if unemployed. She read his long letter and broke into tears as she described her terrorized position. She is a Catholic, married to a Jewish journalist of democratic faith whose son-in-law here is constantly in danger of losing his life. She wept and wept. I consoled her the best I could. She said she had money enough in Prague to take her to the United States the moment her son obtained employment.

He is a brilliant young doctor of philosophy from a German university. I told her I would do what I could to help her son but the immediate prospect was not good as her son was not a full citizen and young American scholars would naturally take precedence over him in college work.

Nothing, however, seemed to appease her sorrow. She broke out: "This system here is terrible. You can imagine how much we suffer and thousands of others likewise. There is no way out but for someone to murder the great murderer who rules us. Someone will do it, must do it." As she retired from my office, tears streaming from her eyes, I told her to wait, compose herself and go upon the streets, always watched by the Secret Police, in a more normal condition.

At 12:00, a new American correspondent came to introduce himself. He immediately revealed his pro-Nazi sentiment in respect to recent events in Vienna. Curious, but newspaper men are human and there are rewards here and elsewhere for men who preach the new doctrine to the outside world.

August 11. Saturday. We left at 10 this morning for Köln where my wife and the children wish to begin an auto trip up the Rhine to Mainz. The road was good and the weather delightful. We lunched at Eisenach and Martha and I went through the old Luther Museum where many interesting pictures, pamphlets, books and Luther letters were shown us. It is peculiar that all this evidence of the great preacher's demand for religious freedom is still exhibited in a country and a region where the Hitler-Rosenberg paganism prevails. From Eisenach we drove on to a beautiful resort town near Kassel where we spent the night in a most comfortable hotel. It cost only some five marks each.

August 13. Monday. We reached Frankfurt today where we looked into the Consulate for a while and then Martha and I wandered through Goethe's home where the guide told rather filthy stories about the great artist's early life. Our next stop was for lunch, then to Heidelberg where the wonderful castle entertained us for an hour or so. From Heidelberg, we drove over a good road toward Stuttgart in medieval Württemberg where ancient villages and monasteries revealed much of the age that has long passed. I have never seen better revelations of medieval Germany than in this fertile, prosperous country. We reached Stuttgart at 7 o'clock and had a good dinner in a modern hotel. Then I found my way to the railway station and took a sleeper for Berlin. The family remained for another week in southern Germany, Austria and Hungary.

August 14. Tuesday. I was back at my task at 10 o'clock. At 4:30 Albert Lepawsky, University of Chicago instructor, and an American friend came in to explain how a Nazi marcher had stepped out of ranks the night before and struck Lepawsky in the face for not saluting the Hakenkreuz flag. The blow was insulting enough, but not serious otherwise.

Lepawsky said he was bringing the story to us on a silver platter and thought I ought to hurry at once to the Foreign Office and demand an apology. He did not wish to see the offender punished. He had not hit hard enough. I reminded him that punishment was the first thing the government would order and that as he was not hurt, I would advise no publicity since we had not had such a thing happen since January. He was not pleased exactly. The pair went away with instructions to lay the facts, under oath, before the Consul General.

August 15. Wednesday. I called at 12 o'clock on Ambassador François-Poncet to learn whether he knew anything more definite than I did about the war-like purposes of the Hitler regime in order that I might write President Roosevelt a letter that might not be misleading. As to facts about Nazi rearmament, the French cite: one million and a half trained soldiers, an ample supply of small arms, and the avowed purpose of carrying the pan-German annexations into effect at the first possible opportunity. François-Poncet was, as he has been since the date of my arrival here a year ago, fully convinced that France is to be attacked and Alsace-Lorraine, Austria and western Poland to be annexed. He reported some evidence of new airfields in Mecklenburg, a larger number of heavy flying machines, and the expectation that next winter the Saar territory will be the occasion for war. The Ambassador was most cordial. I walked back to my office, having taken a taxi to the Brandenburger Tor, and walked thence to the French Embassy to escape the vigilance of the German Secret Police, though I doubt whether I was successful. Nazi Germany is certainly watchful.

At 4:30 Colonel Wuest, our Military Attaché here, called and reported the discovery of a new and heavily equipped airfield as he flew a few days before to Bremen. The German officer in the machine, as they flew westward, affected not to see what he had observed and Wuest asked no questions. This only supports the French evidence. Colonel Wuest is a good man with many contacts. He knows German well, and is watchful of his opportunities, but the military appeal is strong and he instinctively approves of the army drills and demonstrations —contradictory as these are to the interests of the United States.

August 16. Thursday. Young Baron von Blomberg, American-born adopted member of General von Blomberg's family here (the General being the Nazi Secretary of War), came to see me this morning at 11 o'clock. I was a little shy of him in view of reliable reports we have had about General von Blomberg's share in the June 30 terror and in the elevation of Hitler to Von Hindenburg's post without any constitutional or lawful authority to cover it. Young Von Blomberg reported his friendly relations with Assistant Secretary Phillips of the State Department and showed strong opposition to the methods of June 30, which I thought was a bid for frank statements from me which he would get to his patron, and thus enable the government to make out a case against my partisanship, if it could be called such.

He then remarked that Nazi propaganda in the United States did Germany harm. I let him know I agreed fully, but gave no names here responsible for such performances, like Ivy Lee and the rest. Then he said General von Blomberg was much against propaganda and that he was urging the dismissal of Dr. Goebbels. He did not quite say that his kinsman in the Cabinet was urging the abolition of the Propaganda Ministry, but I inferred as much. The young fellow went away talking favorably of the foreign press opposition to all ruthlessness here. It was a rather questionable mission, if such it was.

August 17. Friday. Mr. McMaster, Quaker relief representative who maintains an office here and formerly distributed many millions of American dollars for the relief of German sufferers from 1919 to 1921, reported the difficulties of his people and his efforts, on all proper occasions, to procure the release of innocent Germans from prison. He had many stories to tell, but they are similar to others already recorded and so I do not repeat them. He offered his service in cases in which I cannot intervene in any way.

One case I called to his attention: An innocent man now in a concentration camp had been invited by the president of Dartmouth College to lecture there. Charles A. Beard, president last year of the American Historical Association, had wired to ask whether I would convey the invitation to the prisoner. I asked Consul Geist to sound out the Secret Police here. He did so and reported that any such invitation extended from the United States, if known to the government, would cause rough treatment to the prisoner. I wired Beard that we must await events.

Dr. Henry Smith Leiper, representative of the Federation of Churches, came at 12 o'clock. He told of the attitude of American Protestants and said the representatives of all these churches are meeting in a few days near Copenhagen to discuss international religious problems. He reported that the German Reichsbishop Müller had opposed any German Protestants attending and that the government had refused visas to German preachers who wished to attend. The federation people had disliked this and the German Protestants were greatly offended. Eight or ten had decided to go to a German village a few miles from the Danish border and there consult with their fellow Christians of the outside world. Such action would endanger their freedom, perhaps their lives.

Professor M. McMeyer of the University of Boston, who has traveled all about Germany, reported today prosperity everywhere and almost unanimous enthusiasm for Hitler and his regime. The June 30 killings had not affronted anybody, according to him. There was, he said, free discussion and the same old German *Gemütlichkeit* he had known years before. Has he simply fallen for the Nazi propaganda and will he go back to Boston to argue for the strange medievalism which has escaped his attention? He is a Protestant preacher and teacher of naïve mentality unless I myself am of strange and perverse mental traits!

August 18. Saturday. Mr. John Garrett, of the old B. & O. railroad family in Baltimore, a former Ambassador to Rome, called to pay his respects and to talk a little about Europe. Although his inherited social point of view is so different from mine, his assessment of German life today is the same as mine. I am sorry my family is away, else I would have given him the expected dinner. We closed our conversation by my raising the interesting point about his grandfather's contribution to the saving of the American union of states by the building of the B. & O. railroad to Chicago just before 1860 and the management of the road during the war against Virginia and the South. He was delighted that I knew the facts—an advantage, for once in this atmosphere, of knowing history.

At 12:30 Henry Mann called with Mr. Jolles, vice president of the National City Company, New York, who came to talk about the possibility of American credits to Germany. I could see no safe way. There is no evidence that Hitler, Goering or Goebbels has the slightest compunction about non-payment of any kind of debt to the United States, and these men have the decisive power here. Much as I dislike to have the United States lose its cotton, copper and meat markets, worth hundreds of millions a year, I cannot advise bankers to loan money here. It would simply mean a sacrifice of American savings, as things now look. They went away depressed but in agreement.

Captain Crockett, Assistant Military Attaché here, gave a dinner tonight. It was a nice little party, though nothing worthwhile was said. To repeat what I have said before: Army and Navy Attachés here, and I think all over Europe, are utterly unequal to their supposed functions. They simply have never received good training, except in drill and tactics. They may know a little formal history, but they really do not grasp the social and economic problems in countries to which they are accredited. Nor are they clever enough to spy on German military performances. Spying is really what governments expect in such fields.

August 19. Sunday. I was driven out to Ambassador François-Poncet's country mansion on the shore of Wannsee, where all wealthy Germans like to have summer residences unless they can afford an estate in Bavaria. The Ambassador's mansion is a beautiful building and the lake lies just in the rear.

François-Poncet has no better knowledge than others, but he is very uneasy and with some justification. Germany may readily venture into a war about the Saar Territory next winter or spring, especially if Japan breaks loose at the same time. According to reports, Hitler has sent word to François-Poncet that he will never see him again. This is on account of the charge that he was conspiring last spring with Roehm and Von Schleicher to overthrow the Chancellor. This angers the Ambassador extremely.

In view of repeated attacks by Hitler and Goering upon all democratic and parliamentary governments, we discussed a possible retort sometime. He had no suggestions. I intimated that he, the British Ambassador and I ought possibly to ask our recall simultaneously if attacks and charges of conspiracy were repeated. He did not commit himself. I am beginning to feel that we ought to sound out our governments on the subject of a concerted withdrawal. It might temporarily prevent war if done properly.

After this conversation the party took to a boat and spent an hour on the Wannsee. It was surprisingly cold for August. Having no overcoat, I wrapped myself in a large red shawl, and Madame François-Poncet said she would like to have a picture. There was fortunately no photographer on board and so I escaped. Finally, I could politely leave and I was glad to be home and quiet again.

August 20. Monday. Herr Hecke of the Reichsbank brought me a curious pamphlet recently published here by a philosopher who describes all of German philosophy from Immanuel Kant to Friedrich Nietzsche as merely the prelude to the social philosophy which underlies the Nazi regime. The second part summarizes Hitler's social attitude and political purposes; in the third, Roosevelt's work and purposes are analyzed. According to the author and the bank official who gave me the pamphlet, Hitler and Roosevelt have the same ideals and purposes and both synchronize with the general German philosophy from Kant to Hegel to Nietzsche.

I was earnestly besought to send the pamphlet to the President. The banker was typically naïve. I agreed, however, to send the absurd pamphlet to the State Department but expressed the fear that Mr. Roosevelt would not be able to read it. Imagine such a man as this in high position in the German Reichsbank!

Mr. Francis Hickman of New Orleans called. He wished an interview with Hitler which I did not care to ask for, especially as the Chancellor is in Bavaria. I teased him a little about Huey Long, the Louisiana "Hitler." Hickman gave me the impression that he really wishes to see some kind of dictatorship in America. Perhaps I ought to have arranged an interview with the German dictator so that he could publish his story in the United States and see what the public would say.

August 22. Wednesday. I went with my family to the famous Passion Play at Oberammergau, escorted by the mayor who had kindly sent us tickets. The mayor gave the Hitler greeting whenever he met any acquaintance on the street. We were all seated together in the reserved section but I think few if any of our neighbors knew who we were.

The play during the morning portrayed the early life of Jesus and the Old Testament prophecies and scenes showing what the Christian churches have always claimed were the connecting links between the Old and New Testaments. I saw no Jews present. There were 6,000 people in the beautiful hall. It is open at the end where the stage is located, and one gazes constantly upon a most beautiful mountain scene. It is a wonderful setting.

The chief actor is Lang, son of the man who gave the play its present form some thirty years ago. The Lang family are the masters of the town, Oberammergau having normally 3,000 inhabitants whose main income each year is from visitors, foreign and German, who go there to see the Jesus tragedy. I think Lang is an excellent actor and the choir which sings or recites interludes in a grand style is impressive.

At 2 o'clock we took our places again in the great hall and the tragedy slowly moved to its culmination: the betrayal by Judas, the trial of Jesus and the awful scene of the executions on the cross, with law officers climbing short ladders to the crucified individuals and beating them before their deaths. When Jesus was tried before the angry Jewish court, a well-dressed German, looking very solemn, said to me: "Es ist unser Hitler." Ida Horne, a distant kinswoman of mine, sitting in another part of the hall, told me as we came out together: "A woman near me said, as Judas received his thirty pieces of silver, 'Es ist Roehm!'" I suspect half the audience, the German part, considers Hitler as Germany's Messiah.

About 6:30 I took third class passage to Munich which enables me to get natural reactions of German people toward the existing regime. It was a crowded train but, like all others, I had a clean and comfortable seat. The people, however, seemed to know little of what happens in Germany, though a school teacher and a peasant woman, both educated so that they spoke good German, referred favorably to Hitler. They said nothing of his terrorist conduct. There was much frank talk on this journey, as I had observed last year on my third class journey from Dresden to Berlin. While Bavarian small town and peasant folk have good schools for the young people, they are reported to be the most simple and naïve element of the German Reich.

August 23. Thursday. My friend Louis Brownlow of the Rockefeller Foundation and the University of Chicago called and reported many interesting things about the university and its troubles. Brownlow knows American urban problems as well as anyone in the country. He is talking with officials of German cities to see if the Nazi regime is neglecting the city housing projects, where administration was particularly efficient, which had prevailed here for half a century or more. He knows many prominent pre-Hitler leaders.

In the afternoon Ivy Lee came with his smooth young son. The young son, last winter, thought a speech of mine implied criticism of Fascist Europe, which it did most gently and indirectly. Later I learned of the elder Lee's relations with the German Government.

Today the old man looked broken and in spite of talk about his cure I am sure his health is very poor. He has made his millions the last twenty years and now the world knows how it was done. I talked frankly with him and he turned red in the face more than once. He asked if I had reported on him to Washington. He hoped I could write something favorable to Secretary Phillips.

He then said: "Ilgner of the Carl Schurz Foundation here said you were an anti-Nazi, or perhaps merely against the Foundation." I answered that I was opposed to all propaganda, but had urged the Carl Schurz people last spring to go on with their work if it remained simply cultural and permitted no propaganda. Ilgner wished to see me, according to Lee. I told him to extend an invitation. Ilgner is head of the great I. G. Farben corporation in Germany.

The Lees went away, kindly asking about my family and their sojourn in Austria. It is only another of the thousands of cases where love of money ruins men's lives. I cannot say a commendatory word about him to the State Department.

August 24. Friday. Mrs. Sinclair Lewis, whose ability as a writer and artist equals that of her famous husband, called today at 11 and talked for half an hour about a plan of hers to study and describe the present German socio-philosophical system, if one may call it a system. She impressed me most favorably.

A little after she left, Dr. Dieckhoff paid the conventional call after his vacation in Switzerland, where he has the safe retreat of his father-in-law's residence. I thought also that he wished to hear me talk a little about the strange events that had occurred while he had been away, on June 30 and July 25. We had talked frankly, being rather intimate acquaintances, for a few minutes when Mrs. Lewis called from her hotel, the Adlon, and said she had just received an order from the Secret Police to leave the country in twenty-four hours! "What shall I do?" she asked. I said: Go at once to Acting Consul General Geist. She thanked me and hung up the phone receiver.

I turned to Dieckhoff and said: Did you hear that? He said: "No." I was almost sure he had. I explained and added that this would make a nation-wide sensation. He agreed and said he would do all he could to restrain the Secret Police. We both recognized that whether Mrs. Lewis had given cause or not, her expulsion from Germany would advertise everything she had said all over the democratic world.

August 28. Tuesday. Dr. Max Ilgner of the great I. G. Farben Company and president of the Carl Schurz Verein called by appointment this morning ostensibly to talk about the Verein functions. He had reported to Ivy Lee that I was very unfriendly to the Verein. Ilgner impressed me as unconscious of the real opportunities of his organization. There was little said, however, and I did not press him to explain the propaganda work which I know he represents. He did not mention Ivy Lee who received a large fee from his concern.

He did talk a good deal about a business trip he is undertaking to Manchuria where he said his company had bought 400,000 bushels of soy beans. I suspect he is on a mission to exchange poison gases and explosives for Japanese products. Perhaps I am unfair, but I could not avoid this drift of thought when he talked so freely and profusely about the beans.

August 31. Friday. Professor Vernon McKenzie of the University of Washington came to talk of his interviews in Warsaw and Prague. He said: "The Poles are not planning any annexations at the expense of Russia or Czechoslovakia. They made their pact with Germany because France was so exacting and arbitrary in everything, and in the hope of making peace in the Corridor possible. I am convinced they have succeeded. The French are exasperated."

As to Prague, he continued, "There is great anxiety lest Germany make war on Austria, which would at once force the Czechoslovaks into war. Otto Strasser, brother of the Gregor Strasser recently killed here, said to me he would see to it that the Fuehrer is killed in six or eight months. That looked to me exceedingly unwise to report if he really meant it. But Strasser is inveterately hostile and I look for some efforts in that direction."

I went home to get ready to journey to Dahlem by taxi, to lunch with Dr. Dieckhoff. It was a cold day and I was a little uncomfortable in the draughty dining room. The company was small and all German. Nothing of confidential nature was mentioned until I was about to leave, when Dieckhoff gladly informed me that the Foreign Office had at last persuaded Hitler to stop hostile treatment of the Jews. He hoped that the people of the United States would come gradually to think better of Germany and to allow treaty negotiations in Washington between the two countries. He added that Von Neurath had pressed the matter since my return last spring.

I was surprised and I did not inform Dieckhoff that a few days before I had received a copy of formal instructions to the Nazi Party that they must refuse all association with Jews, must not, if lawyers, assist Jews in any way, and, if clerks in Jewish stores, must not wear their Party badges. And the "wicked race" must in no public places be recognized or allowed to associate with the Aryans. These are the instructions that have been before the Party for a year and a half. This copy bore the name of Rudolf Hess, personal adjutant to Hitler, and the date was August 16, 1934. It was proof that while Hitler supposedly promised the Foreign Office to do what its wisest officials asked, he allowed his most intimate and trusted counselor to do the opposite of what he promised. If this were the first time a promise of this sort had been made to me, I might think there was some error and that the new order was simply the old one renewed by some inside extremist. But it looks real. Sometime when I see Von Neurath or Dieckhoff, I shall show the new order.

September 1. Saturday. Professor McKenzie, Professor Lingelbach and E. T. Colton, Y.M.C.A. representative from New York, lunched with me. The conversation was most frank and searching. McKenzie told of his visit to West German towns where he learned of four or five great underground aircraft hangars, the number of heavy aircraft now ready for war, and the amount of poison gas they could put over Paris or London in two or three hours. Lingelbach, who was quite pro-German during the World War period, and Colton, who gave me a most sympathetic picture of the Nazi regime when I came here in July, 1933, took the story sadly and showed great sorrow that Germany has behaved in a way to make the United States more generally hostile than in 1917. I gave some stories of the treatment of innocent individuals which only made the feeling more unanimous. Nobody came to the defense of other countries that are arming: France, England, the United States and Japan. We parted rather discouraged. It is such an unwise world and war means such terrible disaster.

V

September 5, 1934 to December 21, 1934

September 5. Wednesday. Somewhere today, either at the British Embassy or in the office, I heard another story of the intimacy of General von Schleicher and the French Ambassador all last winter. The informant, recently in Paris, says there is no doubt of Monsieur François-Poncet's share in the Roehm plan to overthrow Hitler last June. I doubted any conspiracy, but felt sure there was political intrigue going on in the hope of overthrowing a regime which all Frenchmen think is aiming directly at the destruction of the French Republic. I hear constantly stories that certain eminent Nazis were listed to be killed July 1. The list has never been published.

The British Ambassador, as usual, asked me many questions today but gave no useful answers to questions about the Far East which I put to him. He said he had not stopped in London on his way to Berlin. He attends the ceremony in honor of Hitler's "elevation" next week. He told me that he had read the Nuncio's manuscript address and recommended omission of one paragraph which flattered the President. I understand the French and the Italian Ambassadors are to be present.

September 6. Thursday. A busy day preparing an address I am to make at Bremen Sunday afternoon. Last evening, Orme Wilson, to whom I submitted parts of the first draft of the address, expressed great fear that my account of belligerent attitudes in Europe would make a sensation, perhaps bring a rebuke from the State Department. I submitted a copy to one of the American correspondents and he hoped I would not omit any passages bearing on international relations; he thought great good might be done at Geneva. I have restated a few sentences and given final form to the paper, and I expect to take the risk of delivering it as written. I shall read it in English as I have no time to put it into German. I shall give a copy tomorrow to the Foreign Office here, also to Washington.

September 7. Friday. Mr. Gannon, vice president of the Chase National Bank of New York, came to learn my attitude about the German debt problem. He had talked long with Dr. Schacht and was to see him again. Gannon lives in London, Paris and Berlin and tries to arrange loans for German purchases of cotton, copper and oil, short term loans at 4 per cent of which there are now some $600,000,000 outstanding in New York banks. I told Gannon that it was my opinion that all European peoples thought the debts due the United States should not be paid at all. Schacht would pay in order to continue exports but would not even try to pay if exports direct to the United States were not greatly increased.

Gannon described a complicated scheme whereby loans might be continued with safety. He would present this to Schacht before leaving for London. I frankly told Gannon that I was not expert enough in financial matters to catch his points in conversation and asked for a written memorandum. He said he would send me one as soon as he reached London and hoped I would write the State Department in support of his plan.

September 8. Saturday. I took the train, second class, at 9 o'clock for Bremen. The car was a little cold the first two hours, but I managed to keep in the sunshine and fairly comfortable. German cars are not heated until weather is really cold.

I sat next to a neat-looking fellow passenger who was quite desirous of talking freely. He said he was born and reared in Germany. He now lives in New York. He had spent the summer in Italy, Germany and Russia and he seemed to have made good contacts and learned much. He was troubled and shocked at the Hitler ruthlessness and cruelty. He thought the German people did not approve, but were helpless. When another well-dressed fellow passenger who sat opposite me indicated a disposition to talk, the New Yorker asked him frankly how he liked the regime. The reply was enthusiastic: "Hitler ist unser grosser Führer; wir sind überall für ihn, und diese Franzosen, die uns umklammern, ach! wir werden diesem bösen Feinde ein Ende machen!" ("Hitler is our great Leader; we are for him everywhere; and these French who encircle us, ach! we will make an end of these evil enemies!") All the world, he went on, is hostile. He had fought in the last war and was ready any day to go to war with France again. He was certain the Germans would make an end of France the next time.

The New Yorker said little more. The German left the train at some town about halfway between Berlin and Bremen. Two officers of the German Reichswehr, returning from Nürnberg, came into the car, but I did not care to begin conversation with them; and the New Yorker also kept quiet.

After luncheon I walked about the old part of Bremen and, finding an old bookshop near the canal, bought a volume of Macaulay's *Essays:* on Frederick the Great, John Bunyan and Barère, the French evil genius. I had failed to take a book to read during the idle hours of my journey.

September 9. Sunday. At 12:30 I was asked to speak briefly before the assembled Y.M.C.A. folk. I was greeted with more enthusiasm than I had expected. In the afternoon there was a gathering of some 5,000 people from all parts of Germany and western Europe. I was embarrassed because I had expected an educated audience of 400 or 500. However, I read my address, *A Troubled World,* and received applause as if all had understood me. What I said was directed against war preparations and increasing commercial barriers.

I climbed into my berth at 10 P.M. and traveled slowly via Hanover to Berlin where I arrived at 7 A.M. and took a taxi to the house, not feeling too well, for sleep in a narrow German berth is next to impossible. I read Macaulay's *Essays* until my eyes were too tired. His Barère essay is a terrible criticism of one of the sinister officials of the Robespierre regime. It is probably correct, but one may infer that part of the great historian's motive was a dislike of France and condemnation of the "wild democracy" of the revolutionary period in France.

September 10. Monday. I had an appointment with Wallace Deuel, new correspondent of the Chicago *Daily News,* this afternoon. Deuel is succeeding Junius Wood, an exceedingly able news gatherer. The former has been in Rome two years and knows the European tangle well, but not the German language. He wished to give me what he had learned the last two weeks and then get light on the characters of Hitler, Goering and Goebbels and their supporting chiefs.

The fifteen or twenty American newspaper correspondents here are by far the cleverest information-finders I know. I think they are cleverer than the French and British spies, who are sometimes a bit too shrewd, for they endanger the lives of Germans who give them information occasionally. I gave Deuel what facts and leads I thought fair and safe to give. He impresses me as a good man, but so unsympathetic with the Mussolini autocracy that it will be difficult for him to be entirely poised in his work here, where Hitler is equally ruthless and curiously repulsive to anyone with English or American background.

September 11. Tuesday. Oechsner of the United Press and Webb Miller, London representative of the same news service, gave me today much light on the publicity methods of the Goebbels propaganda office. Miller was more depressed at German autocracy methods than Oechsner. They report the establishment of a new Secret Police unit assigned to catch every foreigner's opinion over telephones and in hotels.

September 12. Wednesday. At 12:30 I went to the Presidential palace on the Wilhelmstrasse, in full evening dress, to pay formal respects to the new self-made President, Adolf Hitler. Some days ago the Spanish Ambassador came to me to indicate that he felt he would have to go, although he disliked to think of shaking hands with him. I agreed that we could not stay away as we had done in the Nürnberg case. It was a government affair. I had also talked with the British Ambassador on September 6 and he was of the same mind, though Hitler was most repulsive to him.

When I arrived, the whole yard was surrounded by soldiers stiffly at attention. The palace was also duly guarded. All the diplomatic corps was present including the Nuncio who has been ill in the hospital for a month. The Nuncio is the senior member of the corps and it is his function to read the formal greetings on such occasions. Monsieur François-Poncet, in perfect garb and with medals and ribbons to show his distinction, was next in order to the Nuncio. Young Bérard, attaché of the French Embassy, had told me in August that Hitler had declared he would never again see the French Ambassador. That would have been tantamount to his dismissal if Hitler had adhered to it. There was no sign of such trouble today. They shook hands with seeming cordiality.

When the corps, some fifty in all, were properly arranged around the reception salon, Hitler, Von Neurath, Von Bülow and Von Bassewitz came into the room in full dress, and the Nuncio read his conventional document congratulating the enemy of Rome, political as well as religious, upon his marvelous success in assuming the place of Von Hindenburg. There were some hints and warnings against war, which everybody here believes to be the main purpose of the present regime. I certainly agree.

Hitler replied in German avowing his good will to all the outside world and his one objective: peace. When he finished, he advanced in perfect form, bowed and shook hands with the Papal representative. He might as well have embraced him, as far as formal behavior went. Then Hitler came to François-Poncet and they appeared to be even more friendly. For a minute or two they gossiped together in German in a most amiable fashion; but I was not near enough to understand what was said. Then the Chancellor addressed Cerruti, Italian Ambassador, but there was less evidence of warmth. The Italian has not the social *savoir faire* of the Frenchman. He cannot hide his dislikes and he hates the Nazi regime, as his wife, a distinguished Jewess from Hungary, also hates it.

When Hitler came to the Japanese Ambassador who stood on my right he made a point of thanking him for his attendance at Nürnberg and for a speech which he said the Ambassador made. Nobody misunderstood this: it was intended as a rebuke to the French, Italian, English and Spanish representatives and myself who had declined to attend the show both this year and last. As the happy Fuehrer extended his hand to me I reminded him quickly of the peace note in his speech to us and said that it would be approved in the United States, especially by our President, who had asked me to say to him that these peace speeches always interested him. Hitler bowed pointedly and talked for a moment as though he were a pacifist, a type he always damns in his public statements. As he passed on to the Spanish and British Ambassadors, I felt a little badly because he seemed not to have understood my ironical meaning. He assumed that I actually believed what he had said!

I have never seen Hitler quite so happy-looking as while he went down the line greeting the representatives of all foreign countries. Neither Von Neurath nor Von Bülow showed any sense of shame for their country. We all adjourned about one o'clock and drove to our homes, wondering as ever whether the most medieval regime known to Europe can endure.

Newspaper people who came in the afternoon were very anxious to get my impressions of the reception. I could say nothing more than that the keynote was peace and that all the Germans seemed happy.

September 14. Friday. Mattie and I went to the great opera house at Charlottenburg, as guests of the Foreign Office, to attend the opening opera: *Tannhäuser.* Hitler, Von Papen, Goebbels and Generals von Blomberg and Von Fritsch were together in the old royal stalls. Next to us sat Ambassador and Madame Cerruti. Across the hall sat Ambassador and Madame François-Poncet. The boxes were all occupied by diplomatic people and the house was crowded. The music began promptly after the German manner. At the first intermission all the main floor people rose, faced the Hitler box and stood for a time giving the Hitler greeting. This was done again at the second intermission. The vast audience including the actors and singers were enthusiastic about the Chancellor's presence, more, I was told, than was evidenced when the Hohenzollerns used to sit in the royal box.

Von Papen, in spite of what happened to him on June 30 and all he told me, stood during the intermission talking with Goebbels whom he had denounced to me and who, according to Von Papen's son, had tried to have the Vice-Chancellor killed. Curious facts: Von Papen hates Goebbels, Von Blomberg had let me know that he hated Goebbels and would like to see him dismissed, Von Fritsch hates Von Blomberg, and both were reported to have hated Hitler before June 30. Now all of them sit together and appear to be intimate friends!

Madame Cerruti came to me during one of the intermissions and after observing the pretended diplomatic intimacies, said: "You recall what I said at your table June 29?" I had not forgotten. Of course the Cerrutis know I have no more liking for their dictator than I do for the German autocrat. As I meditate upon the problems and the ills of our civilization, I wonder whether the United States should not recall me. I would be willing to go.

September 16. Sunday. We had dinner with Orme Wilson, whose chief guest was Counselor Marriner of our Paris Embassy, returning from a trip to Warsaw where he had been trying to assess the Polish policy toward France and the League. He is highly protocol. We attended the dinner so as not to appear offish, but there was no real discussion, no new information about any subject. It would have been far better to have dined at home and read a good book, in case one could find a good book these days.

September 19. Wednesday. I called on Dr. Schacht, on request of our Secretary of State, at 11 o'clock. He was very cordial. When we had greeted each other, I said very frankly that the relations of our two countries could hardly improve so long as everybody in the United States was convinced that Germany was making ready to precipitate another war. What good can I do in Berlin if all Germany is moving toward a world or European conflict? If I am to fail here, would it not be better to return home and stay? He was a little stunned and replied: "You must not retire; it would do harm." But what can one, of my way of thinking, do in a country where the atmosphere is so disagreeable?

He then said: "All the world is combining against us; everybody is attacking Germany and trying to boycott her." Yes, I replied, but you know the way to stop such things is not to arm to the teeth. If you went to war and won, you would lose more than you could gain. Everybody would lose. When he declared that the Germans are not arming so intensively, I said: Last January and February Germany bought from American aircraft people $1,000,000 worth of high class war flying machinery and paid in gold. He looked embarrassed and was about to deny it, but as he saw I was going to produce a document, he said: "Yes, I suppose you know all about it, but we must arm."

He then acknowledged that the Hitler party is absolutely committed to war, and the people, too, are ready and willing. Only a few government officials are aware of the dangers and are opposed. He concluded: "But we shall postpone it ten years. Then it may be we can avoid war."

I reminded him of his Bad Eilsen speech some two weeks ago and said: I agree with you about commercial and financial matters in the main. But why do you not, when you speak before the public, tell the German people they must abandon a war attitude? He replied: "I dare not say that. I can only speak on my special subjects."

How, then, can German people ever learn the real dangers of war if nobody ever presents that side of the question? He once more emphasized his opposition to war and added that he had used his influence with Hitler, "a very great man," he interjected, to prevent war. I said: The German papers printed what I said at Bremen about commercial relations between our countries, but not a word about the terrible effects and barbarism of war. He acknowledged that and talked very disapprovingly of the Propaganda Ministry which suppresses everything it dislikes. He added as I was leaving: "You know a party comes into office by propaganda and then cannot disavow it or stop it."

On my return to the Chancery, I left my car standing near the Brandenburger Tor and walked into the British Embassy on the Wilhelmstrasse. Sir Eric Phipps was in his office and I talked fifteen minutes about the accumulating evidence in our office of Germany's intense war activity. His consular officials seem not to have given him information we have received from ours, especially from Stuttgart and Munich. He pretended to be surprised when I gave him the facts about German purchases of aircraft from the United States in the last six months.

I also let him know that Schacht had acknowledged to me the war purposes of the Nazi party. My talk with Phipps was confidential and preparatory to future conversations with him if President Roosevelt tries again to bring American arms manufacture under government control. My hope was to enlist him in a move to persuade his government to set up an investigation like that of Senator Nye, now causing so much excitement in all countries. Although I knew England had protested against the exposure of the corrupt practices of its arms manufacturers, I bluntly alluded to the good effects of the Nye exposures. He agreed, though he did not indicate a desire to say anything further. The arms manufacturers over the world are the cause of most of this trouble in Europe.

At 2:30 I went as guest of the Foreign Office to the Kroll Opera House to hear discussions of the great road work now going on in Germany. A number of Germans were present, as also the English and French Ambassadors. It turned out to be merely an occasion for Von Neurath to explain German foreign policy "and peaceful purposes. The Fuehrer desires peace above all else." The idea was to explain Germany's attitude toward Russian admission to the League and the forthcoming plebiscite in the Saar Territory where the people are to decide January 11, I believe, whether they will return to the fatherland or remain under League of Nations rule.

All the members of the diplomatic corps were present and remained in their places until Von Neurath had finished. When the translator began to give English translations, the British and French Ambassadors retired. A little later the Italian and I left. We had had enough of it. Von Neurath was not bad, but no one believed his assertions about the peace purposes of the present regime.

September 24. Monday. The Spanish Ambassador came to tell me that he intended to attend the Bücheberg Thanksgiving festival on September 30, mainly because he has been absent from so many demonstrations and propaganda shows the last few months. I told him I had declined already and could not reverse my decision. These propaganda affairs are so naïve and even repulsive that I cannot endure them unless it is obvious that my official position requires it. I think I shall explain these absences to Secretary Hull and get his reaction.

September 26. Wednesday. The Belgian Minister returned from his long summer vacation, called to talk over the German problems and the Hitler menace. He was certain that no immediate war is coming, but that war is the first object of the present regime, war not upon France or Belgium, but upon Austria and Czechoslovakia. "That is the Hitler objective and it is much safer than the western drive which would unite France, England and Belgium."

It is plain that the Belgian and French Governments are not in harmony; the English and Belgians seem closer together. He was very curious to know whether there is any prospect of the United States entering the League of Nations while Roosevelt is President. I could not give him any information, except that I personally favor American entrance and that I know Roosevelt had also from 1920 to 1930.

We talked a little about the importance of the Far East and the needful co-operation of the United States, England and France in that region if world peace is to be maintained. We were in entire agreement, but I said in conclusion that public opinion in these countries seems far from co-operative. As the Minister departed, I feared I had been too frank as there was at the end a little evidence that he might have been trying to size me up for a report to the clever Sir Eric Phipps, the British

Ambassador. Anyway I had given no assurances of any attitudes in Washington.

September 27. Thursday. Dr. Carl Wehner and Dr. Willy Beer of the *Berliner Tageblatt* called today and we reviewed the whole German back-to-the-land movement. My conclusion was that no real success had been attained. The city unemployed will not go to farms unless compelled and the Hitler government has not applied force in this matter. The large land owners will not part with their lands at prices which the government can afford to pay. Nearly all the unemployed who have been on farms this summer will be back in the cities before the end of October. Mayor Sahms' claim to have relieved Berlin of 100,000 unemployed applies only to summer workers, and they were not welcome workers to the peasants.

September 28. Friday. At 9 o'clock, I appeared, upon invitation, at the Carl Schurz Verein where a professor of the University of Berlin spoke on President Roosevelt's New Deal and the economic prospects in the United States. It was a good and scientific presentation without bias or Nazi propaganda. There were about forty university and government people present. It was such a real affair that I felt free to raise three serious questions when the meeting was thrown open for general discussion: (1) Would the absence of free or near free lands in the United States make recovery on the Roosevelt lines difficult or impossible? (2) Would the fact that neither European emigrants nor American unemployed were willing to accept homesteads compel a new sort of social program? (3) Finally, would the important fact that the population increase of all highly civilized countries will come to a standstill about 1970 not make a difference in economic and social remedies?

There was a good deal of interest shown in these social and moral factors and some discussion, but no answers. It was 11:30 before the party adjourned.

October 1. Monday. The wife of a Secretary of a German Legation in the Balkans called this morning to see if it would be possible for me to assist her in a difficulty forced upon her and her husband by Hitler's representative, Rudolf Hess, who has ordered her husband to prove that none of his ancestors or his wife's were Jews. This lady was born here, of American-German parents. If she cannot prove that neither of her grand-parents were Jewish, her husband must resign his position in the German Foreign Service. She handed me a document which merely showed that her family had been citizens of the United States. Of course I could do nothing; but I referred her to Consul Geist, thinking he might say a friendly word to some German official and possibly ease her situation. The woman revealed no sign of non-Aryan blood. This illustrates the German anti-Jewish policy.

October 4. Thursday. My old friend Quincy Wright, of the University of Chicago, called to talk over the League of Nations problems as revealed at the recent conference at Geneva. The prospect is not good. The Nye investigations in Washington revealed the futility of previous League disarmament discussions while British, American and French armament manufacturers were selling enormous supplies of arms to all the world and even maintaining secret agents at Geneva to defeat the very purpose of the Disarmament Conferences.

Wright thinks the British Conservatives are opposed to the purposes of the League. And the Washington investigations showed that the different armament manufacturers have sold great quantities of arms to Germany for gold, contrary to the treaty between Germany and the United States. Nor have the English been better. They have themselves violated the Versailles Treaty in selling aircraft and other war materials to Germany.

October 5. Friday. At luncheon, the Japanese and Spanish Ambassadors, Von Prittwitz and his wife, Professor and Mrs. Hoetzsch of the University of Berlin, Mr. and Mrs. Wright, Mrs. Baum of Chicago and Miss Sigrid Schultz, among others, composed the party. The Japanese was very clever and also very careful. He talked much and said nothing. The Spanish Ambassador is the opposite type; he revealed his real opinions whenever he spoke and he was very frank.

Countess von Prittwitz, whose husband was Ambassador to the United States from 1926 to 1932, sat on my right. She was far more outspoken in her remarks about conditions and persons in Germany than I dared be. Well as I know the Von Prittwitzes, I do not feel that I can say to any German how terrible the Hitler autocracy is. On my left sat a scientist's wife who showed equal freedom. She said, "German universities are about to be ruined. Half their professors would migrate to the United States if it were possible to get positions." I felt keenly for her and her husband, one of the foremost authorities in his field in Europe. This sort of talk comes to us almost every week.

October 6. Saturday. The newspapers indicate the emergence of a Fascist regime in Spain. I shall almost weep for my Spanish friend if it turns out that way. He is a genuine democrat with a fine mind and much learning. It would spoil his whole life if his country turned Fascist. But Europe is crazy; no one can say what is in store for us.

I spent the morning reading masses of documents and reports on conditions in Germany. At any other time in modern German history I would say a revolution is immediately ahead, but evidence has no significance if all communications are in the hands of a single man and he a monomaniac. He thinks himself called by some God to redeem Germany, and hence no German scholar or statesman dares say one word in criticism of anything. A report yesterday said: Two young S.S. soldiers, brothers, quietly opposed to the harsh drilling system they must endure, spoke mildly against the Hitler autocracy and declined to attend some meeting of the Party. One of them was seized when away from home, killed and burned. His ashes were handed in a package to the surviving brother two days later. That is not proved, but it accords with so many facts about other executions that I cannot refuse credence. Such things are supposed to terrorize all Germans so that they will submit to everything.

October 7. Sunday. I worked all day today on an address I am to deliver in Washington December 28 or 29 before the American Historical Association. Previous presidential addresses have generally dealt with "how history should be written" or "what is the proper realm of history." I think this has been overdone, and feel I should make a definite historical contribution instead. I shall talk on the origin and development of African slavery in the South, with the title: "The First Social Order in the United States." At this distance, and in a position where free time is not easy to get, this means much work.

October 8. Monday. Martha's birthday. Her friends and acquaintances were invited to come at 10, rather late for a party and dance. There were many agreeable people, including many troubled Germans like young Stresemann, the able son of the former Chancellor Gustav Stresemann, whose mother is a Jewess and whose deceased father is loudly denounced by leaders of the present regime. Young Stresemann can have no official position and it is not easy to get legal work because of his Jewish mother. The evening was, however, quite agreeably spent, except that many guests, after the diplomatic and German fashion, remained long after midnight, at which time I retire.

October 9. Tuesday. Luis Zulueta, Spanish Ambassador, and the one personal friend I have here in the diplomatic corps, a real personal friend, came to the office today to inform me that he had resigned and was going back to Madrid where he resumes his work as a professor of philosophy. He said the new government of Spain is a combination of Fascists and Catholic reactionaries with the support of Mussolini and the Pope, an autocratic regime which he could not serve. I had no doubt as to what he said. The news from his unhappy country has been such for some weeks that I could easily see what his situation was. I am afraid his successor will be a Fascist with whom I shall not be able to associate in any but a purely formal manner. I am distressed to lose my only friend here.

At 7 o'clock Oechsner of the United Press called me at the house to say that the King of Yugoslavia had been killed in Marseilles a few hours ago. Barthou, the French Foreign Secretary, was in the auto with the King, and was wounded. It was a shock, especially because the visit to France was for the purpose of binding France, Italy and Yugoslavia into closer relations against Germany and Poland. At 7:30, another call informed me that Barthou was dying. These assassinations may bring international trouble, in view of the tense relations.

At 8:30 in full evening dress, we went to dine with the Egyptian Minister, a rich man who has little to do here but who likes to parade his wealth. There were uniformed servants everywhere and the dining room was huge. There were about forty people present, all in grand style and with all sorts of badges and medals of honor hanging on their conspicuous fronts, the women with costly diamonds and naked backs and breasts, red lips and finger nails. Such expense and show and dress seems out of taste, especially when indulged in by representatives of countries which do not pretend to pay their debts.

There was little conversation at table, the party being too big. Afterwards there was some discussion of the terrible Marseilles events of today, said by a German general to have been due to negligence of the French police. Their conduct does seem to have been very bad. One German baroness asked the general whether war is imminent. She said she had three sons who would be called to the front. The General said, "No," but when I told him of the warlike talk I have heard, though I did not mention Dr. Schacht, he admitted that the war spirit is strong. The baroness changed her tone and seemed rather willing to have her sons go to the front to fight France. Sir Eric and Lady Phipps came to us a few minutes before eleven and indicated that they would like to go but as we are seniors here we must move first—silly protocol. We said farewell in a little while and were at home at 11.

October 10. Wednesday. The new Consul General, Douglas Jenkins, called. He comes from China and takes the place Messersmith held for three years. He is a South Carolinian but by no means provincial or sectional in his attitudes. He has been in the service nearly twenty years. His knowledge of German is pretty good and will soon, I believe, be equal to the demands of his office.

October 11. Thursday. I went to see Secretary von Bülow at 12 o'clock. On the 9th, I received a cable from Washington to make a sharp and positive demand that Germany cease discriminating against American creditors of Germany. I have protested half a dozen times without success. The interest payment of about $2,000,000, due on October 15, had been ordered by Germany to be paid only to the extent of some 60 per cent. Washington complained again and asked me to demand more. No one could receive me yesterday at the Foreign Office and today I had no idea I would succeed.

When I handed my aide-memoire to Von Bülow, he looked it through carefully and said: "Let me read you a copy of a cable we sent to Secretary Hull, through Ambassador Luther, yesterday." The telegram in German expressed regret that no negotiations for a trade treaty had been agreed to in Washington last spring. It then informed Secretary Hull that about one million dollars in registered marks had been cabled over to New York on the 10th. Von Bülow said: "That is the best we can do and it meets the bondholders' demands." And it is substantially true. The marks will be transferred to Americans for the purchase of German goods or to travelers coming to Germany.

We talked a few minutes about the possibility of trade negotiations. He acknowledged serious doubts about the working of autarchy here. Commerce must be freer or we shall all be sufferers. I was favorably impressed by what he said, though I had the feeling the Germans had somehow learned the content of my aide-memoire, delayed my interview, and sent the money to New York. Is there a leak in our office? Or did it get to the German Embassy in Washington?

October 14. Sunday. I worked all day on the address I am booked to read before the American Historical Association in Washington on December 27. I wish I were not in this position, president of the association this year. My hope is to make some historical contribution to men's appreciation of current difficulties in the western world.

October 17. Wednesday. Dr. Schacht came to lunch today directly from a Cabinet meeting at which Hitler exacted a new oath of loyalty to himself. All the Reichswehr were required to take a special oath early in August when Hitler assumed the functions of President in addition to those of Chancellor. On

August 19 everybody was committed to the new autocracy by an election in which 90 per cent of the people voluntarily or by coercion voted "Ja." Now, at the first formal session of the Cabinet, every member was compelled to swear allegiance again. It was announced that every Cabinet member was answerable solely to the Chancellor, that the Parliament or Reichstag had nothing to do with any of the business of government, and that Hitler was sole spokesman of the people.

These facts were in the minds of everybody as they came together today. I asked Mr. White, our Counselor, to be present and keep in mind all that was said about public affairs. In view of the fact that several people were killed here last June because they were reported to have talked freely to Ambassadors of France and England, I never do more than listen and occasionally ask a question when eminent Germans are here. Dr. Schacht was frank and outspoken in a way no other German has been since our arrival here. We made a summary mentally amongst ourselves as soon as he went away, as he said, to his Reichsbank duties.

At table he said: "The whole modern world is crazy. The system of closed national barriers is suicidal and we must all collapse here and the standard of living everywhere be reduced. Everybody is crazy. And so am I. Five years ago I would have said it would be impossible to make me so crazy. But I am compelled to be crazy. We are excluding raw materials all the time and must in time be ruined if we cannot export goods and the exports decline all the time. We have no money to pay our debts and soon shall have no credit anywhere. England and France are recommending the constant decrease of exports to us. Switzerland, Holland and Sweden are taking the same direction, and the United States hates us so that we can never renegotiate our commercial treaty."

Prince Louis Ferdinand remarked: "The United States may have a dictator too. Huey Long is absolute master of Louisiana and expects to be master of the whole country." Schacht did not say directly: "Imitate us!" but he made it clear that such was the Prince's meaning. When Schacht spoke of the impossible dilemma into which he was drifting, I said: You will have to invent something new. He laughed.

Frau Dr. Schacht, who sat next to me at the table, showed as much discouragement as had Madame Cerruti on June 29, the day before the purge, when she had predicted war and said she was leaving Germany the next day. Frau Schacht talked of a food shortage, and of compulsory contributions which would be impossible to bear very long. There is no chance of her leaving Germany, no matter how bad conditions become. In case of collapse I fear Schacht will be made the goat by Hitler partisans and be put out. If Hitler were to be assassinated, Schacht would probably be called upon to become head of the chaotic German state.

October 18. Thursday. William Hillman, Hearst International News Service man in London, called to see me today. He reported: (1) Great Britain and Holland have a pact by which Holland's eastern border will be England's eastern border in case Germany goes to war upon France, and the British army will enter Antwerp on its way to Germany. For this concession from Holland, Great Britain has agreed to protect Dutch possessions in the Far East against Japan. (2) Premier MacDonald is ill and must retire before long. Baldwin and Chamberlain are planning an election before that happens, if any excuse can be found. An election with MacDonald leading would give victory, and after that he would retire and Baldwin would be Premier. (3) Towards the United States, the British Government is increasingly hostile though not warlike, and there is no prospect of a pact with the United States.

October 19. Friday. I visited Sir Eric Phipps and repeated in all confidence a report that Armstrong-Vickers, the great British armament concern, had negotiated a sale of war material here last week, just before a British Government commission arrived to negotiate some plan with Schacht for payment of short-term debts of £5,000,000 due on current deliveries of British cotton yarn from Lancaster. It is impossible, Schacht said to me yesterday, to pay the British debts. Yet last Friday, I reported to Sir Eric, the British arms people were selling for cash enormous quantities of war supplies. And I was frank enough—or indiscreet enough—to add that I understood that representatives of Curtiss-Wright from the United States were here this week to negotiate similar sales. The British Ambassador pretended to be surprised, and said he would let me know if my information was correct.

About a British-Dutch pact he knew nothing. Yet he said it might be. I believe he knows there is such an agreement but is not allowed to admit it. Our conversation was most cordial, though I felt, as I left, that he was more reserved than heretofore when we have exchanged views. Perhaps I was too frank, but he promised solemnly not to reveal anything I had said.

Armand Bérard was visiting the children—no longer children—when we came home from a call on one of our staff. He asked me to sit aside a moment with him and consider the present German-French situation. I laughingly referred to the problem as not acute enough to keep us awake nights. He remained solemn. He said that Goering and Goebbels want war this winter with the French over the Saar Territory where there is a plebiscite scheduled for January 13. He went on to say that troops are being collected on the border of the disputed zone, barracks being built and men trained daily for another war.

I expressed the idea that Hitler would be afraid to risk war now. He insisted that Germany thinks she can win and that if any pretext at all arises—violence of unfavorable nature in the Saar valley or economic collapse here—there would be an immediate attack upon France. I reminded him of England's position and the probability that France and England are stronger in the air than is commonly reported. He was not very hopeful of prompt action by England, fearing that the French capital and nation would be terrorized or destroyed, even if Germany were beaten in the end.

Bérard hoped we would not go home for Christmas, as we had planned, since too much might happen. I said: I have an engagement on December 27 in Washington. You might telegraph President Roosevelt that you need me here! He laughed, but went away troubled. This shows how tense the atmosphere is here, and there is some reason. Our Agricultural Attaché who studies food conditions said to me today: "I would not be surprised if the German Government seized the Swift stores of lard in and around Hamburg any day. There is no lard in Germany and none available. Swift & Co. has refused to take marks in payment."

Josephus Daniels, United States Ambassador to Mexico, has been accused publicly at home of having approved the antireligious program of the Mexican Government. He is under fire from a number of American Catholic associations. Since 1889, when he advised me to take the competitive examination in Raleigh, N. C., for West Point—in which I came out second—I have always felt close to him. What he has done in Mexico I do not know, but he is an able, democratic-minded man, and I believe the President will not recall him. It would make a hero of Daniels among Protestants at home, and among all liberal democrats. The Catholics of the United States have no right to dictate to the Mexican people what they shall do.

October 22. Monday. William Hillman came to lunch today. He had spent Sunday in Dresden with Hanfstaengl, who is the subject of much jesting in diplomatic circles, and with the Nazi Governor of Saxony. He reported a dinner conversation in which the Austrian Consul General in Dresden avowed himself a Nazi and was proud of authoritarian Germany. My guess is that he has probably been bribed and is aiding the Nazis to force Austria into accepting annexation.

Hillman said the Governor of Saxony, a Hitler appointee, impressed him as a brutish man ready for any ruthlessness. Hanfstaengl seemed to him very much more clever than he had expected him to be. He told me that Hitler is about to offer England a pact under which each power will agree not to attack the other with aircraft.

October 24. Wednesday. This morning Dr. Max Sering, eminent professor emeritus of economics and political philosophy of the University of Berlin, called to see me to talk over a letter he is writing to Secretary Wallace. He traveled all over the United States in 1930, as he had done in 1882, studying economic and agricultural life there. Secretary Wallace had written me to see him and let him use the government pouch for correspondence if he wished.

Dr. Sering is seventy-seven years old, but very vigorous. He delivered a lecture a month ago at the Bad Eilsen international conference where Dr. Schacht spoke on the German financial situation. After reading to me a draft of his letter to Mr. Wallace, he talked of the present German economic situation with great anxiety. He said: "These people do not know anything about economic and historical problems. They are sacrificing the culture and intellectual life of Germany for their fantastic ideals of perfect unity and complete independence of all the world, which is impossible for a great nation." I gave him bits of experience I have had here and part of my remarks to Hitler and Rust on March 7, 1934, about academic freedom and its meaning for modern civilization. Dr. Sering was surprised but most happy to learn what I had said. He then dwelt at some length on what he regards as the impossible world complex.

He spoke of the present German leadership which he said "has got itself into a warlike attitude toward all neighbors, and war would ruin Western civilization. This leadership demands submission from the universities, the churches and the people, to its childish ideal. It allows no freedom of speech, conscience or initiative. That will ruin us. We cannot endure it. I am no longer young. I oppose the system and I express my opinions when opportunity offers. If they want to kill me, they can do it. I shall not submit."

I was greatly impressed by the old gentleman's courage and expressed purpose. When he said the system cannot last here, I wondered how he imagined effective opposition could be made. The Reichswehr accepted the absolutism of Hitler as demanded when Von Hindenburg died. The Cabinet surrendered entirely when the new "laws" were decreed early in August, and an election was called for August 17 in such a way that any German who voted "no" ran the risk of imprisonment, perhaps death. At the first formal meeting of the Cabinet in October Hitler compelled every member to take a new oath of complete submission to him. Only one member—Eltz-Rubenach—resisted. If all had refused there could have been a revolution, but half the Cabinet is absolutely submissive, the other half actually so when it comes to a real contest.

Dr. Sering said the system cannot last. I think its end not near, and if the economic situation does not become impossible, the regime is apt to go on for years. However, Dr. Sering is in danger—serious danger—although I shall keep what he said entirely confidential.

October 25. Thursday. I asked Schacht today about the registered mark exchange business and the rights of our staff to send dollars home when they can have only small amounts of marks with which to buy dollars. He said at once: "I want students in Germany and travelers to buy registered marks up to a hundred a day and spend them here in order to help American exchange. That is the way to pay the interest on American bonds." He then added that all diplomatic people may buy dollars up to ten per cent of their salaries to send back home. It was clear then just what the bank wishes. However, a good many diplomatic people, in my opinion, buy German marks and trade in devious ways at German expense. I do not know this, but I have seen several signs which pointed that way.

Curiously enough, Schacht asked me to see Hitler about the church issue here and advise him what to do. Two Lutheran bishops in South Germany are in prison because they refuse to accept the *Deutsche Christen* faith and submit to the Hitler idea of one faith and one single state, with complete unity and subordination of all youth to the Hitler religious view. I agreed with Schacht that the imprisonment of bishops and dismissal of preachers because of religious disagreement greatly affronted American church people, especially the Lutherans. He added that it hurts us more in America than our Jewish persecutions. But I said: I can't talk to the Chancellor about internal affairs of this kind. It would be intermeddling. He added: "Von Neurath has argued for hours with Hitler about this, as I have done. But he is so surrounded by S.A. and Party men that he never seems to understand. You might do more than some of us." He wished to make an appointment for me but I declined.

October 26. Friday. Colonel Wuest, our Military Attaché and a flying machine observer, came into the office to tell me about German military preparations. He had been driving about the country for ten days. He was excited. "War is imminent, preparations everywhere," but he was not specific and I had little time to listen.

October 27. Saturday. At Konstanz today, I met Rexford G. Tugwell, so-called "brain-truster." He said he had been especially instructed to discuss with me the situation in Germany. He had been definitely instructed not to visit me in Berlin. I guessed this had been to avoid publicity of a conference between two "brain-trusters," as I have at times been associated with Warren and Tugwell, although this is not really true in any sense.

We talked freely. I was told that Roosevelt holds Cabinet meetings but does not allow frank discussions. I presume that is because men like Hull, Roper and Wallace are strongly opposed to Ickes and Miss Perkins and Lewis Douglas. Tugwell said real discussions were taking place between the President and specialists who are trying to administer the New Deal. I remarked to Tugwell that I would not care to sit in such a Cabinet, free discussion, in my opinion, being the function of Cabinet advisers. Tugwell revealed a sharp dislike of Secretary Hull, one of the most competent men in the government. We agreed that the election of Upton Sinclair as Governor of California, especially since so much money had been poured into that state to discredit him, would be a help to Roosevelt. It would be a solemn warning to the extreme capitalistic people who still think they know how to govern the country.

October 28. Sunday. At 11:30 William and I drove our car onto the ferry that took us back across Lake Constance and we continued on toward Stuttgart. At Hechingen, we lunched in a fair hotel on the main street. As I finished, I asked the host, who had just watched 2,000 Hitler Youth march past his window, whether he could give me a copy of a placard, issued by Goering's Air Ministry, on the wall near our table. It was a color map of Germany which called on all Germans to learn to fly and which showed in sharp colors the parts of the Baltic region, Poland, Denmark and France that should be annexed. The man gave me a copy of his placard.

I said: Are you all learning to fly? He said: "We have twenty good flyers in Hechingen and they have 2,000 in Stuttgart, capital of Württemberg. All big business wants war; the common people do not." The speaker did not know who we were and of course he spoke German. It was a rather touching conversation as he showed not a little concern.

We drove on to Stuttgart where we made no stop. There was nowhere any sign of unemployment or distress in Beyreuth, Nürnberg or Stuttgart. In Konstanz there had been distinct signs of economic decline. Hotels were closed, for instance, though that may have been due to the fact that the summer season is the time when they are really in use.

October 29. Monday. All through this region, we have seen signs as we drove into towns which read: *"Keine Juden erwünscht"* (Jews are not wanted), *"Juden sind unser Unglück"* (Jews are our misfortune), and so on, sometimes done with bitter humor. At Erfurt there was every evidence of prosperity, and in Goethe's famous town, Weimar, there was the same evidence of industrial activity. We drove through Bitterfeld, a town with a huge munitions development, aglow with industrial activity, every smokestack busy and all the great industrial houses lighted from top to bottom. In the little hotel at Wittenberg nearly every table was taken, the great poison gas manufacturing plant keeping people busy here and giving Luther's town a most lively appearance. On the walls of the old hotel there were pictures of Von Hindenburg and Hitler, the same size and make; there was a third and smaller picture of Dr. Goebbels. I asked the servant why General Goering was not represented. He turned away with a smile.

From Wittenberg we reached Berlin in two hours, a beautiful night drive. It had been a long journey of four days. The cost was about 200 marks for both of us, not including the gas purchased on credit, the diplomatic way, the bills to be forwarded to me in Berlin.

October 30. Tuesday. My usual routine began at 9:30, the
staff members and clerks trailing in after me. They think a
diplomat should not enter his office until 10:30 or 11, the clerks
and typists coming at 10. This is especially true of Americans
here. The French and English begin at 9 and continue until
6 or 7.

At 12 o'clock the new Russian Ambassador, Jacob Suritz,
called in all form and ceremony, a distinguished-looking man,
perfectly dressed and very protocol in manner, very much like
the French Ambassador. We talked German nearly an hour on
economic subjects.

November 1. Thursday. At 12 o'clock, Professor Coar came
in. He was much the same but rather more unfriendly to the
Nazi regime than during the summer of 1933. The stories he
told would seem to indicate increasing hostility to Hitler in
Germany. He had sat in a hotel here a day or two before, waiting for a friend whom he dared not visit in his house. Near him
were two women who were knitting, after eating their breakfast. One of them said to the other: "You know my nephew
has been put to death." The other seemed not to be surprised
but was quite angry.

In Hamburg, Coar said, hostility in a luncheon room was so
outspoken that he had had to leave lest he be reported as a
participant. Yet Coar is beginning a series of lectures before
German universities on cultural subjects, and he has been guaranteed perfect freedom. He reported that Hitler had sent word
that he would attend his first lecture in Munich.

Dr. George Solmssen, long time president of the Deutsche
Bank-Disconto Gesellschaft and one of the rich Jews of Germany, called a second time. He had told me a good deal of
his sad story a year ago, soon after my Chamber of Commerce
address. He now seems somewhat reconciled to the Hitler regime and wishes to spend a month in New York, Chicago and
Washington. Since he knows the European financial situation so
well, I gave him letters of introduction to Henry Morgenthau,
Jr., and Daniel Roper. I suspect his real mission is to pacify
the American Jews, as he said he was having conferences with

Dr. Schacht. He will find Morgenthau, father and son, most impatient with the German regime.

At 6 o'clock, I returned the formal call of the Soviet Ambassador, Suritz. He talked rather freely about Russian economic life and gave me an inkling of negotiations with Hitler in spite of the Nazi hatred of everything Russian. I believe Hitler is trying to negotiate a pact with the Soviets like that with the Poles, mainly to scare the French. I shall watch all signs.

November 2. Friday. Frederick Oechsner, the United Press representative, called to explain how badly, in his report to his news agency, he had assessed the Lutheran Church situation last week when I went to Munich. I had asked him at that time to let me know the exact state of things in Bavaria and Württemberg where two bishops were in prison, and his report showed that the Associated Press and London accounts were mostly incorrect. This morning he said: "I want to explain and correct my former report; it was wrong. I do not know how our man in southern Germany got it so badly mixed." I knew that his local reporter, a German, was a Nazi sympathizer who dared not let him learn the facts. I was glad to note that Oechsner was willing to acknowledge his error. I think his organization in New York wishes him to be as favorable to the Hitler regime as possible.

I lunched today in the magnificent Esplanade Hotel dining room, one of the handsomest I have ever seen anywhere, with the American Club, where the new Consul General Jenkins was the speaker and Dr. Dieckhoff was the German official representative. Jenkins read a careful address on Chinese life and culture and in no way made statements that would in any way be compromising here. My thought has always been to say something or not speak at all, though I endeavor never, in this atmosphere, to say anything that can be quoted as applying directly to the existing regime.

November 6. Tuesday. Professor Wolfgang Windelband, modern historian at the University of Berlin, came to walk with me. At 5:30 it was already dark, a fact which I was sure pleased Windelband. He talked about a lecture he is giving on

November 14, before the American Women's Club, on Bismarck in 1870 and 1871. He said he would dwell upon the mistake the military men made when they demanded Alsace-Lorraine and not merely German-speaking Alsace. I have never known a German historian who seemed to understand Bismarck's position when the treaty of 1871 was being forced upon France. Windelband, however, opposed Bismarck's inclusion of Lorraine in the Reich.

Windelband drifted quickly to a discussion of the position of universities under the Hitler regime. It is a very critical situation, he said. It cannot continue two more years without ruining university life in Germany. He then told me of his part in conducting state examinations for history teachers in high schools. The chairman of the examination board was a local Nazi leader. Two other examiners, also Nazis, tried to force the candidate to answer a number of questions in their ideological way. The candidate adhered strictly to history as written and taught before 1933. Windelband voted that the candidate was right. The two Nazi examiners voted that the candidate had failed. The matter was hotly discussed and the board finally decided the candidate had passed in spite of protests from several of the Nazis. The Nazi presiding officer had voted with the regular professors. Windelband thought this a significant result.

He added that the church struggle was helping the universities immensely. I think there is a chance, but doubt whether the Catholics will support the Lutherans in their contest and believe this failure will defeat the university people. Catholics do not always practice religious freedom or freedom of speech, and the Pope is in alliance with the autocratic Fascist crowd in Spain who are killing their opponents after the Italian-German manner.

Perhaps the Lutheran-Calvinist people of Germany will win. More than a thousand of their preachers have been dismissed because they would not surrender and they are now threatened with starvation, almost all of them having families. Of course if all church folk of Protestant faith would hold firmly together, they would succeed, but how can they co-operate when communication with one another is almost impossible?

November 8. Thursday. Mattie, Martha and I lunched today with the British Ambassador and Richard Strauss, the great Austrian musician. About October 13, as I recall, I had asked Sir Eric Phipps whether there was a pact between England and Holland under which England guarantees the Dutch position in the Far East and Holland opens her harbors to England in case of another war provoked by Germany or Japan or both. He then said he knew of no such pact. I had also asked him whether the Armstrong-Vickers concern, closely linked to the British Government, had sold war materials to Germany just before the arrival of the British committee to negotiate Lancaster debts. He had said "no" to both questions, but added that he would call me if he learned anything. He had not called me between October 13 and this date.

At table there was no exchange of remarks that might in any way be called intimate. After all of us retired from the table, he managed to avoid seeing me alone, even making this conspicuous. We had no exchange of words on any subject except in the presence of others. It is the first experience of this kind I have had with him. I am convinced the Armstrong people sold war material to Germans for gold at the very moment the Lancaster cotton people were being told they could not be paid. I shall investigate this and carry facts to Washington when I go.

At 4 o'clock, I called on the Dutch Minister and asked him about the Dutch-English pact. He said there was none, but acknowledged he had been in London in the hope of doing something on the subject. He said Holland would be compelled to enter the next European war or be annexed to Germany. He was certain that war is coming.

I told him that Sir Henri Deterding was supposed to be coming to see Hitler soon. He had not heard it. I said: Does Sir Henri support Sir Oswald Mosley, England's Fascist Fuehrer? He said: "I know him well and I am sure he would give Mosley £100,000 to help him win." Will he come here then to make a deal with Hitler to get a monopoly of the German markets for his oil and gasoline? The reply was: "I have heard recently there was a conference in London with Standard Oil Company about their relations in Europe, and so I do not believe Sir Henri has such a plan in mind." After some further talk in which we agreed on every essential point about the war danger in Europe, also in the Far East, I bade him good-by. He said he was leaving tomorrow for The Hague and would call to see me after his return.

November 9. Friday. I learned this morning that there are negotiations between Germany and Russia for sales of goods to Russia on a five-year credit scheme. To make a little more sure of this story, I sent for Armand Bérard. He came and I told him in confidence what I had heard. He was a little perturbed but not surprised and said he would let me know if he obtained further facts. As Bullitt has failed to make any real agreement about the Russian debt of $200,000,000 to the United States and is now on his way back to Washington, I shall press this case if I have an opportunity and wire information to the State Department.

The fact that a great number of high German officials and generals of the Reichswehr were most conspicuous at the Russian reception two days ago indicated something, though Hitler, Goering and Goebbels were not present. In my judgment the Reichswehr, the Foreign Office and the royalists are all pressing Hitler for a Russian pact like that with Poland, which was a surprise to all the world in 1933. The idea is to isolate France and find a market for German goods, as the former regime found. The Russian idea is to let the United States know that they are not so important. It all points to peace for a few years, that is, until Germany can be entirely ready to command Europe.

November 10. Saturday. We went tonight to the Italian concert where Ambassador and Madame Cerruti received all the diplomatic corps. The concert was good. At the close of the first part, I spoke a moment with the Polish Ambassador, recently raised to this rank. He said he thought a German-Russian pact was in process, perhaps already signed.

November 11. Sunday. James McDonald came yesterday in the hope of seeing officials of the German Government. Dr. Schacht refused to see him, though he had made an appointment for the 9th. He is to see Schacht's assistant tomorrow, his hope being to get Germans to allow Jews who leave the country under heavy pressure to take some of their property with them.

At luncheon today we had Professor Sering who knows the economic and agricultural life of the modern world better than anybody I know. He was again most vigorous and outspoken in his opposition to the Hitler philosophy and practice. His wife was even more venturesome in my presence. They are not orthodox Christians but they attend Dr. Niemoeller's church at Dahlem regularly and rejoice at the Lutheran revolt against the present effort to force all Germans into one church—the *Deutsche Christen.*

Count von Bernstorff, nephew of the former Ambassador to Washington, was also present and was equally frank in criticism of the autarchy which he says will ruin Germany for decades to come. There was another guest who had talked very frankly sometime before at the Berlin Sport Club. He wore today the regular Party badge and to my surprise, seemed to be preparing a report to the Propaganda Ministry of what he heard at our table. He got nothing from me. The professor paid no attention to the Nazi party man, except to talk more frankly and mention to me that the son of the famous Admiral von Tirpitz was related to him, which interested the Party man somewhat. It was a unique luncheon. When all were gone, Martha reported that Von Bernstorff had said so much in the presence of the Nazi leader that she feared he would be reported.

November 12. Monday. The manager of the American Fox Film Company here came to the office to say that in a conference of film people in the Propaganda Ministry a few days ago he had been ordered to put unfriendly interpretations into American films presented in Germany. He had protested, saying that such propaganda would still further exasperate American public opinion. The German film officials replied they did not care what Americans thought or said of the Germans. He wished me to intervene in his behalf in case trouble came to him for not obeying orders. All I could say was that I would ask our Consul General Jenkins to do whatever the law or treaties allowed. I am expecting the Fox Film Company to be ordered out of the country, as some other companies are now about to be.

November 13. Tuesday. This morning I violated my usual rule and went to the City Hall to hear General Goering address the Academy for German Justice, a kind of German bar association. The wonderful hall was crowded to utmost capacity when I arrived. On every desk in my part of the room there was a large envelope filled with beautifully printed pamphlets describing German grievances against the world, especially the Saar question. Von Neurath had contributed a brief plea for the German claims.

Hans Frank, head of the Ministry of Justice here, presided. Last summer, Frank was about to be killed because he ventured to inquire about certain prisoners in a concentration camp near Munich. He escaped somehow. It was June 30. I could not help thinking of this story when he rose to greet Goering with the "Heil Hitler" salute which every German official is compelled to give on every possible occasion.

Goering entered the hall in a Brown Shirt uniform, his chest covered with medals and badges of honor. He turned toward the audience as he approached the platform, raised his right hand, bowed and shouted "Heil Hitler." I did not enjoy these demonstrations. They have always seemed so absurd to me. But several of the other diplomats did heil Hitler effectively. Von Neurath and Von Schwerin-Krosigk, the Finance Minister, joined reluctantly, as it appeared to me.

The audience sat down and Goering read an address which re-emphasized the absolute dependence of every German citizen upon the Fuehrer. There was to be no sort of resistance at any time. When the speaker briefly explained the murders of June 30, he showed no sign whatever of any consciousness of error on that occasion. All foreign peoples had denounced the acts of the Fuehrer although he pretended he was saving the German people from disaster; but this was stupid. "We needed to have no indictments, proofs or trials. We were killing enemies of the people."

Everybody knew Goering had ordered the killing of men and women against whom there was no feeling or evidence anywhere that they were guilty of treason. At one place the fat general said heads will simply be chopped off if men do not obey the inspired Hitler and submit to his decrees. A good many of these statements were interjected. They did not appear in the printed copy when it came out in the papers. Since correspondents of the foreign press were not present there was no likelihood of a sensation anywhere, and German judges and lawyers were instructed emphatically what they must do.

November 15. Thursday. Consul General Jenkins called to review some of his work and then told me that a clerk in the Propaganda Ministry had met one of the consulate clerks at luncheon today, had told him that Jenkins was as real an enemy of Germany as was former Consul General Messersmith, and had added that they had a copy of Jenkins' last report to Washington which proved the point. That was a little exasperating to the Consul General. He had made only one report and that at the request of the President. It was a survey of agricultural relief for the unemployed, and I had read it carefully. There was no criticism, simply a summary of all the reports made by Minister Darre, head of the Ministry of Agriculture.

It was certainly stupid for anyone in Goebbels' office to reveal such a thing even if it had been true. It annoys a new and very important American official here, and it reveals an espionage which puts us all on our guard. The document had lain on my desk three days, not being regarded as specially confidential.

At 8:30 I went to the Adlon Hotel to hear Minister of Education Rust lecture on German culture and education. The host of the evening was Alfred Rosenberg who met me at the entrance to the hall. The photographers snapped us as we shook hands. It was not delightful to me, for there is no German official who thinks less clearly or indulges in more bunk. I was again photographed as I shook hands with General von Fritsch, chief of the Reichswehr and an opponent, I am sure, of all that Rosenberg and Rust represent.

When Rust began speaking it was clear that we were to hear only propaganda. He talked of the heroic Party struggle, of the inspired work of Hitler, and of the absolute necessity of keeping all children from learning anything but loyalty to the State and rigid discipline, both mental and physical. The best way to bring up young people was to put them in farm homes the first six years of their lives, then in country primary schools, and finally, from twelve to eighteen, in classical schools. This would make good Hitlerites and heroic Germans ready to die for their race and country. No religious influence should be allowed until after the twelfth year. The audience applauded warmly. It was all just another revelation of the type of thought or absence of thought that prevails here. Will intellectual Germany submit?

November 16. Friday. L. V. Steere, our Agricultural Attaché, called after a month's sojourn in the United States. He reported two conferences of the Under-Secretaries of State and Agriculture in which the majority opinion was very strong against their chiefs, Hull and Wallace, exponents of free trade policy as far as it can be practiced now. It is not unnatural that bureaucratic under-secretaries from former administrations should still adhere to the old protective philosophy, although most enlightened men recognize that protectionism was one of the great causes of the disaster of 1929-1934.

Mr. Pierce of the International General Electric Company came to urge a favorable report to the State Department on a Siemens proposition to lay a cable between Germany and the United States. This scheme of the greatest European electric power companies in co-operation with the cotton importers of Bremen is designed to connect Germany and the United States without touching England, by cable. Germany would be able to buy cotton with the money ($10,000,000 or $12,000,000) obtained from the United States as payment for the laying of the cable. Two difficulties are in the way: England has a monopoly of the cable business now and may not allow contact at any point in Ireland, and the American Telephone & Telegraph Company in New York may not accept this new project as a connecting link between the United States and the German systems. Mr. Pierce explained and argued for a time and I became convinced it seemed to be a reasonable undertaking and agreed to have our Commercial Attaché make a study of the matter.

November 17. Saturday. The Polish Ambassador, Lipski, called for the usual greetings after his promotion from Minister to Ambassador and remained nearly an hour. He was frank in the discussion of Polish-German relations: "The pact of last winter is only a temporary affair. Germany intends to re-annex part of our country, the maps posted all over Germany show this clearly. I protested against these a few days ago, but received no satisfactory answer from the Foreign Office. The Russians and the Germans are negotiating a commercial treaty which I think has a political and military pact attached, but it is secret, and these negotiations are going on largely to isolate France." He did not say that it was the same motivation that actuated his government last year, but he let it be inferred.

Germany, he went on, intends to re-annex Alsace-Lorraine and large parts of Poland as well as Austria and Czechoslovakia. Then she will control the Balkan region zone and all the Baltic Sea. Europe will be a German realm if she succeeds. This was nothing new, but coming from one who had helped his country humiliate France in 1933, it was interesting. However, it was plain that he still regards France and England as the only hope of the Poles. He believes firmly in the French-English-Belgian pact of last July. Co-operation of the western powers, he stated, is the only salvation for all the smaller states of Europe.

It seems to me that Monsieur Lipski is not entirely in sympathy with autocracies, although he has never indicated dislike of the reactionary Polish regime. Like a diplomat, he obeys orders from home and always maintains a smooth countenance even when embarrassing questions are raised.

We went to dine with Professor Hermann Oncken at his house in Dahlem. The library which was filled with books, perhaps 4,000 volumes, was crowded with guests, all standing until we went to the dinner table. Oncken is a German historian of highest rank and author of many books, though none that I have seen shows the non-partisanship that seems to me necessary if history is to serve its purpose.

When the dinner service was about half finished, one of the guests rose to pay tribute to the host on the occasion of his sixty-fifth birthday. The speaker read a marvelous poem which paid appropriate tribute to Oncken but satirically warned Oncken of the terrible misfortune which might hang over him if there were a possibility that some one of his ancestors was of non-Aryan blood. The author gave a seemingly solemn admonition to all present in a language as witty and clever as I have ever heard. Although the present Nazi philosophy was ridiculed in every verse, no quotation could have been found that the Nazis could use to convict the author before a German court.

A second speaker, Dr. Friedrich Schmidt-Ott, paraphrased Schiller's poetry in a similar vein, showing the greatness of the famous poet of Goethe's time and the distressing liberality of the one German poet whom Nazi Germany claims to be its model. Still another speaker spoke in a like strain for ten minutes, and finally Dr. Ferdinand Sauerbruch, the famous Von Hindenburg physician, concluded the tributes of the occasion in a witty summary of what had been said and closed by clever compliments to Frau Oncken. From the beginning to the end there was sharp fun-making of the Hitler-Rosenberg philosophy and conduct, and everybody seemed to enjoy all that was said.

Although we have attended many dinners in Berlin, some in honor of President von Hindenburg, some at the French and English Embassies, I have nowhere seen such clever people. All the guests were specialists in certain fields of history, literature and art, and several had held high positions in former governments here. It was a challenge to any person of learning and the whole performance showed by contrast the emptiness of diplomatic dinners where no one ever feels free to say anything about the fields of history and literary criticism, because nobody knows history and literature and because no one trusts anyone else. We came away at 11 o'clock.

November 20. Tuesday. We lunched today with Mr. and Mrs. White. There was one really intellectual person present, a former German Cabinet official who had resigned when his chief, Stresemann, disagreed sharply with him about official policy. His name is Hans von Raumer. Another guest was Dr. Wilhelm Solf, the German Ambassador to Japan in 1905, who lives half time here and half in Switzerland on account of delicate health, and perhaps a delicate position under the Hitler regime.

Von Raumer indulged after luncheon in the first real assessment of the Bismarck era I have ever heard from a German: "Bismarck had done great work, but his greatest mistake consisted in the clever shaping of the German Imperial constitution so that the German people thought they had parliamentary government when in fact it was a dictatorship of Prussia, speaking through the Reich's Supreme Council in which Prussia always had a majority—seventeen to sixteen—when all members were present. In this way the people of Germany were dominated by an utterly undemocratic group."

Von Raumer had been a member of the Reichstag from 1920 to 1930 and I realized that he spoke from experience under the democratic Weimar constitution of 1919. He did not mention the fact that the Bismarck suffrage system also stalled popular opinion in the old Reichstag, even though, as he said, that body really had no power against the Prussian Junkers, who dominated the Council majority. All this was familiar to me from my Leipzig student days, but I had never heard a German scholar acknowledge this undemocratic system as a great Bismarckian blunder. He said it was that system which prevented German people from earning parliamentary government. It also caused the World War.

November 22. Thursday. Frank C. Lee, American Consul General at Prague, who has been appointed First Secretary here to take the place of Mr. Wilson, called this afternoon. Mr. Lee has served twenty years as Consul, speaks Russian and German well, and knows the European complex fairly well, judged from occasional reports which have come to me here. There is no doubt in my mind of Lee's capacity or industry, but his visit to look things over reminds me of certain interesting facts.

When I accepted this post, I stipulated that there was to be no complaint if I lived within my official income. I could not play the rich man's game as Walter Hines Page had done in London at the expense of his family and friends. However, I had not been in Berlin long before I received notice that the then Counselor, George Gordon, was to be recalled and J. C. White was to succeed him. In fact, William Phillips, Assistant Secretary of State, had told me this was contemplated. I did not realize the purpose of this appointment until some months later when I learned that White was one of the richest men in the service.

At the same time, I learned that Orme Wilson was to come with the Whites, and he was reported also to be a very wealthy man. This was clearly intended to supplement my want of millions of dollars. Furthermore, I saw that Jay Pierrepont Moffat, brother-in-law of White, and Phillips, uncle of Wilson, both in high positions in the State Department, intended to have White and Wilson manage the Embassy.

This is the background to Lee's visit today. White and Wilson show no enthusiasm. I believe Lee is superior in character to anybody on the staff here.

November 23. Friday. Frank Gannett, a personal friend of President Roosevelt, came in today and asked for an interview with Hitler if possible. He reported that London was very fearful that Goering would send a thousand aircraft over that city during some fog and destroy it before the English could begin a defense. I rather doubted the story, and suspected it was all a means of getting appropriations from Parliament for enlarging the British air forces.

Mr. Gannett is the owner of a dozen New York State newspapers. He said there are many well-to-do people at home who are arguing for a Fascist system there, with a sort of Hitler to head it. They use the facts of perfect order and absence of crime in Germany as arguments for such a move. I told him there were other phases of the regime which would shock Americans to the limit.

At 12:30 I went to the Foreign Office to present a protest once more against German discrimination in debt payments. Von Bülow received me and I gave him the document, this being about the fifth or sixth time I have presented the same words, or nearly the same. Von Bülow repeated the old excuse: "We sell no goods to the United States and so can pay no debts."

I replied: I understand that argument, but our bondholders cannot see its value. They think the bonds were not issued on any such understanding. They would be willing to take lower interest payments if other peoples, English and French, did the same. When he referred again to lack of trade, I said: That is unfortunate and you know our government is now reducing tariff rates as fast as public opinion will allow. I may say that Secretary Hull delivered an address early this month in New York in which he said the protective system has been a curse to our people. I said I agreed with the Secretary, but that we cannot suddenly abandon a policy when so many thousands of workers are certain to be unemployed. As fast as we can change this we shall do so. But just as we abandon our barriers, you set up even higher ones and create a system which you cannot change without even greater losses and disturbances. How can we have better economic relations when such systems are applied? There was a half-hearted assent to my remark about the present German autarchy.

November 26. Monday. Dr. Arnold Brecht, formerly a Cabinet member here, now a lecturer at the New School for Social Research in New York, came to see me. I had not known that he lived in Berlin and was sorry we had not had him to dine or lunch with us. He seems to me to be a very able and truly patriotic German. He remains one year more in New York, and I wonder what he will do when he comes back next June. He is not welcome here and unemployed in the United States. He is not a Jew, but just as helpless, or will be.

November 30. Friday. At 4:30 I called to see Sir Eric Phipps, thinking he might tell me something of recent moves in London which look like definite warnings to Germany about their intense rearmament. He said: "I went to London Friday night, November 23. I spent Sunday, the 25th, in the country with Sir John Simon, the Foreign Secretary. He told me what was planned for debate in the House of Commons for Wednesday, the 28th, and Monday morning I sat with the Cabinet for an hour or more reviewing facts and circumstances here. I returned early on Tuesday the 27th, with a memorandum to be presented to the German Foreign Secretary. I read the memorandum to von Neurath at 12 o'clock." Sir Eric then read the document to me. It was a positive warning to Germany on two subjects: the reported and accepted accounts of German secret arming, especially air preparations, and the effects of this secret and perpetual rearmament upon world opinion. The British Cabinet members were willing to have their views corrected by Von Neurath if they were wrong. Sir Eric then said:

"I was asked to see the Chancellor at 5 the same day. I read him some of the items of the British document. After a moment, he jumped up, ran about the room, waved his arms and declared 'all countries around me are arming, they have ten thousand airplanes and yet they complain that we Germans have 1,000!' He went on shouting and fussing and Von Neurath joined him. I came away not a little disgusted. Next morning Von Neurath called and begged me to see him. I went to his office and he tried indirectly to correct the impression the Chancellor had made and especially to explain his own conduct. You see the Foreign Secretary here is never consistent or firm." I said: Of course Von Neurath is afraid of Hitler and consequently always appears in the presence of outsiders to agree with him.

Sir Eric then explained the British policy and the debate in Parliament of Wednesday night, November 28. I said: It seems to me your government has acted very wisely and I am glad the information has been conveyed to the American State Department. I then asked him about the possibility of a British-American agreement as to the Far Eastern naval problem. He said he had not had any reactions to that problem while in London, but was convinced our two countries could agree. In case Japan broke away and hastened her naval armament, England would not object to American increases of naval strength. This naval race looked foolish to him, but Japan seemed bent upon an imperialist program.

Once more I come to my 1933 solution of these dangerous problems: If Great Britain and the United States unite upon a guarantee of Philippine independence and the existing status in the Far East, the dangerous naval race will cease, and there will be peace in the Pacific. After this success, the two countries can present a united front against warlike Germany at the next disarmament conference, with Russia and France supporting them, and peace in Europe will be guaranteed. All this has been carefully described to the State Department and the President, and both the British and French Ambassadors have seemed to agree with me entirely, also the Dutch Minister who is always alert and deeply interested.

As if I had not done enough for one day, we went to the Berlin Staatsoper to hear a concert conducted by Eric Kleiber, reported to be a half-Jew who managed somehow to continue his art in Berlin. It was an interesting performance, a truckload of police guarding the building. The police were there because a demonstration by the Nazi part of the audience was expected against the music composed by the Austrian-Jewish artist, Berg, forbidden by German decrees. But when the Berg part was finished, one man in a prominent box shouted "Heil Mozart"— a signal for a protest from the audience. There was no protest.

December 1. Saturday. The foreign press gave their usual dinner and ball at the Adlon Hotel. We arrived as guests of Miss Sigrid Schultz. The British Ambassador, General von Reichenau, acting Chief of Staff, and some English and American visitors were at the same table. The French Ambassador, the Russian, General von Fritsch and Dr. Goebbels were at another table. They seemed very friendly although hatreds between François-Poncet and Goebbels, and between Von Fritsch and Goebbels are known to be tense. Von Neurath came late and went away without dining. The reports were that he was not offered proper seating rank. He should have been placed at the table with Goebbels and that would have been most embarrassing.

December 2. Sunday. I received a report today from Stuttgart which described a happening there on Wednesday, November 28. Alfred Rosenberg who is the official philosopher of the present regime went to Stuttgart, the capital of Württemberg, the home of Von Neurath, to lecture to the South Germans on their loyalty to the sacred state. He reviewed the unhappy relations of the ancient Catholic Church with the Holy Roman Empire, the first Reich. "No religion shall be permitted to weaken the hold of the state on the people. Only what is useful to Germany can be regarded as true and we claim the absolute right to remold all things in Germany as they should be. National Socialists in Germany will form in the future a social order with all the holy mysticisms of the medieval age." He concluded: "You all know that there is a senatorial hall with sixty-one seats in the Brown House in Munich which has never yet been in use. We only await the signal of the Leader to lay the foundations of this holy order of Germany in this hall."

This reveals a little of what was said, and of the strange mysticism which has gripped the vast majority of the German people, if votes on two occasions, November 12, 1933, and August 19, 1934, prove anything. This sort of talk is repeated almost every day by Hitler, Goering, Goebbels, Darre, Ley and minor characters, never by university professors or preachers, except the *Deutsche Christen* people. The newspapers repeat these ideas always with approval.

In Stuttgart all the officials of the city, the S.S. and S.A. men and officers and some Reichswehr people attended under compulsion. The audience was 8,000 strong, shouting "Heil Hitler" and roaring with applause when Rosenberg attacked the churches for their resistance to Gleichsanschaltung (complete subordination to the state). It had been only a week since the Bishop of the Protestant Church of Württemberg had been released from prison and reinstated in his office because of the overwhelming demands of church people. Yet Rosenberg went the limit in the same city in attacking all church people who do not submit to the Wotan religion which Rosenberg is trying to establish. Hitler was in Stuttgart a week before and acted in a similar way. Is Rosenberg now renewing the religious war?

Another interesting illustration: A member of a university student organization which was dissolved some time ago by order of the government reported to a member of our staff that a few days ago a prominent man invited a group of students who had been members of the club to dine with him. To their surprise, as the company was about to sit down around the table, an S.A. leader appeared at the door with a detachment of soldiers around him. The S.A. leader forbade the entertainment and was about to order the party to leave when a student from the Saar country remarked that this sort of thing was very interesting to him and added that he would describe it to his friends in the Saar country where he lived. The dinner was at once authorized to proceed. I am not sure of this but it resembles other rulings I know about and so I record it.

December 3. Monday. A professor from Cologne, an eminent architect who had just returned from Washington where he had met and talked with Roper and other members of the Cabinet, called for a short visit. He showed great interest in and enthusiasm for the United States. But the significant part of his conversation showed how troubled and embarrassed Ambassador Luther must be in Washington. He seems not to be a Nazi and he dislikes the whole system now prevailing in Germany. Yet he must fight for German interests and justify the dangerous policy which prevails here. If he resigned, his status at home in Essen would be very difficult. If he remains in Washington, he must maintain a false attitude. Such is the position of many eminent Germans everywhere.

December 4. Tuesday. Colonel Deeds called. He represents the National Cash Register Company and also the National City Bank of New York. His son was brought before the Nye committee of the Senate last September to explain sales of arms to Germany by a company of which he is an officer, allegedly in violation of the American treaty with Germany. I have seen Deeds many times. He is the good-natured big business type and affects to be enthusiastic for Roosevelt's New Deal. He considers me a naïve academic who is not aware of the under-cover armaments deals which business men have tried again and again to put over here in the last eighteen months. He said he strongly favored international disarmament. Yet he told me his register company was doing a vast business here with the famous Krupps of Essen. Krupp receives 20 per cent of the profits of sales to Germany.

From Vienna, I learn that Messersmith is doing fair, even excellent, work at his difficult post. I understand the German Minister, Von Papen, is doing nothing, that he is most un-welcome there and that the whole diplomatic corps practically ignores him. This is probably correct; Von Papen was to have been shot here last June, and his dismissal as Vice Chancellor preceded the nomination, against the Foreign Office's wish, to Vienna. All Europe knows what double-dealing Von Papen has engaged in from the time of his residence in Washington until now. The poor scamp is now in Berlin. His son is in an *Arbeitsdienst* camp at Jüterbog and even more miserable than his father. I think he is an excellent young man, but he cannot get any position in Germany, he does not know how to work his own way upwards and he can only take ten marks, $3.00, if he leaves Germany.

Other news from Vienna is that Mussolini has agreed to a mutual assistance treaty with Austria, and that Hungary has tightened its relations with Italy, especially economic, which annoys Germany. Yugoslavia is still threatening Italy because Mussolini's hired assassins killed their autocratic and murderous King. Russia, Poland, Germany, Turkey and Austria all have been playing this medieval game for years.

December 5. Wednesday. Norman Ebbutt of the London *Times* came in to give me a report on the effects of the London protest to Hitler about rearming—a protest made after England and the United States have sold millions of dollars worth of arms to Germany. Ebbutt thought the British Government was pressing for a disarmament conference in February or March. He had written a true story of church troubles here two days before. The Germans forbade the sale of the *Times* and rebuked Ebbutt. He was not a little annoyed. I reminded him of the frequency of this treatment of British and American press people.

December 7. Friday. At 8:30 we went to dinner at the house of our Military Attaché, Colonel Wuest. We met the wife of General von Fritsch, head of the Reichswehr, who said she and her husband were not permitted to attend diplomatic dinners and receptions. The commander of the Reichswehr of all Germany north and east of the Elbe was also present, but there was no reference to the rearmament work now going on all over Germany. The German Military Attaché at Washington was most interesting in his discussion of American military history. He knows the Civil War as no American Attaché here knows German war history.

I believe that after the Saar election, on January 13, there will be trouble. In case it comes to an open issue, half of Germany will rank themselves among the opponents of the existing regime. If the Catholics support the Protestants, Hitler's regime will begin to slip. If Catholics hold aloof, Hitler will murder a lot of preachers and force all into submission. I look for no trouble, however, until February.

December 10. Monday. A small party came to lunch. Ebbutt confirmed the report of mid-October that a British woman, connected with Hitler's inner group, was here just before the British negotiations on Lancaster debts, to sell war equipment for Armstrong-Vickers. The British Ambassador "had not known about it," according to previous conversations. I am sure now the British staff members did know.

I had a long talk with the French Ambassador, François-Poncet. He agreed that the British move of two weeks ago had brought the Germans to recognize the danger of their position and to agree to a conference on international armaments after the Saar election, January 13. But he added: "The Germans will demand annexations somewhere when the conference be-gins and, in view of their belligerent attitude, we will have to refuse. That will defeat the conference."

At 11 this morning the Dutch Minister told me the same thing that the Belgian told me last week. "Germany will annex Holland if she wins a European war." He was very positive in this, and also perturbed about the Japanese denunciation of the Treaty of Washington. "It means war if the United States and England do not unite in their Far Eastern policy. England will lose her Hongkong and other Chinese concessions, the United States will find the Philippines annexed to Japan, and we, the Dutch people, will lose our three-hundred-year-old Far Eastern holdings."

December 11. Tuesday. We went to say farewell at 12 o'clock to Von Neurath. He kept me waiting ten minutes or more and did not apologize, although he was very cordial for fifteen min-utes. As I bade the Minister adieu and wished him a Merry Christmas, he sent his best wishes to Secretary Hull and added: "I agree entirely with him in his commercial policy and do not agree with the present German quota and bilateral scheme. It cannot succeed." That is the same attitude Schacht expressed at our house before several representatives of foreign countries in September.

Returning for a few minutes to the Chancery, I then went to the Automobile Club to lunch at 1:30 with Dieckhoff, David-son and Ritter, all experts of the Foreign Office. For an hour and a half they belabored me to press in Washington for a treaty between Germany and the United States, allowing lower tariffs to them in return for their buying more cotton, copper and lard. I replied in different ways: first, the present treaty had not been kept; second, there is a tough public opinion in the United States, as a result of the June 30 events, church treatment, and the general feeling that Germany is preparing for aggressive war. We then discussed the recent compromise between Germany and France about the Saar plebiscite as being an important move against war.

When they came back to the urgent treaty business, I said:

In view of the present attitude in the United States, if you had not denounced the existing treaty last October 14, without asking us, it might be much easier for the State Department to renew the treaty, or prolong it for a year or two, without having to get Senate approval. But now, with the treaty abandoned by Germany, it will be hard to get Congress to give a new treaty consideration. The Nye Committee will discuss war and the German purchases of war supplies (I had told them before how bad it was to pay gold to American arms manufacturers and deny their ability to pay interest on bonds) during the month of January, and also the whole debt matter. So we shall hardly be able to get a treaty considered before Congress adjourns.

One of the experts said: "We shall have to withdraw our abrogation of the treaty." Dieckhoff said, "No, we cannot do that. Can't you get the President to appoint a committee of three American business men to go to Washington to discuss the matter?" Later, according to a plan suggested by Schacht, they could come to Germany to inform themselves of German conditions. Their study might be used as a basis for future negotiations. I said: I can ask the State Department to consider the matter—that is all—unless I am questioned about it by the President.

This closed our luncheon discussion. I was convinced that all of them realized how inconsiderate the German attitudes were toward the outside world. Dieckhoff, whom I know well and sympathize with rather closely, escorted me to the cloakroom. I said: You know what a terrible impression the events of June 30 made in the United States and you must see how unpopular a treaty would be. He agreed, but did not say too much by way of explanation.

Realizing how troubled the liberal element of Germany is, and this includes nearly all the Foreign Office people, I called Dieckhoff in the afternoon and asked if we might not drive together a little as he went away from his office. He agreed and we drove around the Tiergarten and talked the problem over again. I told him how universal is the feeling that Germany is preparing for aggressive war, mentioning the Goering flying-machine maps circulating all over the country and even saying that ministers of neighboring countries had recently said to me that Germany means to annex them. I had in mind what the Belgian and Dutch representatives had said recently. He was not surprised. Though he expressed regrets and hoped I would try to disabuse the President's mind if he has such feelings, I could hardly hope to do much in that direction, for my own reports during October and November had given much evidence of Germany's intense militaristic feeling. I asked Dieckhoff to look at the maps in the halls of the University of Berlin which I had recently seen. It was all a personal affair, though I had some feeling that he might not keep his promise. We parted where the Tiergartenstrasse crosses the trolley line which runs southward toward the canal.

December 13. Thursday. We drove from Berlin to Hamburg to catch our ship for New York.

December 18. Tuesday. About 11 o'clock yesterday the ocean began to roll. At 1 o'clock it was wild. All day and night— about thirty hours—the waves were so high that the ship frequently stood almost still for hours at a time, lest it be overwhelmed by the storm. A Norwegian freighter was caught in the same storm. Our ship was called upon for assistance as the freighter was about to sink, but a German ship arrived first, spread oil over the water around the distressed ship and finally rescued all the officers and sailors. The captain of our ship was not disposed to let anybody know all this, but the story was noised about the *Manhattan* this afternoon. This is the third time I have experienced this sort of rough sailing over this part of the Atlantic and the second time the ship I was on tried to rescue a sinking crew or ship. It is not very agreeable.

December 19. Wednesday. W. H. Hassen, representative of the Sinclair Oil Company, whose president and manipulator was in jail three months, sat at table with us today. He sells oil products all over Europe, a very active, clever business man, as I estimate him.

He said: "I am a staunch Republican. Our American people

are not national-minded. They must become so. We must forbid all imports except rubber, coffee and one or two other necessities and sell all we can to other peoples, arm and drill our people."

I said: You mean by this that all the world should arm to the teeth and later either destroy all your arms material because they are obsolete, or start a war and kill your people, thereby using the arms. That stopped him for a moment but he came back: "Yes, it is a struggle for the survival of the fittest." I said: No; destruction of the civilized peoples and the survival of the least fit.

Notwithstanding the logic of my reply, he held to his point, argued for American arming of all Europe and sharply opposed the reduction of American tariffs. Such is the view I know of many eminent business men everywhere: the Du Ponts of the United States, the Krupps and Thyssens of Germany, the Armstrong-Vickers people in England, and the Schneider-Crusot interests in France. It is the talk of Mussolini, whom Hassen regards as a great statesman. I suppose Roosevelt will find this type of man very difficult to control. If he does not vigorously control them, his New Deal will fail.

December 21. Friday. This voyage as well as the studies I have made of seventeenth century seafaring convince me that historians have never assessed correctly the courage and bravery of the men and women who settled North America. It was no small thing for a poor family, whose members knew the Atlantic only from the stories told by neighbors, to venture across this terrible sea on a ship of 200 tons burden. They did it by the thousands and for the reason that they wanted to make homes for themselves. Thousands and tens of thousands in a single year! In my judgment, people of such character were apt to make any country great and enterprising.

VI

December 23, 1934 to May 21, 1935

December 23. Sunday. We reached New York at 4 this afternoon, a day and half late.

December 25. Tuesday. The thirty-third anniversary of our marriage at Auburn, N. C., we celebrated simply here in Raleigh. Mattie was with her family part of the time, I visiting my father in nearby Clayton, my birthplace.

December 27. Thursday. Having been chosen president of the American Historical Association, I delivered this evening a formal address which I had prepared under pressure in Berlin on the emergence of the first social order in the United States. Professor Owsley of Vanderbilt, one of my students who took his doctorate soon after the World War ended, rose to present me a volume of essays on American history written by my students. That had been done before, especially in 1932 at Toronto, and I was not so much surprised as I might otherwise have been, though I had not been warned at all. I made acknowledgments to my students as best I could and then read the formal paper which was a little new to most of the audience. It was a summary of three chapters of Volume i of my *Old South*.

December 29. Saturday. I had an engagement to lunch with the President today. We sat down together in a second-floor room of the White House, a little late. For an hour and a quarter we talked about the European situation. I presented my plan to prevent war and bring all nations into some sort of co-operation.

The United States, I said, must co-operate with England and Holland in the Far East, give the Philippines their independence and guarantee the existing status in that region, allowing Japan the privilege of coming into the agreement. Then the United States ought to join the League of Nations, forcing Germany and Italy into co-operation with England and France for peace and reduction of armaments. If the President pressed a joint resolution upon Congress at the right moment, I thought he would succeed and in a year or two the commercial relations of the United States would greatly improve. Then perhaps the next disarmament conference would really succeed.

The President said: "I agree as to the Far East and think we must do something in that region. Japan is annexing parts of China and plans to annex more and control all of Asia including India. We shall spend a billion dollars building warships, and all of them will be antiquated in ten years."

As to a joint resolution to join the League, he said, "I am skeptical of public opinion, but I have asked the Senate to approve our joining the World Court and later I shall ask for authority to send an ambassador to Geneva." I thought both moves might test public opinion, but indicated that delay might defeat the final purpose. I also told him that Baron von Bülow, second ranking official in the Foreign Office, and wisest man there, had said to me: "We would return to the League immediately the United States joined."

Many other subjects were touched upon: German militancy, Italian aggressiveness and British fear of another depression, as well as the British desire to co-operate in world affairs with the United States.

December 30. Sunday. A telegram came that my wife's mother was dead. Much as we had rejoiced at being able to see her on this return to America, I now felt that our visit and the presence of several of her children on Christmas Day, perhaps the entertaining of us so handsomely, had hastened her end. The attention and the pleasure of seeing us all were too much for her. Anyway a very unselfish, kindly soul had passed away. Mattie hurried away for the funeral.

January 16, 1935. Wednesday. Professor Thomas J. Wertenbaker met me this afternoon at Trenton in his car. We stopped on the way to his house at the home of Albert Einstein where we had tea and talked a little about troubles in Berlin. There were no personal complaints. Einstein had been expelled from the University of Berlin in 1933 with all his property confiscated. A few days ago the American press carried the news from Berlin that Einstein's daughter had had all of her property, a home and a little stretch of land in Potsdam, confiscated. One daughter had died recently and her husband was part owner; her sister, the only surviving child of the Einsteins, was also part owner. These people are now helpless in Germany where their father was considered the first scientist of his age. In spite of this rough treatment not a word was said of the Hitler regime that could have been counted unpatriotic, from the German point of view.

After taking dinner with the Wertenbakers where Abraham Flexner, long an active representative of the Rockefeller Foundation, was one of the guests, I went to the Princeton auditorium where I delivered a lecture on Washington and his problems, giving special emphasis to American foreign policy. Once more the audience seemed to sense the mistakes of American attitudes since 1918. Certainly the university people of the country wish to see the federal Government do what it can to advance the cause of the League of Nations as a means of avoiding war.

January 17. Thursday. I reached New York at 11. Immediately calls came from different people: The National City Bank, the Siemens concern and the Foreign Policy Association. I saw the bankers at 4 and the Siemens president at 4:30.

I had an engagement with Colonel House for luncheon. He seemed very well, though he had been ill for a week with a cold. He talked a good deal about foreign policy; the need of

American entrance into the League, of co-operation with England in the Far East and of a means of coaxing Japan from her imperialistic drive against China. I had my doubts about his Japan scheme but he told me that the Ambassador from Japan was to see him tomorrow. I asked him to write me if Japan indicated a disposition to co-operate. He promised to do so.

As to President Roosevelt's attitude, we agreed that he looks upon the world dilemma much as we do, but that he fears violent opposition to any progressive move that he might make. My view is that violent opposition will always be made to any far-reaching and unselfish policy that may be offered. Besides, no President has ever been able to accomplish anything worthwhile during his second term, except for two moves of Washington, which he had to make but which led to his denunciation all over the land. Roosevelt must act this year or surrender in matters of American relations to distraught Europe.

House said he would try to see the President during the next month or two. He approved the President's statement of January 29 that he might send an ambassador to Geneva as a beginning of our entrance into the League. I said: It would be far preferable to ask Congress to approve our entrance at once, because of the economic and political difficulties at home, since there could be no real economic recovery in less than four or six years. The President would have no real power during his second term, if re-elected. Colonel House agreed. However, I doubt whether Roosevelt or any other President of our time would venture such an unpopular move with the masses who have been propagandized for fourteen years against any connection or co-operation anywhere.

January 31. Thursday. This morning the newspapers brought the story of the Senate defeat of Roosevelt's request for American entrance into the World Court. Two days before the vote, I saw Senator Robinson, majority leader, and he was sure of winning by a margin of seven votes. I was a little doubtful when I left him. Now he is defeated. Borah, Johnson and McAdoo were the outstanding opponents of that mild move in the direction of world co-operation. Borah has long been silly about foreign relations; Johnson has howled about debts due the United States as though our states had not repudiated hundreds of millions due European creditors; and McAdoo is reported to be under the Hearst banner.

My first reaction was to write the State Department asking if it would not be wise for me to resign in protest against Senate minority domination of American foreign policy. It would create a sensation, but it would give me the chance to say to the country how foolish it seemed to me for our people to denounce minority dictatorships in Europe and then allow a minority of men, largely under Hearst and Coughlin influence, to rule the United States in such an important matter.

February 1. Friday. I saw Judge Walton Moore, and he advised against resignation. He said, "We must all fight our cause out to the end and stick together." He said that was Secretary Hull's position too. But Moore added: "I have never felt quite so discouraged. Our recovery work is apt to fail if our foreign policy is dictated by the Senate minority and I see no way to circumvent that group."

I said: If I were the President I would await a strategic moment and then appeal to the country for entrance into the League of Nations. After that I would have the Democratic majority present a joint resolution and press it through both houses. I would challenge all my opponents and have a definite line-up, even if I had to refuse to run a second time.

Moore was quite struck by this and wondered whether Roosevelt had really made up his mind as to the importance of better world relations. I was also doubtful whether the President was really concerned, whether the so-called "economic nationalist" idea of some of his "brain trusters" had not won him over, or at least confused his thinking a little. Moore was very anxious for me to see the President. I wrote Secretary McIntyre of the White House to let Roosevelt know we are sailing February 14 and that if he wished to see me I was ready to call. However, I was not too optimistic.

At 6 o'clock, I was with Representative Lewis, most courageous member of the House I know. He offered a day or two ago a joint resolution to the House to overrule the Senate decision against the World Court. He showed me his preliminary speech and I told him a good deal about the German, Italian and Japanese dictatorships and their menace to the whole modern world. He was much interested and said he would wage his battle the best he could. I think the House could be rallied almost unanimously if the President's support were given to Lewis.

I also told Lewis that Hearst has been supporting and visiting Mussolini for five or six years. I gave him an account of the Hearst visit to Berlin last September and his reported bargain with Goebbels under which the German Propaganda Ministry is to have all the Hearst European news at the same time it goes over to the United States. Lewis vowed utmost secrecy unless he could get the facts from somebody else. I took the risk in the hope of rendering him some aid in his struggle.

Leaving Representative Lewis, I drove to Georgetown to dine with Rexford Tugwell, Assistant Secretary of Agriculture, though he knows little of agriculture. A certain well-known senator was one of the guests; several others included Representatives Carter (Mass.) and Frank (Ill.) and Senator Josiah Bailey (North Carolina). From the very beginning, this senator attacked Roosevelt. He was angry with the President because he had not backed Senator Cutting, a former supporter of Roosevelt. He was also disgruntled because Roosevelt had not agreed with the Progressive group on huge appropriations which would have led to national bankruptcy. He claimed that he and Huey Long, the pirate of Louisiana, had caused Roosevelt's nomination in 1932.

The attitudes of this man were amazing. He talks like a National Socialist. He would stop trade with Europe. He advocated German domination of all Europe, our domination of the Americas, and Japanese domination of the Far East. He wishes to see England dominated by Germany, with Canada falling naturally to the United States. Most of the people at the dinner agreed with this big business idea of three great world powers uniting and dominating smaller peoples like the Poles and the Dutch. It seemed to be based upon hatred of

England and France, on ignorance of the teachings of history, and on indifference to the cultural appeals of such peoples as the English, the French and the Dutch, not to mention the great German intellectual element now so helpless.

I departed with a sense of surprise, wondering whether they really meant what they advocated. But the senator must have been sincere when he said he had persuaded Long to vote against the World Court idea about which Long knew nothing. I remarked at a quiet moment that I would not speak to Long. He said, "We shall soon be shooting up people here, like Hitler does."

February 2. Saturday. I called on Secretary Hull at 10 o'clock. After talking a moment, Secretary Moore came in. It was a rather sad half hour we had together. Hull said: "I hope you won't resign even if you can do nothing now in Berlin. We also are helpless. All peoples are economically crazy, and our people are being misled all the time. I cannot see how domestic recovery can come anywhere so long as international relations remain so chaotic." At 11 o'clock I returned by automobile slowly to our remote mountain home which serves me as my one retreat from a crazy world.

February 6. Wednesday. I drove slowly down to Washington to lunch with the President. He was far more cheerful and optimistic than I or anyone in the State Department had been.

I repeated in confidence the senator's statements at Mr. Tugwell's on February 1: that he had actually persuaded Senator Long to vote against the World Court resolution, and that he had talked of our coming "shooting-up game." But I did not give the senator's name. Roosevelt at once said: "It sounds like Senator X———." I did not say yes or no—though he had guessed right—merely that the conversation had been confidential.

The President went on: Long plans to be a candidate of the Hitler type for the presidency in 1936. He thinks he will have a hundred votes in the Democratic convention. Then he will set up as an independent with Southern and mid-western Progressives, Senator X——— and others. Thus he hopes to defeat the Democratic party and put in a reactionary Republican. That would bring the country to such a state by 1940 that Long thinks he would be made a dictator. There are in fact some Southerners looking that way, and some Progressives are drifting that way. But Cutting of New Mexico wants the presidency too. He paid tremendous sums in order not to be defeated for the Senate last fall. He will divide the Progressives and perhaps defeat Long. Thus it is an ominous situation.

I then talked about German affairs, Hitler's attitude and the possible return of Germany to the League of Nations. I added: If the Senate had adopted your recommendation on January 30, the United States would have made this certain. The Government's prestige would have been raised immensely, and American commercial relations would have been greatly improved. Roosevelt agreed but did not seem too regretful about the Senate vote. I had the feeling that he had not pressed the case strongly.

I told him Hearst had really done the stunt, and that I believed Hearst to be close to Nazi Germany. I told him I would send him proof of Hearst's help of the Italian dictatorship when I got back to Berlin. He said he would be greatly interested. After a few minutes' talk about the foreign service and a little about the waste of American diplomats (he said, "Since Theodore Roosevelt's time, rich men have injured the service by enormous expenditures"), I bade him farewell and emphasized my hopes of his success.

I have the feeling, however, that I am in a position in Germany in which nothing can be done. No amount of optimism relieves my doubts. Since the January 30 vote of the Senate, a minority of old-timers in the Senate will insist on guiding American foreign policy.

February 8. Friday. I lunched today with the Senate Committee on Foreign Relations. Borah was absent, but Robinson, Johnson, George and others were present. Johnson began the conversations by alluding to the falsities of written history. This gave me an opportunity and I referred to the debt payments under Washington and the repudiations of 1830 to 1850. The California Senator pretended not to be surprised. When I was asked about European relations, I said: The Senate's action on the World Court was a great blunder. It set back our commercial relations and prevented our asking Germany to account for her treaty violations of last summer before a body which might not enforce payment of damage but which would give world publicity to the matter, give the United States great bargaining advantage, and enhance the government's prestige by 50 per cent all over the world.

Senator Robinson, Roosevelt's spokesman in the Senate, agreed at once. Bulkley of Ohio also agreed though he revealed an isolationist's attitude which surprised me a little. Senator George of Georgia also agreed but later argued for a protectionist policy which Democrats are supposed always to oppose. Before we adjourned I was told that two Senators had voted against the World Court adhesion but when they saw that the President's resolution was going to be defeated anyway they changed to the other side. They had voted to please their constituents who did not know much about the subject. This is one of the weak spots in American democracy. I had the feeling as the luncheon broke up that a real discussion of the merits of foreign relations would have changed the Senate's attitude, i.e., if there had been a real presentation of the facts and their probable consequences to the Foreign Relations Committee.

There was some urgent matter before the Senate and all the members of the committee hurried to their places to vote. A little later Senator Bulkley introduced me to Senator Nye, who discussed his armaments investigation most intelligently. He was far better informed about foreign attitudes than I had expected. He surprised me when he said: "Secretaries Hull and Roper have helped me very freely and have only warned against publicity which might prevent their representatives abroad from obtaining information so much needed." The press had given the public the impression that Hull and Roper had tried to prevent information from going to the committee which Nye headed. Nye impressed me as a true public servant.

February 13. Wednesday. I lunched today in New York with Adolph Ochs and the staff of the *New York Times.* John Finley and eight or ten other distinguished newspaper folk were present. The conversation was most interesting; nearly everyone on the *Times* was familiar with the European situation. The simple directness of Ochs, the owner of the *Times,* was interesting. There was no evidence of any sectarian anger.

February 14. Thursday. We are on our way back to the critical post in Berlin. The ocean is expected to be stormy again, though we are hoping for a better sea than in December.

February 23. Saturday. At last we are here, and the delicate work of watching and carefully doing nothing begins. I am not happy. I feel the constant risk of never finishing my *Old South.*

February 26. Tuesday. Today at 12 o'clock I was at the Foreign Office to pay customary respects to Secretary von Neurath. I gave him special greetings from Secretary Hull, and he was most cordial, more so than at any other time since I came here in July, 1933. I wondered if he had heard the rumor that I was not coming back to Berlin and that Washington would leave the position vacant indefinitely, a report which a Washington newspaper man had told me he had from Berlin by wire.

Von Neurath discussed frankly the critical economic and social situation here, saying it could not endure long unless world trade improved. I agreed that I feared similar troubles lay ahead in the United States unless world trade improved. He was specially strong in his approval of President Roosevelt's plan of recovery, and fearful of the Senate's opposition, which he said was quite similar to the Reichstag behavior preceding the Hitler putsch. So much was said that I returned at once and wrote a summary to Washington. Von Neurath said he was afraid our political deals between one sectional interest and another against real national interests might cause the overthrow of democracy in the United States.

March 1. Friday. We went tonight to our first formal diplomatic dinner at the Soviet Ambassador's palace, the greatest of all the diplomatic mansions in Berlin, more elaborate even than the famous old Hindenburg palace on the Wilhelmstrasse where Bismarck lived for a time. There were forty guests, Von Neurath being the guest of honor, with François-Poncet, French Ambassador, next in rank. I had met most of the people, but I could not remember half of them. Poor Eric Kleiber, the conductor who had been dismissed in December, was present. He is a Hebrew, though he had made his peace with the regime here and we thought him safe. He was dismissed because he allowed a piece of music written by a Jew to be given in one of his concerts in the Staatsoper. He hung on to me a little and Von Neurath noticed it. Kleiber goes to the famous Salzburg festival next summer.

March 4. Monday. All our staff including the attachés went with us to be presented formally to the new Japanese Ambassador here. It was the usual, formal, useless affair attended by about 500 people. The Minister of Uruguay, under some excitement, called me aside to say he had news of a Japanese commission in Chaco trying to buy oil lands and settle 80,000 families there. He asked me to wire Washington. I was doubtful but listened.

March 5. Tuesday. We dined this evening with Von Bülow and a group of ten or twelve Germans. Finance Minister von Schwerin-Krosigk was the most distinguished of the guests. The only noteworthy bit of conversation I had was with Von Bülow and La Bougle, Minister from Argentina. The topic was Hitler's refusal yesterday to receive Sir John Simon who was due here for a conference about armament control and aircraft limitation. MacDonald, the British Prime Minister, had announced in a White Book yesterday that the German people were preparing their youth for war and that England must, therefore, arm to the limit of her ability to defend herself against possible attack. This so affronted Hitler that he contracted a deep cold and cabled Sir John Simon, Foreign Secretary under MacDonald, not to come to Berlin!

This had made a sensation of the first order. I remarked to Von Bülow that I agreed that the English Prime Minister had made a blunder, but that if I had been the responsible official here, I would have met Sir John with a big official delegation at the railway station and given him a cordial greeting.

Von Bülow looked nonplused for a moment and then replied: "I incline to agree with you; it would have compelled the British to apologize and be agreeable." The Argentine Minister also agreed with me. When I said good evening to Von Bülow he repeated: "You and I always agree." I was not quite sure he meant it, but two or three times when we have debated American demands about debts we have actually been in agreement. He is a representative of the old aristocracy and is thought to be uncomfortable in his present high position.

March 7. Thursday. I went to the Kaiserhof Hotel to hear the Labor Front leader, Ley, talk about German labor difficulties. I sat down with the Cuban Minister at a quiet side table where beer was promptly served. In a little while Rosenberg, under whose direction these meetings are held about once a month, came to greet me and ask me to join him at his table where high officials sat. The table was occupied and I asked to be excused as I liked a quiet corner. It seemed satisfactory.

The lecture was not unlike Rust's address early in December, rather cheap, with no real discussion of basic troubles here or elsewhere. Three times Ley emphasized the idea that all German workers must never forget that they are soldiers owing absolute obedience to the state and permitted to have little thought of their earnings. Personal dignity and self-sustenance were not mentioned. "The employer, under the Nazi regime, does not think of his great plant, his machines or his earnings; he thinks his greatest obligation is to give work to his employees, and render service to Germany. The laborer is absolutely loyal to his employer and has no idea of resisting or of organizing for strikes." There may be some people of these qualities but I do not believe half what Ley said. There is no way, however, to learn the truth since no one dares express his convictions.

March 8. Friday. My wife and I dined with the Fürstenbergs, a wealthy banker family living in a beautiful home on the old Königin Augustastrasse, not far from us. Dr. Kühlmann, former Cabinet member, wealthy head of great steel plants in the Saar Territory and a clever writer for American periodicals, was one of the guests. Another was Max Warburg, so uneasy last August or September when he visited me in the Embassy. His brother is Felix Warburg of New York. Both are bankers of great wealth. Warburg seemed quite secure this evening. His brother was not so confident when I saw him in New York on January 17.

There were other guests claiming to be friends of Dr. Schacht, as they indicated more than once. One of them, also a bank president in Berlin, remarked that Hitler's attitude toward paying debts contracted under the Bruening regime, his predecessor, was like the Soviets' attitude towards debts contracted with the United States by the Kerensky regime. Both believed it was an honor not to pay them. I wonder whether this is not also Schacht's attitude. The best of the Germans find it impossible to forgive the United States for participating in the World War. The Germans do not discuss this, even friends like Oncken, Marcks or Windelband, but they feel that a great victory over all Europe was denied them. So the debts due the United States, though contracted after 1924, are really of doubtful obligation, so far as the National Socialist nation is concerned.

March 11. Monday. I drove out to Professor Hermann Oncken's, where I met an interesting crowd last autumn. He told me that one of his students, only twenty-nine years old but an influential Party member, had violently attacked a book of his some time ago because of a description of the Cromwell regime which seemed to parallel the Hitler autarchy here. The attack was given wide publicity and Rosenberg, the editor of the *Völkischer Beobachter*, official organ of the Nazi Party, intervened with Rust and caused Oncken to be retired from his position as head of the history department in the University of Berlin. But the protest of university students was so nearly unanimous when his "retirement" was announced that Rust withdrew the recall for the rest of the winter semester. However, he does not know whether he is to go on with his work in the coming spring semester or not.

Oncken is perhaps the foremost historian in Germany and his "retirement" without reference to his health condition or his own wishes will be widely discussed in the United States. I do not think Oncken is in any way radically opposed to the present regime, now that it has swung so completely over to the conservative side. He does, however, insist on a professor's right to publish a book without submitting it for the approval of the government.

Professor Oncken said, however, that nearly all university people in Germany are uneasy and that they are writing him their sympathies and approval. He also added that the university people are allying themselves with the Lutheran Church and contending for the rights of free teaching and preaching. He expects another struggle during the next few months.

I am inclined to think Hitler will side with Rosenberg whose constant preaching of a new German Christianity—the worship of Wotan and other ancient German gods—is the new Nazi religion. Curiously enough, the defeat of Rosenberg's reversion to German barbarism depends on the Roman Catholics' support of Lutheranism. The Pope is in a tight place. He must help Lutherans and Lutheran universities to save Catholicism in Germany. At the same time he must support Nazi philosophy in the hope of defeating Communism in Russia and checking the advance of socialism in France and Spain.

March 15. Friday. I told President Roosevelt on February 6 that I was fairly certain that William Randolph Hearst, who had helped to defeat the President's plan to have the United States enter the World Court, was a sympathizer of Mussolini and Hitler, and promised to confirm my opinion if I received further proof upon return to Berlin. This is the story I have learned.

In 1924 Hearst had been violently opposed to the Mussolini dictatorship. He sent a clever Italian correspondent to Rome to take the place of the United Press man as far as Hearst service was concerned; the United Press man had been serving the

Hearst papers. When the first of a series of articles reached headquarters in New York, Hearst sent another man to Rome to negotiate a deal with Mussolini by which Hearst would give him $1.00 a word for anything he would dictate for the Hearst press. It was widely known that a Pacific coast bank had loaned Hearst some millions of dollars and that this bank was in sympathy with Mussolini. Thereafter, Hearst newspapers all over the United States praised the Italian dictatorship and Mussolini received large sums of money. From 1924 until now, Hearst has advocated dictatorship in Italy.

In the summer of 1934, Hearst traveled to Germany with a party of friends in several cars. He spent some weeks at Nauheim, and was reported to be strongly opposed to the Hitler dictatorship. It was a little after the June 30 murders. However, Hanfstaengl and Rosenberg made visits to him and early in September Hearst flew to Berlin. He had an interview with Hitler and went away less unsympathetic.

The German officials demanded that Von Wiegand and Knickerbocker, who has written a book on Nazi Germany and who is a world traveler and reporter for Hearst, be forbidden to re-enter the Reich. Hearst agreed that Knickerbocker should never come here again, but officials of the Reichswehr, who had never forgotten Von Wiegand's relations with the Kaiser's regime and his friendliness during the World War, protested and his right to return was not denied.

March 16. Saturday. Von Wiegand was again in my office. As to the drift of German international policy, he had nothing new but confirmed his former view that war is the program and that the situation is analogous to 1912-1914 when Western Europe was trying to persuade Germany not to go to war. I am doubtful of the parallel. Today's German papers are full of violent denunciations of the French anxiety revealed in Premier Flandin's speech yesterday before the French Chamber of Deputies. Flandin's speech and French approval of the plan to increase the French army by doubling the term of each soldier's service were both replies to Goering's announcement last Monday of increased air training here for defense against bombing planes. All German papers, acting upon instructions from the government, declared that the French act was a scrapping of European disarmament. I think the Goering air program is truly belligerent but France, Italy and England have armed in violation of the Versailles Treaty too.

However, this afternoon a *New York Times* correspondent called to tell me that at 5 o'clock the German Propaganda Ministry officials had called in all the press people to inform the world that Germany had begun to reorganize the Reichswehr into a standing army of 400,000 to 500,000 men. This seems to have excited the press people, but the work has been going on for at least a year. This is the German reply to the French decision of yesterday that they would increase their strength. All this adds to the significance of the coming Sir John Simon visit on March 26. This is what Von Wiegand says is a repetition of the events preceding 1914 when the British sent a Cabinet official here to know what the Germans meant by increasing their army and navy at that time. I picked up the facts from newspaper folk, for no official note had been sent to the Embassy when I left, and cabled them to Washington.

March 17. Sunday. After an hour in the Chancery office, I drove with Captain Keppler, our Naval Attaché and Captain Crockett, enthusiastic military attaché, to the famous Staatsoper on Unter den Linden to hear a talk about the fallen heroes of Germany—a sort of German Decoration Day service. As I entered the reservation for the diplomatic corps, Von Bassewitz showed me to the ranking place in the box. I asked: Is not the French Ambassador here? "No, nor the Nuncio," he replied. Being seated some ten minutes I was a little troubled by the absence of all ambassadors except myself.

The papers this morning had announced that the French, English, Italian and Polish representatives had been before the Chancellor to hear an official declaration of his enlargement of the army. It now occurred to me that they had all agreed not to come. Why had not the British informed me? We had for more than a year co-operated in most matters of this sort. Also the Japanese Ambassador was not present. Why? The Japanese are known to approve of German attitudes. I suspect it was hinted to him by the German Foreign Office not to come. He would be counted an ally. I was the only one of whom no complaint could be made on either side. So here I was.

March 18. Monday. Monsieur Bérard came to see me at my request at 12 o'clock. He said his government was pressing actively for an agreement between England, France and Italy to present a united protest against German military preparations. His ambassador was even thinking of recommending the withdrawal of the ambassadors of those countries if the Germans continued violations of the Treaty of Versailles. I said, half jokingly: I believe I would ask to be recalled too, if those three powers withdraw. However, England has already indicated a disposition to send Sir John Simon, her Foreign Secretary, here in a few days, notwithstanding the affronts of the last ten days. This greatly perturbs the French. Italy is reported to be co-operating with France.

At 5:30 I called on Dr. Schacht to ask him what he had learned at Basle when he had met with the international bankers to discuss the tangled financial situation. He reported that Montagu Norman, head of the Bank of England, was in favor of stabilizing the pound and dollar, but that the British Treasury was opposed. This means the British Government is using the cheap pound in order to compete with American industrialists who are trying to capture British colonial trade, having already a monopoly of the American home market. The cheap pound is a means of competing with American high tariffs. Schacht was not optimistic. He said: "In case there is no stabilization, we shall have an economic crash next October." I am not of contrary opinion though my knowledge of the complicated financial structure of modern society is so vague that I cannot have definite convictions.

Turning to Schacht, who seemed to wish to talk about general subjects, I said: How about the universal military service which was decreed yesterday? He replied: "It means peace for Europe. My son is now serving his year and all Germans must do this for the security of their country." I reported the military show which I had witnessed yesterday. But he said, "This doesn't mean war." This is absolutely contrary to his earnest statement to me last autumn.

He then added: "Hitler quoted Wilson's Fourteen Points as a bid for a European conference on that basis; will your country enter such a conference?" I expressed doubt, though I did not disagree with him as to the world-wide benefits of American co-operation in a League conference. I told him the President had favored co-operation with the League but that public opinion in the United States seemed to be hostile. I mentioned the Senate's vote on the World Court on January 30, but I did not consider that as indicating public opinion accurately, Hearst having made a great row and scared some senators. Schacht re-emphasized Hitler's use of the Fourteen Points and seemed to think it was really serious. I thought it was simply to irritate France.

At 8:30 I asked Bérard to call a moment at our house. He came in hurriedly just as we finished dinner. I wished to refer to the confidential talk I had had today, which I did. I gave him in all confidence Schacht's statement about Hitler's reference to the Fourteen Points. Bérard said: "I never trust Schacht." Berard was hurrying off to Paris with instructions from his ambassador.

March 21. Thursday. Events have remained exciting for the last two days, England agreeing to send Sir John Simon to Berlin next Sunday and Germany agreeing that Hitler will discuss world peace matters, possibly a disarmament conference. France and Italy made their protests today and the German Foreign Office replied in such a way as to try to separate the two Latin powers. The French Ambassador was treated a little coldly and the public given to understand this.

Learning this morning that a French economic journal had published an article saying I had sent the President a twenty-page survey of Germany and predicted an economic collapse next April, I wrote a note to the French Ambassador asking if it were possible that Monsieur Bérard had given out anything like that after conversations we had had. In the afternoon

Monsieur Bérard came to the office and denied all responsibility for the story. He had just returned from Paris and had not seen the sensational article. I was then convinced that he had not been responsible. But the article claimed that our Embassy, on the basis of a scientific survey, had warned the United States against continued investments, predicting Hitler would continue in power only a few years, that war was in prospect and that collapse was coming. I gave a statement to the press people that I had sent no such document, and at 6 o'clock, after I had returned to the house, the Havas agency called asking for a statement to send to Paris. This I gave, though I added that we sent economic studies each month, but without any such prophecies as to a definite collapse. I cannot imagine how this story got out for it is said to have come from a French correspondent here.

March 22. Friday. At 9 o'clock my wife and I went, as Ernst Hanfstaengl's guests, to Mussolini's play called *The Hundred Days*—a description of Napoleon's last phase. We were in the same box with Madame Cerruti. The film showed how the Italians and Germans regard their leaders as modern Napoleons. The audience was not displeased and Napoleon, portrayed by a German actor, Krauss, received much, but not wild, applause.

When I was a student in Leipzig, I noticed a German-erected monument of Napoleon on the field of that famous slaughter and I also noticed that professors regarded him as a model leader and commander. If only he had been a German! Hitler now regards himself as a Napoleon abolishing democratic governments all over Germany and making Germany the dominating power in Europe. Hanfstaengl thinks he is advancing his own rating with his Fuehrer by giving these shows to great masses of people. I am not sure the Germans will really like *The Hundred Days*.

March 25. Monday. This morning the Japanese Ambassador called. He pressed me to call with him at the British Embassy and ask for an interview with Sir John Simon to learn what was being planned about the German navy and a possible Russian pact. I talked as agreeably as I could but declined an immediate answer to his request. I would not think of going with him on such a mission. It would make a sensation all over the United States.

It was clearer than ever to me that there is an agreement between Germany and Japan. The Ambassador spoke of dining or lunching with Goering, Goebbels and other high German officials the last few days. He referred to them in a way showing personal vanity and satisfaction. I would not have alluded to such appointments if I had made them. I have an instinctive distaste of shaking hands with such men, even though they consider themselves modern Caesars. I suspected the Japanese Ambassador or his government had planned to see if I could be maneuvered into this position. He went away bowing and scraping in protocol style. I promised to call him in case I saw "any prospect of seeing Sir John Simon."

At 8:30 we appeared in the elaborate palace of the Belgian Minister's to dine. There were about forty guests at table, all in full dress. There was the usual cordiality but no talk of value. Later in the evening, sitting at a table with the host, a German general, the Swiss Minister and one other German, I said in humorous strain: I had a strange dream Sunday night. "What was it?" said the Swiss. I said: It might be dangerous to tell. "Oh, no, no," were the replies. I then said that I had dreamed that the Hohenzollerns had been restored and that I had a talk with the Crown Prince on the throne or near it.

The Belgian was silent; the Swiss seemed puzzled. But the German general commented that Von Blomberg had paid no tribute to the Kaiser or the Crown Prince at the memorial service Sunday, although he had complimented the famous Ludendorff, now an enemy of Hitler, and lauded Von Hindenburg's military services. Von Blomberg, the general said, had thought of praising the Kaiser but had purposely omitted it at the time. The general said Von Blomberg was entirely in sympathy with the Hohenzollerns.

March 27. Wednesday. This afternoon we gave a reception to about 250 German official and private folk and to the diplomatic corps. It was not disagreeable, though tiresome. Most official Germans gave all kinds of excuses for not being able to be present, part of which were perfectly honest, as I judge, but some were not.

The most distinguished of the German guests was the well-known General von Hammerstein who slipped out of Berlin last June lest he be murdered, according to stories told me at the time. He seemed comfortable and would have talked freely if there had been time and a chance to sit in a quiet corner.

March 31. Sunday. I was in bed all day yesterday. Today I went to the Embassy office and found it too cold, as I did most of last week. A German janitor can hardly imagine keeping the temperature at 24° Centigrade or 75° Fahrenheit to be important, especially if he must rise early in the morning. I gave him another warning and came home.

Rabbi Lazaron of Baltimore, a generous, humane man who is in Berlin in the hope of helping his people but fearful that he may be ordered out of the country—I am also—lunched with us. Others were the famous Hoetzsch, my classmate at Leipzig, whose recent work on the diplomatic correspondence on the Russian side in the World War was featured in the London *Times* last week, and Dr. Richter, formerly Minister of Education, with his wife.

They were most interesting and witty conversationalists. Richter's father-in-law, Professor Schmitt, was rector of the University of Berlin for a time under the Ebert regime. Richter himself was dismissed from the university faculty in 1933 because he was not in sympathy with the Hitler program. Hoetzsch was a member of the Reichstag under the republic but is now very guarded in all his references to controversial subjects. He will be entitled to a pension from the university in a year or two unless he publishes some book or article which puts him in bad, which is very difficult to avoid since he is an internationalist of wide reputation.

Poor Lazaron revealed great concern because so many wealthy Jews have surrendered to the Nazi leadership and are influential financial aids to Dr. Schacht who thinks their assistance is very important in the present economic situation.

April 4. Thursday. I received a telegram from Secretary Hull asking whether war in Europe is imminent. I had an engagement with Von Neurath at 12 o'clock to speak about a minor matter. So I decided to see Sir Eric Phipps, whose office is near the German Foreign Office, at 11:30. He happened to be free. In the conversation it was made clear that the visits of Sir John Simon and the young Eden had been of negative value.

Hitler had sat in the conference in his brown-shirted S.A. uniform, the others all in civilian clothes. Hitler made it clear he would not agree to the so-called "eastern Locarno pacts" or guarantees of existing boundaries between Germany, Poland, the little Baltic states and Russia. But he said he would not go to war, only insist upon treaties being kept. As to the annexation of Austria, he vowed that there would be no German aggression. However, he insisted on the same right to send help to his cohorts there as the Italians had sent to theirs, both countries being engaged simultaneously in rival propaganda. As to Russian-German co-operation, Hitler said there was no possibility. Most of these points I had telegraphed to Washington. Sir Eric simply confirmed them and indicated once more grave doubts as to the maintenance of peace in Europe. One thing is certain: Hitler aims at war. When he will strike depends on preparations and a proper incident.

At 12:00 I sat down for a talk with Von Neurath. After offering him the twenty-one-volume diary and documents prepared some years ago by Hunter Miller, historical adviser to the State Department, and receiving his cordial thanks, I raised the question of German military policy. I told him first how general is the feeling in the United States that Germany aims to go to war relatively soon. He vowed there is no move toward war. He pretended great concern that Mussolini should have almost doubled the strength of the Italian army by recent orders, also that Mussolini should have published a statement two days ago demanding the encirclement of Germany and blaming England for not uniting with France and Italy to make it possible. In spite of this he said we shall have a general peace agreement within a few weeks. I inferred that he meant the coming conference at Geneva, where the League chiefs are to meet on April 15.

I reminded Von Neurath that all Germans seem military-minded, that all their public demonstrations are in full war equipment. I also said that Germany circulated, widely, imperialistic maps, that is, maps which show that the Nazi leaders demand the annexation of border countries like Holland, Austria, parts of Switzerland and the Polish Corridor. He said these maps were published by irresponsible people. But I said they bear Goering's name and are to be seen all over Germany in hotels and railway stations. He allowed that to be true but said it meant nothing as to German foreign policy.

I said: It convinces the outside world that Germany means to re-apply the old imperialist policy, not unlike that of Theodore Roosevelt. Marching everywhere in uniforms and claiming all border areas where German-speaking people live are strong evidences of the war spirit here. The Foreign Minister said: "Imperialistic talk and attitudes worry me too." The conversation lasted half an hour and it convinced me once more that Von Neurath and perhaps all the higher officials of the Foreign Office are fully aware of the dangers of Hitlerism and that they press for their points of view in vain. Hitler really aims to annex all these areas and will in due time go to war for that purpose.

I came away without any valid assurances, just as I left the British Embassy without being convinced that England was doing anything but playing politics. Perhaps that is all the present government in London can do. Lloyd George is playing a clever game and radical Labor is, as always, strongly pacifist. The encirclement of Germany is at present not possible and the 1914 situation is reproduced in most of its features. Will Europe go to war? I think not in a year or two.

At 4:30 I sat down to get the reactions of François-Poncet, the French Ambassador. Without telling him that Washington had wired about the danger of war, I pressed for his opinion as to the possibilities of the Stresa conference on April 11. He at once revealed the French exasperation at the English procedure of the last month. He was not sure what Mussolini and the

French Foreign Minister, Laval, could do except to agree on encirclement of Germany as the only means of keeping the peace and then put the agreement before Sir John Simon. Then he said the English would refuse and another adjournment would follow, leaving Germany again free to arm.

He said he did not think Hitler would precipitate war, but only because he is not yet ready. "We shall not have war the next year or two unless some break comes over Austria, Danzig or Czechoslovakia. Then Hitler would persuade the whole German people to march again. If England won't join us now there is going to be war." I learned of a confidential interview with Beneš, about the end of March, in which the Czech Premier said his country would fight for its independence if their allies came to their aid; otherwise, there was nothing to do but capitulate to Germany's terms of friendship. I wonder if Beneš doubts the validity of French and English promises.

I went to dinner this evening at Minister La Bougle's, of the Argentine. Sitting on the right of Madame La Bougle, I heard from her that Goering had given her and her husband a grand dinner the night before which indicated the present vain Nazi hope of winning South American countries to their side in the event of war. She indicated confidentially her very severe criticism of the present regime.

On my right sat the wife of the Swiss Minister who, on Monday last, made a formal protest against the Nazi kidnapping of a Jew, named Jacob, who has been writing able anti-Nazi articles for the Swiss and French press the last two years. Jacob was a German citizen before 1933. He is now in jail, to be tried for treason. Von Bülow declared to the Swiss Minister that Germany would not release Jacob nor would they submit evidence that Jacob had not been kidnapped, which was the Swiss claim. The German-Swiss treaty of 1921 is to be ignored.

As the Swiss Minister's wife drifted a little in her conversation from subject to subject, I said: I have just been reading what Leckey, the great British historian, said about your famous Zwingli and his devotion to the idea of personal freedom, two hundred years before the rest of Europe recognized the valuable philosophy of freedom of thought and speech. She affected not to know anything of Zwingli; perhaps she did not, for few diplomats know anything of history, only the mere conventions.

April 5. Friday. I wired Secretary Hull the facts about the war danger here: The regime is aggressive. The responsible or irresponsible trio, Hitler, Goering and Goebbels, might easily do a wild thing, knowing so little of past history. All of them are of a murderous frame of mind. The economic dilemma might precipitate war as a possible way out, but Schacht has absolute power and this the German people so respect in any leader that they will submit to other temporary solutions. Hence I think no debacle is imminent.

The Foreign Secretary says: "No war," though he is troubled about Mussolini. The British Ambassador says: "No war in a year or two but war is the purpose here." Finally the French Ambassador says: "No war yet, unless some break in Danzig or Austria gives the regime a chance to arouse German enthusiasm." It was a sad story; but I think a true one. If the telegram were to be revealed as the Miller report of last October was, it might greatly anger the German authorities.

April 9. Tuesday. We had been engaged for weeks to dine with the Solmssens, so we could not get to the first Goering wedding show at the Opera House on time. The talk at Solmssens was in ridicule of the Nazi leaders, Goering, Goebbels and Hess, for trying to terrorize all Danzig people into voting for Nazi Party control there last Sunday. Many violences were visited upon the people who did not have Nazi flags over their houses. Consuls of some countries had their windows smashed because they had not erected flags. The Nazi chiefs thought they would surely win 75 per cent of the vote and then control the Danzig Council by two-thirds and demand that the League of Nations allow Danzig to return to Germany. All reports show that Danzig would have voted 90 per cent to return to Germany, but not while the Nazis were in power. In consequence the vote was lower than in 1933.

The criticism of the lack of wisdom in sending Goering, Goebbels and Hess to Danzig to overawe the people was sharp.

There was also rather free fun-making of the wedding show that Goering is giving tonight and tomorrow in the Cathedral.

We had to beg to be excused after we rose from the table in order to appear at the Goering reception in the Opera House at 9:15. We were sorry to leave but the French Ambassador, in the absence of the Nuncio, had been compelled, as he said, to agree to attend the wedding and advise other members of the diplomatic crowd to be there. Hence we had accepted the tickets.

We arrived just in time to join the rush of guests to shake hands with the bride and groom, who were standing in the great hall on the second floor of the Opera. The ceremony continued for an hour. Then all went to their places and witnessed the completion of the opera. Krauss was the Austrian Nazi conductor brought here to take the place of Furtwaengler, removed last December. Krauss gave every sign of great joy at the opportunity to give a musical show for Goering. Not a judge of music, I cannot say whether the performance was good or not. I did not enjoy it.

April 12. Friday. I learned from the French Counselor tonight that Counselor Newton of the British Embassy went to the German Foreign Office to know if Germany would approve the French-Russian treaty of a day or two ago, as it was only a defense guarantee. Perhaps the Germans might then fall in with English demands at Stresa where the English, French and Italians were in conference about armaments and additional peace pacts. Von Neurath replied, to Newton's surprise, that Germany would approve, or at least not oppose, any peaceful treaty. This was telegraphed to Stresa. While this surprised the French not a little, it did not surprise me, since I have repeatedly been told by the Foreign Office people that Germany would return to the League of Nations whenever other powers agreed to recognize her equal rights.

We were dining at the house of the Greek Minister who had been in great distress, until a week or two ago, about the Venizelos revolt in his country, so much so that he had withdrawn invitations to a dinner about the middle of March. There were twenty-one guests including the Russian and the Japanese Ambassadors. I noticed the heavy silver plates on which we were all served. "English silver," the hostess said as I remarked its beauty. After the second course, I noticed the same silver plates come in again. This is one of the common habits of diplomatic people to impress their guests with evidence of wealth. How far this goes one can only know by attending dinners. Home at 11:15, after a wasted evening.

April 13. Saturday. William Bullitt, Ambassador to Russia, was with us today and we had a party of twelve people. The Russian and Polish Ambassadors and the Ministers from Yugoslavia and Venezuela attended. Dr. Dieckhoff and Dr. Hoetzsch were also with us. Bullitt still impressed me as quite proud of himself, and rather more boyish than one would expect for a man of his years. He told me of a conversation with the French Foreign Minister, Laval, in which the defensive alliance between France and Russia was discussed. It is to be signed on April 23.

A peculiar story, perhaps characteristic of Nazi Germany, came to me today from a reliable but secret source. It only reveals what must happen in a society which permits autocracy, especially one commanded by three such men as rule here.

From S.S. circles, I hear that General von Schleicher's next of kin, incited by the head of the army, General von Fritsch, are suing the German state for damages in connection with the shooting of their distinguished kinsman last June. It will be recalled that the Reichswehr Ministry refused to give back to the S.S. the files and records of the shooting, after having obtained them for examination. The day before yesterday, four S.S. men called on the major in the Reichswehr Ministry in whose keeping these files are held. At the point of a pistol they demanded the records. Feigning to acquiesce, he bent down as if to take the documents out of his desk drawer but instead pressed an alarm button concealed there and gave them other papers to gain time. Shortly thereafter, the guards responded to the bell and came and arrested the four S.S. men, took them

to the cellar of the building and there shot them. The ashes of
the bodies were sent in a box to Himmler.

April 16. Tuesday. In view of the tense situation all over
Europe, I went at 12 o'clock to talk with Von Bülow. He has
impressed me as more frank and liberal than Von Neurath, but
I can never be quite certain. We talked a half hour and I
learned little. He said Hitler could never join an eastern
Locarno pact for the maintenance of existing boundaries, though
he did not use direct statements from Hitler. He was certain
Hitler meant to maintain peace, but Soviet Russia, he said, had
a treaty with Czechoslovakia whereby a vast number of Soviet
planes could land at their air fields. "This means a close alliance with France and aggression against Germany."

I said: We have information that Czechoslovakia is moving
toward the English compromise viewpoint, and is not so close
to France as before. Von Bülow answered, "No, Beneš, the
Prime Minister, is, as usual, deceiving your Minister at Prague.
The Czechs are absolutely allied to France, and the new
French-Russian treaty only strengthens this alliance."

I asked him if Germany would send delegates to the Rome
Conference on May 20, called by Mussolini. He said: "Yes, but
we have not yet been invited." Will you agree to Austrian independence? "Oh, yes, we could not stand an *Anschluss*, although we know most Austrians wish to join Germany. But
Italy pays the salaries of Austrian generals and other officials.
That is the way the government goes on." He was not hopeful
of results from the Rome Conference, because Bulgaria will
not co-operate with Hungary and Rumania and because there
can be no agreement with Italy and France about Austria. This
seemed inconsistent since he had said Hitler would not have an
Anschluss with Austria. If so, then, why no agreement as to
Austrian independence?

He asked about American attitudes and I said: Nearly everybody over there thinks Germany is headed for war and that
affects our policy very seriously. He repeated the peace idea but
remarked that a returning German official had said that when
he was in Washington all the papers were saying Hitler de-

manded the Corridor from Poland, the German districts in
Czechoslovakia and Austria. The press people had gone to Ambassador Luther to know if this were true and Luther had refused to deny it, which convinced the American people that
Hitler would demand this much. Then said Von Bülow:
"Luther cabled us and we at once denied the story; only it was
too late as news."

I thought, but did not say, that this meant the Ambassador
feared Hitler did demand the areas named and hence had not
felt free to make a denial. In my opinion, Hitler does intend
to take these eastern areas at the first opportunity, but he wishes
some other nation to make the first aggressive move. Then Hitler would claim he was repelling aggression and demand annexations. Von Bülow remarked that the Geneva Conference
today would not amount to anything. France would defeat anything Germany might propose.

The Polish Ambassador, Lipski, lunched with me and we
talked an hour afterward, but the only information was that
Poland, despite the pact of January, 1934, is still uneasy as to
her situation and must try to get on with Germany and Russia
too, or there will be an invasion.

April 19. Friday. The conversations of the 16th were serious
enough, but events of the 17th were more serious. The Stresa
agreement of England, France and Italy on the 12th had been
troublesome, but the calling of a Little Entente conference in
Rome on May 25 to settle the fate of Austria was more serious
than Von Bülow indicated. He had said to me that Von Papen
had been here on April 15 and reported that practically all
Austrians wished to be annexed to Germany. I had not asked
any question on this point except: Would Germany participate
in the Rome Conference and would Germany give up the
Anschluss idea, so dear to Hitler? He had said: "*Anschluss*
would be a terrible thing for Germany." I suppose he meant:
now. Certainly all Germans I know wish annexation.

I do not know what Sir Eric Phipps said on the 16th after
my interview. But yesterday I learned that on Wednesday, the
17th, Hitler, at Berchtesgaden in upper Bavaria, ordered Von

Bülow to ask Sir Eric to the Foreign Office and give him a rebuke from Hitler, to be cabled to London. It is said Von Bülow
was violent and insulting. Today the Berlin papers say the Italian Ambassador was included in the rebuke. Anyway the press
of Paris and London is reported this morning to have been
greatly excited, some English papers saying 10,000 airplanes
are the only guarantees of British security against Nazi Germany.

The reason for Von Bülow's rebuke was the unanimous rulings of the League meeting on the evening of the 17th and the
morning of the 18th that Germany's armament decree of March
16 was a violation of the Versailles Treaty which could not be
permitted again. The warning clause was that if Germany
placed any soldiers in the neutralized zone along the Rhine it
would be considered as the beginning of war.

The situation of Europe is certainly critical, but the announcement of the details of the French-Russian Treaty as given out
yesterday at Geneva is proof of the encirclement of Germany
which Hitler might have foreseen in October, 1933, when he
suddenly left the League of Nations and ordered his first plebiscite. England, France, Italy and Russia are all in agreement to
fight if Germany makes an unfriendly move anywhere. They
would be tough even for a thoroughly armed Third Reich.

Moreover Belgium, Holland, Norway, Sweden and trem-
bling Denmark are all on the side of England and France.
Perhaps they would not fight, except Belgium, in the case of
war. But unlike 1914-18, they would all aid England as much
as they could in a peaceful way. In my judgment, the Rome
Conference should declare Austria finally and absolutely independent, and Rumania, Yugoslavia, Czechoslovakia and Austria should all join a co-operative union, with Hungary and
Bulgaria sympathetic. Germany would be helpless, and an economic boycott could follow if Germany should go on arming.

Never, in my opinion, has a great people been guided by a
less sensible group. Hitler knows no history, Goering is even
less informed, Goebbels is utterly incompetent except in his German propaganda, and success in this may not be real. These
three supremely egotistical men are supposed to be together at

Berchtesgaden today trying to decide upon German policy, all pretending to think that 90 per cent of all Germans are behind them. What they will do, one can hardly guess, but wisdom can scarcely be expected of three such men.

April 20. Saturday. According to the custom of diplomats here I went this morning to the old Bismarck-Hindenburg palace to write my name in a book of congratulations to Hitler, President and Fuehrer of deluded, helpless Germany. As I drove into the Wilhelmstrasse from Unter den Linden, I noted that tens of thousands of Germans, men, women and children, stood behind ropes on both sides of the street for two whole blocks, waiting for a glimpse of the Fuehrer whenever he may come out of the palace where he is spending the day in conferences, I suppose, with officers of the Reichswehr, perhaps with Von Neurath.

Entering the hall I met the new Minister Gie from South Africa in top hat and formal clothes, gloves and cane in hand. He was a little embarrassed for me when I shook hands with him without gloves or top hat. The Minister from unhappy and poverty-stricken Rumania was not quite so formally dressed as Mr. Gie. In a half-minute my name was on the book and I drove past the soldiers again.

At 12 o'clock, Dr. Goebbels delivered an address. It was written in the best German I hear or read these days. He spoke over the radio to all Germans, also to Latin and North Americans who cared to listen. I wonder how many cut their radios off. I was in the office, busy getting off dispatches to Washington, and consequently had no chance to listen to the shrewd propagandist whose role here is so important that Hitler would not dare dismiss him, much as the more sensible Germans hate him. What he said about Hitler represents, however, almost exactly what 80 per cent of the Germans think. In one part of the address Goebbels indicated what a calamity it would be if any one of the three "immortals," Hitler, Goering and Goebbels, were to be killed. I am a little surprised that he said this, since there are thousands of Germans who would kill the Fuehrer if they had a chance and pay the penalty with their own lives. At least this is common talk in indirect ways.

We sent a telegram to Washington at 5 o'clock giving the gist of a defiant reply of Hitler to the League of Nations members who voted for resolutions in which the German proclamation of March 16 was denounced. When the Chancellor-President handed his document to his publicity department, he mounted his airplane and went back to Berchtesgaden where he spends more time than here in the executive office which once held Bismarck so closely. Hitler holds Cabinet sessions only occasionally, and issues decrees which the members never really sanction by voting their convictions. That is all he does in his high office.

April 21. Sunday. Easter. Strange that Hitler's birthday should happen to be the day after Good Friday. Since Goering was a national hero last week when he was married and received such extraordinary gifts, it was necessary to give Hitler an equally sensational "Heil." So we hear today he is to receive from the people a gift of twenty-seven war aircraft. Easter time!

It turns out to be an interesting season, four days in succession, just after the League of Nations rebuke of Germany for its rearmament challenge. Friday, the crucifixion day; Saturday, Hitler's birthday; Sunday, resurrection day; and Monday, the usual holiday. Everybody in official circles here is out of town, most of them in South Germany. I am quiet at home trying to put in a little time on my long-delayed *Old South*.

April 25. Thursday. We had our first formal dinner tonight since our return from Washington, two months ago, although we had had many luncheons and dinners for groups of ten or twelve. It was a party of twenty. The most interesting person present was the Yugoslav Minister, about seventy years old but witty and outspoken in his fun-making of the Rosenberg activity in Germany. The Japanese Ambassador talked again of his close relations with Goering and Goebbels whom nearly all diplomats dread to see. I have been at Goering's house, a palace more elaborate than Hitler's, and have had dinner at

Goebbels' rather modest place. Neither of them has ever been in our house though both had been invited a little before June 30, 1934.

April 26. Friday. A party of some twenty young people came in on a sort of welcoming party for Martha who arrived today. Some were interesting persons. The most troubled, though it was wonderfully concealed, was Prince Louis Ferdinand, grandson of the exiled Kaiser, heir to the imperial throne if it ever be re-created. He is about twenty-seven years old, tall, handsome and very clever. He loves to talk about Henry Ford—"a great administrator," he says, then about flying machines which he pilots in preparation for war which he hates. He talks only to my daughter, now and then, about the Hohenzollern tragedy. He has a faint hope of becoming Kaiser some time. If he were sure that would not happen, he would go to the United States to live. I tell him he ought to study German history and write the story of the family just as it happened. He was too young in 1914 to know much, but he has seen enough since 1914 never to forget the points in the tragedy.

April 27. Saturday. We were with Sir Eric and Lady Phipps for lunch today, forty people present. Goering's assistant, Air General Milch, was present, his wife sitting on my right at the table. Nothing worth while was said, however, except Sir Eric's report to my wife that Germany is building twelve submarines and several large war vessels in violation of the Treaty of Versailles. He had seen Von Bülow the day before, but no agreement had been made to negotiate. Why plan this great navy when Germany has no long stretch of coast? Only for a thrust at England.

April 29. Monday. At 11 o'clock this morning Von Wiegand stopped by. His information confirmed our reports of war aircraft work and of German navy building. He reported that General von Reichenau had just told him that the Reichswehr was very much disturbed over Hitler's challenge to all Germany's neighbors and that they demanded a treaty with Russia now that the French were weakening a little toward the Soviet

Union. It's the one opportunity to break the encirclement which France, England and Italy are making. Hitler is much troubled and dreads terribly to approach Russia, his one enemy never to be dealt with. However, Von Reichenau said he had replied to one of the Reichswehr spokesmen: "Well, I will make a treaty with the devil for Germany's sake."

May 1. Wednesday. The annual Labor Day in Germany has been converted under the present regime to a National Socialist demonstration, not unlike July 4 at home, the difference being that all workers must attend meetings in honor of Hitler whether they wish or not. We were to have gone to the Tempelhof airfield to witness the demonstration, but snow and rain alternated and I called up the Foreign Office to be excused. It was readily granted. Reports estimated the crowd at 1,700,000. I doubt the figures but it was an immense show and Hitler made a rather pessimistic speech. He warned the public they might look for hard times, but all must hang together. He said he would rather be a German peasant without a home than a citizen of any other country. He is an Austrian and is reported to be a millionaire.

The great day passed without other events than the speeches here of Hitler and Goebbels, the latter having compared his chief to Joan of Arc as the one person who converses with God Almighty about his country's affairs.

May 2. Thursday. Mr. Dunn, chief of our State Department's Division of Western European Affairs, amused me a little today by his interpretations of events and attitudes. He is traveling about and making contacts as best he can, not knowing any language but his own.

May 6. Monday. Oechsner of the United Press reported from a secret but absolutely reliable source great activity in submarine and other war vessel building at Wilhelmshaven. He described also some light ships which carry a few bombs and go 60 knots an hour. These increasing German naval activities have changed the friendly British attitude of the last three months to serious concern, revealed by debates in the House of Commons as well as by Sir Eric Phipps. Last Sunday, May 5, I met Sir Eric walking in the Tiergarten and he indicated his growing anxiety, since Germany has no exposed sea front of any extent and no colonies. Yet she violates the Versailles Treaty (of course unfair at many points, like all treaties which end wars) in this respect too, risking England's hostility. It seems to me most unwise at the very moment Italy, France, England and Russia are working out their encirclement alliance. England has been hesitant about the Russian phase of this, but German behavior at this moment is apt to swing England into co-operation.

Lord Lothian, who as Philip Kerr was secretary to Lloyd George during the World War, wrote me about this in a letter which I received today. He expressed the opinion that the opportunity to bring Germany into the League of Nations had been missed because of the failure of France to face reality and Great Britain's failure to alter her course. Consequently he believed the League would be reduced to merely an anti-Nazi combination giving Germany additional reason to follow its own path of power politics. He indicated clearly that he favors a coalition of the democracies to block any German move in their direction and to turn Germany's course eastwards. That this might lead to a war between Russia and Germany does not seem to disturb him seriously. In fact he seems to feel this would be a good solution of the difficulties imposed on Germany by the Versailles Treaty. The problem of the democracies, as he sees it, is to find for Japan and Germany a stronger place in world affairs to which, in his opinion, they are entitled because of their power and tradition. He hopes this can be accomplished without any sacrifice to the British Empire and with as little destruction to human liberty as possible.

May 7. Tuesday. Rabbi Lazaron returning from a trip to Geneva and Rome, reported that a member of the Pope's cabinet had said to him that the Catholics could not co-operate with the Lutherans in Germany, although their situation was identical. The 400-year-old hatred of Martin Luther and his work is still responsible for Catholic hostility. But Lazaron was more troubled about the terrible Jewish plight here. He had seen Max Warburg of Hamburg and he was very disturbed too. Neither of them could see what is to be done.

May 10. Friday. The new Minister from Bulgaria called in all good form at the conventional hour. He surprised me with his liberality and knowledge of affairs in Europe. His explanation of the situation in his country showed a breadth of view and appreciation of the international situation which surpassed the knowledge of American ambassadors I have met: Bullitt in Russia, Cudahy in Poland and Long in Italy. I do not know Bingham in London and Straus in Paris well enough to compare them. But I am convinced that the ministers here from Bulgaria, Rumania, Czechoslovakia and Jugoslavia are each superior to the American ambassadors indicated above.

All these ministers from backward little countries know three languages and the history of Europe over long stretches of time. American ambassadors and ministers and even staff members almost ignore the need of two or three languages and make no effort to understand the history of the people to whom they are accredited. I am ashamed of my lack of knowledge of French, though my German serves me fairly well, and my understanding of history gives me some rating with the German Foreign Office people who know many languages but not much of their own history, due to the partisan teaching in German universities since Von Treitschke.

May 15. Wednesday. Wishing to get some knowledge from German officials about the international situation, now that Germany is so completely encircled by so-called pacts, I asked Von Neurath for an unofficial conversation. I saw him at 12 o'clock.

He said that Hitler would speak before a session of the Reichstag on May 21. What he would say he could not guess, though he had sent Hitler a memorandum on what ought to be said. The date was set for the 21st because of the death of Pilsudski who was to be buried on May 18. Von Neurath spoke of the so-called "eastern Locarno pact" without animus, though Hitler rages when the suggestion of his joining it is raised. The Secretary wished it to be delayed until England, Germany and

France could agree upon an aircraft pact whereby each country is to limit its building of machines. I did not say that England and France would probably not agree to this until an eastern Locarno treaty is agreed to by Germany, France being absolutely sure Germany will not keep any of her promises about disarmament. That point was left open because I am myself sure Germany intends to annex areas in the north and east and so will not cease arming soon.

I then asked him about the Italian position and the Danube Conference proposed at Stresa on May 11, and much discussed since. He was surprised, he said, at Mussolini's lack of wisdom in sending troops into Abyssinia. The result, if war comes, will cost Italy a great many soldiers, will not be successful for a long time, and will probably bring financial bankruptcy to Italy. He described the Italian situation as very dangerous: armed to the hilt, in debt to the limit, and without markets. The position is exactly parallel to that in which Germany will find herself by 1937. He said: "Mussolini cannot dismiss his million soldiers without huge unemployment; he cannot go on arming further without bankruptcy and he cannot fail in war without being overthrown." Von Neurath described this in a way which made me think constantly of Germany's similar position even now, though her debts are not yet so critical as Italy's and war is not quite so imminent.

While nothing directly significant was said, I came away convinced that the Foreign Office people are doing their utmost to restrain Hitler and coax England into a breach with France and Italy. There is real uneasiness, especially since the Polish dictator Pilsudski's death.

May 17. Friday. Richard J. Davis of Chicago, a Christian Science lecturer, finishing a month's lecture tour of Germany, called to describe the peculiar attitudes of German audiences in all parts of the country. He thought there was an increasing interest in religion, contrary to the Rosenberg drift. I am not sure of his appraisal, but it was surprising that houses where he lectured were always crowded. He thinks the population very uneasy. Perhaps at least the church people are.

May 18. Saturday. I went to the Catholic Cathedral near the old Kaiser's palace to attend the service in honor of Pilsudski, who was being buried in Cracow, Poland, at the same time. The church was crowded. Hitler took the seat of honor on the right of the altar. Von Neurath, Goebbels, and generals of the Reichswehr were seated in the first row behind Hitler, whose distinguished position in a chair with an altar just in front of him looked suggestive.

It was amusing to note all the white gloves in the church on a moderately warm day. It was strictly formal, though swords in a Christian church seemed to me to be bad taste. What would Jesus have said if he had seen such evidences of war spirit? He would probably have left the place.

Promptly at 11, the Papal Nuncio came up the aisle with an escort of twelve priests, a long, red robe suspended from his shoulders and extending at least twelve feet behind him, two men holding it up so it would not drag along the floor. He took his seat on a sort of throne on the right side of the great altar where candles were burning and priests were chanting in Latin, which no one understood, and occasionally falling upon their knees and scattering incense, which I think Jesus never used. It was the medieval ceremony from beginning to end and nobody, save perhaps the priests, understood anything that was said or sung.

To me it was all half-absurd. I do not know much about Pilsudski, except that he was a dictator who put people to death when they opposed him. Why so much religious ceremony when no one could have imagined him to be a Christian? But there was probably not one follower of Jesus in the whole congregation. I wondered how German Lutherans and Catholics would honor Hitler, a professed Catholic, if he should die. He has murdered or caused to be murdered hundreds of innocent people. Yet all of us diplomats would be called into the churches to pay tribute to him as a Christian in case of his death.

I came away from the Cathedral at 12:20 rather relieved to be free from so much hypocrisy. Some people may not feel as I do. To me the actual teachings of the simple, direct-minded

Jesus were exceedingly important and early Christianity really democratic. Now neither the Catholics nor the Protestants believe in, nor practice, Christian or democratic principles. Since my college days, when I was president of the Virginia Polytechnic Institute student Y.M.C.A., I have come slowly to recognize the insincerity of people who call themselves Christians and I have been compelled out of honesty to cease attending church services, save on certain official occasions. If men were Christians there would be no war, also none of the terrible exploitations which our business men have applied to our people.

May 21. Tuesday. At eight o'clock I went to the Kroll Opera House near the old, discredited Reichstag Building to hear Hitler speak to the world about his situation and his policy as Fuehrer. I was five minutes early, but all the seats in the diplomatic reserved section, except one, were taken: the French, Italian, British, Japanese, and Polish Ambassadors in the front row. Madame von Neurath and Madame Cerruti had taken two front-row seats, so there was none for me. Von Bassewitz placed a special chair at the end of the row for me, but the chair was not comfortable-looking, and knowing the speech was to last two hours I took the one vacant seat in the third row, very undiplomatic but comfortable.

The Chancellor began promptly. For twenty minutes he talked about the German economic situation, without real understanding. Then he discussed the German situation at the close of the World War (assuming that his country was entirely innocent of any wrongdoing) and the wicked Versailles Treaty. I noted the self-consciousness of the French Ambassador, especially as he spoke of the Fourteen Points of 1918-19. The last hour of the address dealt severe blows to the League of Nations and Communism. He was not far wrong in this either, but exaggerated greatly the faults of both. He did not indicate, as formerly, his willingness to return to the League in case of the granting of equality, so often discussed since October, 1933.

What Hitler said about Lithuania and eastern border troubles revealed more freely than he intended his real purpose never to surrender his hope of annexations. Many times he has said that colonies would not be worth anything to Germany, as Dr. Schacht so often insists they would, and that therefore annexations of regions of half-industrialized peoples like Lithuanians, western Poles and Esthonians must be made. His reference to a Lithuanian annexation was veiled but it brought the wildest hurrahs of the whole evening. Similar references to Austria brought equal applause.

There was nothing said which directly indicated German war purposes. The references to a navy equal to 35 per cent of British strength and the suggestion that England and France ought to enter into an agreement with Germany to limit aircraft suggested two approaches to an agreement with England which I think pleased the British Ambassador. It is quite possible that Hitler might be compelled to come to some international agreement, if the other powers are wise enough to make careful moves. But they will not do this.

Earnest and emphatic as Hitler appeared, he certainly does not fool me. He once avowed to me that he would throw any German official into the North Sea if he sent propaganda to the United States and when I arrived in New York during the last days of March, 1934, his Consul General brought me a cabled order to German officials in America to the same effect. I gave the order to the State Department. But there are now 600 employees in the foreign propaganda division now active in Berlin. Nor was there any let-up in the United States in 1934, although perhaps the Consuls for a time suspended open activity. This is one of many evidences of the complete insincerity of their promises. Much as I dislike the thought, I believe all the powers of Europe must unite and keep united and armed to the limit, unless they soon give the Chancellor an ultimatum compelling him to cease arming beyond a certain point, and his response to that might mean the outbreak of war.

VII

May 22, 1935 to November 25, 1935

May 22. Wednesday. I had an interesting talk at noon today
with Armand Bérard. He frankly said: "France is perturbed,
especially at England's acceptance of Hitler's promises as sincere. We cannot believe he is pacific, but the French people
will not go to war. We made a pact with Italy last year, much
as we disliked Mussolini, simply to stop German aggression
and we had to promise him the annexation of Abyssinia. I
hope Mussolini has sense enough to annex a little of the country at a time, as we did in Morocco. We have urged that upon
the Italians. They may not observe this and precipitate trouble." This is the European way. I was a little surprised at his
frankness.

He then said: "Laval, our Foreign Minister, wishes to come
here and talk with Hitler. My Ambassador is leaving for Paris
tonight in order to stop this if possible. We do not think any
agreement with Germany can be made." I think some agreement could be made if France agreed that Austria might be
annexed, and that would mean later attempts to annex Czechoslovakia and Hungary. Of course the French do not like to
think of a Third Reich of eighty million people.

Monsieur Bérard then said that France is soon to reduce the
value of the franc in order to check gold shipments to New
York—over a million dollars this week, a carload on the *Washington* today! But this devaluation will not change British or

American devaluation attitudes. Washington wished to stabilize when I was there. Now there seems to be no wish to do it.

At 4:15 I talked with Sir Eric Phipps who seemed quite a bit pleased at the reactions of the London press to what we heard Hitler say last night. I was not surprised. The British seem to have fallen for the Fuehrer's proposals. If they keep on like this, six months from now there will be no real disarmament agreement, and Germany will be far more completely prepared for another 1914 stroke than now.

We talked a little about the possibility of influencing the Germans to stop their ruthless and cruel treatment of the Jews. Poor Rabbi Lazaron of Baltimore has been here three months, coming to my office far too often, and hoping always to get a hearing with Hess or Goering. Not a chance in the world! I have warned him that he had perhaps better leave the country, as something might happen. Sir Eric said he would see Lazaron because he represents the leading Jews of England and the United States.

"But it can do no good," he said. "Hitler is fanatical on the subject and if you and I were to go to the Foreign Office to argue the matter there would be a sensation and perhaps a dozen Jews would be beaten, even killed, within a few days." I am not quite so pessimistic as that, but such a move would do no good at all. The Hitler Party is bent upon putting all the Jews out of Germany and confiscating their property.

May 25. Saturday. Louis Lochner sent me information from someone in the Foreign Office with whom he talks intimately that the German Government has a military alliance with Japan and that seventy army officers are coming here to coordinate their activities with German Army officials. Ilgner of I. G. Farben, the Chemical Trust, who has been in the Far East for a year, is said to have negotiated part of the pact and to have sold Japan vast supplies of war chemicals and gases. I have believed there was a secret pact of this kind for several months. While this story may not be true I am enough impressed to have telegraphed the State Department.

Rabbi Lazaron came in unwisely again, calling first on the

telephone. He was aware, though, of his danger and is getting away in a day or two. It would not surprise me if he should be arrested in Cologne or Frankfurt where Jews are being watched more closely than here. He reported that a good friend came to him this morning, very uneasy lest he be killed. I expect Jews to be put into prison and maltreated if not killed. Thousands are reported to be in concentration camps now, especially Jews who have returned. Lazaron goes to London in a week or two in the hope of influencing the British Government to ask the Germans to cease or limit their drastic behavior. I do not think any results can be obtained.

May 26. Sunday. I met Sir Eric Phipps for a walk in the Tiergarten. I gave him the confidential information about the Japanese. He was not as much impressed as I had expected. He said: "We have three army officers here studying German methods. That's not seventy, of course. It might be a serious thing for Japan to make such a pact, but I would not be surprised." After a good deal of talk about consequences in the Far East, he promised to inquire in London whether they knew of such a military alliance.

On the general subject of Germany's policy he was still optimistic and seemed to expect an air Locarno involving limitations and international inspection. I indicated my doubts, but said that if Germany makes a real concession and permits an international commission to pass upon such things it may mean real progress. I added: Have you heard that Germany is to help Poland get Lithuania, and Poland is to cut off the Baltic end of the Corridor so that East Prussia can be definitely connected through Danzig with Germany? He said: "No, but I would not be surprised, since Lithuania has been so foolish the last year." I agreed entirely as to her folly, but the German propaganda in Memel had a lot to do with the trouble.

Of course Germany's position in the Danzig zone is very difficult. But Poland for 150 years before 1914 was shamefully treated and exploited by Prussia, and by Russia too. Poland has some right to a bit of sea coast, especially when her population extends to the sea.

Sir Eric indicated that the English are more optimistic of German co-operation than I am. Perhaps the domestic situation in his country is responsible. The evidence that comes to me every day seems to show no change whatsoever in Germany's aggressive conduct.

May 27. Monday. I was a half hour with Dr. Schacht today to learn what he thinks about the existing economic dilemma in Germany. He was so enthusiastic about the effects of Hitler's May 21 speech that I learned nothing. Instead of expecting collapse next October he now says: "We shall go on successfully until next January, perhaps until the United States and England stabilize their currencies."

May 29. Wednesday. We had to go to the home of the Japanese Ambassador to dinner last night. A large company was there, including the Russian Ambassador, Dr. Schacht, and Von Ribbentrop, who expected to be put into Von Bülow's place, with Von Neurath going to London. Von Ribbentrop acknowledged that he goes to London on June 4 to negotiate a naval agreement, by which Germany is to have 35 per cent of England's strength. There was, of course, no worth-while conversation, but we were shown an hour's film about Japan which kept us rather late for me. We were the first to leave. The Japanese will return to Tokyo in a few days to remain five months, they said.

The Russian Ambassador said to me while we were a moment alone together: "Yes, I think there is a German-Japanese treaty, but I have no proof."

June 2. Sunday. We had a rather sad luncheon today. A young prince belonging to one of Germany's royal families spoke with deep feeling against the murders that were committed here last year. He said the Reichswehr officers are all against the present regime, but dare not open their mouths. I have other evidence in the same direction, but nobody ever says anything openly. The Prince spoke of the ruthless treatment of Professors Oncken and Hoetzsch, dismissed because they insisted on their right to express their opinions in their special fields. He said, "Our Kaiser never permitted such a thing to be done."

I recall a certain lack of freedom, when I was in Leipzig as a student, on the subject of the Kaiser. Otherwise there was considerable freedom in historical and philosophic fields. I remember that Mommsen once attacked Bismarck violently in the Reichstag and nothing was done to him. Such an attack now would cause one's death, or long term imprisonment. When the Prince went away all of us felt depressed for him. A liberal who would like to play some role in the affairs of his country, he can only serve as an officer in the army and he hates the idea of war.

June 8. Saturday. Lochner showed me a copy of secret instructions sent to the German press about the necessity of conciliating the Jews who supposedly have the world film business in their control. Goebbels had dictated this explanation to the press because recent instructions against Jews had been so drastic. Lochner said he could not send the report over the A.P. wires because it was so confidential.

June 13. Thursday. McMaster, the Quaker leader here since the World War, came in today to tell me about an eminent man in prison, Carl von Ossietzky, whom Jane Addams before her death recommended for the Nobel peace prize. He was editor of a German paper of liberal type, not unlike the *New Republic*, before Hitler came to power. It was at once confiscated and forbidden to appear and he was imprisoned early in 1933. He has been in prison ever since and frequently beaten, so McMaster reports. But he has been spared during the last few months. McMaster thinks him a very fine man, though perhaps his work was not important enough to justify the Nobel prize. Strange as it might appear, I believe Miss Addams' advice might wisely be accepted. It would emphasize *peace* so strikingly that all the world would discuss it for a month.

Another prisoner of the same character, about whom Professor Charles A. Beard has written me twice, is also still in prison but likely to be released. However, McMaster says he will not be permitted to leave the country—"he knows too much."

This McMaster is a unique man. He knows practically every high official here, he distributed millions of American dollars in food for the hungry in 1919-21, and has seen so much of the good and the bad of German behavior that he cannot be denied a hearing. Yet he said to me the last time he called: "Do not call me on the telephone or write letters under Embassy heading." So when I wish to consult him, I send a messenger with a note.

He is one of the most humane and useful men in Berlin. Von Hindenburg was a friend of his; Von Hindenburg's secretary, Meissner, is always glad to see him and report his requests to Hitler. But McMaster never reports anything as coming from me. Although the economic status here is very dangerous, McMaster says the regime will last a long time, unless the death of Hitler should occur. That is exactly my view, and if Hitler continues five years more in power, there is apt to be war. The German population is being trained to the limit for war, its national debt is piling up every day, like that of Italy, and both the Polish Corridor and Austria are expecting aggression.

June 14. Friday. Having been asked several times to speak before the Carl Schurz Verein, I accepted for this evening and went to Schadowstrasse No. 7 in the older part of the city. The hall was packed. I spoke on the Lincoln crisis in 1861 showing just how the Civil War began. My conclusion was that war rarely solves any problem. The enthusiasm of the Germans, including officials, was such that I concluded they are afraid of the Hitler war program. Since the American press asked especially for a copy, I am a little afraid my statements may be so printed over there as to arouse criticism. I shall wait and see.

June 15. Saturday. We had a score of guests at tea today, the most interesting being Sir Eric Phipps, who pulled me aside and said: "Our situation is very difficult, if not dangerous. The Germans insist upon their 35 per cent new navy and they are otherwise belligerent. Two months ago I talked with Hitler. He then demanded the same size navy as ours. I said you do not need so many ships since your coast line is so limited. He said: 'Yes, but we must have warships all over the Baltic Sea.' Later I argued with him and he was uncompromising, even impolite in his manner."

We talked a little about British-American relations in the Far East, both agreeing that co-operation of the two countries was about the only means of preventing a world war within a few years. "But public opinion in both our countries is opposed to any common action," he said. It was a sad conversation, the British Ambassador revealing more concern than I have before noted this year.

I told him I owed a letter to Lord Lothian, former secretary to David Lloyd George. He said, "Won't you write him frankly about the real situation here? It would do more good than one of my letters." I promised to do so. "Lothian," he said, "is a close friend of Lord Astor and the *Observer* people. They need some more accurate information."

June 21. Friday. I read a lecture tonight on the American Revolution before Professor Windelband's seminar. There was a large crowd. I spoke German and the students seemed to understand all that was said. There were five or six professors present, but no Hitler greetings were exchanged. My old professor, Erich Marcks, was present and asked some interesting questions when I finished. The discussion of certain phases of the Revolution continued almost an hour.

I omitted to note the fact that we had a luncheon today in honor of Charles R. Crane. Dr. Schacht was one of the guests and he took considerable interest in Mr. Crane particularly, I noticed, after I told him of Crane's business connections. Mr. Stewart of the State Department was also with us. His hope was to find some way to sell Germany some hundred thousand bales of cotton. Schacht gave him an appointment for an hour late in the afternoon. Schacht is even more anxious to buy than Stewart is to sell, but how to pay?

No man in Germany, perhaps none in Europe, is quite so

clever as this "economic dictator." His position is always delicate and even dangerous. When I saw him early in July, 1934,
his first remark was: *"Ich lebe noch"* (I am still living), which
I felt was rather dangerous. His wife says they "are on a train
going at full speed near the end of the road."

June 25. Tuesday. A foreign correspondent told me today
his conviction that both England and France are absolutely
opposed to any move that may lead to war, even if Germany
were to annex Lithuania, and that Hitler is bent on dominating
the Baltic Sea, annexing what he wishes on the east side of
that sea in order to block Russian expansion. He said he had
seen a letter received by Lord Rothermere a month ago from
Hearst in which the latter had urged a German-English-Amer-
ican alliance. This would permit the domination of the world
by these nations. Lord Rothermere was reported not too hopeful of the scheme.

He then said he had heard in Paris that Germany and Japan
have a secret entente, to be used any time Germany chooses to
move in the Baltic area. If Russia protests, or becomes involved
in war with Germany, Japan will attack her eastern frontier.
Finally, he attached great importance to a conference about
to take place in Paris between Laval, Litvinov, Titulescu of
Rumania and Beneš of Czechoslovakia. It is to conclude a pact
between France, Czechoslovakia, Rumania and Russia to block
Hitler's plans in the Baltic area.

It is not a little curious, but no German official has ever intimated to me a German desire for an understanding with the
United States.

Douglas Miller, our Commercial Attaché, asked today to
send a long telegram under my name. It explained a meeting
he had had the day before with leading German industrialists
who think they can pay for 600,000 bales of cotton in goods
which American firms wish to import, Montgomery Ward and
Company of Chicago being one of the main importers. This is
in disregard of the boycott by the Jews and the labor people.
I sent the telegram, giving the facts but making no recommendation, since that would involve the State Department in

some responsibility for the credit New York banks are propos-
ing to give. Having failed always to get any real consideration
when I have asked for payment of the two billions on which
the Germans pay no interest, I could hardly say anything now
even though payment seemed rather promising. $30,000,000
would be something of an item.

The last thing on this busy day was a visit to the Minister
from Holland. He is convinced, as I am, that there is an entente between Germany and Japan, but he has no proof. Of
England's position he was as skeptical as I am. Both of us are
of the opinion that England and the United States might stop
Japan's annexation of China if they co-operated. Curiously
enough the English-speaking peoples do not like each other
though neither ever thinks of direct hostility toward the other.
He thought the British-German naval pact of a week or two
ago a dangerous thing though he approved of the Russians
being held firmly in their isolated position. Germany will control the Baltic absolutely, Turkey will never allow Russia
access to the Mediterranean, and Japan watches Russia's little
front on the Pacific like a hawk.

Before leaving I suggested that he ask his government to
make approaches to universities in the United States for exchange professorships. I told him I would suggest the same to
Chicago where such lectureships are always welcome. He
agreed at once, saying that if our peoples could know each
other better and the English could also co-operate, we might
do something for peace. I suppose all such moves are useless,
yet one dislikes to do nothing in a world in such a dangerous
position.

July 4. Thursday. At 5 o'clock hundreds of Americans living
in Berlin and Americans visiting Germany came to our annual
reception, some of them very interesting people. I made a short
speech at 6:15 on *The American Idealists of 1776.* This address had been written for delivery at a dinner tonight of the
American colony, but the dinner was called off, and since
American press people had wired copies to the United States,
I felt I had to deliver it sometime today. The guests stood

fifteen minutes while I delivered it and some wealthy Americans declared they agreed with my comments on the great leaders of American history who have represented the principles of 1776: Lincoln, Wilson and F. D. Roosevelt.

July 6. Saturday. At noon I saw Secretary von Neurath for half an hour, the State Department having requested information by wire on reports which I had sent in the last pouch. Von Neurath talked freely about the British-German agreement on naval armament.

"Germany is proud of the good understanding and hopes France will co-operate," he said, "but I do not think we could enter the League of Nations even if England and France agreed to an anti-Italian war policy. We would, however, give moral support because we think Mussolini's war plan very foolish. Yet he must go to war since he can do nothing new at home. If he does not fight he is in danger. If he does go to war against Abyssinia, he can hardly win anything worth while and may even be defeated, which would mean his overthrow. I know him well and am sure he will not change his attitude, no matter how much England, France and even the United States may protest."

When we talked of the recent German-Polish conference here, he said, "We are on the best of terms. Our object was to defeat the French-Russian pact and prevent the Danube agreement proposed at Stresa. There were no Hungarian alliance or agreements discussed." This he said in spite of the fact that the chief of staff of the Hungarian Army was here under cover. "Nor was there any agreement with Poland about our control of the Baltic Sea. We must control that area to keep Russia off the ocean." That is the historic German policy, though Kaiser Wilhelm II allowed the Russian fleet to sail around France, Spain and Italy on its way to fight Japan in 1905.

When the Secretary referred again to a British-German entente and I asked about the coming naval conference, he expressed much hope that all nations would meet together and agree on naval reductions, "but we cannot join the conference if Japan refuses to attend." This surprised me a little because I had not expected such an open hint of a German-Japanese entente. He stated this with a positiveness that confirmed my belief that there was an alliance.

Japan must dominate the Far East and capture Vladivostok. Germany must dominate Europe, but first the Baltic, and if Russia resists, Japan will attack the Russian eastern border. This is certain to happen if the League of Nations fails. Then France and Italy will become minor powers and the Balkan zone will become subordinate to Germany, with Russia hemmed into her old historic position. Finally the United States will have to bring both Americas into co-operation or be subordinated.

July 8. Monday. The Germans celebrate Sabbath days with soldiers drilling and marching. Yet Hitler always declares he will never allow war. Perhaps some of these poor fellows dread the dangers of a European conflict, but most of them think warfare something that ennobles the German character. It is the one way in their minds to serve one's country.

July 11. Thursday. I did not want high officials here to know I wished to see Von Ribbentrop, the personal negotiator of Hitler, about naval and other agreements with England. I had heard that the Foreign Office had shipped Baron Lersner, a former Army official, to London to spy on Von Ribbentrop while he was there negotiating the naval pact. Lersner is a very shrewd man and one could hardly tell that he is a German, he speaks English so fluently. For these reasons I asked the Carl Schurz Verein secretary to invite Von Ribbentrop to meet me there today at 12 o'clock.

We talked half an hour. His answers to questions paralleled everything Von Neurath said except on the subject of Japan. Three times I managed to ask him about Germany's position in case Japan refused to take part in next year's naval discussions, on expiration of the Washington Treaty. He evaded answering every time. He did this in a way which made me think there is a German-Japanese treaty. He expressed the hope twice that I would press upon Washington to urge France to co-operate with England and Germany in navy matters. I mentioned the matter in a telegram, but did not give personal advice. There was little else discussed.

It is commonly said here that Hitler will soon assume the Foreign Secretary's functions, as Mussolini has done, and that Von Ribbentrop will then become the real and active Secretary for Foreign Affairs. In that case, I should be still further embarrassed. It would be most disagreeable to see Hitler himself when important messages from Washington were sent. I could not stand it long.

July 12. Friday. At 12:30 I sat down for a half hour with the French Ambassador to ask about some problems I had discussed with Von Ribbentrop. He said he thinks there is an understanding with Japan whereby the Germans will lend indirect aid in case of any war. He said: "I think this, but have no proof. As to naval co-operation, France cannot think of it. We must build new warships to keep pace with the new German navy. As to Mussolini, I do not think he will go to war with Abyssinia." The Ambassador's reason was clear: Mussolini could not afford to take the risk of a great setback, for then Germany might easily seize Austria.

July 14. Sunday. We had a most interesting luncheon party. Paul Scheffer of the *Berliner Tageblatt* and Louis Lochner of the Associated Press were the most interesting guests. Scheffer, who edits the once famous liberal paper read all over Germany, is well informed. He was once well known in the United States and he traveled with Roosevelt on his famous campaign of 1932, but he had to come home after Hitler suppressed so many newspapers and denied liberty to those which survived.

Scheffer said: "The readers of newspapers in all Germany have declined in number by more than six millions since 1933." His paper has about a tenth of the subscribers it once had, and he barely earns his living. His wife and children are living in Washington and supporting themselves, no one being permitted to send money out of this country.

He said he had heard the day before that at the last Cabinet meeting the economic situation of Germany was solemnly dis-

cussed. The demand of Goebbels was that Dr. Darre, the Agricultural Minister who is an extremist, be made economic dictator in place of Dr. Schacht. Von Schwerin-Krosigk, Finance
Minister, and Von Neurath opposed Goebbels. Schacht said: "I
cannot be sure we shall succeed, but I cannot change my policy.
I shall stand my ground even if put to death." When Schacht
sat down, Hitler rose and said: "Often as we disagree, Dr.
Schacht, I shall not permit any such thing to happen to you."
Goebbels, who hates Schacht to the *n*th degree, was defeated.

July 17. Wednesday. We sat down to dinner tonight with
the French Ambassador, twenty miles out of town on Lake
Wannsee. It was a beautiful evening. The leading guests were
the Papal Nuncio in his blood-red frock, the Italian Ambassador who is about to leave for Paris, the Belgian, the Austrian
and the Swiss Ministers. But the tone was rather solemn. The
Nuncio talked about the increasing violence against the Catholics all over Germany. He expected trouble. The Pope had
just published a denunciation of the German violations of the
Concordat of 1933 guaranteeing Catholic freedom. The Austrian said that the drift in his country was toward restoration
of the Hapsburgs, but that this would cause danger, if not intervention, from Hitler. The Italian assured the French that
"nothing would halt Mussolini." This reversed a French statement to me a few days ago. We came home about 12 o'clock
none too happy. It was an interesting evening, though diplomatic food does not agree with me.

July 18. Thursday. I called on Secretary von Bülow to get
the German view on the Italian-Abyssinian conflict and to learn
what the German authorities would do if Washington pressed
for enforcement of the famous Briand-Kellogg pact against
war. The Secretary was quite positive that Mussolini would go
on, that Germany would hold aloof, and that pressure for the
Briand-Kellogg pact would do harm. It was clear to me that
Germany hopes the Italians will go to war and lose. That will
give Germany her chance in the Balkans. It was plain that Von
Bülow would be embarrassed if the United States pressed its
peace ideas.

In the afternoon the *Berlin Am Mittag* carried glaring red ink headlines calling attention to Goering's declaration of war upon the Catholics. Henceforth they are to have no freedom of speech, no right to have youth organizations, and no right to criticize anything.

July 21. Sunday. We drove out to Neudeck and I sent my card into the palace of the deceased President. After a few minutes, Paul von Hindenburg and his wife met us a little way from the house and we walked about the old estate for an hour. There were 12,000 acres of very good land, a great barn for 150 horses, cows enough to produce a hundred gallons of milk a day, 500 sheep and wide fields of wheat, rye and barley. It is a great estate which Von Hindenburg's ancestors had owned for 200 years. The Hitler Party had bought the greater part of the land now included and given it to the President in the hope of gaining his support. This is the common story. Anyway Von Hindenburg sanctioned autocracy in January, 1933, and never protested publicly when Hitler's aide, Goering, set fire to the famous Reichstag building, about the time the Fuehrer took office as Chancellor.

Knowledge of these circumstances embarrassed me a little, but the son was most agreeable and showed us the marvelous house and its interesting paintings and sculpture, all rather warlike. They then begged us to remain for dinner, but we declined. There was not a picture or bust or flag of Hitler in or about the place. The Kaiser's likeness was most conspicuous in the Hindenburgs' library. Frederick II's picture was equally attractive. A painting of Ludendorff was also there, though the two generals are said to have been bitter enemies all their later years.

July 22. Monday. A long, fast drive to Berlin. The trip showed how prosperous the whole region north of Berlin seemed to be. I have never seen such wonderful grain crops. Even the Polish crops are extraordinary. I cannot help thinking Germany will have plenty to eat next year and a reasonable surplus for war emergency. But the journey did not cure my digestive ailment. Stopping at the office, I found many letters and documents awaiting my attention.

July 23. Tuesday. Too unwell for office work, I remained in bed until late in the afternoon when Henry Haskell, editor of the *Kansas City Star*, came to tea. I listened to him describe the attitudes of leading American papers of the Middle West. He predicted Roosevelt's re-election, but he is doubtful of the constructive work necessary for a real recovery from our economic troubles. The party situations are that the Republicans are divided hopelessly and without a single leader of any real promise while the Democrats are only a little more united, Roosevelt being the only man who can hold liberal groups together and thwart the extremists of left and right.

What he said about Farley was most deprecating, but he added, "We cannot in years to come get on without chiefs tied in with city politicians, almost American Fascists." From the one independent, liberal paper in the West this is a sad comment. One paper in St. Louis, the *Post-Dispatch*, is perhaps of the same temper. The politics of the United States is certainly none too appealing.

July 24. Wednesday. When I entered the office, I was informed that officials of the Von Steuben Society of New York, ally of the Carl Schurz Foundation here, and financed by the Oberlaender Trust Fund of Philadelphia, had so affronted members of our staff, our consulate members, and our press people at the *Bierabend* given last evening that no one would attend the dinner this evening at the Kroll restaurant. Mr. White asked to be excused from going to Magdeburg tomorrow where he was expected to speak in honor of Von Steuben. Our Military Attaché, Captain Crockett, called me on the phone and asked to be excused. He could not attend a meeting of American travelers here who insulted American citizens and officers.

The question I had to answer was: Shall I keep my fortnight-old promise to be at the dinner and speak briefly tonight? Since all other members of our official group had given notice they would not attend the dinner, it seemed to me that if I declined at the last minute, though I was really half-sick, it might appear as a diplomatic affront and perhaps receive publicity of an unfavorable nature. I decided to go, especially as Ambassador Luther was to be present. But I determined to make a careful, brief speech advising them not to indulge in offensive propaganda and to remember who Carl Schurz was.

Ambassador Luther came to see me in the morning. We talked half an hour and said nothing. I could not say anything about conditions in Germany without being critical. He could hardly say anything about things in Washington without being critical. He did talk somewhat freely because Americans do not resent rational criticism. Acknowledging that neither of us had really done anything, he said farewell. He is sailing for New York on August 1. He is a conservative and quite agreeable. I intimated that both of us ought to resign.

My wife and I went to the dinner. There was a company of about a hundred Germans and Americans. I sat down by the side of Mr. Hoffman, the chief of the Von Steuben crowd, the man who had spoken so offensively last evening. At the appropriate time, Hanfstaengl spoke for the German official element, repeating what he had said two weeks before when the International Chamber of Commerce people gave a dinner at the Adlon Hotel. I then spoke briefly and urged the German society to cultivate friendly relations between the two countries by exchanging lectures of distinguished scholars and scientists, by stressing cultural relations and university connections and, above all, by opposing war moves or attitudes. I even stressed free press relations and the value of publishing the truth so that people could know what was actually going on all over the world. There was some hearty applause as I closed, and some significant silence.

Hoffman followed with an offensive description of what he said had been the American attitude toward Germany. Although he did not again attack the American press, he did attack the Wilson plan at the end of the World War and he treated the American boycott as though it had no provocation from the German side. I was insulted but I did not get up, nor did I say anything that could cause hot discussion. Hanf-staengl criticized Hoffman in private conversation. It was the most disagreeable meeting I have attended since I came here in 1933.

July 25. Thursday. Minister Gie of South Africa came to ask me whether evidences of unrest in Germany indicated another "shoot-up" like that of June 30, 1934. We discussed the idea for some time and concluded that it all depended on whether Hitler yielded to the demand of Goering, Goebbels and Darre to dismiss Dr. Schacht. As yet I have no evidence that Schacht is to be dismissed, but if I were Schacht and had any money in the bank at Basle, where he is a director, I would leave Germany and stay away as long as the Nazi regime lasts.

July 26. Friday. At 11 o'clock, I held a conference with members of the Embassy staff, Mr. White, Mr. Lee, Mr. Flack and Mr. Beam, all close students of events here, also Miller, our Commercial Attaché, Steere, our Agricultural Attaché, and Captain Crockett as well as the Naval Attaché. We made an interesting survey which revealed ample evidence of sharp differences of opinion in the German Cabinet. Darre wishes to control economic policy and confiscate the wealth of all Jews, great industrialists and great landlords in order to place the unemployed on farms and train the army for service at any moment. Miller said Schacht is dead against confiscation and that Hitler supports him.

Captain Crockett, after traveling all about Germany, says the country is covered with barracks, training grounds and air-fields, and that munition plants are now scattered all over the country, especially in residential sections of big cities. He added that army officials had reported 2,000,000 volunteer soldiers now awaiting their turn on the drill grounds, that the plan is for 8,000,000 to be ready for service within three or four years. To my surprise, army officers of high rank are supporting confiscation of wealth to be used for army equipment, drills, and uniforms. This is contrary to former army attitudes. It may mean that Hitler will yield to Darre who is supported by Goering and Goebbels. That would put Schacht out of office. With him would go Von Neurath, Von Schwerin-Krosigk and others of the moderate wing. The effect? No one can tell.

This was also a day for letters from home. Colonel House wrote from his summer residence in Manchester, Mass., that he hoped I would resign in October and return home where I might render better service than here. I am inclined to retire but do not wish to do so until next spring. There is nothing one can do here, much as one may try. I replied to Colonel House indicating how difficult it would be for me to do anything there: I am not fitted for expert work in the government and any speeches I might make would probably be embarrassing, as was revealed last winter when I spoke in Baltimore.

August 2. Friday. Yesterday there was a riotous attack in New York on the German ship, the *Bremen,* its flag being thrown into the Hudson River. Senator King recently offered a resolution in Washington asking our government to sever diplomatic relations. And President Green of the American Federation of Labor called on all Americans to cease commercial relations with Germany. If this is not enough to make our relations with Germany critical, I do not know what could make them critical.

August 3. Saturday. A correspondent came to me this morning and reported that an official of the Reichswehr met him by appointment last night and said: "Conditions are worse than you have reported and the propaganda people know it. Between 50 and 150 Stahlhelm people have been killed in Saxony in the last few days as they resisted arrest. How many S.S. men who tried to arrest them were killed I do not know." This information came from Von Reichenau's office, a general soon to be sent to one of the provinces to command a division of the new army. I am not sure of course whether this story was told to get the correspondent to make a "blunder" or whether it is genuine. We shall not mention it in our telegram of today.

We sent a telegram about the dismissal of Italian and Swiss press correspondents this week and the threats to two Dutch news men. Their lives are not safe here, according to the Dutch Legation.

August 6. Tuesday. Martha and I arrived today at Budingen Sanitarium, in Constance, for the purpose of a real vacation.

August 26. Monday. After three weeks in Constance, I set out for Berlin this morning. The ship took me to Friedrichshafen in two hours. Another hour and I was at Ulm, but had no time to stop and look over the famous medieval city. I reached Augsburg in time for lunch. Then I wandered about the marvelous old city. The most striking thing I saw was the Jacob Fugger bank and business house. The whole building covers at least two acres of ground, more than eighty yards fronting on the leading street of the town. It was all so interesting that I bought a biography of the first Morgan of modern Europe. Looking into five or six bookstores, I saw only two Nazi books: *Mein Kampf* and Rosenberg's banned book on Catholicism and the new German faith. Nor did I see more than five Hitler flags.

This reminds me of similar evidences noted in Constance. The last week I was there, solemn warnings of the German Government against Catholics and any sort of criticism of the Hitler regime were posted about the streets of the ancient town. Within three or four days all were torn down, although such an act is treason under German law. On August 25, I went to the Munster Catholic church. There were not enough seats for the people, scores standing through the service. The sermon began at 9:15 and the preacher very cleverly criticized the German Government, calling upon all Catholics to train their children, to profess publicly their faith and to let everybody know their loyalty. At 11 o'clock, I went to the St. Stephen church where hundreds of German soldiers had reserved seats. I expected a sermon of the Nazi faith or perhaps a Catholic endorsement of Hitler's system. The church was even more crowded than Munster, but the sermon was much the same as the other.

The aisles were full of people who could not find seats. I asked those standing near me about this extraordinary church attendance. The reply was: "It is this way all the time and with all the churches." Constance is certainly religious-minded. If the eight or ten other churches were as well attended, there must have been more than 20,000 worshipers that day. I was not able to attend a Protestant church, but reports were, "they are equally well attended." Germany for once in the last half century seems really religious, or is it an expression of political opposition silently registered through the Church?

At 11 o'clock I took a sleeper for Berlin. I was quite tired, but greatly impressed with the spirit of the people in South Germany. I saw no demonstrations of Nazi enthusiasm, and very few flags anywhere. Farmers and small townsfolk seemed very busy and prosperous.

My three weeks off duty and on a strict regime of diet, massages and exercise did considerable good. My headaches had almost ceased. However, I think it was more relaxation, exercise and sunshine than anything else.

August 27. Tuesday. In Berlin at 8 and in the office again at 10. A pile of letters lay on my desk. The new Italian Ambassador called to pay his respects to the American Government and to talk about a Jewish difficulty he has on his hands here. A prominent Italian art collector who had decorated German Government buildings is now to be expelled from Germany but forbidden to take any of his property with him. The Ambassador asked about my experiences in similar difficulties. I could not encourage him. I let him know that I had tried often to persuade Hitler people to cease their violence and ruthless treatment, but said, although the Foreign Office officials had tried to do something, there had been no results. He also reported that there was no genuine feeling for support of war in his country.

September 4. Wednesday. Mr. Williams of the *Christian Science Monitor,* a friend of Lord Astor, is here after a visit to London. He reported that England is about to make a loan to Germany. I have heard already that such a thing is on foot, Schacht being active in negotiations. The English are in a very dangerous position as Italy goes on with her war program. If pacifist England does not actually begin war or threaten Mussolini, she will lose the Suez Canal.

September 9. Monday. We had a luncheon with the interesting Dr. Schmitt, former Minister of Economics, as the honor guest. Schmitt was an able, courageous German who often spoke his mind in public addresses. He is now head of an association of insurance companies, but the fact that he still lives in Berlin has not been announced in a single paper. His talk today revealed his hope, a common hope here, that Germany and England would never again come into conflict. He is strongly opposed to Mussolini's war moves. The Egyptian Minister was also with us—his outstanding fear is that Italy intends to conquer the Suez Canal Zone and control Egypt. "I have warned the British for a year that this is the object of the Duce," he said.

September 14. Saturday. Mr. and Mrs. S. R. Fuller called at the house today. Mr. Fuller, who is a friend of President Roosevelt, owns large rayon interests in Tennessee, is connected with Dutch and Italian interests manufacturing rayon, and is also a part owner of similar corporations in Germany, including a large industrial plant in Hanover. He is not allowed to go into this plant any longer. "The German Government is probably making use of our inventions and does not wish me to know it," he said.

The Dutch Minister called. He said three Dutch Jews engaged in business here had been ordered to close their shops, leave the country and not take their property. "I went at once to the Foreign Office and reported that my government would confiscate the property of three Germans in Holland if the Germans confiscated the property of the Dutch Jews. I was promised the matter would be delayed until January 1."

September 19. Thursday. The new Italian Ambassador Attolico called. He reported interesting facts about the Nürnberg meeting which he was practically compelled to attend. Hitler set forward the date of his formal reception so as to see him the day before the show began and invite him personally. He said he went and really liked it better than he expected. His belief is that Germany begins to worship Hitler. I agreed to the extent of 40 per cent of the people. They consider Hitler a sort of Jesus Christ and show a semi-religious attitude, but I am convinced that the Catholics are not even half Hitlerite. Half the Lutherans are perhaps submissive, but the Evangelicals (Calvinists) are not one third sympathetic. The Ambassador talked quite a while about Mussolini whom he does not like at all, though he did not say so. He is opposed to the Abyssinian war but only showed this indirectly.

September 25. Wednesday. Sigrid Schultz came to talk about the drift of things. She told a curious story of a German high school teacher being dismissed because he said to his history class that Frederick II made some mistakes. The man is not allowed to resume his teaching.

September 27. Friday. Hoping to get information about the Italian-Ethiopian war, about to break, I called on the French Ambassador. We talked half an hour but I gained only a little information about the French position. He is more concerned all the time about the German situation, also about the divided opinion in France over everything. He has no particular liking for the English.

I then went to the British Embassy where Sir Eric Phipps talked freely enough but gave no information except that he was very uneasy lest a war break out in the Mediterranean Sea, where one of his sons is an officer on a warship. He agreed that Mussolini really aims at getting control of the Suez Canal and of Egypt. That means the beginning of the decline of the British Empire, not unlike the decline of Holland after 1713, I said. He did not say "no" and I did not press the point for discussion. It is plain to me that if Italy wins the struggle against Abyssinia, the League of Nations will mean nothing in the future and England's position will be increasingly difficult. What a pity to have the leader of modern civilization lose its power and prestige! The land of Shakespeare and Milton going under.

October 7. Monday. I had a curious official talk today with Dr. Dieckhoff about the 1923 treaty with the United States, article 7 of which was denounced a year ago without any consultation with me. It was done a year ago in the hope that the United States would be pressed into amending the treaty favorably. That has not happened, and today we sat down together solemnly and signed duplicate documents confirming the annulment of the part of the treaty which gave Germany the only prospect of lower tariffs on her goods exported to the United States. We signed our names and after friendly regrets on both sides, parted.

It was a little strange that Von Neurath had made a point of being out of town for several days when it was his business to hold this conference with me. I had notified him two weeks before that I was ready to call and sign with him. Secretary Hull had done the same with Ambassador Luther in Washington. I think Von Neurath wished to have Dieckhoff manage the matter as a sort of complaint to the State Department in Washington, perhaps as a rebuff to me because of my absence from the great Party show in Nürnberg. However, I gave no hint that I noticed the little jilt.

October 8. Tuesday. Ambassador Cudahy from Poland came in for greetings. He impressed me more favorably than any other diplomat we have seen. He was inexperienced when he came in 1933, but he has worked hard in his position and seems to me to be a useful representative of his country, even though he is a rich American. His story of things in Washington and Chicago was quite revealing. In spite of his privileged position, he is a real supporter of Roosevelt and wishes to go home in 1936 to canvass for him, perhaps to spend his money.

Cudahy's knowledge of Poland's position and relations with Germany seems to me to be good. He departed, urging us to drive up to Warsaw and spend a week with him. I could not promise. I have no time, much as I would like to go to poor Poland—its people so incapable of democratic government, even more than the Germans.

October 10. Thursday. We had former Ambassador Schurman to lunch today, with an interesting group of Germans who knew him when he was here. Schurman was president of Cornell University, succeeding Andrew D. White who had been Minister in Berlin under McKinley. Schurman was in Berlin from 1925 to 1930. He is now eighty-one years old and still a very active man. He was particular to ask me whether he should request an interview with Hitler. I declined definite advice because I thought he might call at the Foreign Office and it would then be polite for the Chancellor to invite him to call. When Schurman was here, he got Americans to give Heidelberg University a building and he was very popular. When he visited Berlin in April, 1933, Von Hindenburg invited him to call, and they had a long conversation about American affairs and German problems. Schurman quickly concluded not to call on Hitler, though not on my advice. I simply suggested he call on his acquaintances in the Foreign Office.

I came to my office a little late. I found the Russian Ambassador was coming in a few minutes. I had not seen him in some time. He is a very agreeable and clever man, but a Communist. Berlin almost ignores him, except for the French Ambassador. I was glad to see him. What he came for I could not guess, perhaps in the hope of meeting Ambassador Bullitt who is due tomorrow, but we had already made up our party and I had not thought the Russian would be comfortable since we had to have some eminent German officials. Anyway we talked nearly an hour and I learned what he hoped the League of Nations would do in spite of his sharp dislike of England. I intend to return his call soon.

October 14. Monday. Dr. Schurman brought a friend, Ben Smith of New York City, to see me. After a good deal of talk about conditions at home, Smith quite frankly remarked: "I am a New York speculator, but also a close friend of President Roosevelt." That surprised me a little: first, that he would acknowledge such a profession; second, that he had confidential relations with the President. Dr. Schurman told me, in an aside, as they were leaving, that his friend Smith was a clever speculator who violated all bankers' advice in 1929 and sold stock short in such enormous amounts as to make many millions. Was that patriotic?

October 16. Wednesday. I went at 5 o'clock to the Kaiserhof Hotel to attend a Nazi tea and to hear Hanns Kerrl, Minister for Church Affairs, explain the Party attitude to the Evangelical churches of Germany. Kerrl is supposed to succeed Reichsbishop Mueller who has made church matters exceedingly difficult, keeping scores of dissenting Lutherans in jail.

Many of the diplomatic people were present, the French, English, Italian and others, also many German professors and scientific people. Kerrl spoke for an hour and a half: The Nazi Party members are the true Christians of Germany and all church folk must ultimately become Nazi Christians. I asked a man who sat near me if Kerrl had ever read the Sermon on the Mount. My neighbor laughed but would not talk. Kerrl argued that Hitler had done for modern civilization what Copernicus had done when he discovered proof that the world was round, not flat as all Christians then believed. With all kinds of naïve arguments he carried the parallel to the limit. All the world, he said, would ultimately accept the Hitler idea as "our ancestors had ultimately accepted Copernicus." He preached a sermon calling upon us all to surrender to the new discovery.

The audience did not applaud except mildly at the close of the speech. Very few gave the Hitler gesture in response to the speaker's salute as he sat down. In my opinion, three-fourths of the audience did not treat seriously what had been said.

October 18. Friday. I sat by Dr. Schacht at luncheon today. Twenty people were there, some Americans and many Germans. Dr. Schurman was the guest of honor. Schacht indicated in rather sharp language his pro-Italian attitude and his great dislike of England and the League of Nations. "Why apply those sanctions to defeat Italy's legitimate demand for colonial possessions?" He showed no concern at all about the cruelty of seizing other people's territory and killing thousands of people. He did not protest against the attitude of the United States, but made it plain that he was opposed to it. He seemed to fear Italy would be defeated and, if so, that it would mean a sharp limitation on Germany when she comes to the point of seizing territory. He was more anti-League than I had ever noticed before.

October 20. Sunday. One has no rest here even on Sunday. I go to the office each Sunday about 10 A.M. There is always a radio report of events in Washington and the United States which one has to read closely. Sometimes there is a cable asking information, and half the Sundays there is a bunch of letters to be read, sometimes answered at once. Since the government furnishes no stenographer, I have to write very many letters by hand and Sunday is the best time.

Today Louis Fischer, of *The Nation*, New York, came directly from Moscow where he has lived for many years. Knowing the attitude of *The Nation*, I intimated early in our conversation that propaganda was the curse of our time. When he seemed a little troubled and asked what I meant, I told him the story of my experience with the New York Von Steuben Society which escorted about fifty German-American Nazis through Germany. This made Fischer's defense of propaganda difficult, for if Communist propaganda is right in the United States then Nazi propagandists have a similar right to press their philosophy upon our country.

Fischer was really puzzled to find a defense. We talked about the misrepresentations and omissions of history, and about the duty of each country to have its real history taught to its people. He was surprised at several facts of our history and it became clear that he had never really studied Jefferson. He did not know that Jefferson tried all his life to bring about gradual abolition of slavery. It was clear that, although a widely read reporter on Communism, he was less well informed about the history of the long struggle for democracy in the United States. He did not know what sort of propaganda Lincoln sent to England in 1862: Henry Ward Beecher and Harriet B. Stowe and a score of others. At 12:30 I was out for my hour's walk.

October 24. Thursday. Senator James Hamilton Lewis of Chicago, here a month ago, came back from Moscow where he was desperately ill some two or three weeks. I called on him at the Adlon Hotel. He looked quite feeble. He insisted on thanking me and my wife for sending a nurse to him from Berlin and especially for sending hominy grits to eat when he began to recover from pneumonia. He could find none in Russia and he could not digest other food for some days. It was a curious incident: At 12 o'clock one night when all of us here were in bed, there came a phone call from Russia through the *New York Times* office. It urged shipment of grits by aircraft next morning at 7:30. My wife was the only one in the house who heard the call. She answered and agreed to furnish two boxes if the *Times* man would call and take the boxes to the airfield. He agreed and the foodstuff was thus forwarded. The Senator insisted that we had saved his life.

October 25. Friday. Robert H. Jackson, a very able young lawyer from the Treasury Department in Washington, was one of my callers this morning. He talked freely of the great difficulty President Roosevelt has had to bring utility men and financiers to see what must be done if we are to escape another depression and a worse social dilemma. What he said about his chief Morgenthau was reassuring. The President knows his difficulty and is doing his utmost to avoid any moves that might lead to a Tory victory in 1936. He thinks Roosevelt will win, but fears the American people will not know what the economic situation is and elect a Congress which will be unwilling to cooperate in constructive work. That is my fear, even if Roosevelt should win with as big a majority as in 1932. Mr. Jackson seems to me to be the ablest and wisest man who has come here from the United States in a long time.

At 5:30 my friend Professor Wolfgang Windelband called and sadly informed me that he had been ordered to give up his position and go to Halle. He says he will resign rather than obey the arbitrary order. "If I went to Halle there would be Hitler Jugend demonstrations against me, no students would register for my work, and in a few months I would be dismissed." This looks to me to be a true explanation.

The embarrassed professor, indignant to the limit, wondered if there were a possibility of his finding a position in the United

States. I could not promise anything more than some friendly letters to American university presidents. We have so many unemployed young scholars at home that I could not give much encouragement.

Only a day or two ago Attaché Miller had brought me the story that the German Government had ordered automobile, typewriter and sewing machine companies in the United States to cease sending parts free of charge to their branch offices here. This means that the 60,000 American cars in Germany must be repaired by Germans who cannot reproduce patented parts. This will compel the owners of the cars to buy new ones of German make when their cars are in need of serious repairs. This looks like an American barrier of 1930 days, and is certain to cause agitation for further United States discrimination against German goods.

November 2. Saturday. I drove as unobtrusively as possible in a taxi to the office of Dr. Schmitt, former Minister of Economics under Hitler. Schmitt is the only real statesman I know in Germany who has held office under Hitler, though Schacht is a financial wizard of the highest order. I reported in all confidence the facts about Professor Windelband. He had not heard of the case, but he knew of the scheme of Rosenberg and Frank to force upon German universities the teaching and writing of propaganda instead of history. He said it was a crazy scheme but that Hitler was committed to it. However, he said he would try to influence Hitler when he saw him again, and then asked me to speak to Von Neurath. I said that would not do, as the whole thing was personal and in no way official. Schmitt agreed, however, that relations with the United States could not improve as long as such men as Rosenberg and Frank play the roles they do.

Schmitt then talked about the very dangerous position Germany is in, especially its financial situation, so long as so much of the national income is devoted to rearmament. He went so far as to say Germany was headed for war and that any war she might precipitate would bring upon his country a worse disaster than that of 1918-19. He argued that the only way of salvation for Germany lay in re-entrance into the League of Nations and renewal of better economic relations between Germany, England and the United States. I said National Socialism was contrary to such a policy. He agreed, but added that Hitler is more open to reason on this policy than ever before. Dr. Schacht, he said, had indicated a certain drift in that direction, contrary to what Schacht said to me the last time I saw him. I am certainly not convinced of this. Schmitt argued that Germany must have colonial possessions and that England was ready to grant these through the League if Germany returned. He said that Italy ought to be defeated because her invasion of Abyssinia was not the way to get new colonial possessions.

November 7. Thursday. At 7 o'clock, we sat down in a box of a Berlin theater with the French Ambassador and his wife. The performance was to be Goethe's famous *Egmont.* Hitler came on time, Goering by his side. The audience rose and cheered, but very moderately. They did not turn around in their places and heil Hitler as I had witnessed more than once before. Hitler looked our way and we bowed but of course did not give the Party salute.

Then the play began, Furtwaengler was again leading the orchestra; he had been restored to favor. For an hour it went on. It was well done. Then came the intermission. All guests moved in the direction where Hitler and Goering, our hosts, were supposed to be. They were not to be found, but Dr. Goebbels stood at the entrance to the Hitler stall to greet all who approached him. Most of us did, but there was of course no real conversation.

I asked Von Ribbentrop teasingly what he was doing to keep the peace of Europe. He said: "All I can," but he was in no sense communicative, though the common talk of the last week or two has been that he is negotiating with secret agents of Laval, the French Foreign Secretary. M. François-Poncet said to me: "There are negotiations; but I do not know what is up. However, nothing is to be expected within quite a time." I suspect something between France, England and Germany whenever Mussolini is brought to terms.

November 12. Tuesday. The next caller was Cornelius Lothrop, member, he claimed, of a famous Boston family of that name. He said he was unemployed at home and had come to Berlin to teach English to Germans. He wanted a gift of money to help him along until January 1, when he expected a position. I felt obliged to decline. Perhaps I was wrong, but so many people come for similar purposes, especially to sing.

In the afternoon John L. Spivak called, with a letter from a Chicago friend of mine, R. M. Lovett, to get possible information for a book about Italy, Germany and Poland. I asked, Why not Russia? As he won a national reputation last winter with a book on German propaganda in the United States, I felt that he must include Russia or his work would be regarded as anti-German and pro-Russian. He was a little surprised. But I gave him certain information, confidentially, and told him whom to see in Germany, and if possible to travel about the country speaking German and learning for himself. He was rather uneasy lest he be arrested and thrust into prison incommunicado. I was a little disposed to agree, since similar people have been thrown out of the country or imprisoned without trial.

November 13. Wednesday. Since we are so well acquainted, I asked the Dutch Minister today how he felt about meeting Hitler, Goering and Goebbels. He said he never had interviews with Hitler and never accepted invitations to their spectacles or entertainments. I have not talked with Hitler since February 6, 1934, or Goering since June of the same year. Goebbels had us to dinner in early June, 1934. It is rather difficult to remain in my position here and never have any of the triumvirate with us socially. They are the governors of Germany and I represent the United States here. But it is so humiliating to me to shake hands with known and confessed murderers. I am inclined to do the same as the Dutch Minister to the end of my service, May, 1936, as I now think.

November 16. Saturday. We lunched with the Italian Ambassador. The reception room was cold, about 60° Fahrenheit. The dining room was not much warmer. I was as uncomfortable as I had been in September at Professor Windelband's. The palace is a wonderfully elaborate and roomy house, representing a great cost for a country that owes the United States two billions or something like that and never even apologizes for not paying any part of the interest due. The furniture and paintings are very valuable, everything beautiful and in good taste, but I would be ashamed, if I were the Ambassador, to invite an American official to the place. I left early because I had a cold coming. I went to bed and took aspirin in the hope of fighting off another attack.

November 19. Tuesday. At 11:30 I called on the Soviet Ambassador here, in his magnificent palace, far greater than that of the Italian. But only one butler showed me to the office, other embassies having several such servants. He showed no disposition to take, or expect, a tip, the only place in Berlin where one does not give a half or a whole mark every time one calls.

The Ambassador had just returned from Moscow at a moment of uneasiness about the Japanese invasion of North China. I intimated that if the Russian Government had kept its promises of 1933, our President and the English Government might have made a joint protest in Tokyo, and that might have prevented this sort of aggressive conduct in North China. He did not say he agreed, but I was sure he did agree. I added: If these countries were to protest and threaten a boycott of Japan, the war would be stopped. He at once said he wished to cable my remarks to Moscow. I said: If you do, do not intimate that it is anything more than my opinion.

November 21. Thursday. An expert of the Department of Labor in Washington called for a short visit this morning. He is one of the many Americans who try to study Germany although they know no German. He seemed to be a well-informed official and by no means disposed to parade himself.

November 25. Monday. Ambassador Bullitt from Moscow came in this morning. He showed a real recovery from the disease which troubled him when he was here last September. His remarks about Russia were directly contradictory to the attitudes he held when he passed this way last year. Then he was to all intents and purposes enthusiastic. But Bullitt is the heir to a great fortune and was known as a liberal contributor to the Roosevelt campaign in 1932. My gift was $25.

One thing he told me which surprised me was that when he left Moscow last autumn President Roosevelt asked him to visit China and report on Japanese plans and activity in the Far East. He says now that China will make a terrible and determined resistance if Japan presses for domination of North China. One general alone there has 100,000 troops who will put the Japanese army out of existence. I do not accept this. Bullitt said Russia had no business trying to hold the peninsula which projects into the Japanese sea at Vladivostok. That is all going to be taken soon by Japan. I said: You agree that if the Germans have their way Russia with 160,000,000 people shall be denied access to the Pacific, and be excluded from the Baltic? He said: "Oh, that makes no difference." But I could not help adding: "You know this treatment of Russia over the last two hundred years has caused many wars." He replied only: "Ireland keeps England off the seas."

I was amazed at this kind of talk from a responsible diplomat who had done much to get Russia recognized in 1933. The President must know the man's mentality, but if so, how could he have appointed him Ambassador to Soviet Russia?

VIII

November 26, 1935 to February 1, 1936

November 26. Tuesday. I include a report from a French source about Schacht's troubles:

The trouble that Schacht is in is this: He began to question and investigate and think curious the number of German bank notes in foreign countries which he had not checked out. The exact financial details of this I didn't understand. Anyway he suspected something was wrong. So he began to investigate the loads of coal that went from Germany and discovered several old boxes, etc., concealed in the piles of coal which apparently the Jews had put there as a means of smuggling out their own money. However, even this did not account for the tremendous sums in other countries. He began to suspect an official leakage. So he marked with a special number and system some hundreds of thousands of marks in bank notes that went to Rosenberg, Himmler and Goebbels. These same bank notes turned up in foreign countries, revealing, with a little spy work, that these three men were financing their agents of propaganda abroad, not only with the money set aside officially for propaganda by Schacht but also with tremendous sums they could scrape together through other sources of income, not allowed, according to Schacht, to leave the country.

They have been pocketing these private funds and using them abroad for their agents. Schacht went in a fury to Hitler and told him the whole thing had to stop or Germany would be bankrupt. Hitler has not as yet taken sides but this is the reason that Schacht is in danger.

November 27. Wednesday. Max Warburg reported today that he and Dr. Schacht had not been able to do anything to relieve the Jewish situation. His information about the financial abuses here, especially the Goebbels group activity, was the same I had heard from other sources.

November 28. Thursday. Thomas J. Watson of New York City, business man with a salary amounting to $1,000 a day from several big corporations, spent an hour with me. Strangely enough, he is strongly Rooseveltian and convinced that if big business insists on defeating democracy in the United States there will be a revolution which may lose business men all they have. He favors income tax at rates like those of the British, which are very high, and he is for lowering tariffs. He is opposing the attitudes of Newton Baker and John W. Davis in their fight against the Federal Utility Act.

November 29. Friday. We dined with thirty other guests at the home of Herr Karl Trutz. Many people were present, some university men with their wives. Whenever the conversation bore at all upon the present regime here, great dissatisfaction was expressed. Not a favorable word was spoken. I was at one end of the dining room, my wife at the other. She heard nothing but critcism, so much that she did not venture any remarks that could reveal her attitude. I was perhaps a little freer. These poor German people!

To complete my hard day's work we all went to the Adlon Hotel as guests of the foreign press people to a supper and dance. Prince Louis Ferdinand went with Martha and even in our car, which I had gently discouraged. I thought his being with us might cause trouble to him. But he insisted. There was some surprise shown as we entered the large dining hall. Frau Sahm, wife of the dismissed Mayor of Berlin, sat on my right, the Mayor on the left of Sigrid Schultz, our hostess. These poor people were most unhappy and conversation was quite distressed. The Mayor was the foremost in German mayoralty service, thirty years at the head of cities. He was dismissed with the approval of Hitler because he was not an enthusiastic Party member.

Herr Lewald, the Olympic Games chief, sat opposite. Nor was he happy, news having come over that Americans might not participate in the great show next summer. We could not talk about that. But Lewald is a quarter Jew, a fact recently discovered here and published in the newspapers. I wondered what his real thoughts were. I was asked in January, 1935, by a German official in America to aid in securing permission of the United States War Department for the purchase of a new model of rifle made at the army arsenal in Springfield. This was a peculiar request because it seemed to me all such things should go directly through our War Department. The official said that the Olympic Committee wanted such arms for "training purposes."

The next table to us accommodated the British and Russian Ambassadors, who hardly spoke to each other, and Monsieur François-Poncet who seemed to be cordial to both. The poor Russian, perhaps the best intellect in the diplomatic service here, was left almost alone. Prince Louis Ferdinand went over to greet him though he had sent word to Miss Schultz that he could not sit at her table if the Russian were there, Communist executions of his Imperial kinsfolk in 1917 being the cause. It is my opinion the Russian Ambassador is not a proselytizing Communist. Von Neurath was equally indifferent, though he sat opposite the Russian. The last time we were at the Russian Embassy, Von Neurath was very cordial and many of the highest military men were equally friendly. At that time a treaty was being talked of and the old Bismarckian element of Germany has always been pro-Russian in a measure.

December 1. Sunday. There is no end to entertainments. At 9 o'clock we went to the Swiss Minister's place, where there were an enormous crowd and about fifteen musicians. For two hours we listened to Bach and other eighteenth century German music composers. It was exceedingly good, though my poor taste for that sort of art prevented my enjoyment to the full. To me Bach was the best. When the performers ceased their functions and received long applause, the crowd jammed into a dining room so crowded one could hardly move. They ate and drank for an hour, but I kept out of the room. Home again a little after 12 o'clock. I must say the Swiss Minister and his wife were, as usual, most agreeable and entertaining. They have been here many years, and are very much troubled now.

December 2. Monday. Our new Counselor is here and ready to take up the work Mr. White is leaving. The Counselor, Mr. Mayer, is from Indianapolis, and has served three years at Geneva. I accompanied him to the Foreign Office and introduced him to Von Bülow and Dr. Dieckhoff. We had a very agreeable conversation.

December 3. Tuesday. Sir Alexander Lawrence, a rather famous Englishman, was more than an hour with me. He understands German plans as well as any German outside the governing group. I raised the question of the British attitude on oil sanctions against Italy. He said he was in entire agreement and hoped his country, France and the United States would offer a solid front, compel Italy to surrender and try to force Mussolini's overthrow. He said he had a home for winter residence in the neighborhood of Florence, I believe, and that the people very frankly condemned and denounced the war scheme the last time he was there. He was convinced the people of Italy would gladly get rid of the Duce if they ever had a chance.

As to Germany, he said he was certain the scheme of Hitler's *Mein Kampf* to conquer a large part of Russia had not changed at all. He added that England was a lot more interested in Germany than Italy. Yet he agreed with Minister Eden who demands a boycott of Italy's oil supply until she collapses. He also expressed great hope that the President of the United States could co-operate.

I said: Yes, the sanctions would be useful and would probably be applied if England really did what she was discussing. I then raised the question of England's attitude toward Japanese aggression. He said: "Sir John Simon made our greatest blunder since the League began by refusing to co-operate with the United States when Manchoukuo was seized in 1931."

I talked then about the World War. He had no belief that Germany would have won even if Wilson had not entered the war in 1917. It was a peculiar attitude for an intelligent and highly experienced observer. Perhaps all Englishmen have overlooked the fact that France was about to collapse in March and April, 1918, just as 300,000 American soldiers were arriving each month. That stopped Von Hindenburg's and Ludendorff's great drive which began about March 18. No real obligation to the United States was recognized, nor have I ever heard a single Frenchman admit that Woodrow Wilson saved France, though all Germans say: "Wilson defeated us, the treacherous Wilson."

December 5. Thursday. Colonel Edward A. Deeds of Akron, Ohio, and New York City, president or director of twenty great American industrial concerns including the National Cash Register and the National City Bank, came to lunch today with a score of others, Americans and Germans, including James Hazen Hyde. Deeds had negotiated a deal with a German corporation for sending over our airplane patents so that the German company could manufacture and sell a hundred planes to Italy, the American company to share the profits. This seemed to me contrary to the spirit of the United States statute of neutrality which had been enacted last August. This sort of thing is done all the time in this European war atmosphere. I telegraphed a report of this deal to Washington a day or two ago. This news had come confidentially from a German aircraft man.

Deeds talked all the time as though he were a good Roosevelt friend and real American democrat. He is another of the rich men who hang around European industrial centers, like the Japanese, and sell war materials at high profits without fully considering the real interests of their country. How should one treat such persons who always claim to be enthusiastic friends? A score of people talked two hours but said nothing—one of the evils of diplomatic life.

December 6. Friday. We sat down to dinner with the famous Dr. Max Sering, a friend of Secretary Wallace and foremost agricultural economist in Europe. Frau Sering was on my left and Countess von Tirpitz, widow of the famous German Admiral who did so much to anticipate American participation in the World War, on my right. There was frank talk all the evening.

One woman openly hoped I would help prevent Americans from participating in the Olympic Games here next summer, a risky remark to make. Another was even more positive when, describing her residence in the mountains of Bavaria, she said she could never think of living in Berlin under such a regime as that of Hitler. She denounced the constant and amazing preparations for war. In spite of all her past connections with the autocratic Hohenzollern regime she said war was a horror and should never be provoked again. Her contempt for Mussolini was complete. I did not say much; but it was evident that almost all present were of the same attitude.

Before we left Dr. Sering and I talked together a few minutes. Getting off the general subject of complaint against the present regime, he said: "Germany's economic interests must spread over the Balkan zone, where there must be an exchange of industrial for agricultural goods." I did not say to him that under the policy of Hitler and the present barter system which works so badly, Germany produces so nearly all the foodstuffs she needs that the Balkan folk cannot sell their meats and grains here.

He added: "Of course political co-operation must follow." This was not discussed because I did not care to remind him that the old Kaiser's policy of expanding toward Constantinople was the chief cause of the World War. It is an instinctive policy of national-minded and even moderate Germans to annex parts of the Balkan states and dominate the others, just as Mussolini thinks the Mediterranean Sea and the countries bordering it are properly his, perhaps excepting France.

December 9. Monday. We dined at the house of the former Finance Minister, Dr. Dietrich, of the Bruening period. There were some thirty people present, former officials and university folk, and the sentiment was as critical and hopeless as at the two preceding dinners. Although there were some Nazi uniforms present, I heard not a single statement in praise of the present-day system. What can all this mean? Eminent official and unofficial people are all of the same mind even in the presence of Nazi officials. I cannot recall their names, as I cannot possibly remember German and French names unless I hear them pronounced several times.

The Minister of Rumania singled me out and talked almost violently about the Hoare-Laval proposition sent to Mussolini last Saturday and discussed in the press here today. He said his country was ready any time to apply oil sanctions to Italy, "and now, when all of us smaller nations and the United States are ready to stop oil shipments to Italy, England and France make a surrender without consulting us or the League." He was indignant.

I had heard previously that the reason for the Hoare-Laval proposition was the English-French fear that Communism might come to Italy in case Mussolini falls. I think this is probably partly true, and that Nazi Germany certainly wants to see Mussolini successful. Perhaps these two dictators have already made an agreement.

December 12. Thursday. These are busy days. Mr. Mayer and I called on Monsieur François-Poncet at 12 o'clock and remained half an hour. He mentioned to us the Hoare-Laval matter and thought Mussolini would make an agreement with England and France and so end the Ethiopian crime. I at once disagreed. If Mussolini does accept, which I doubt, it means control of the Mediterranean and collapse of the League of Nations. Mussolini thinks himself a Julius Caesar.

François-Poncet argued strongly for the Hoare-Laval proposition. I said: It's the biggest mistake since the World War. It means an Italian-German combination for redistribution of eastern and southern Europe, and such a combination cannot be defeated by England and France. Why did your governments not apply the oil sanction through the League with American co-operation and bring Mussolini to terms?

He said: "Mussolini would have made war even if the oil sanctions had been applied. We, the French Government, were unwilling to go to war, even if England were attacked." It was an honest, frank discussion and Mr. Mayer agreed with me at every point, which was significant since he had been at Geneva three years. As we came away, François-Poncet said: "Mr. Ambassador, you are too logical." Mr. Mayer said: "How can a Frenchman ever blame anyone for being logical?"

December 13. Friday. Mrs. Anne O'Hare McCormick, who writes for the *New York Times* so cleverly, came to ask for an interview with Hitler, having had one a year ago. Her husband was with her. They talked of their interview with Mussolini and said: "The Duce reported a conversation he had last spring with Sir John Simon, British Foreign Secretary. He had no liking for the English. Sir John sat in conference at Stresa with his eyes closed, perhaps asleep, until the Duce said: 'You know, all of you, that the Germans intend to annex everything to Bagdad!' That awakened the British Foreign Secretary."

Mrs. McCormick told other things about Italy and its policy, revealing that she was interested in the personality of the Roman dictator. I pointed out to her that the Caesarian boasts of Mussolini resembled the Frederick Barbarossa aims of Hitler, both men being ill-informed and highly romantic, at the same time cruel to the last degree. She saw something of my interpretation of things, but she was very hopeful of seeing the Fuehrer here. I told her we would suggest means of doing so, but were very doubtful since Hitler has refused so often the last few months. I suggested that she see Dr. Schacht who would talk more frankly.

December 14. Saturday. I learned last evening from a secretary of the French Embassy here that the British Ambassador had an hour's interview with Hitler and that he had pressed again the idea of a general peace agreement among all the greater powers including the Russians. Hitler pretended to be willing to come to an armament agreement with the Western powers, but broke into a furious denunciation of Russia, saying that Germany must go to war against the Communists, the wicked Communists, forgetting how much the Nazis here have learned from Communist propaganda. Nothing seemed to be agreed to, but two German officials were to depart soon for London. I suspect this has merely to do with the naval conference which can hardly amount to anything, Germany and Japan being united in naval matters.

I think Sir Eric Phipps was sent to Hitler as a sort of gesture to distract public attention from the terrible blunder of the Hoare-Laval proposition. However, the papers gave no attention to the incident but preached daily against the League of Nations for having tried to apply sanctions, as if there were any other way to stop a war except by applying them. For two months the German Foreign Office people had been amazingly silent, gently intimating now and then that Germany might apply sanctions if the United States continued its policy in that direction. The real thing was that Nazi Germany feared to take any attitude until she could see what happened to Mussolini whom Hitler hates, although he imitates him. All military and naval experts here report the utmost speed in German rearmament. They are building the greatest military machine in the world.

But now that England and France have taken a move that threatens to break up the League, every German paper rejoices and is almost willing to join Italy in her adventures.

At a tea gathering at our home this afternoon, the one subject of concern was the Hoare-Laval proposal and the abandonment of the sanctions policy of the League. The Russian Ambassador, the Rumanian and the Czechoslovak Ministers were in conference half the time. They said the small powers of the Balkan region would withdraw from the League if England's policy were applied: "There would be no safety for little states in Europe in a League which does not prevent annexations like that which Italy is attempting in East Africa."

December 16. Monday. Since Von Neurath was with Hitler when Sir Eric saw him, I called on him today. There were two ministers of small countries with the Foreign Secretary when I arrived, and they stayed fifteen minutes, talking about the Balkan attitude toward the recent English-French policy. One of them is on the way to Paris tonight.

Von Neurath was as agreeable as ever but gave no inkling of Germany's position. When I asked him what Germany would do if Mussolini annexed Egypt, he said: "Nothing." I then said: Palestine and Greece would fall into Mussolini's hands, isn't that true? He said: "Yes, but we shall do nothing even if England and Italy go to war." Since he is closer to Hitler now than at any time since I came to Berlin, this seemed significant. The real point, however, is as always here: "We are not yet armed."

December 19. Thursday. Colonel Claude A. Tupper, an engineer and business man from Chicago, was here for half an hour. He revealed conflicting attitudes: much of Nazi work seemed promising to him, a good deal of it unreasonable, especially the propaganda in the United States. He had been an hour with Dr. Schacht whom he had known when in Chicago some years ago. "Schacht said to me," he reported confidentially, "his address delivered in Leipzig had been submitted to Hitler and Hitler had approved it, yet the German newspapers did not print a word of the critical parts." This looks strange, but is not unusual here. In a few days there will be a violent attack upon the Jews either by Goebbels or Streicher, the Nürnberg propagandist, and Hitler will have approved what is said.

The Colonel added that Schacht had said his situation is most critical here, "so difficult that I would like to jump off a ship into the ocean." I am quite sure Schacht said something like this, for several times he has talked the same way to me. One thing is fairly certain: If Schacht fails, there is apt to be a collapse and a financial collapse might bring the Hohenzollerns to the throne. Schacht would almost certainly be the Chancellor under a parliamentary restoration. However, the Hohenzollerns would have a hard time if they went on with the war policy.

When Tupper spoke of the State Department in Washington as receiving ridicule here and elsewhere in Europe I was a little skeptical. He made an exception of Secretary Hull and I believe Hull's trade liberalism is the one thing that is criticized here though it seems to me the only promising policy of the

United States for Germany, even if Hull is not in sympathy with the present Nazi regime.

December 20. Friday. The Dutch Minister reported that he had heard no news that Dutch-English-American oil companies—Shell, Sinclair and Standard—had brought pressure to bear in London and Paris to stop the League sanctions against Italy, especially oil sanctions. I had heard indirectly that a Sinclair Oil man in Paris and some big business man in London had applied pressure, and consequently I had dropped the Dutch Minister a note on the subject. I am still of the opinion that the oil companies used pressure. They have interests at stake, especially the Standard Oil Company, in Rumania and Persia, and their interests have in the past caused extraordinary performances in America.

The German papers have suddenly ceased their fun-making of the League. The House of Commons voted yesterday such a sharp criticism of the Hoare-Laval scheme that Hoare resigned. There is talk of Austen Chamberlain being made Foreign Secretary, a man whose newspaper articles against Nazi Germany have been so severe that the government here sent a violent protest to London a few weeks ago. Imagine him being appointed Foreign Secretary!

At 8 o'clock, I sat down by Von Papen, at a dinner given at the Herren Club, the oldest and most aristocratic organization in Berlin, I believe. There were forty or fifty men at the tables. On my right sat the owner of the *Frankfurter Zeitung,* intimating his strong opposition to the Nazi regime. As I was not free to respond, Von Papen being on my left, there could be no outspoken criticism. To my surprise Von Papen quite openly said: "Well, I see that your people have got rid of Huey Long." He then asked if there were real opposition to Roosevelt. I said: Yes, big business is almost unanimously opposed, and Father Coughlin is always breaking loose. Von Papen is a Catholic, but he showed no sympathy with Coughlin.

When we all rose from the tables and found places in the large library of the club there was group conversation which indicated a strong approval of the British abandonment of the

Hoare-Laval business. One elderly man spoke with enthusiasm of Woodrow Wilson as the one statesman of the World War era—"a man who meant to put an end to war," he said. I am sorry I did not get his name. He added: "There is far more approval of Wilson in Germany than you suppose."

December 21. Saturday. We lunched with the kindly, friendly Eichbergs. Both are extremely miserable, no escape from Germany being possible for them unless they give a big sum to the Nazi Party and swear themselves no longer Jews or perhaps illegitimate children of other people, reared by Jews, as some Jews here have done. They have a beautiful library. There were some people of high station at dinner, and the wife of General von Seeckt of the army. Criticism was common talk, but not by the host and hostess.

December 22. Sunday. At 4 o'clock, we had a tea party for Marriner, Counselor in Paris, who stopped here on his way to Warsaw. What Marriner said about events in Paris was very interesting. Laval had put over on Sir Samuel Hoare his scheme of extreme concessions to Mussolini. Now the French people are more anti-Laval than before. We learned today, I said, that Anthony Eden is to succeed Hoare. Marriner replied, "That would trouble Laval, but would not cause the weakening of England's position in Paris, the people being even more against Mussolini than against the Laval Government."

Marriner reported that Bullitt's interview in Berlin on December 1 was telegraphed to Paris that day, and that Herriot's wife had read the telegram before Bullitt had arrived in Paris about December 3. What Bullitt said here was astounding to me in view of his past record. When Madame Herriot reported to Marriner that Bullitt had spoken against Russia and in favor of Japan, he was amazed. I had been so shocked at his advice to the French Ambassador in Berlin not to favor the Russian-French peace pact that I reported to the State Department. I suspect Bullitt's words were telegraphed to Washington before he reached Paris.

There was much interesting talk about Eden's appointment in London and its meaning here. There is not apt to be any more unfriendly League talk in German official circles. Mussolini is a puzzle to Hitler, who is reported to hate him, yet he must praise him for seizing Ethiopian territory.

December 23. Monday. I received a letter from our Minister in Prague saying that an American journalist has been in the terrible Dachau concentration camp near Munich for several months, not allowed to write to me or to the Consul in Berlin, where he was seized. I referred the matter at once to Consul Geist, the best-informed person here to run down such stories.

December 29. Sunday. We had some free time this last week, though my wife and daughter were busy half the time filling the house with Christmas decorations, a tall tree, flowers and little lights to make the house look joyful. Everything was beautiful enough, but restful hours were of chief importance for me.

I received a letter today from a friend in the State Department, asking me to cable what it was best in my opinion to do to check the Italian war which threatens now to involve France, England and the little Mediterranean powers. I reviewed the situation as best I could and had a brief statement in mind as I went home to dinner today, after two hours in the office.

We had information a few days ago that Secretary William Phillips, in London for the naval conference, is to arrive here tomorrow. We have arranged to have twenty people to meet him, including the British and French Ambassadors, Dieckhoff and Ritter from the German Foreign Office, and others like young Prince Louis Ferdinand. Von Neurath and Dr. Schacht as well as nearly all other higher German officials are at their country estates until January 8, the German custom at Christmas time. Mr. Phillips told Mr. Mayer of the staff here by long distance phone that he wishes to meet Hitler. We had to say: There is no chance unless you can remain past January 8, 1936, Hitler being at Berchtesgaden in Bavaria.

December 30. Monday. Secretary Phillips spent an hour talking over the difficulties in the United States and the almost certain failure of the naval conference in London where he renews his task on January 5. The outlook is not good, "and all high officials in London expect war with Italy." How foolish are these European governments, especially the dictatorships, not to find some way to settle their difficulties peaceably! Nor is our country any wiser. The folly was when America refused to co-operate with the League of Nations and now must spend nearly a billion a year of the people's money preparing for war.

At 11:30 we had all our experts, including the staff members, come to meet Mr. Phillips and give him up-to-date information about all phases of German activity. "Germany is one vast military camp," said Major Smith, Military Attaché. Our Commercial Attaché said, "In two years Germany will be manufacturing oil and gas enough out of soft coal for a long war, the Standard Oil Company of New York furnishing millions of dollars to help." "The substitutes for cotton which the Germans are making are rapidly reaching such a stage that American cotton can be dispensed with" was the opinion of Captain Crockett who described the wonderful cloths and war-stuffs made from combinations of wood and straw of various kinds.

Mr. Phillips was amazed and distressed, although all this information has been going to the Department for two whole years. But no high official can master all the reports as they pile up there. Major Smith agreed to take Phillips to see the vast camps and airfields tomorrow.

At 12 o'clock, some thirty press people came to hear what Mr. Phillips might say and to answer questions as to what may happen to them if they are expelled from the country, as is frequently rumored here. I could not remain for the whole hour they were to exchange views. Our press people are exceedingly well informed and absolutely trustworthy if one warns them what is not to be reported.

At 1:30, our party sat down together and after we finished luncheon, there were intimate conversations with Secretary Phillips about the dangerous situation in Germany and the possible attitudes of the United States. The English and the French guests were the most solemn. So things go here always.

January 1, 1936. Wednesday. Another troubled year begins.

At 5 o'clock today, we received all the American and English journalists here, also members of the Embassy staff, the various attachés and other helpers, clerks and stenographers. It was a party of eighty or ninety people and quite a strain for me. Secretary Phillips was also with us for a half hour, and two German editors who have seen much of the world and are none too happy, though they showed no signs.

January 4. Saturday. This morning's German papers report on the front page the gist of Representative McReynolds's proposal in Congress to give Roosevelt and the State Department the right and the power to apply a boycott to any aggressor nation when it starts a war, the time to do it being indicated by events. This is almost exactly what I telegraphed and wrote on Sunday, December 29. If Congress enacts this proposal the United States is going to recover the power in international affairs it lost in 1920, and Roosevelt may be able to do what Wilson tried so earnestly to accomplish in 1919.

The German papers all reported this proposition to their readers but made no editorial comment. When I went to the office at 9:30, a radio copy of Roosevelt's speech of last night to both houses of Congress came promptly to my desk. It is a marvelous but very shrewd indictment of all dictatorships, of all nations which persist in organizing great armies and pretending they have a right to annex smaller nations' territory. No German official can read this address without serious concern. It tells the whole world about the suppression of freedom here and the complete subordination of the people. I do not think any paper will dare print any part of this address. Editors would be imprisoned, perhaps even be executed, if they printed it verbatim. The speech seemed to me so timely and far-seeing that I sent a cable of congratulations and a promise to cable the effects or reactions here in a day or two.

In the afternoon, the German papers broke out in denunciations of Roosevelt's proclamation to all the world, defending themselves as a people who had been unjustly handled in treaties. The *Börsen Zeitung* said Roosevelt is another Woodrow Wilson trying to subordinate and betray the poor German people who are not allowed to migrate to the United States. The *Angriff*, Goebbels' paper, attacked the President all over the first page. The *Berliner Tageblatt* was not unfair, but it did not speak favorably of this great effort to stop wars. No paper which I have seen quoted a single paragraph verbatim. They all drew conclusions aimed at inciting the Germans. In my judgment, most Germans actually admire the President even though they get only half-truth on any point. I shall see many of them before long.

Realizing the importance of co-operation when the League meets on January 20, I sent Martha to the Russian Embassy with a brief note saying that I would like to see the Ambassador. My wife had told me it was unwise to see the Communist representative. Martha went to the Adlon Hotel, only a block from the Embassy, dismissed the chauffeur and then walked to the Embassy. The card was delivered. The Ambassador was away. Martha told the Counselor not to telephone me. The Counselor agreed but said, "Tell your father to come at 7, anyway." So as I went back to my office at 4, I planned to drive over near the proper place and then walk alone to the Ambassador's office.

To my surprise when I returned to the house at 6:45, the Russian Ambassador called on the phone and said he was at home and would be glad to see me. After all my precautions, the Secret Police thus had proof in their office of my visit to the wicked Communist Ambassador. It was his blunder. I am not sure he did not do it on purpose, in order that the Germans might learn of my supposed friendly relations.

So I went to see the Soviet leader here, who is so unwelcome that one rarely sees him at an official luncheon or dinner. He told me his government was ready to co-operate at once with the League in sanctions against Italy. He also said Rumania was even more ready for prompt action. He said the French Ambassador had made it plain to him that he feared a defeat of Mussolini would mean the German annexation of Austria.

When we were through talking about the effects of Roosevelt's attitude, I said to him: I hope your government will manage to stop propaganda in the United States where it does no good. Let the two countries learn how to co-operate in commercial matters and help keep the peace of the world. We are a democracy and your people are Communist. Each people has its right to its own method of government, but it must not interfere with other peoples. He agreed and said he would do all he could.

January 6. Monday. Concerned about the German attitudes toward the new sanctions question and the solid front England and France are reported to be forming against Mussolini's crazy policy, I wrote a note in hand to the former Secretary of Economics, Dr. Kurt Schmitt, and asked if he could stop at my office on his way home. The note was taken by one of our messenger boys to avoid exposing Schmitt to the Secret Police.

We talked more than half an hour. His reactions to the American attitude about sanctions were less favorable than two months ago when I saw him. He is still opposed to Mussolini's aggression but less so than before, indicating he thought the emergence of Communism in Italy would ensue in the event of Mussolini's defeat or compulsory overthrow under the pressure of England and France and even the Pope, who is not too much opposed to dictatorships. When I raised the question of Austrian relations with Germany he said there was no interest here in the annexation of Austria now.

When I alluded to vast army expansion, he said: "You know all Germans have been taught militarism for fifty years and all Prussian Germans for nearly 200 years. This has given the people an attitude which no other people has. Every man has served his term in the army and he thinks it an honor to have his son serve and have his chance to become an officer. This basic national attitude is what gives the Germans the appearance of wishing war. We do not want war and this is one reason nothing will be done about Austria, though everybody knows Austria is German."

On all three points Dr. Schmitt, considered a liberal opponent of the present regime, showed a modified attitude, milder by far than when I last saw him. What has happened? He is still in control of the German life insurance companies. My guess is that he has been given considerable attention by Hitler whom he said he had talked with before Christmas. He thinks American attitudes are less important, though he is still an advocate of German-English-United States co-operation. The Italian dictatorship is more agreeable to him because Communism may arise there, and vast armament is not so dangerous because Germany is naturally inclined toward big armies! But when I alluded to the Jewish difficulties, he flared up a little and his references to the university situation were of the same character as before: a big blunder on the part of Germany.

As he went away I said: I sent a messenger with my note to avoid possible embarrassment to you. He replied: "I had no hesitancy about calling you on the telephone because I have no idea the police believe I give private information, which of course I don't. I shall talk about these things to Hitler when I see him."

January 9. Thursday. Most Germans I see stress the peace objectives of the Third Reich, including some men who are entitled to real consideration. But this evening my wife and I went to the great movie theater, the UFA Palast, to see the widely advertised *Unser Wehrmacht* (Our Defense Power) film. For an hour a huge audience watched and applauded the scenes: vast army fields with tanks and machine guns operating and soldiers falling to the ground, all shooting and some killed; great parades of heavy trucks and big cannon; air attacks with hundreds of flying machines dropping bombs on a city. At strategic moments Hitler, Goering and even Goebbels appeared on the scene indicating their approval of all that was going on. The audience applauded many times. I could hardly endure the scene and what seemed to me the brutal performances.

If this means German devotion to peace, I cannot understand this psychology. When Hitler speaks he stresses his peace objectives, yet he and Goering parade on every possible occasion in their elaborate uniforms, all the soldiers shouting "Heil

Hitler." The generals of the Reichswehr seem less enthusiastic but they never condemn war as a means of advancing Germany's interests.

January 10. Friday. At 11:30 I went in full dress to the annual reception which Hitler gives to the diplomatic corps. Practically every ambassador and minister was present, all dressed in formal style, some with old-time hats and wonderful gilt-finished clothes. It reminded me of the eighteenth century. We waited nearly half an hour before the Chancellor arrived. The Italian Ambassador was the only one who seemed embarrassed, the Soviet man simply keeping still unless approached by others.

At 12 o'clock, Hitler, Von Neurath, Von Bülow, Lammers and Meissner came into the reception room where the diplomats were all lined up according to rank, the red-dressed Papal Nuncio at the head of the long circular line. The gay French Ambassador stood next to him, I was third in line and the English representative was next to me. The Nuncio read a meaningless essay of congratulations in French which Hitler did not understand any better than I did. The Chancellor replied in briefer form, boasting a little of unemployment relief which he had given the German people, not explaining that nearly all the relief was due to the armament boom.

When Hitler came along the line he talked at some length to the Nuncio about a certain Catholic cloister which he had known and something of Church history. When he shook hands with the Frenchman, he asked about the floods of the Seine in Paris. Turning toward me, I said to him that I noticed that he talked history with the Nuncio and that I supposed he read history with real interest. He replied: "Yes, history is far better for me than politics which wears me out." Before he turned to my English colleague, he asked: "When are you moving into the Blücher Palace?" I had to say I did not know. He showed considerable interest, referring to the unfortunate effects of the subway which has caused the palace to show signs of possible collapse of the walls. Then he went on down the line and to my surprise talked with the Russian more freely than with several others.

We were all free to leave at 12:30. While it is regarded as necessary, this kind of show seems to me useless. The cars all departed in order, everybody dropping a tip in the hands of servants who were at the door.

January 11. Saturday. Three days ago I received a letter from the University of Chicago offering Professor Otto Hoetzsch proper compensation if he would lecture there next spring, April and May, on European affairs between 1920 and 1930. Hoetzsch was one of the best-known and most popular professors in Berlin. He was so affected by his dismissal that he was seriously ill for a month. Having known him fairly well and remembering our work together in Leipzig in 1899, I did what I could to get the University of Chicago to extend this invitation

As soon as the offer came I sent word to him to call at the office. He visited me on January 7 and I asked him if he could accept and promised to forward his answer by cable to Chicago, as requested. I also told him he would probably be asked to repeat some of his lectures at the Universities of Michigan, Illinois and Wisconsin. I was somewhat surprised at his hesitancy to accept, knowing how much it meant to him. He went away agreeing to give me an answer in three days.

This morning, January 11, he came in and promptly said he could not accept the offer. He had talked with Dr. Dieckhoff of the Foreign Office and learned that the German Government disapproved of anyone's lecturing in any country, perhaps also at home, on the European situation following the World War. They are not even willing for anyone to discuss the war. Dieckhoff made it plain that Hoetzsch might lose his pension if he lectured on anything after 1914.

Hoetzsch tried to persuade me to ask Chicago again to give him the opportunity of lecturing there next fall on European history between 1856 and 1915. While I agreed to mention the matter and I took a list of the subjects he proposed, I made no promise. These subjects are better handled by Chicago historians than here, and I am convinced now that no German historian dares to tell the plain truth about his country. I cannot really press the matter again.

Curious, these scholars, even the ablest, have no real conception of true history. They know the facts fairly, but cannot recognize a single error on the part of their governments. The idea of a great people not knowing important items of its past and eminent professors not allowed to give their interpretations of events is discouraging to me. Hoetzsch was a member of the Reichstag here from 1920 to 1930, chairman of its Foreign Relations Committee which worked out the Dawes-Young arrangements. He has traveled all over Europe and the United States and his experience as a writer has been ample. Yet he cannot lecture objectively on subjects he knows most about! I shook hands with him sadly when he left.

January 13. Monday. There was a great deal of comment in the press today about the Goering parade, all ambassadors except myself having been present, also the unhappy Crown Prince and his wife. But Hitler and Goebbels were not there.

At 11 o'clock Max Sering came to talk about another international agricultural conference to be held in England next summer. He showed me a letter from Secretary Wallace. He is a man of eighty-four or eighty-five but still vigorous. His daughter married the son of the famous Admiral von Tirpitz. Sering is a Lutheran who is resentful of the Nazi church control and reorganization. He is also an old-time royalist who prays for Hohenzollern restoration. Yet he believes Hitler to be a real statesman as contrasted with Goebbels and Goering.

When he said: "Germany does not want war again," I could not help mentioning the film we saw on the 9th at the UFA Palast. I saw that he, like most Germans, does not grasp the military and aggressive attitudes behind such shows and the sale of millions of little bombs and tanks to children as Christmas presents. I did not wish to add to his unhappiness so we discussed his agricultural problems as he appraises them. He will undoubtedly have something worth while to say if he goes to the conference, half of the delegates coming from the United States. If the educated German people only understood their own history!

January 16. Thursday. I was at a dinner given in honor of R. L. Hague of the Standard Oil Company of New Jersey which ships great quantities of oil to Hamburg in return for 15,000-ton tank ships. The president of the German shipbuilding company in Hamburg which makes the tankers said they employed 1,000 men as a consequence of the Standard Oil contract. He also said he made similar ships for England and that all of them are so built that they can be readily converted into warships. However, the Hamburg business man made it perfectly plain that he disliked the Hitler regime, though not Hitler so much. He said his children in the Hamburg school had to learn great falsehoods at the command of Nazi teachers, compelled by Rosenberg to teach nonsense.

January 17. Friday. About noon today a staff member sent down a detailed telegram which he wished I would sign for the code men to get off. It was more than twice as long as it should have been, and about the fifth time since his arrival here that he has sent long, detailed and even unimportant cables, the cost of some of them being over $100. I had shown him several times how to abbreviate them and save half the cost. He had yielded, but had sometimes failed to do what he had promised. So I rewrote this one with omission of all unessential sentences, making it only half as long as his original. I sent it back to him to be sent as my telegram duly signed. I went away for my usual noonday walk.

When I returned to the office in the afternoon, my secretary reported that the man in question had been angry and complaining. But I have made up my mind to write telegrams myself, if he cannot learn how to write.

This illustrates the spirit of the diplomatic service people. They are graduates of Harvard, Princeton and one or two other universities. Being the sons of rich men, hardly one in ten has ever learned anything about clear-cut, succinct writing, even less about history. They think it perfectly right to load off $1,000 a month on their government, and at the same time they think they are free to come to their offices at 10 or 11 o'clock each morning, remain two hours, clerks doing their work, and then go away to some luncheon and remain until 4 o'clock. One or two more hours in the office and then they feel free to go to a card party or a little later to a dinner where they remain until 12 or 1 o'clock. I have tried to correct all this, set definite hours for office work and urge a more regulated social life. Most of the staff members have become cooperative, though I believe they do not regard the Embassy here as too serious a business.

Although the present staff members have learned painfully to come promptly each morning and have tried to write good telegrams, they carry a society burden almost impossible for anyone who hopes to keep his health.

January 18. Saturday. A journalist of the Hearst press in the United States came in for a talk this afternoon. I had seen him before and asked him to report any interview he might get with high German officials, as far as he felt free to do so. He is not exactly a pro-Nazi journalist though he is a good Hearstite. So he reported today he had seen Von Ribbentrop, the diplomatic specialist of Hitler who negotiated the English-German naval pact of last June. Von Ribbentrop is clever but most unwelcome to Von Neurath and Von Bülow.

He said, in his interview: "Germany has an understanding with Mussolini; the Ethiopian war will end in his favor; then Germany and Italy will demand restoration of German pre-war colonies." He showed maps of all the German colonies and tried to prove them rich in mineral and other raw materials. "It really means war if the League of Nations does not restore German colonies," the Hearst man said. I said: No, not so soon. Germany is not ready for war, but will be in two years.

I told him of German-Japanese relations since I have been in Berlin, and my feeling that there is an unwritten treaty under which the two countries will make war upon Russia at the strategic time. I continued: Now you say there is a pact between Germany and Italy. That means what I have prophesied for more than a year: a dictatorial front in Europe which may give the world much trouble.

January 21. Tuesday. I talked with Dr. Schacht half an hour this morning. He spent two weeks in Italy about Christmas time. He then went to Basle for the International Bank conference where he is one of the directors. I had hardly taken seat opposite him at his desk in the palatial Reichsbank before he referred to the Senate investigation of munitions and finance which Senator Nye has managed. Schacht wanted to know if I thought Wilson had entered the World War for financial and trade advantage. I replied in the negative, giving Wilson's statement to me August 15, 1916, about his attitude which was to intervene in case it became clear that the Berlin military dictators were about to dominate all Europe.

Schacht avoided a reply, except to say that he did not believe Wilson was pulled into the war by the New York bankers.

I then asked about German-Italian relations. He said, "You know Hitler and Mussolini had a long conference at Venice in 1934, but the two leaders agreed about nothing. They disliked each other so much. Now, however, there is a better feeling. Both countries must have colonial possessions, and while we have no alliance there is a rapprochement."

I answered: Restoration of colonial possessions to Germany would be right and fair, but you know colonies no longer yield profits. We have lost immensely on every colony we took from Spain in 1898. He replied, "But your people would not go to those possessions," and I added that modern conditions are such that unemployed nowhere, except in Japan, will migrate. He let the subject drop. But I am sure Germany means to make an issue of colonial restoration soon. Hitler says, "We will not go to war for colonies," but he will probably press the matter in such a way as to incite war.

Then Schacht referred to German economic and financial conditions. He indicated that American claimants for interest on bonds are soon to come to see him about payments due

April 1. I said: Well, our latest telegram, on January 20, showed that your income has improved a lot the last few months. He was interested and asked if he could see parts of my telegram to the Secretary of the Treasury. I replied that I might *tell* him something of what we reported on the German financial situation. Then he said he had paid interest on bonds last autumn hoping to get better commercial treaty arrangements with the United States, but that there had been no improvement.

I replied: There are so many other matters that affect public opinion with us that a really low tariff treaty would hardly pass the Senate if negotiated. You know what these difficulties are. If everybody here understood things and made public statements similar to yours, things would go much better. The United States does not like bilateral agreements. What Secretary Hull wants is lower barriers everywhere, and I think that would everywhere raise standards of living. He halfway assented, but made it plain that no change of the present autarchy policy and no religious freedom with fair treatment of the Jews are possible at present. I bade him good-by and best wishes, aware that our half hour's talk had only cleared the atmosphere a little, not given evidence of any better relations between the countries.

January 23. Thursday. Our Commercial Attaché brought Dr. Engelbrecht, chairman of the Vacuum Oil Company in Hamburg, to see me. Engelbrecht repeated what he had said a year ago: "The Standard Oil Company of New York, the parent company of the Vacuum, has spent 10,000,000 marks in Germany trying to find oil resources and building a great refinery near the Hamburg harbor." Engelbrecht is still boring wells and finding a good deal of crude oil in the Hanover region, but he has no hope of great deposits. He hopes Dr. Schacht will subsidize his company as he does some German companies that have found no crude oil. The Vacuum spends all its earnings here, employs 1,000 men and never sends any of its money home. I could give him no encouragement for the German

Government is hardly willing to do anything for an outsider, even if he does spend millions here. Mr. Miller was of the same opinion.

January 24. Friday. John Foster Dulles, who writes for the *American* magazine about European affairs but who is also connected with a large banking business in New York, reported his difficulties in financial matters here.

He said: "My sister lives here. She is an enthusiastic Hitlerite, and anxious to show me the German attitude for peace. So we went this afternoon to the movie, *Unser Wehrmacht* [Our Defense Power], which she said was proof of the German desire for peace. I sat through the show, but the war planes, big guns, pictures of violent attacks upon cities and the enthusiastic attitudes of Hitler, Goering and Goebbels, as they stood looking at the devastating work, took from my mind all thought of peace as an object of the show." His impressions were the same as mine two weeks ago when I witnessed the same demonstration of Germany at war. Dulles said he could not understand his sister's attitude, and added that such a display in the United States would be hissed off the screen.

Dulles said he had served in the State Department with Secretary Lansing when Wilson was President and that he was indignant at the charges of the Senate Committee that Wilson entered the World War to make money for the United States. He recognized the bankers' role and attitude during 1915-16, but denied that the President had any contacts with the Morgans. This accords with my information, though I am inclined to the belief that Lansing was not altogether free from strong banking influences.

January 25. Saturday. Louis Lochner reports that at the meeting of the Foreign Press Association this morning he was re-elected by a vote of 59 out of a total of 65, six members not voting. This gives him a status which may prevent Dr. Goebbels from ordering his departure from the country next autumn because of too free reports of conditions and troubles here. Last summer there was serious danger of this. When the Olympic

Games are over, there are apt to be sharper attacks. I congratulated him on his re-election and hoped no trouble would occur.

January 30. Thursday. Today is regarded by the Hitler regime as a German July 4. I had accepted an invitation to hear Hitler and Goebbels speak at 11:30. But the weather was bad and I had learned that the affair was an outdoor show, with 30,000 S.A. soldiers marching past the Fuehrer. The weather made it risky for me to attend and I wrote a note declining.

I now understand that the people and soldiers did not shout and hurrah as they have formerly done. Is there a declining popularity? One often hears this, but I doubt whether Hitler has lost many followers. Absolutism denies anybody a chance to protest or criticize; all important organizations in Germany are official, the churches alone excepted; and these can do nothing. At night there was an amazing torch-light procession through the Wilhelmstrasse, once more in honor of the Fuehrer.

January 31. Friday. There are many rumors of German uneasiness about a possible solid front of England, France, Italy and all the Balkan states against further German armament and against any demand by Hitler for a restoration of German colonies. For this reason I called at noon today on the Czechoslovak Minister, just returned from Prague where he had been for a week.

He said: "Austria is uneasy lest a Nazi drive be made for the overthrow of the regime there. Czechoslovakia is also tense and listening to Austrian Catholic leaders who are urging close co-operation between the two countries. England is supporting Austria in concert with France and there is trouble in Hungary where the English have ceased buying fats and thus upset the economic life very much. All the states of the Balkan zone are disposed to co-operate in the League of Nations against Italy, later against Germany if she becomes aggressive toward her small neighbors."

He said, however, that he had no definite information as to how far League action was to go. He would see the French Ambassador in a day or two and ascertain whether there is any decisive policy, especially whether England and France were about to announce approval of the pact with Russia against any aggressor, particularly Germany or Japan. He promised to let me know if there were definite moves. The one thing Germany opposes is the Russian pact for keeping the peace.

At 4:30 Major Archibald Church of Bristol, England, long-time visitor and observer here, dropped in. He was a leader in the Labor Government of MacDonald and had been a private secretary to Bruening. He talked an hour and a half about the English situation, the League, Italy and especially Germany. He gave me the name of a prominent Cabinet member here between 1920 and 1933 who let him know how much money had been secretly used for armaments and the training of soldiers, beyond the treaty allowance. Stresemann and Bruening, though claiming to be sincerely co-operative with England and France, he said, granted these allowances out of a huge secret fund voted by the Reichstag. So, he said, there were far more trained soldiers in 1933 than the Reichswehr acknowledged.

Church impressed me as exceedingly well informed about internal matters here. According to reports, he slipped Bruening out of the country, June 30, 1934, when the former Chancellor was in danger of being killed, and several others he also helped out in clever ways. Bruening, he said, had not shown appreciation of the service rendered. He had lived a year in London in fashionable style at the expense of English friends and had failed to earn money by giving lectures at Oxford and elsewhere, though he was invited frequently. I suspect Bruening felt that lectures from him would cause spies to be put on his trail and perhaps lead to his death. Church did not think this likely. "Now," he said, "Bruening is in Canada and the United States, I hope paying his own expenses."

February 1. Saturday. We went with James H. Hyde to the great indoor horse-jumping contest, with German, Italian, Polish and Japanese horses in the show. It was quite good. After the horse-jumping, there was an amazing army demonstration: a cavalry parade (not bad), Black Shirt soldiers marching, then cannon wagons pulled around for us all to see, with tank and machine-gun operations. It was intended as a sham battle, the machine guns being fired by soldiers prostrate on the ground.

The vast audience, 20,000 perhaps, applauded, and Hitler and Goering gave salutes. No one could fail to see that the Nazi spirit is fundamentally warlike. Ambassadors of other countries, also many military and naval attachés, were witnesses to this demonstration.

What Europe is to do with 68,000,000 people bent upon another war I cannot guess. If all states combine and remain armed to the teeth, the struggle may be delayed, but not actually avoided. Not to form a solid front will mean annexations east, west and north, and 90,000,000 people in the German Reich. The French and English peoples have become overwhelmingly pacifist and the Germans know this. Pacifism is the attitude of the United States also, but pacifism will mean a great war and the subordination of all Europe to Germany if the pacifist peoples do not act courageously at this critical moment in their history.

IX

February 5, 1936 to July 29, 1936

February 5. Wednesday. Suppose the Hohenzollerns were restored, would they avoid another great war? The German people have so long submitted to militarism and the Hohenzollerns have so long advocated aggression east, north and west, that they might fall again into this antiquated form of national behavior.

Prince Louis Ferdinand was one of the guests at a party of Martha's tonight. He asked to talk to me for a moment. I told him what the Franco-Russian entente, with the hope of a united Balkan zone, was intended for. He was depressed because he saw it meant German encirclement and perhaps another war. He asked me what I thought was the way out for Germany. I said to him quite confidentially, though I suspect he will tell his father, that the liberal people of Germany would have to have a more progressive government, a parliament freely elected, freedom of religion, a let-up on the Jews and freedom of the press. He agreed. Certainly Louis Ferdinand himself would favor this.

February 12. Wednesday. This morning Ambassador Bullitt, on his way to Russia, came to see me, reporting the optimistic attitude of the President, also greetings from Secretary Hull and Judge Moore. Bullitt said: "Pennsylvania will be a crucial state in next November's election, but in Philadelphia the old

Republican group no longer rules. The Irish and the Jews are a unit for Roosevelt and they are apt to carry the city."

This may be true. It is a curious combination in our country. Bullitt seems to think he will have to go back in late summer to campaign for the President, perhaps become an intimate adviser to take the place of poor Howe who is about to die. I doubt if these hopes will be realized.

Bullitt sounds like an emotional friend of the President but not one whose judgment can be relied on. He is ambitious for promotion to high position but does not seem to me to appraise situations too well. For example, this morning he condemned sharply the co-operation between England, France and the Balkan states in the hope of bringing Russia into a moderate policy and keeping the peace of Europe. He said Germany would capture Austria and Czechoslovakia in two weeks' time and quickly bring all Europe under her control.

I questioned: Do you think this would be good for the United States and England? He cared "not a damn" for England and reported that both Lord Lothian and Lloyd George are against the English, French, Russian co-operation with the Balkan entente. He added that Lothian preferred to let Germany go on her conquering way towards European domination rather than to impose limitation upon Germany by his country. While I said little, I did add that the Lothian policy would mean the decline of England to a position like that of Holland. To me it would be a calamity for a people which has so long led in culture and democratic attitudes to lose its position and power.

Then Bullitt said that before he sailed last December for Washington he knew that England had declined a great loan to Russia. Learning that France was about to loan her old Russian ally of 1914 one billion francs, it is reported that Bullitt went to a strategic person in the French Government and convinced him that Russia would never repay the loan. Thus he had defeated the Russian negotiations. I was not sure myself whether the Russians would pay, but it seemed unusual for an American Ambassador to Russia to defeat Russo-French negotiations.

I shall not speak of this to anyone here, but it seemed to me an unwise thing to do. Whether the story is altogether correct or not, it is certain that no loan was made. While I doubt the wisdom of any nation or great bank making a big loan to Germany, I would certainly not prevent negotiations, if England or Holland, for instance, were to lend money to Germany. My position here would not allow it, according to my philosophy.

Sir Eric Phipps reported what he could upon English attitudes. He was more outspoken than he had been in a year: "England has abandoned her disarmament policy of the last fourteen years. She will spend nearly £300,000,000 a year now in order to have a greater army, a bigger navy and ample air defense. This is a sad move, but we have argued with Germany since last February to agree to disarmament proposals. The Fuehrer has always said 'No' to me. We shall not bother the Germans again; but after the French elections next April, we shall unite with France and other European members of the League of Nations and say to the Germans, 'You can agree now to an international limitation of armaments or else we shall all, including Russia, unite to defend any state that is attacked.' "Russia," he added, "is now emerging into a more rational state and we can afford to co-operate with her to keep the peace. If we do not succeed in persuading Germany, there will be war in a few years and Europe, including Germany, will collapse."

He then told me that the French Ambassador had recently had Goering to dinner and that, when there was talk of the possibility of Hitler's retiring or his health failing, Goering put his fat hands upon his chest and said: "I am to succeed the Fuehrer." This was so disturbing to the Frenchman that he went to Phipps and indicated his anxiety.

Goering is the one member of the triumvirate here who frequently makes challenging speeches on the French and Polish borders. I think Goering is almost a complete Mussolini and ready to risk war at any time. This story only confirmed me in the view that the encirclement program, if supported by all the border states east and west of Germany, and by England, France and Russia, is about the only promise of peace there is in Europe.

I came home to luncheon rather more troubled than usual, the two conversations having revealed once more the angles of the dilemma here. Poor German people!

February 19. Wednesday. Today the newspapers reported that the Swiss Government has forbidden all Nazi organizations. This reveals once more the sad state of things in this famous country. A week ago a Nazi propagandist in Switzerland, named Gustloff, was murdered by a German Jew who had become a subject of Yugoslavia. Gustloff had troubled the Swiss people for several years and their Minister here had more than once protested in vain, as I did in 1934, against similar propaganda in the United States. When the murder was known here, all German flags were put at half mast. Not even Von Hindenburg's death was treated with more public attention. The dead man was brought slowly through Germany to his burial place in Mecklenburg. Hitler made an amazingly aggressive attack on all Jews. Other addresses were made in Hamburg and in other cities, tens of thousands of people listening, compelled to be present. Secretary Dieckhoff was ordered to represent the German Foreign Office where Hitler spoke.

Today's papers are full of attacks upon the Swiss, claiming that Nazi organizations abroad ought to be allowed to function, forgetting that Hitler published an order to the German Consulates in the United States late in December that at the end of that month all Nazi organizations must be dissolved, even in our country where there are millions of Germans. Now Switzerland is denounced throughout the country for doing what he said he had ordered in America.

In addition to regular press attacks there was passed out to the press from Goebbels' office a sarcastic statement that the Swiss would probably build a monument to honor the murderer of Gustloff. They forget that the German Nazi leaders built a monument to the murderers of Rathenau, the greatest of ministers here since the war, and that each year flowers are laid about the monument to the murderers. How can the press complain now if the Swiss newspapers call attention to the German monument to a murderer?

February 20. Thursday. A New York *Times* man called this morning to report on a little trouble Birchall got into on account of his story of Sir Eric Phipps' interview with Hitler on December 13. His report corresponds with what I had learned from different sources. It indicated that Hitler had gesticulated rather violently and denounced the Russians as enemies whom he must be ready to fight; that he had no idea of limiting arms of any kind and would enter into no international conference on the subjects of aircraft or warships. When this was reprinted from the *Times* account in the London *Daily Telegraph,* the German Foreign Office, Dieckhoff and others, informed the *Times* people here that Birchall must not return to Germany, that the police were instructed to keep him out.

Somehow, Birchall is in Berlin and had a long talk with Dieckhoff yesterday. As yet no one knows what is to be done. However, Birchall reported so favorably the German courtesy and treatment of the Olympic Games participants in Germany during the last two weeks that he was quoted a few days ago in the German press. Evidently Birchall made his peace, though I believe his story of the Hitler attitude of December 13 was correct. Anyway he is here. The *Times* man said: "I only wish I could leave this country. Everything here is in such a condition and all of us newspaper people kept in such a state of mind that life is miserable." But the American press authorities at home are so bent upon keeping their cleverest reporters here that I think these people will remain. The Olympic Games will occur in the summer and they involve the expenditure of millions of dollars by foreigners in Germany, one of the greatest hopes of Dr. Schacht.

Later in the day the finance expert of our staff brought me a typed German report quoting me as saying that on account of Hitler's illness, it had been decided that Goering, General von Blomberg and Hess will be the next German triumvirate. The man who sent this circular is an intimate of finance circles here and receives pay for notices of this sort.

I have telegraphed to Washington that rumors here over many weeks indicate that Hitler's throat is in bad condition, supposed to be cancer, and that the generals of the army about

January 1, 1936, had held a meeting and agreed to this triumvirate in the order given. The Czech Minister told me this.
I also had it from another official source. My telegram did not
say it was a fact, only that the above reports had come to me.

Now, how does this story get back to Germany? It is possible
that the British Ambassador mentioned it as coming from me,
but he told me first about Goering's being designated as the
coming Fuehrer, a few days ago. I then told him the other part
of the story. It is possible once more that somebody in the State
Department let this story out and that it was cabled over here.
It may be true that somebody in Paris reported the contents
of the telegram, as a copy was sent there. It is not an agreeable
matter.

February 25. Tuesday. I lunched with Oechsner and Roy
Howard, head of the United Press, who has been around the
world. Howard is to see Hitler tomorrow at 12:30. He was not
a little pleased at the prospect, though I told him he need not
expect much. I did not say that I would not see Hitler or Goering at any time on my own volition. However, newspaper people feel it to be a duty to see Hitler and Mussolini when in
Berlin and Rome.

February 27. Thursday. Oechsner came to report what Hitler
had said yesterday to Howard and himself. They noticed that
the Chancellor was very much troubled about something, but
they had not observed that the armed guards about the palace
were twice as numerous as hitherto. This Mr. Flack of the Embassy had noticed yesterday as he came from the Foreign Office.
The reason was, he thought, the recent reports of the murderous putsch in Tokyo when three high officials were killed by
army officers. There was cause for some concern when everybody knows there is much unhappiness in Germany. The possibility always exists of another "June 30."

February 28. Friday. I received a report today from Cologne
of a long conversation with Fritz Thyssen, the greatest manufacturer of arms after the Krupps. Thyssen said he had given
a great part of his fortune to help Hitler win his long struggle

for his dictatorship. He said he was troubled about the present situation and added that another June 30 purge was necessary to save Hitler's regime. He did not name the persons involved. He was fearful that the radical wing of the Nazi Party was becoming almost Communist. However, he condemned severely the persecution of Catholics and Protestants which has been going on for two years.

I guess that his aim is to have Goebbels, Rosenberg, Darre and the labor chiefs dismissed. There have been many rumors in Berlin about a possible shooting, and people who are supposed to know a good deal think Goering is the man who will once more rid the country of people he does not like. One story is that he will put Hitler out of the way and himself become the dictator.

Of the arrests already made, Catholics have been among the principal victims: reports say 200, preachers and others, perhaps half of them later released, though one can never know the facts. One thing the Nazis insist upon is the absolute control of all the young people, their religious instruction and general education, under the same methods applied now for nearly twenty years by the Communists of Russia.

February 29. Saturday. At 12:30 I had a long talk with Secretary von Neurath, entirely unofficial. He was more frank with me than on any previous occasion. I suspect that serious disputes have been going on between his wing of the government and that dominated by Goering. He did not acknowledge such disputes, but when I asked him about the Franco-Soviet pact which has been denounced so often in the German press, he said that the plan of the French and the Russians really was not belligerent, that the Communist system was not equal to a war outside of Russian boundaries. They might fight bravely if attacked at home but they could not fight an offensive war, although they did have a vast army.

That was my idea, too, for I do not see how 170,000,000 people can be too submissive to a Party government with hardly more than two million Party members. I did not say so, but I believe Germany's 68,000,000 would not offer complete unity if called upon to invade Belgium again, or Holland.

Then I reported to the Secretary that most of the ministers from the Balkan states here had repeatedly said to me since the second summer of my residence in Berlin that the independence of those states could be guaranteed only through the formation of a confederation for defense and peace. I asked him: Would you consider such a union as a menace to Germany? He replied: "No, so long as neither France nor Russia nor Italy dominates it."

This raised the question of German "encirclement," so much talked of since universal military service began in March, 1935. I said "encirclement," or alliances, is the natural consequence of the declining power and influence of the League of Nations from which Germany has withdrawn. If this process goes on we shall have the condition of 1914 again. In fact we do have a similar situation, all states arming to the limit with France, England, Russia on one side, and Italy, Germany and Japan on the other, but this I did not stress directly with Von Neurath. He agreed that the danger is acute.

I said the Balkan states, if united, would be a strong guarantee of peace. I urged: Why not restore the League and settle boundary problems through conferences? He surprised me by saying: "We are contemplating a return to the League on the condition that the Western powers agree to restore our colonies, allow us to re-enter, with our army, the demilitarized zone on the Rhine, and make certain concessions as to naval parity." He insisted that colonies must be restored, that the Rhine zone might possibly await diplomatic negotiations, that the Franco-Russian pact was not serious and that England had received German assent to naval arrangements about to be made in London.

After some remarks about the folly of militarism and war, I asked him if Germany were about to make a special alliance with Japan, which had been so often rumored recently. He evaded this with, "We might as well commit suicide as enter another war," but insisted that there was no sort of entente between Germany and Italy, also that Germany would not be drawn into a war with Russia even if Japan did attack the Soviet Union. So I got an answer to an important query without direct question.

I agree with him that Italy and Germany are not apt to co-operate unless both find themselves in a defensive position outside the League. But I cannot avoid the belief that Germany would support Japan against Russia if it came to war. There is much evidence here that Germany and Japan are in some way tied up. Both Von Neurath and Schacht have said things which lead to that conclusion.

As I came away, Von Neurath emphasized the fact that he was arguing things out with Hitler. He insisted that the Fuehrer showed signs of compromise, especially about returning to Geneva. This surprised me a little.

March 5. Thursday. There is considerable uneasiness these days. The Minister from Czechoslovakia came in this afternoon to talk of the difficulties of his country. I told him in confidence that Von Neurath had agreed with me that the union of the Balkan states for mutual defense and co-operation would not be an affront to Germany as long as no outside country was a party to it. This contradicted what he had heard was the Foreign Office attitude. I cannot always be quite sure that Von Neurath speaks the exact truth to me. However, I believe what he told me last Saturday was quite sincere.

Then I added to my Czech friend: In view of the dangerous position of all smaller states bordering Germany, if I were an official of the Balkan zone, I would do my utmost to bring about such a union, not a strict union, like ours in the United States, but a confederation for mutual aid, economic and political. He agreed with me, but indicated the great difficulties: Austria wants to restore the Hapsburgs: Yugoslavia is very hostile to that idea; Hungary is most hostile to Czechoslovakia; and Bulgaria is not yet ready to do anything.

I replied: If the Balkan populations of more than 80,000,000 do not find a way to unite, your independence will be lost. Imperialism is too strong in Germany, as you know. We parted, both in agreement but doubtful that peoples of Europe know how to co-operate. He said he was leaving that evening for Prague where he was to be the guest of President Beneš.

March 6. Friday. The story is going around that Hitler is calling the Reichstag together for March 13, the day after the announced French ratification of the agreement with Russia. The idea is that Hitler will issue some violent reply. Whatever is planned, there is considerable anxiety here, with meetings of the dictator and his associates supposed to be held frequently.

At 5:30 Mr. Gie, Minister from South Africa, called to report what he had learned during the League Commission session this week. He said Foreign Secretary Eden of England had insisted on oil sanctions against the Italians, but that the French Foreign Secretary, Flandin, had opposed sanctions almost as sternly as Laval had done last December. It surprised and angered Eden. The French were still bound, as they thought, by their pact of January, 1935, which guaranteed Italy as much of Ethiopia as she wished. It was a repetition of the blunder of December, 1935, one more surrender to dictator Mussolini with 6,000 war planes ready to attack the British fleet in the Mediterranean Sea.

Mr. Gie was quite depressed to report Eden's defeat and England's danger of losing her position in Egypt. While all these powers have done things similar to Italy's conquest of poor Ethiopia, it would seem that the League could find a way to stop such performances. Germany looks on and wonders when she will be able to seize weaker peoples.

When I told Gie confidentially that Germany was considering a return to the League on condition that her colonies of 1914 be restored, he said: "That was discussed between Eden and myself and he said England would agree to the granting of colonies to Germany only as mandates, so as to avoid arming the natives, as France has done in Morocco." He talked a little of the tense attitude here, but neither of us could guess what would be done when the Reichstag was called.

March 7. Saturday. When I reached my office at 9:30 Counselor Mayer reported that he must go at once to the Foreign

Office to receive information which Dr. Dieckhoff had been asked to give us. Already the news had come that Hitler was to address the Reichstag assembly today at 12 o'clock! When Mayer returned at 11 o'clock, he brought a summary of Hitler's propositions: he was sending some 30,000 troops into the demilitarized zone of the Rhineland; he proposed an agreement with France and Belgium to demilitarize both sides of the Rhine, also the Dutch border on the German side; he would denounce the Locarno pact between Germany, France, Italy and England because France was signing a pact with Russia; he would return to the League of Nations and be ready to limit aircraft with Western powers, and would demand the restoration of German colonies.

Dieckhoff hoped we would give this document to the American press people here so they would cable at once to the United States what Hitler was doing and saying before the Reichstag. We called the newspaper offices and gave them the information which was immediately sent across the Atlantic.

Mayer and I then went to the Kroll Theatre near the old Reichstag building to hear what was to be said. The hall was crowded. On the main floor were the members of the Reichstag, all in Nazi uniforms, men named by Hitler and paid by the government just as if they were actually serving as legislators. They had been called together on short notice and they were to vote unanimously for whatever Hitler proposed. Of course it was ridiculous, but the assembled men did not show any signs of a sense of humor.

The space reserved for the diplomats was fairly filled, though the French, the English, the Russian and the Polish Ambassadors were absent. At least the English and French had been informed what was coming, and they remained away on purpose. I sat next to the Turk, and next to him sat the Italian.

When Hitler rose to speak there was enormous applause, the diplomats all silent as is usual here. Madame von Neurath sat next to the Italian and she applauded, though I knew she was insincere in doing so. To the rear of Hitler sat Goering who looked very proud. To the right sat Lammers, one of his chief secretaries, in uniform; on the left sat Frank, the head of the

Nazi Bar Association. The Cabinet members were further to
the right; Von Neurath, Gürtner, Minister of Justice, and
Goebbels, who read the pages of a copy of Hitler's speech and
turned the leaves just as Hitler himself turned his pages. Behind Von Neurath sat Dr. Schacht with other members of the
Cabinet to his right. Hundreds of press people were in the gal-
lery. It was designed as a great occasion, Hitler speaking over
the radio to all Germany and the world.

The speech lasted an hour and a half. It enumerated the
points already sent to us and dwelt at length upon the vicious-
ness of the Franco-Russian pact and also on the idea that German culture has been greatly improved and advanced since
1933.

It seemed to me very inconsistent to talk about Wilson's
Fourteen Points and world peace and then devote fifteen minutes to a denunciation of the Franco-Russian peace pact, its one
purpose being proclaimed to be simply defense against an attack. At the same time Czechoslovakia was similarly denounced.
Anyone knows that little country of 14,000,000 people would
never attack Germany. The long praise of Nazi culture was of
course absurd, though it may be that Hitler is still fanatic
enough to think Nazism is culture. The other points of the address were cleverly designed to weaken the relations between
England and France. It seemed to me Germany and Italy were
acting in common. If that is true, it will mean trouble for
France.

At 1:40 I left the hall, Hitler having been escorted away by
hundreds of armed soldiers. He is never without a vast guard.
As I came out of the room, the Dutch Minister showed much
indignation. He said to me: "The Russian and Czechoslovak
representatives here may consider resigning and I think the
French Ambassador will go to Paris tonight." I had not thought
this would happen, but I agreed with him that the denunciations he alluded to were certainly belligerent.

Mr. Mayer who did not understand German very well was
enthusiastic. He had never seen such enthusiasm and he thought
Hitler's oratory was marvelous. I indicated certain doubts but
agreed the address was cleverly planned and thought it another

strategic moment to call a national election. The reoccupation
of the Rhine country and the humiliation of France are likely
to give Hitler's candidates for the new Reichstag overwhelming support. Since Hitler nominates one candidate for each
district and allows no other nomination, there is no choice for
voters. They may cast blank ballots or not vote at all, but they
risk imprisonment by doing so.

It was high time for luncheon. The rest of the day was spent
in the office where rumors from anxious Paris and London were
reported. One crisis after another has been the rule here since
our arrival in July, 1933.

March 9. Monday. My friend, Limburg-Stirum, called about
12 o'clock. He is a democratic aristocrat, member of a 400-year-
old Dutch family, and has been in Berlin for ten or twelve
years. His own government is very doubtful what to do in case
France succeeds in applying sanctions to Germany on account
of the march into the Rhine and the German denunciation of
the Locarno Treaty. The economic life of the Netherlands depends very much on exports to Germany. Also Germany owes
the Dutch people a great deal of money.

But the Minister's personal opinion is bitterly opposed to the
Hitler policy which he says is aimed at annexations in the
Balkan and Baltic zones. In case the Rhineland is made neutral
as Hitler suggests—a stretch of country from Basle, Switzerland, to northern Holland thirty miles wide on each side of the
historic river—there can be no interference from the French
side when Germany annexes Czechoslovakia, Austria, Lithuania
or Esthonia. The Minister thinks that is the scheme and that
Holland too is considered as ripe for annexation. I am inclined
to agree. Certainly the vast preparations here and the unprecedented propaganda for annexations of countries where Germans
live would indicate this.

March 10. Tuesday. Baron Albert Dufour von Feronce, descendant of French Huguenots who have lived here since the
end of the seventeenth century, came apparently to persuade me
that Hitler means no aggression, that the French-Soviet pact
was contrary to the Locarno Treaty and that the march of

36,000 troops into the Rhineland was entirely justified. He was formerly German Minister to Yugoslavia, was long in the diplomatic service and is now on a pension. He revealed the enthusiasm almost of a Nazi Party chief, though he is supposed to be in opposition to the Hitler regime. He was enthusiastic about what he calls German honor and the right to violate a treaty in order to militarize the area demilitarized in 1919. He represents, as I believe, 90 per cent of Germany although it is the general supposition that no more than 40 per cent of the population is actually Nazi in faith. This shows how clever Hitler was in planning his stroke of March 7.

March 12. Thursday. On account of the tense feeling here I went to see the Polish Ambassador, Lipski, at 12 o'clock in the hope of learning what the Polish Government actually thinks about its situation. He indicated great anxiety: "Germany owes us $15,000,000 for freight and passenger service between Germany and East Prussia; Schacht says Germany can pay only in goods; we insist on gold or foreign exchange payment; the two months' dispute is now referred to Hitler. What he will do I cannot guess." But, I said, the Germans plan going back and forth to East Prussia over the Baltic Sea on German boats. What will you do? He said: "We can make no objections, but we want the payment of a perfectly honest debt and shall close the railroad across the Corridor if we are not paid."

When I asked about the German-French quarrel over the Locarno pact, he said: "We are with France if it comes to war, but we have a treaty with Germany which is valuable as long as peace prevails. Our treaty with France takes precedence in case Germany attacks France." He added: "We do not favor applying sanctions against Germany because of her violation of the Locarno Treaty. That would be terrible for Germany and cause a repudiation of debts and perhaps produce war."

When I asked what could be done at the London conference, he said he could not see what could be done, but that Poland would support England, not France. This seemed to me in violation of the French-Polish treaty of which he had spoken so approvingly. He revealed what one notes every day here: the complicated nature of relations, racial, economic and political. Poland owes her independence to the United States, England and France. She was to have been practically annexed to Germany under the treaty of Brest-Litovsk, but the entrance of the United States into the war defeated the enforcement of that treaty. Yet Poland can hardly move right, rear or left without a conflict and a possible subordination to Germany.

March 13. Friday. This evening Hitler spoke to a vast crowd in Karlsruhe on the Rhine. He repeated much of the speech of March 7, with the suggestion that France and Germany embrace each other as friends. He was emotional as usual. His crowd may have been half voluntary, but as usual vast crowds were ordered to attend from cities as far away as Freiburg. One can never say in Germany what an audience really thinks of Hitler, Goering or Goebbels, because no one dares oppose what these members of the triumvirate have to say on any subject.

March 14. Saturday. I am told Hitler held Cabinet and official conferences all day today, that Sir Eric Phipps saw Von Neurath to give the British view of what Germany must do to avoid possible war, and that Von Neurath argued long with the Fuehrer. There is much anxiety. However, Hitler speaks at Munich tonight, taking a flying machine about 8 P.M. He will repeat what he said at Karlsruhe and have hundreds of thousands of hearers in the city.

March 15. Sunday. Hitler returned early today for another conference about the German-French dilemma and I hear the British Ambassador spoke with him rather violently. This is surprising to me for Sir Eric is a most gentle and suave Englishman. It only means that the situation is dangerous, though I think war unlikely.

March 16. Monday. We all went rather late to a musical at the Soviet Embassy. The music was extremely good. There was a large crowd but only a few Germans were there, nobody in official positions. It was rather unfortunate as the Germans need very much to sell goods in Russia for gold. However, Hitler's formal denunciation of Russia in his March 7 speech had already had the effect of closing trade negotiations with a Soviet commission which had been here some time. Wisdom is not a Hitler-Goering-Goebbels quality, though cleverness as to domestic affairs cannot be denied them.

The former Ambassador to Soviet Russia, Nadolny, was present and very frank in his criticism of the present system here. The Soviet Ambassador was a perfect gentleman in every way: manners, dress and bearing such as even the French Ambassador could not surpass. Although the Russian officials and servants eat together in the kitchen each day, according to reports, and are very simple in every way privately, there was the most protocol bearing all evening in the enormous palace rooms, and a vast and wonderful spread of foods of all varieties in the most costly dishes on a long, broad table. Some 200 crowded into the dining hall about 11:30 as we were leaving.

March 18. Wednesday. I went to see Von Neurath at 11:30 to get his reactions to events since March 7. He was suave and smiling as if everything he had discussed with me February 29 had worked out according to his advice. He even denied what he told me on the former occasion, namely, that he was urging a diplomatic solution of the Rhine demilitarization matter. I suppose it is impossible to trust even the more conservative members of the government. His attitude on the Rhine decision was rather more surprising because I was sure he did not favor marching soldiers into the Rhine zone in violation of the Locarno pact. He talked as if everything were going in the best possible way. His hope was that the London negotiations would be delayed until May when both Germany and France will have had elections. As if Hitler ever had real elections!

I went from the Foreign Office to the Reichsbank to talk with Dr. Schacht who I know is not a Nazi. Schacht talked nearly an hour. He was of the same temper and tone as Von Neurath. Everything is going fine. Germany has her Rhine territory again, she will soon have a restoration of colonies, then perhaps join the League and re-establish peace all over Europe. His only anxiety was about German exports which he said were declining on account of the nervousness of other countries. But that he thought would not continue. I never saw the great finance chief so optimistic in my life. Certainly Hitler's stroke of March 7 has had effects. I did not consider all I heard worth a half-page telegram, and so sent nothing.

March 23. Monday. We sent a long careful telegram last Friday giving the facts about the possible exchange of the Blücher Palace at Brandenburger Tor for a large place on the Tiergartenstrasse. The palace is under the very doors of a German Government building and on such a busy street that I have doubted its value as offices and residence for the U. S. Embassy. It would require $1,000,000 or more to put it into order, having cost us $1,700,000 in 1931. The German authorities have offered to give us offices and residences for all our officials here and two acres of open park around them in exchange for the palace. Secretary Phillips, when he was here, was enthusiastic for the exchange. Former Ambassador Schurman, here in November, was of the same opinion. So we sent all possible information and I urged a quick decision in Washington. As we were about ready to get the message off, Consul General Jenkins sent a protest preferring the Blücher Palace in spite of all the extra expense. I included his statement with the rest.

March 26. Thursday. Professor Richter, one-half or one-fourth Jew, dismissed from the University of Berlin in 1934, a very able man interested mainly in the history of German literature, came this morning to say farewell. He is moving to Baden about two miles from Basle, Switzerland, where he wishes to send his children to school. It is a very attractive and agreeable family. My son spent some months in their house to learn German, and also to study history, in 1935. I was depressed by the story he told. But such conditions are reported to me nearly every day.

Two people, Jews, who had lived in England nearly two years, returned a year ago thinking they could teach in a Jewish school here. They were promptly thrust into jail where they still remain. The husband's mother lives in Chicago and my friend Professor Ferdinand Schevill wrote me a few days ago begging me to get them out of jail if possible. They would at once depart for Palestine.

I asked Mr. Geist to speak quite personally on his own account to the Secret Police chief here, Himmler, when he had occasion to see him about other matters. He did so and showed Schevill's letter to him. Himmler said he would release the couple before long, but asked Geist to assist him to locate Communists here whom he would imprison and perhaps even put to death. I am doubtful about the release of the poor Jews, entirely guiltless as far as we can learn.

March 27. Friday. Mattie and I drove through Leipzig to Wartburg in the neighborhood of Weimar where we wished to see the famous medieval castle where Luther was hidden away from the Imperial authorities for nearly a year. We had had beautiful weather for a week and had thought the prospect good for a delightful journey.

March 28. Saturday. A grand demonstration has been given all the way from Berlin to Eisenach of the enthusiasm of the German people for the Fuehrer and his recent drive of troops into the demilitarized zone in the Rhineland. As noted earlier, Hitler, Goering and Goebbels have made speeches almost every day or night all over Germany calling upon everybody to vote approval of the March 7 announcement of foreign policy. In Leipzig, where one can hardly imagine everybody ready to shout, all hurrahed for the Fuehrer. There were flags flying from nearly every house and apartment, big flags and little, all the *Hakenkreuz*, hideous to look at when one thinks of what they mean.

While we were in Weimar, Goering was speaking over the radio and people were gathered in the streets to listen, where there were radio loud-speakers. The people would raise their right hands and say "Heil Hitler" as they left. The managers of the Goethe-Schiller houses did the same when we entered. I simply said "Good evening." They showed no resentment.

It was a rather striking thing to note in old Weimar, the one-time center of German civilization, that almost all the houses were flying Hitler flags. How much of all this was coerced I could not guess. In Eisleben, where Luther represented the famous German ideal of religious liberty in 1521, there were the same hurrahs for the regime which now denies all freedom. On our way to Berlin today we stopped an hour in Halle to get luncheon. The old university town of Lutheran ideals for three centuries and more showed the same sort of enthusiasm we had seen everywhere else.

All this is over an election in which there is no choice of candidates. Hitler had issued a list of names of candidates for all the districts of Germany soon after his speech March 7, with no alternative names. Ballots were printed with a circle in which the voter was to indicate approval. He might write "No," but if he did so he was liable to be arrested and imprisoned. Only people willing to risk their lives could write "No." This was understood from the beginning. Yet Leipzig, Weimar, Eisleben, Eisenach and Halle were shouting approval of the whole campaign.

As we drove into Berlin about 5 P.M., two great Zeppelins were flying slowly over the city. People were crowded everywhere to watch them and pick up cards and leaflets dropped down which asked people to vote unanimously for "liberty, equality and peace." Eckener, the captain of the new Zeppelin, the *Hindenburg*, was supposed to direct the flights.

March 29. Sunday. Today was election day. All the servants who help keep our house in order, men and women, voted joyously, it appeared, though some compulsion was evident in their behavior. However, Fritz the butler, who fought as a private on the Russian front during the World War, showed his rejoicing spirit in reference to the reoccupation of the demilitarized zone, symbolizing a hatred of France which he freely indicated.

March 30. Monday. Returns from yesterday's plebiscite showed about 95 per cent of all Germans had voted approval of Hitler's policies. The papers had little else this morning, no indication anywhere of the slightest displeasure about a coerced election or a Reichstag body which meets perhaps once a year to shout "Heil Hitler" when he makes a speech. I have attended two of these so-called Reichstag gatherings and on both occasions not a word was spoken by members, except "Heil Hitler" at pauses in his speech.

Our newspapers reported yesterday's election and a reporter told me that in the old Communist areas of Berlin there were 25 per cent opposition votes. These negative votes were not allowed to be reported. Dr. Goebbels is shouting thanks in all the German papers for the amazing, free election and the unprecedented enthusiasm of the great, free German population!

April 4. Saturday. To my surprise the Soviet Ambassador came to the office this morning. He stayed nearly an hour, talking about the French dilemma, the lessening of the tension between Russia and Japan and the dangers in the Balkan zone. He agreed with me as to the importance of friendly co-operation of those little states, but doubted its possibility. He insisted as before that Russia is not aggressive anywhere. She only wants peace.

The Fuehrer, after two or three days of conferences with a Cabinet whose members dare not oppose him, except in conversations before final decisions, has disappeared for a two or three weeks' vacation in south Germany, I think at Berchtesgaden in the mountain area of Bavaria where he looks longingly over the Austrian border at his homeland.

We learn today that some Austrian and Czechoslovak Germans are new members of the Reichstag. The fact that Hitler decreed them members is symbolic of his so-called peace policy. The claim of the right to annex parts or all of these countries is thus subtly announced. If the United States made Americans who have homes in Mexico and are Mexican citizens members of Congress there would be a world-wide commotion. Yet not a word is said here or elsewhere about these new Reichstag members. The German propagandist in Switzerland, killed two months ago by a Jew, only represented a similar feeling of the Hitler party toward Switzerland.

Naturally all small countries lying next to Germany are uneasy. The maps which show them as parts of the Third Reich are still circulating. If Hitler is able to build his fortifications along the French front to match the French fortifications, then he may at any convenient moment put his great army on the Austrian or even the Polish frontier, annex as much territory as he wishes and then call upon the enthusiastic German people to give him another unanimous vote of approval. A ten-year peace would enable him to do anything he wished; therefore, "peace and prosperity" are his slogans.

Yet today's papers announce that 4,000,000 boys between ten and fourteen are to be compelled to wear knives. These are evidences of honor. They are to be worn, as are the daggers, by boys between fourteen and eighteen, and the young boys are to be trained in military performances in all the schools, as are the older ones. Even young women are trained in certain war services. This spells "peace" in the Hitler language. How can Von Schirach and Rosenberg, intimate counselors of the Fuehrer, proclaim Hitler a second Jesus Christ before vast public gatherings and be applauded to the limit?

Roy Howard had a long interview with the Fuehrer two months ago. When Hitler complained violently about the 340 Germans per square mile with no land to go to, Howard said, "Why do you then pay every woman for her third child, with more for her fourth one, and why pay people to marry?" The Fuehrer could not reply without giving his real motive. He refused to answer and later forbade publication of this in the interview. In yesterday's Paris *Herald*, it was announced from Berlin that the German Government had given $125,000,000 to couples who have married since 1933. An increasing population for the Third Reich means either war or "peaceful" seizure of other peoples' land.

April 6. Monday. Messersmith came to our house for a luncheon today where some twenty-five people took seats at the table, the wife of the unhappy French Ambassador on my right. Others were the new Chinese Ambassador, who reports that he attended my history lectures in Chicago; the Austrian Minister; Udet, the great pilot and air adviser to Goering; Consul General Jenkins; and Mr. Wright, a mining expert of the Interior Department in Washington who is making a com-

plete survey of European mineral resources. This was the usual
"show" luncheon we give, absolutely necessary from the diplomatic point of view, perhaps not so bad since we always have
a number of Germans whom we have met and they can thus
see what sort of folk Americans are.

Messersmith reported that the Austrians are very uneasy.
Schuschnigg, the Chancellor, had been in conference with Mussolini on March 18 and 19 and as a result Austria ordered universal military service which the Italian dictator had recommended. Messersmith was convinced the Italians would help
Austria in case of a German attack.

I told him I had my doubts because Italy wants to annex
Egypt and if Germany will approve that, Mussolini will approve German annexation of Austria. He reported that Mussolini had said he hated Hitler, the very sight of him. That I
thought was for effect on Schuschnigg rather than an expression of real hatred, though I do not think the two dictators love
each other. Germans hate Italy to the limit and Italians feel
the same towards the Germans, much as the latter spend their
savings in Venice, Florence, Rome and Naples.

I expressed my opinion to Messersmith that Italy will hold
Albania, keep close to Austria and threaten Yugoslavia until
the Mediterranean struggle comes. Then she will yield Austria, take Egypt and allow Germany to have the Balkan states
she demands if she has control of Palestine, Greece and Syria.
Mussolini will re-establish the Roman dictatorship, Germany
will become the master of Austria, Czechoslovakia and Hungary. If the Germans build their fortifications as planned on
the French frontier, there will be nobody to stop her moves.
Messersmith was not of a really different view, and he agreed
that the poor Balkan peoples so hate one another that they invite this.

April 7. Tuesday. I called on Secretary von Bülow today. He
is not a Nazi and is reported never to have conferred with Hitler about anything. Von Bülow answered many questions re-
servedly. He said: "Economically Mussolini owns Albania.
That distresses our friends, the clever Yugoslavs, but we have

made no protests. As to Austria, we are doing nothing, and we would make no protest if Mussolini annexed Egypt. As to the possibility of war, there is none. France is excited but their generals do not favor war now and their people are dead against hostilities on account of Hitler's Rhine occupation."

This was nothing new at all, and I cannot see why he took the time he did. Practically all Germans want to control, if not annex, everything between their present eastern boundary and the Black Sea. Not even an educated republican German objects to the great risks in this direction. That would mean an empire of 150,000,000 people and control of all Europe as the United States once thought of controlling all the two Americas.

Next, I went to see the British Ambassador on the same street. Sir Eric Phipps is not the best-informed man on European history, but he knows contemporary Europe as few others do. In January he was ready to help his government to the limit against German aggression and willing to support the French-Soviet pact, wrangled over in Europe for a year. He had said then that France and England were offering a solid front and Italy was expected to join them.

Today he was uncertain about what his country should do in any direction. All Europe is in a critical situation. Italy may seize all Ethiopia and even Egypt, which would mean immediate war in the Mediterranean. France might break across the German western frontier which England would not support. Germany is preparing to the limit for eastern aggression and England won't do anything. I said: That means a new Europe, with France declining, England losing her empire and Germany becoming the master of all.

April 11. Saturday. William N. Enstrom, representing the Irving Trust Co. of New York, came in for a talk about the financial situation here. I had to refer him to our finance expert, Mr. Flack, and finally to Dr. Schacht who is now on his vacation in South Germany, near Basle where he goes monthly to confer with international bankers. Enstrom revealed an attitude toward Roosevelt which surprised me. Surely he was not simply drawing me out! He predicted the President's re-election by a large margin and he also said a defeat would be a calamity. It is rare that a great bank official expresses such views.

We are at the end of the week during which England and France have labored at Geneva to find some way out of the dilemma which has been growing worse every week since December 15, 1935. The British Foreign Secretary Eden is the only eminent leader in Europe who seems to understand the drift.

Italy is fighting with increasing success in Ethiopia, aiming to control the Mediterranean and cut off England from her vast Far Eastern possessions. Mussolini thinks himself a new Caesar entitled to recover what Rome controlled 2,000 years ago. If he succeeds, England's power declines as did that of the Netherlands after 1713—a sad move for Europe.

Anthony Eden saw this danger and urged the stopping of Mussolini's ruthless war by sanctions on all war supplies. But the Foreign Secretary, Hoare, influenced by great oil and other corporations, agreed with the French Foreign Secretary, Laval, to defeat Eden and leave Mussolini a fairly free course of conquest. France had promised Mussolini everything he asked in January, 1935, in a secret agreement contrary to French obligations as a member of the League of Nations.

When the Hoare-Laval announcement was made in December, Mussolini saw his way to Caesar's position more clearly. England was so perturbed that Hoare was compelled to resign and Eden was appointed Foreign Secretary: too late to save England's case in the League. France still hoped to enlist the Italians on her side in case of a German threat of war. But Hitler quickly saw his opportunity, and Goebbels spoke on December 17 in praise of Mussolini, saying his success meant German recovery of her colonies. From December 15 to March 6, high German officials worked and conferred with army officers for a united front to seize the demilitarized Rhine zone, denouncing the French-Soviet peace pact and asking for all the German colonies of 1914. The German people, who hate Italians as much or more than the French, rallied slowly, and on March 7 came the strategic Hitler appeal to Europe. On March 29 came the plebiscite which gave Hitler a 95 per cent vote.

This week the League and Locarno conferences have been held in the vast palace in Geneva. Eden could do nothing. Flandin, French Foreign Secretary, would do nothing. The two dictators are happier than they have ever been before. The small European states, Holland, Denmark, Czechoslovakia, Rumania and others, are more uneasy than at any time since the end of the World War. Austria is the next objective of Hitler, and Egypt the next ambition of Mussolini. At least this appears to be true from all the evidence available. England and France, having failed to see realities, have put themselves in dangerous positions and practically ruined the League, their one hope of avoiding war.

April 16. Thursday. I went to say good-by to Von Bülow, perhaps the most sensible and charming man in the Foreign Office. He talked about the dangerous and wicked war of Mussolini and agreed that he is certainly a menace to European peace. However, he added, he believes Mussolini is not so near to the mastery of all Ethiopia as he proclaims. He foresees complete surrender because he fears the coming rainy season may defeat him. His economic situation is exceedingly dangerous.

Von Bülow informed me "the French Government is preparing a series of questions to be sent us next week. They have to do with the Locarno question and the proposed peace of Hitler. We can answer the questions fairly well, but they wired us not to reply until the elections are over in France, on May 3, so we are convinced there is nothing very pressing. It seems to me peace is fairly secure for months to come. The League can do nothing but talk and delay. In case France were to agree to have no alliances, I think we all might unite in a European League for Mutual Security."

At luncheon we sat down with some interesting people at our table: Dr. Hugo Eckener, the great Zeppelin engineer who has just returned from Brazil, Karl von Wiegand, the United Press general representative William Philip Simms, and Counselor Mayer. Dr. Eckener was the one man who interested us all. He declined to fly his ship and propagandize for Hitler on

March 28 and 29 when the new Zeppelin, the *Hindenburg,* was ordered to fly all over Germany. That caused Goebbels to see Hitler and ask what should be done to the indispensable captain. It is reported that Hitler ranted and shouted that the man must be dismissed. That was not possible, and Goebbels gave the German press an order never again to mention Dr. Eckener's name. Although the *Hindenburg* was caught in a dangerous storm on the way back from Brazil last week and the machinery damaged, there was no mention of the commander's name.

When Dr. Eckener talked at table about a flight to the United States, I said: "You might take Dr. Goebbels with you and let him see the United States." Dr. Eckener seemed amazed and, after a pause, everybody roared with laughter. The joke was understood. Later the flyer explained his plans for going to the United States and calling on President Roosevelt. But he insisted that Goebbels must recall his order or he would resign and there would be no flight this year across the dangerous North Atlantic. I am wondering what Hitler will order to be done.

April 18. Saturday. I began my long journey back to the United States this morning, driving to Hamburg, my wife and daughter with me. We arrived in Hamburg at 4:15 but lost nearly a half hour in finding the *City of Baltimore.* There had been rain and snow all the way from Berlin to Hamburg. The country looked beautiful for that part of Germany, wheat, barley, rye everywhere and quite green for the season.

April 19. Sunday. In bed all day, but the sea was beautiful, this old sea where thousands of ships, of peace and war, must lie on the bottom, and perhaps millions of men's bones in them. What a sad story if the real history of these waters could be known since the time of Julius Caesar! I never sail over this region without wondering what poor mankind has done here. As night approached, I was out a few minutes on the deck to view the southern coast of England where the Romans first went across to capture the attractive country, where the Saxons in the fifth and sixth centuries entered to crowd the mixed Celts and Romans westward, and where the Normans landed in 1066 to conquer the people who had been organized and made a nation by Alfred the Great, whose monument I pondered upon in October, 1928, in the beautiful English town of Winchester.

Poor, rich, powerful England, for three hundred years the leading cultural country of the world, the builder of the amazing empire of 1600 to 1914—now beginning to decline. If Italy seizes her strategic positions in the Mediterranean, as Mussolini plans to do, the Empire will begin to fall to pieces. If Germany under Hitler or his successor seizes the control of the Balkan states to Constantinople, as planned, then England loses her leadership of western Europe. To me these moves seem logical, tragic but inevitable. They will be calamitous for the ideals of the English people whose leaders during the past six or eight years have made the saddest blunders possible.

April 22. Wednesday. I am instinctively of a nervous nature. My food does not digest properly, headaches spread over the nerve connections between the stomach, shoulders and brain until sleep is almost impossible, and that only adds to the discomfort of ocean travel. While I am never seasick in the ordinary sense, I was in bed all day yesterday reading a German book on *Roosevelt and His Revolution* trying to counteract the influence of the stormy sea and rolling stateroom. There was no quiet until 1 o'clock, the ship moving steadily. The book on the President and his task is good, though not altogether right.

The Atlantic is certainly a rough part of the world, where most sea trade goes on from year to year. Somehow boat life annoys me. I can't imagine myself in the position of an officer or seaman even on the safest of vessels. Such a life is incomprehensible to me. Yet the men on this ship seem to be quite content with their lives.

June 22. Monday. I arrived here, the University of Chicago, Saturday morning in the best of health. Six weeks at my Round Hill farm, "Stoneleigh," were among the best of my life. The State Department agreed to leave me as free from interruption as possible and the arrangement was observed strictly. I was outdoors in the warm sun about ten hours each day, working a little here, a little there, helping to build an annex to my house for a library, improving roads that needed repairs very much, and even supervising the hauling of rocks necessary to build the annex. The work was not too heavy at any time but quite useful to the simple fellows who were working for me.

There were people who seemed amazed that I should work with ordinary laborers, but anyone could see that without my help they would not have done more than half what they did. The weather was so beautiful and my dairy farm was in the best condition I have seen it in years, with a fine corn crop growing in spite of a brief drought in May. The thirty cows yield $175 a month. If the present tenant learns how to raise all needful feed, he will really make a net profit, even with the low milk prices in Washington. The only criticism I had to make of the tenant was about his careless treatment of the horses which I furnished him.

This morning the news came from Berlin that my friend, Secretary von Bülow of the Foreign Office, is dead. It is sad news to me. He was one of the noble figures in the sad complex in Berlin. He took cold a few days ago and the cold drifted into pneumonia and he could not rally against it—one of the things I fear will happen to me. We both were quite sensitive to cold, both having little electric heaters near our desks in our offices. I sent a cable to Secretary von Neurath indicating my great sorrow. Von Bülow was a genuine patriot and many times indicated to me his real feelings about the regime under which he worked.

June 28. Sunday. This university where I first appeared on Andrew C. McLaughlin's invitation in the summer of 1908, is the most appealing to me of any in the world. Perhaps this is partisanship, but certainly there are many real, truth-seeking professors and many promising young scholars coming here every year. President Hutchins, whose call depended in 1929 a good deal on what Professor Charles E. Merriam and I thought of him, is very able and ambitious, sometimes very unwise in his methods of selecting new scholars for different faculties. He is now away; perhaps he is away on purpose while

I am here. He knows my difference of opinion with him in some important matters. His article in the current *Yale Review* shows his theoretical attitude.

I think universities should be free-thinking and free-speaking centers of study and research. He thinks the same, but has the idea that presidents should select professors without the agreement of the faculty members already at work who know the prospective scholars far better than he can know them. He has the dictatorship idea in this and reorganization matters. My way would be faculty recommendation, debate and majority decisions. That would increase the interest and effectiveness of scholars, always tempted to be absorbed in their own fields of work.

July 1. Wednesday. I talked last night on world commerce and free trade, on the industrial-financial revolutions which paralleled the amazing trade profits of 1846 to 1912, on the abnormal building of great cities, and finally on the World War and its effects on economic-social life everywhere between 1918 and 1936. I have never had such close attention and at the end, the applause surpassed anything I have ever experienced. All the papers and press people had a full outline of what I said, but I was sure the Chicago papers would not publish it. This morning I noted that the *Tribune* tried to exploit what I said parenthetically about Woodrow Wilson in the hope of injuring his fame. The *Daily News* put a brief story on page 10, the *Tribune* on page 4. The Hearst papers printed only two inches, after their reporters had spent a half hour with me trying in vain to get an interview on Europe and making half a dozen snapshot pictures.

July 21. Tuesday. I have to leave Chicago tonight for Cleveland where I am to speak once more on the *Dilemma of Modern Civilization*, which the Chicago papers have been unwilling to report. The editors are big business men who think protective tariffs are a blessing, who still think they can sell abroad no matter how little they buy and who do not like my accounts of the way our country has paid its debts after wars. Moreover, every paper here of any wide circulation is dead against Roosevelt and cannot allow even an historic approach to the dilemma. This is an attitude of the press the President has had to contend with from the beginning. But other papers, only a few about the country, call attention to my warnings against the dangers ahead.

My work here has been heavy. Great numbers of most competent students who are teachers in all parts of the country have taken my time. From what they say the university's merging of history into the social sciences as a minor subject is most discouraging. They lament the failure of the university to give American history in a large comprehensive way, and add that they cannot get sufficient knowledge except upon their own initiative and with library work. This is Hutchins' system. I have long feared his scheme of limiting departments and avoiding departmental selection of professors would greatly injure this institution. Nothing is more important than eminent professors developing their subjects their own way, first being sure the professors are worthy of appointment. I am distressed at Chicago University. Sometimes I wish I might again bring pressure to bear here.

July 24. Friday. Driving down to Washington, where the weather was most oppressive, I saw Secretary Hull. We talked freely a few minutes about the failure of the German commissioners who were recently with him and the possibility of Roosevelt's defeat. I regretted that Germany could make no changes in her bilateral commercial treaties. This meant the application of a penalty tariff on German imports, since Germany could not, under Hitler, open her market to American exports: the sad plight of modern industrial countries.

As to Roosevelt's re-election, Hull said he was fairly certain of success, but, he added, the President cannot speak "what you and I believe the truth about tariff follies. The people are now protectionists." If this is correct it is the first time in American history when protective tariffs would receive a majority vote.

Washington is the most disagreeable city I know in some respects. The traffic is concentrated about Pennsylvania and Constitution Avenues in such a way as to make movements in

a car or on foot most difficult and dangerous. The construction
of government buildings close together reminds one of the
stupidity of the Loop district of Chicago where millions of
people labor or move about with great danger. Modern people
think they must pack themselves in cities and refuse to leave
even when starvation confronts them. How different from the
spirit and purposes of the people who founded the North American colonies and later the Union!

July 29. Wednesday. I sailed on the *Washington* today at 12
o'clock. Now comes the renewal of the distressing tension of
my residence in Berlin where democracy is denounced almost
every day.

X

August 7, 1936 to December 25, 1936

August 7. Friday. We arrived in Hamburg after a slow all-day ride in the low-tide river, the Elbe. I hurried in my car to Berlin with our chauffeur. In Berlin at 10:30, after a long and most beneficial vacation in Virginia and Chicago, in spite of my heavy university work. All the way from Hamburg to Berlin, about 200 miles, the countryside looked beautiful and prosperous, as ever in spring and summer.

August 9. Sunday night. I attended the 100-year-old Herren Club where Von Papen, Von Neurath, the French Ambassador and others sat at the table where I was, but I heard no really revealing conversation about anything. It was a large show, with 150 people present, in honor of the Olympic Games which are attracting so much attention. It's the club whose members were expecting to be killed the last week in June, 1934, one of whom came to me for help. Kaiser Wilhelm I, Von Hindenburg and Hitler stood out in great paintings on the main dining room wall.

Aside from the dinner there was nothing worth while, though Von Neurath did say he had been talking over long distance with Madrid this afternoon. Nothing decisive was happening in Spain, he said, and not apt to happen in a month. He said: "All peoples are committing economic suicide by their foolish trade and financial policies. Schacht was right in his recent speech."

August 14. Friday. Fritz Kuhn, Nazi Fuehrer in America, brought a group of German-Americans to my office. Kuhn is a Nazi propagandist who once worked in Henry Ford's factory in Detroit. He is guiding his party of visitors about Germany to convince them that Nazism is the salvation of modern peoples. He kept his purpose from me but I have since learned that he represents Bohle of the Foreign Office of the Nazi Party.

Yesterday we went to Goering's garden party in honor of the Olympic Games commissioners here. It's the old Prussian royal palace where Goering feels so much at home, a mansion far larger and more elaborately fitted out than the White House in Washington. The garden, in the very heart of the city, is about as large as the front lawn of the White House. There were huge spotlights on the tops of surrounding houses which shed light over the area almost as bright as daytime. And there were hundreds of lights suspended from trees about the place. There was hardly anything that modern inventors could have added.

Ministers of the government, Goebbels, Von Neurath, Von Blomberg and others were grouped about with ambassadors and ministers from all over the world. I talked a little with Schacht and walked around the park with Sir Eric Phipps. As we all sat down about 8:30 to eat at hundreds of tables, small and large, the wind was cold and damp, and the electric heaters about the place were of no value, as the breeze took the warmth away. I saw that I would take cold, but my wife argued against my wearing my hat and overcoat which I had left in the palace as we entered. But as the air grew colder and colder, I got my hat and coat. I felt less conspicuous when I saw Lewald, the German chief of the Olympic Games commission, had his hat also, and Sir Eric Phipps was leaving because of the cold.

It was the greatest display I have ever seen, with actors and actresses dancing in eighteenth century garb on the lawn. The famous air pilot Udet had arranged a flying machine performance which showed all the tricks of the expert stunt flyer. We looked at the show for a time, as also at other displays. But the weather was so cold that I decided to leave, at 10:15. I was sure my colds of last year would return.

August 15. Saturday. A report of the American Consul at Stuttgart in southern Germany says the press over that region is quite open in its discussion of Spanish relations. The general idea they suggest is for the Fascist-Nazi powers to assist the revolutionary, or rather the reactionary, army crowd of Spain to regain control there. Then Germany and Italy, having lent assistance, would divide the Spanish colonial possessions and enter into some entente arrangement which would give the three dictatorships control of Europe without war.

While I had not foreseen this immediate Spanish situation, I had forecast the German-Italian control of Europe in private reports to Washington. The events of last autumn pointed toward this outcome. Hitler's speech of March 7 was a master stroke in this direction. The failure of English-French co-operation against Italy in the Ethiopian conquest seemed to me to doom democracy in Europe. In these last weeks the Spanish conflict seems to offer another opportunity to Mussolini and Hitler. They can hardly fail since England is helpless and France so divided that a dictatorship seems unavoidable. The United States, having failed in 1919-20 to co-operate in European affairs, now faces a solid dictatorship front which in due time will give serious trouble. How unwise our minority Senators were and have continued to be!

A member of my staff told me today that our Counselor Mayer, who was sent here last December, decided before I left last April to get into closer relations with Goering, and negotiate a treaty with Germany. He made all sorts of advances to Goering, who received the impression that I would be re-called by Roosevelt soon or retire if Roosevelt should be defeated in November. I thought last March he was cultivating the German dictators far more cordially than either Mr. White or Mr. Gordon, his predecessors.

When Mayer wrote the State Department saying he was

offering to open negotiations, the Secretary advised against it. But when two representatives were urged to come over to talk things over, Goering was most friendly and invited the Counselor more than once to see him. He also gave him a dinner. The State Department sent two representatives to Germany, but they refused to come to Berlin.

Goering, with Hitler's approval, sent a representative to see them in Munich. No real concessions were offered for a treaty and the United States agents went home. Goering, and perhaps Mayer, thought I had defeated the move. Never a word was said to me in Washington. Of course I had nothing to do with the matter.

Then two Senators came over, Wheeler and Barkley. Mayer dined them in grand style and asked Goering to sit with them. Goering accepted but failed to appear at the last moment, apparently angry with Mayer. Wheeler was among those at a dinner in Washington where Germany's right to be dictator of all Europe was approved. He reported to Mayer that I was unpopular over the whole United States. This was in no way evidenced to me when I was there in June and July. These Senators are reported to have said that I would soon be recalled. What they really said or had in mind, I shall try to learn.

August 16. Sunday. We went this afternoon at 1:30 to the Olympic Games Stadium for the closing contests and final announcements. I spoke one minute over the radio to the United States.

As we entered the seven-mile street at the Great Star circle in the Tiergarten, we saw the flags of Germany and many of the other nations flying from hundreds of tall poles. The flags continued all the way to the stadium, with swastika flags flying from the windows of every house. On both sides of the streets, all the way, were uniformed S.A. and S.S. soldiers, standing close together. There must have been 100,000 soldiers.

We took our places with the other ambassadors on the front row of seats. Hitler and Goering and other Nazis, including the generals, were to be seated on reserved seats high above us and a little behind. Hitler arrived at 3 o'clock. The races then began, horse-jumping contests between many countries. They continued until 8 o'clock. Then came announcements and the awarding of medals and honors. The great stadium field was lighted by electric machines from the top rows of the seats all around and by curious electric streams of lights meeting some two or three hundred feet above the performances. I have never seen such an elaborate show.

Last night, we went to Dr. Goebbels' reception for diplomats and Olympic people on a beautiful island near Dahlem, fifteen miles out of town. It was the site of a former Jewish mansion. We shook hands with the host, the man who had helped in June 30, 1934, to murder Germans who have never been shown to have been guilty of anything but opposition to the Nazi regime. I disliked the hand-shake as I did that with Goering at a similar show two days before. We sat down at a small table near Goebbels' main table, although I am second ranking diplomat here, the French Ambassador being first. I preferred this and Goebbels had not asked us to his table.

In a little while the dinner was served, some 2,000 people supposed to be present. There were beautiful lights strung all over the island, some in trees. The French Ambassador and his wife, the Italian Ambassador and his wife, Von Neurath and some Olympic Committee people took their places with Goebbels. We were near enough to note that there was no really cordial conversation, which is a rare thing at diplomatic functions.

When the dinner closed, dancing began on an elevated platform near us. It was not unlike the dancing at Goering's reception, imitating Greek and Victorian performances. About 10 o'clock there was shooting of a kind that suggested war. This continued for a half hour, a great many people complaining at this form of war propaganda. People at our table trembled when the bombing made such a terrible noise. There were of course no real shots or shells, but there were explosions which almost made the ground shake.

This display, like Von Ribbentrop's and Goering's, must have cost 40,000 marks of government money. How much the Olympic show cost one can hardly imagine, though I would guess 75,000,000 marks. The propaganda of it all may have pleased the Germans. It had a bad influence on foreigners, as reported to me, in spite of the fine entertainment of all concerned.

August 18. Tuesday. I talked today with Dr. Schacht who has hitherto been most friendly and frank. I never heard him criticize the United States in such a vehement spirit. He was violent in his language about the decision of the government not to allow German subsidized imports. I asked him if it were understood here that I had done anything in the United States to precipitate this decision. He said: "Oh, no. I know you have always favored freer trade."

He laid the blame on the President and on Secretary Morgenthau. He ridiculed the idea that the tariff law makes the decision necessary, and then said Germany will buy nothing else from America. He never mentioned the subsidy difficulty, but criticized Secretary Hull for his system of treaties and indicated the German anger about the relations between the United States and Brazil which he said had defeated German trade plans in Brazil. I did not know the details of this and hence did not discuss it.

Schacht then said: "Well, we shall not pay interest on your bank bonds. Your people demand 6 and 7 per cent from us when they get only 2 and 3 per cent for loans at home." I let him go on, although I knew most Americans who held German bonds had agreed to 3½ and 4 per cent interest. Schacht further added: "You gave us the League of Nations and then would have nothing to do with it. Now Germany asks for colonies and the right to expand." I said: But that is England's business; we have often said at home Germany ought to have her colonies returned.

He went on urging that Roosevelt call a world conference after his re-election and insist upon Germany's rights, although he blamed the President for his Chautauqua speech about world peace. "We have been arming for three years and have paid all the cost of it."

I replied: But war is apt to mean the collapse of civilization.

"Yes," he agreed, "a general war would mean world-wide Communism and total economic collapse."

It was a revelation of Schacht's hostility never before shown. It seemed clear that he thinks Germany, if she continues to increase her sway in Europe, will and must resist to the limit, perhaps even fight the United States. When I mentioned some blunders Germany had made in religious matters, he replied: "You are right; it was a mistake. Won't you see Hitler about that?" I felt his sarcasm but could not help saying: The Fuehrer would go into a fury and I do not care to witness that.

Although Schacht insisted upon his friendliness to me and agreed to keep our talk confidential, I had the feeling that what we said was registered on a government machine connected with his telephone.

August 23. Sunday. For three days now German official attitudes have been impossible to ascertain. We know that Hitler held a conference here with some Cabinet members and ranted violently about the Spanish search of a German war vessel off their coast beyond the legal zone. Von Blomberg was much opposed to a war-like move. Hitler quieted down after a while and a protest was sent to the helpless Spanish Government.

Miss Schultz, the Chicago *Tribune* correspondent, reported that she knew twenty-five German airplanes had been sent last week from Dusseldorf to the rebels in Spain. At the same time I learned that Von Blomberg had forbidden Dr. Schacht to ship airplanes and war material to Bulgaria, saying: "All war material must remain at home, so imminent is the danger." Schacht was distressed because he so much needed foreign exchange with which to buy foodstuffs and raw materials. I do not see how the Spanish rebels can pay for their imports.

Friday and Saturday the German press was wild in its attack on Russia because it was said they had 12,000,000 soldiers ready for war and forty submarines in the Baltic Sea. Denunciations of Russia were the worst I have ever noticed in my three years here. The denunciation of the Spanish Government was equally violent. There seemed to be grave danger of an immediate war move.

Mr. Wright, an expert student here for six months of German war and other resources, reported to me that a leader, frequently asked to become economic secretary under Schacht, had solemnly said to him that Germany was ready for war soon, but that if she did go to war there would be defeat and that Hitler would be overthrown. He thinks the German masses would not fight as they did in the World War. Mr. Wright reported further the difficulty of supporting a great war very long. It would be impossible to get supplies and foodstuffs. I am inclined to think Wright estimates fairly well, except that war is always more possible than economists think. Oil, gas, and foodstuffs would be the costly necessities.

In spite of all the newspaper and general excitement during the last days of the week, we have a silent press today. There is no repetition of attacks on Russia, France or Spain. Some order has been given out to stop everything. Hitler is in Berchtesgaden, Von Neurath is near Stuttgart, and Von Blomberg is quiet at his suburban place here. I think the demonstrations were to prepare the German people for increased war preparations and for the understanding of and submission to food shortages, already being talked about anxiously.

August 25. Tuesday. We had a luncheon, the third large one since my return from Chicago. Some interesting guests included Dr. Dieckhoff, Dr. Leitner and his wife, for nine years Counselor to the German Embassy in Washington, Dr. Thomsen, personal secretary to Hitler, who is going to Washington to take Leitner's place, Mr. and Mrs. Pierson of the government Import-Export Bank in Washington for assisting international trade, and several others, including the Minister from Nicaragua, supposed to be strongly pro-French. The conversation could not be free or interesting because of the various opposing opinions. So we talked a lot, said nothing, and ate heartily. After the luncheon I sounded Dieckhoff out, but there was no real comment on German policy, except its anti-Communist attitude toward Spain.

Léon Blum, the French Prime Minister, said a few days ago that the great problem in France was substantial unity, a combination of all moderate and radical groups behind a struggle for the sort of real democracy which France has never had in spite of all her efforts since 1789. I doubt Blum's success. If the Italians and Germans set up a Nazi or Fascist regime in Madrid, through their propaganda and secret assistance to General Franco, France is going to be in the most difficult position since the fall of Napoleon I.

August 29. Saturday. Nothing is more oppressive to a democrat, not a Democrat and also not a Communist, than the situation in Europe. Hitler is the absolute master of Germany's 68,000,000 people, Mussolini is master of Italy's 42,000,000, and the dominant groups in Poland, Austria, Hungary and Rumania are already Fascist. We have reports that Mussolini sent word to Franco that any general who precipitated the dictatorship movement in Spain, on July 17, would receive Italian help to overthrow the democratic (partly radical) government of Spain. All the world knows the horrors that have been perpetrated in Spain since August. Hitler is, or was, certainly sending aid to Franco and the Nazi Party here has been maintaining propaganda activity in Spain for several years.

A story comes today from a Vienna newspaper man that Schuschnigg, the dictator of Austria, was with Hitler at Berchtesgaden a few days ago. He also says the situation of Austria is such that it is a pure waste of money to have a United States legation in Vienna. That has been my opinion for more than a year. Another reputable journalist reported that Mussolini told him: "Do not go to Vienna. Rome and Berlin determine Austrian affairs." It is mostly Berlin, however.

A few days ago Dr. Schacht went to Paris on a special mission. There were many rumors as to his purpose. My guess, supported by the French Ambassador's remarks here today, is that he went with instructions from Hitler to work out a deal with the French Fascists before the expected fall of Blum, the Prime Minister there now. Before Schacht left here early this week he talked with François-Poncet, who is not far from being a Fascist. From newspaper stories one might think it was a simple financial mission. I think the second object of the visit was the hope of buying cotton and copper in France from Americans, since the trade situation between Germany and the United States does not allow cotton or copper to be sent directly. These materials are the most necessary of war stuffs. François-Poncet acknowledged this today.

One other story today says Mussolini was with Hitler last Saturday. I doubt it, but Goebbels, shrewdest of all the dictators here, is in Venice. So the pressure everywhere is for dictatorships, in all countries except England, where the foolish Conservatives are in power, in Czechoslovakia, where there is a movement to surrender to Hitler, and in Russia where Communism is again executing its opponents. In the United States, capitalists are pressing in the same Fascist direction, supported by capitalists in England. Nearly all our diplomatic service people here have indicated their drift in the same direction. Violently hostile to the Nazi regime for three years, they are now half supporting it.

August 30. Sunday. The last few days here were quiet, but the newspapers continue their violent agitation against Russia and Communism. Young Armand Bérard of the French Government has been here for several days. His picture of the French dilemma is very discouraging. Prime Minister Blum has a few Jews in his Cabinet, very able and popular men when appointed. Now an anti-Semitic campaign is increasing its activity all the time and this adds to the strength of the Fascists. They now have a leader, the renegade Jacques Doriot, a man who has a certain following among Paris workers and is financed by French industrialists. Next November Blum is almost certain to be overthrown and, if so, a Fascist regime is quite possible. That would be what Schacht wishes. Bérard goes back tomorrow via a flying machine.

September 1. Tuesday. We all went to the flying field at 4 P.M. to meet my son William, returning from Shanghai where he has been working for the International Peace Campaign, a popular-front group with representatives in the United States, England, France, Switzerland, and even Russia. Mr. Bérard waited over a day and he was with us. William's flying plane was two and a half hours late and the young Frenchman had to take his Paris plane back before William arrived.

I was quite uneasy before the plane landed, lest the sharp winds from the North and Baltic Seas might have brought his plane down. He arrived, though, about 6:30 and we had a delightful family reunion.

September 4. Friday. Thomas Wolfe, the American novelist of great popularity, just left. He said a hotel owner and a friend of his publisher here remarked to him today: "All Europe is going Fascist and that keeps the peace."

This afternoon I called on the Dutch Minister, who has just returned from his country. He said soon after I entered his office: "We shall probably never have another happy day in our lives. All people seem so crazy. The English have committed the greatest blunders in their history these last three years."

He spoke of the Nazi Party Day which opens next Monday in Nürnberg. He does not go, as I do not. He agreed that it would be most disagreeable to sit outdoors in the cold on high benches near the Fuehrer and hear him or Goering denounce democracy as they have done each time. I said: It might be more embarrassing to have to get up and leave when such things were said. But the Minister reminded me that the representative here of Sweden had been ordered by his government to attend the Nürnberg Congress. He added: "I see the Czechoslovak Minister and the Rumanian are also attending." This only shows the increasing fear of those little countries of the Hitler Reich. However, the Dutchman has never attended, nor has the Belgian Minister. And neither I nor the French or English Ambassadors has ever accepted these invitations to witness such propaganda on a grand scale. Neither Mussolini nor Stalin asks diplomats to attend their party meetings.

This evening's paper, the *Abendblatt*, announces in great headlines that Mussolini is sending a war vessel, armed, and several thousand soldiers to Barcelona. This seems to me Mussolini's way of finding out what the French and English will do. I think they will do nothing. If they do not, later Mussolini will, in my opinion, send more troops and subordinate General Franco to his will, perhaps take partial control of Spain—one more step toward his Caesar goal.

September 6. Sunday. Since nothing of importance can be discussed or decided in Berlin the next few days, with all high officials in Nürnberg attending the Party Day, we drove away about 11 o'clock for Magdeburg en route to Holland. It was a delightful day. At Magdeburg we stopped long enough to see the famous cathedral where Otto I lies buried, a monument to his Negro servant standing near his impressive tomb. Magdeburg was the place where Martin Luther first went to school.

From Magdeburg we drove along the wonderful German *autobahn*, a road for cars alone, but eventually for war purposes too, toward Hanover. Hanover is one vast farm area with fertile hills and valleys, wheat, potatoes, beets everywhere, harvested or ready to be harvested. Nowhere did I see any signs of erosion although the land has been cultivated a thousand years.

September 11. Friday. About sixty miles east of the Rhine, we were halted today on a lonely road by a road barrier and a military man. He said soldiers were conducting secret attack and defense maneuvers on the road ahead and nobody was allowed to see the performance. He ordered us to turn back toward the Rhine. I said we were bound for Rothenberg where we hoped to be about noon. He said "No" again, but when our driver showed him our credentials and curtly said we were "dienstliche unterwegs" (on official mission), he yielded rather reluctantly. Our chauffeur believed that the officer mistook me for a general due to arrive from Berlin to supervise the army show.

During the next hour we saw army trucks, machine guns and many soldiers. We got caught in a line of tanks and were unable to move along, all the time fearing that at any moment the maneuvers would begin. In the last village we passed through, the officers had to remove an entanglement of barbed wire thrown across the road. I was very nervous and felt we were in the wrong place. Other officers stopped us twice and questioned us angrily, but let us go on when they learned who we were and our destination. I was afraid the officer who let us in first would be arrested. I am still a little fearful that some sensation may come of it.

September 12. Saturday. As we returned from our week of travel about Holland, Belgium and south Germany we picked up Leipzig and Berlin papers filled with articles about Hitler's, Goebbels' and Rosenberg's denunciations of Communists, "dominated everywhere," they said, "by wicked Jews who intend to rule the world." It is amazing what these men have said and how they seem to think Germany and Italy must force all peoples to join them in overthrowing the Russian system, as if one country had the right to dictate to others what sort of government they may have.

At the same time that Hitler talks virulently about democracy, President Roosevelt addresses an international conference in Washington giving some of the basic causes of existing troubles in our world. How little good American attitudes can do! Hitler knows all peoples are horribly afraid of another war and yet he challenges and insults all peoples who do not submit to arbitrary governments. He thinks he can rule all of central Europe, as Napoleon tried to do, because everybody is afraid he will go to war.

September 16. Wednesday. In view of the needs of our government to know whether multitudinous newspaper reports as to German conditions are correct, I asked yesterday to see Dieckhoff. I was hopeful he might talk more frankly than his chief, Von Neurath.

When I entered the waiting room of the Foreign Office, the most conspicuous thing in the room was a large portrait of Hitler on the table where guests or diplomats are expected to sit while waiting a few minutes to be received. This Hitler portrait is a new thing in the Foreign Office. When I entered Dieckhoff's office, I saw another large portrait of Hitler on his desk by which we were to sit a half hour. I wondered whether the same portrait is in Von Neurath's office. When I came to Berlin the officials in this department of the government were all friendly to democratic institutions and resentful that innocent Jews were being so roughly treated. They even expected to be dismissed by Hitler because they were not all Party members. Now all seems different.

Dieckhoff defended all Hitler had said against other countries, but said he did not mean to compel the Russian Ambassador to leave the country, as we had heard from reliable sources. When I asked him about German relations with Spain he said, "Germany is strictly neutral," but he at once justified Portugal's refusal to be neutral on the ground that the democratic government of Spain intends to annex Portugal. I told him I did not believe that. He insisted, and argued for the Franco army coup in Spain, even approving Italy's aid to the army revolt. All that Dieckhoff said showed that he hopes for a Fascist government in Spain. That is Hitler's demand, and I believe Germany is sending aid through Portugal. One day I think we shall learn that Hitler and Mussolini have advised Portugal to take this position.

When I asked Dieckhoff about the Locarno conference, possibly a world peace agreement, he at once said: "Yes, we shall agree to participate, but not if Russia is allowed to be there." I said this would keep France from entering the conference, especially if Germany demanded the abandonment of the Franco-Russian peace pact of last year. He replied: "We can have nothing to do with Russian Communists."

I said: I agree the Communists have been very foolish in sending propaganda all over the world, but your government does the same thing. Why do you complain? He replied at once: "We send propaganda only to German subjects in other countries. We have a right to consider them our own people." I did not tell him what I knew to the contrary in the United States, Switzerland and other countries. I once replied, at a dinner, to his remark that Germany must control the Danube countries: Well, we have millions of citizens of the United States in Canada, or sons and daughters of citizens. Why should we not demand control of Canada? Yet not a single prominent American leader since Champ Clark has made a speech asking the annexation of Canada. I thought of that conversation today and I think Dieckhoff did, too. Nearly all Germans, Nazis and anti-Nazis, regard Germans all over the world, especially in Holland, Switzerland and the Balkan zone, as their own people and hope to annex them, even if they must go to war.

From the Foreign Office I went to Unter den Linden in my car. There I left my car and walked to the Russian Embassy, in order not to be watched by Germans. I saw the Ambassador only a short time. He said he did not expect to be withdrawn because of Hitler's wild attacks. "These attacks are really aimed at forcing France to denounce her treaty with us. My government has not even asked me to make a protest. Hitler expects to force England and France to join Germany and Italy in isolating the Soviet Union." I am much of the same opinion, and think Hitler intends to annex the Baltic states that were formerly parts of Russia, Lithuania, Latvia and Esthonia, the first time there is a break anywhere, especially if France and England agree to have the treaty between Russia and France abandoned.

From the Russian Embassy I walked to see the British Chargé d'Affaires. He said England would not yield to Hitler's demands about Russia, she would insist on a Locarno conference and once more urge reduction and control of armaments. I can see no prospect of success so long as Hitler remains the dictator of Germany and hopes to be dictator of Europe.

September 26. Saturday. It is ten days since we summarized attitudes here and wired them to Washington. Since then, the Germans have been conducting great army maneuvers. Hitler has participated in these operations as commander-in-chief first of one side, then of the other. The poor German people are engaged as never before in drilling, marching, rifle practice, flying and bombing. All Europe is watching with the gravest anxiety.

Today the Minister from the Netherlands said to me: "We are all sure that Germany intends to annex our country in due time, also Switzerland and other countries where people of the medieval German race lived or left descendants." I told him of a recent report that Germany means to get colonies in the

Far East, repeating what Dr. Schacht said about Dutch New Guinea last spring. The Minister had heard similar reports, but he said: "We are arming in our Far Eastern possessions as never before. However, our people, like the English, refuse to allow universal service and will not prepare for war until one actually breaks out. They are so opposed to war."

He was both anxious and pessimistic as he went away, saying: "Unless your country and England and France and Russia work together for world peace there is no way to avoid a world war." He added that all democratic countries in Europe would unite behind such a front if it were formed, even Sweden where Von Neurath said, two years ago, that the Nazis would gain control in three years. But Sweden in spite of all Nazi propaganda held an election a few days ago and not one Nazi won a seat in the legislature.

September 28. Monday. This afternoon Consul General Jenkins came to tell me the story of the trial of an American, Lawrence Simpson, before a special Hitler People's Court for treason cases, of which there are so many. In April 1935, I think, Simpson was caught on the American ship *Manhattan* with Communist pamphlets in his possession. The police took him at once to a local court in Hamburg and he was promptly sent to prison. In July he was sent to a prison in Berlin or near by. The Consul had reported the case to the State Department and had made a protest to German authorities against his imprisonment without trial. The German officials declared there were some seventy Germans co-operating with Simpson and hence the delay. So nothing could be done.

Now, September 28, 1936, the man was tried with one German co-worker. Simpson confessed himself guilty of all that was charged and he was ordered to prison for sixteen months more, having been in jail fourteen months already. The German-American treaty of 1924 does not contain a clause that could be applied in Simpson's behalf. So the Consul General could do nothing though he had tried several times to get some consideration from the German authorities.

The Consul General repeated the story that Simpson had

refused to accept $1,000 brought to him from New York to enable him to employ a German lawyer to defend him. Many stories of the man's arrest and maltreatment by the Germans were printed in American papers.

October 2. Friday. During October and November, 1935, Mussolini was in a dangerous position at home and venturing upon a war in Ethiopia at great cost. The Italian Ambassador and his wife, in my judgment, thought he would fail and that a better system might follow in poor Italy. But the blunders of France and England gave him victory. Hitler came closer to the victorious Italian dictator from December, 1935, to March, 1936, and Mussolini reciprocated. Now both are aiding Franco to become the dictator of Spain, both having sent arms, airplanes and men to assist the rebels there. So the Ambassador marches today alongside German officials, receiving the salutes of the Hitler army and returning the Nazi salute.

Rust and Ley spoke on Monday evening before an immense audience, perhaps ordered to attend, announcing that young people are hereafter to spend seven months of each year in school, and twelve years, instead of thirteen, in getting their education. This reveals again the new German idea that parents have no say as to their children's upbringing, it becoming a government matter. After fourteen, children must drill and prepare for war during five months, not every day to be sure, of each year. And at eighteen both boys and girls are subject to service one way or another for war work and in labor camps.

October 5. Monday. The debt situation here seems to me almost impossible to manage even for so clever a financier as Dr. Schacht. The public debt is 18 million marks, but there is now a secret debt of 25 billion marks. Arms and army expenditure is counted by the English authorities to be £800,000,000, the equivalent of 4 billion dollars or 12 billion marks a year. I can hardly accept the English estimate, but war activities here surpass anything ever known.

The German Government seems willing to risk everything in order to compel England to restore her pre-war colonies. There is much discussion here of a proposed Locarno conference as a means of restoring the colonies, but the people of all races in South Africa demand the right to vote what they will do, and German attacks on all races but Aryans and denunciations of democracies are indulged in regularly. The result has been hostile attitudes among all colonial peoples, especially the blacks of Africa. I can see no prospect of Nazi colonial success now. A wiser discussion of things might have encouraged honest efforts on the part of England and France.

October 10. Saturday. The Russian Ambassador called to see me this afternoon. Although he is exceedingly well informed, he had nothing to add to my information. He talked about Russian aid to the Spaniards and about German-Italian violations of their promises of strict neutrality. I did not doubt the truth of his charges. The Ambassador condemned the English attitude of refusing to act upon violations of the Non-Intervention Agreement, but he thought there was no real danger now of world war. I agreed as to this, but cannot see how universal war activities, with enormous debts and certain unemployment a year or two hence, can have any other result than war.

October 15. Thursday. I went to the Adlon Hotel this evening to hear what Rosenberg, the so-called philosopher of the Hitler regime, might have to say about international relations. It was the third time I had gone to one of his *bierabend* affairs. On my right sat Meissner, private secretary to Von Hindenburg until August, 1934, now secretary to Hitler. On my left sat Rosenberg who directs the rearrangement of all education, especially history, in German schools and universities. On Rosenberg's left was Sir Eric Phipps. Other diplomats and some navy officers sat opposite us.

The conversation was not revealing except that Meissner said to me that our former Ambassador here, Schurman of New York, was in Nürnberg for the grand Party Day. Schurman had announced in the press here that he would attend the congress, but since no reporter from the American papers saw him there, I thought he had foreseen a little of what might be said and hence had not attended the meetings. Meissner said he talked several times with Schurman whom he admired very much.

Rosenberg spoke more than half an hour denouncing once more the Communist system and suggesting that all Western civilization is in danger. He did not attack democracies. There was a very large audience including many representatives of democratic countries. Perhaps he considered it wise for once to leave some countries alone. There was at the close some pretense of international co-operation, though Nazi Germany can co-operate perhaps only with the hated Italians.

October 18. Sunday. As Martha is leaving for the United States on Tuesday, Prince Louis Ferdinand, the hopeful pretender to the throne, came to bid her farewell and send greetings to some friends in America. As Hitler says his regime will continue a thousand years, I do not see how the Hohenzollerns can expect to be restored to power.

October 19. Monday. We lunched today with Sir Eric Phipps and, a little to my surprise, Rosenberg was an honor guest, the same Rosenberg who was compelled in 1933 to leave England where he had been doing propaganda work. Meissner was also present. There was a large company, diplomats and journalists, some quite clever ones. I had a brief confidential talk with Sir Eric about possible co-operation of democratic countries in financial and commercial matters.

October 20. Tuesday. A few days ago, a New York lawyer representing a score of claimants against Germany for destruction of their property before the United States entered the World War came to see me to ask if I could help him put his claims before the government. There is no doubt that hundreds of millions of dollars of American property were destroyed by German sabotage in the United States or seized by the German Government in Germany. A commission representing both countries worked for years on the subject and decided that many millions must be repaid. The commission ceased its work in 1930. The lawyer wished to get some payments for his clients out of the $20,000,000 which Germany has placed in the United

States Treasury—perhaps a tenth of what had been destroyed.

I wired Washington to know whether I should open the question with the German authorities. The reply was: Do or say nothing. But the lawyer went to see Von Neurath and others in high positions here. He got no promises, but somehow he formed an impression that something might be done. So today Captain von Pfeffer, representing General Goering who was willing to pay some of these claims if the United States would sell cotton or copper to Germany on credit, offered a formal document against the lawyer's claims in all ceremony. He was in a Nazi uniform and he had a lieutenant with him, the dignity of his position being thus maintained. I let him read his document and accepted with formal thanks.

These men were hardly out of the building before the lawyer came in again to report his difficulties. I could not do anything. I asked him, however: Why did the Standard Oil Company of New York send $1,000,000 over here in December, 1933, to aid the Germans in making gasoline from soft coal for war emergencies? Why do the International Harvester people continue to manufacture in Germany when their company gets nothing out of the country and when it has failed to collect its war losses? He saw my point and agreed that it looked foolish and that it only means greater losses if another war breaks loose.

October 25. Sunday. Professor and Frau M. had just returned from a two weeks' visit to their daughter whose husband lives outside of Germany. They lived at the expense of their daughter, they said, because they were not allowed to take any money of their own with them.

Herr and Frau M. began to talk freely about the "sad plight" of German universities and schools. He said the German people have been trained so long to be submissive and their national psychology is such that the present dictator can do anything he wishes. They all submit, though they are much opposed to what they have to submit to. He said all universities are now just about ruined as far as their departments of history, philosophy, economics and political science are concerned.

He said university subjects are prescribed by incompetent Party men, and students are instructed to be spies on their teachers. If a student reports anything that does not please the Propaganda Ministry, a professor is dismissed. No reason is given for the dismissal. Nothing can be done to change the situation.

The professor is retired on his pension or part-pension and can never teach, lecture or write again except from a Nazi point of view. To write a true account of existing conditions is so dangerous that one dare not do so, even if kept in handwritten form. He added that what has happened to universities is being applied to all schools, and that no one can be a teacher unless he is a Party member.

"Our civilization is being destroyed. If things go on for ten years more as they have during the last three years, we shall not recover. We are on our way directly to slavery and barbarism." I remained more than an hour listening to the professor's description of his unhappy countrymen. Soon after we began talking, Frau M. put a heavy blanket over her telephone to avoid danger to her husband.

October 26. Monday. All last week Count Ciano, son-in-law of Mussolini, was here. Such demonstrations from day to day! The idea of Mussolini is to persuade Germany to give the world evidence that she would support Italy in her demands that England recognize her conquest of Ethiopia and then England would gradually give up her control of the Mediterranean and share the control of the Suez Canal with Italy. Von Neurath had told me a week before that Hitler would not join another conference of European powers unless England agreed to Italy's demands. Unhappy as Von Neurath indicated himself to be when I came here in 1933, and also in 1934, he is now a complete tool of Hitler.

The demonstrations went on until the 26th when Ciano saw Hitler in Munich. What they said no one seems to know, but I am fairly sure Hitler asked Mussolini to keep his hands off Austria, and not to interfere when his propaganda leads to her annexation. Two Caesars cannot easily agree as to the division of Europe between them.

October 31. Saturday. This is Luther's Day, but there is not a word about it in the papers. When I was a student in Leipzig, the Germans treated Luther's Day much as Americans celebrate July 4. Now, Luther is not mentioned. There has been instead a three-day celebration of Goebbels' success in Berlin ten years ago. Goering made an address in which he challenged the outside powers and called on all Germans to decrease their butter and meat consumption in order to add to the number of cannon Germany is making. On the last night Hitler rushed into the great palace to thank Goebbels for his "splendid work."

November 9. Monday. Nothing of importance for a week. Goering made what was supposed to be an appeal to the German people to co-operate in the Hitler Four-Year Plan. He warned Germans that a food shortage might give some trouble. Germans must tighten their belts so as to save money for rearmament. He attacked England shamelessly, although Lord Londonderry was present as a guest. He said England had stolen German colonies and robbed Germany of her gold. Lord Londonderry, a Nazi Englishman, is reported not to have understood what was said. He was conspicuous at Goering's reception the next day.

According to reports, on January 30, 1937, all German states, Prussia, Saxony, Bavaria and the rest, are to cease to exist. So long as Von Hindenburg lived, this was not allowed although Hitler announced the policy in 1934. It is an unprecedented move to abolish such historic states as Bavaria or Saxony dating back to the time of the Caesars. Hitler, much as he hates France, is imitating Napoleon I who abolished all French states.

Ernst Hanfstaengl, who is said to have saved Hitler's life in 1923, is now in Paris. He is a graduate of Harvard. His mother was a member of a famous Boston Back Bay family, the Sedgwicks, but he came back to Bavaria, where he inherited a handsome estate. He joined the Hitler putsch business before 1923 and contributed handsomely to the Fuehrer. In 1933 he was appointed head of a press bureau designed to propagandize American and foreign correspondents. Before we came here he was counted an intimate of Hitler. In March, 1934, he arranged a private interview with Hitler for me to make a protest for the President against propaganda in the United States. Later Hanfstaengl went to the United States to attend an anniversary meeting of his Harvard classmates. Somehow Hitler came to dislike him, refused to see him any more, deprived him of his office and left him in a dangerous position.

A few days ago he went to Paris and gave out an interview about Roosevelt's re-election which may get him into trouble. He simply indicated his admiration of the country where he would like to live if he could take any of his property with him. I am wondering a little what will be said or done here when he returns. He is supposed to be very clever. I cannot quite say whether he is or is not.

November 12. Thursday. Yesterday we lunched with the Swiss Minister. General von Seeckt, who was the head of the Reichswehr when Hitler seized control of the government in 1933 and who was out of sympathy with the Nazis and was dismissed, was there. He went to China to show the Chinese how to train an army. Now he is again here with some sort of position, not so critical of Nazism as formerly.

His wife today said: "Germany was very foolish to allow the Polish Corridor to be established. Wilson gave the Poles access to the Baltic but we did not have to recognize it. Now we have a ten-year treaty with Poland, but we are going to take that part of Poland in spite of the treaty. Danzig is not a free city. It is our city." This supports recent German attitudes which have practically denied the League of Nations the right to help Danzig if attacked. It would not surprise me if Hitler made some challenge next January 30 in connection with annexing Danzig.

This afternoon Carl Albrecht, a cotton importer of Bremen, called to talk about the possibility of importing some cotton from the United States. I explained the attitude of Secretary Hull about lowering tariff barriers in case Germany abolished subsidies on goods shipped to the United States. He knew of the matter, having spoken to Mr. Pierson of the State Department last August.

Then he talked about our new Consul at Bremen, reporting

what the Consul had said of the Spanish medievalism which was being corrected by the new government there last spring. Albrecht then said it was shameful that other powers shipped arms to the rebels of Spain and prolonged the terrible war. I referred to the habit of arms manufacturers everywhere to sell arms to warring countries, even to incite wars.

He said: "Yes, last winter when Italy was warring upon Ethiopia, the head of a long-established German munitions company came to me and asked a loan to help them sell Italy shiploads of arms, promising high interest. I was disgusted and of course refused, but I think they shipped arms all the same." I referred to English and American arms people who did the same, even when their governments were opposed. He replied that he was sure munitions makers of all industrial countries operate in this way and admitted that Germany and Italy are doing it for the rebels in Spain.

November 15. Sunday. Three times in the last few days the Italian Ambassador here, who has avoided me since my return in early August, has approached me to find out what President Roosevelt means to do through the Latin-American conference in December in Buenos Aires. As I have had no specific instructions I could not even intimate anything more than the general American peace attitude.

Yesterday the Ambassador from Argentina called, pro forma, but at once began talking about the conference. He said: "There is great concern among German officials about the American objectives." Since he had been received by Hitler two days before and had not been at the Foreign Office more than once, I felt that the Minister's questions had been suggested by Nazi officials who hesitate to ask me about such matters. They know I am a Democrat and the recent overwhelming vote for Roosevelt whom they had hoped to see defeated, is really disturbing to them.

The Argentine Minister said, further, that Paul Scheffer of the *Berliner Tageblatt*, who had been visiting Latin American representatives here, spent an hour with him. Scheffer had represented the Foreign Office, he thought, and perhaps the

Propaganda Ministry. He criticized the whole American program in Latin America, said it was a renewal of the Monroe Doctrine in its former aggressive shape and that Roosevelt had no right to influence South American policy. This talk irritated my Argentine friend who said he was wholly in sympathy with the President's peace and commercial attitudes. I have been watchful of this Scheffer who was several years in the United States as correspondent for the German free press before returning to the *Tageblatt*.

The real fear here and in Rome is that the President may organize all American peoples against Fascist Europe and even boycott any power that starts another war.

The Hitler way of doing things is revealed in the Berlin press today. He decreed last evening that all German rivers, especially the Rhine, Elbe and Oder, are no longer under any jurisdiction of the League of Nations. Hitler must have known that Bismarck negotiated a treaty in 1886 under which Dutch, Belgian and Swiss ships might carry cargoes up and down the Rhine. Then the Versailles Treaty stipulated that Switzerland, Czechoslovakia and Poland might export goods through the Rhine, Elbe and Oder. These countries need such access to the sea. Since Hitler announces that none of these peoples are to be deprived of these privileges, actually beneficial to Germany, why could he not have the Foreign Office call a conference with the League members and arrive at a general agreement? But the Fuehrer thinks of himself as the supreme power and so announces a violation of treaties simply upon his own authority. It may please the Germans but it is not a politic way to do things. I look for England and France to denounce this sort of practice tomorrow. But they can do nothing. Next January 30, I suspect Hitler will announce his seizure of Danzig, "his own city."

November 18. Wednesday. A day or two ago reports here revealed Hitler's anxiety lest the rebels of Spain be defeated by the legal government. Our Consul General in Hamburg wrote us on Monday that he had been informed that three ships loaded with arms had been sent from Hamburg recently.

The situation in Madrid must be disappointing to Hitler and Mussolini who, I'm sure, will do their best to establish a third dictatorship around France.

A few days ago about twenty German residents in Moscow were imprisoned as conspirators against the government there. This might have been expected as a reply to the repeated attacks of Hitler, Goering and Goebbels. The German Foreign Office protested, but the Russian Ambassador protested also because the Germans had arrested Communists in Germany without proof of anything in the nature of conspiracy. But what can Communism and Nazism do to each other without crossing Poland? That would incite Poles, Czechs, French and even Rumanians to attack Germany.

Today Germany and Italy recognized Franco as the head of the Spanish people, which he certainly is not. This will probably mean French, English, American and other democratic refusals to recognize him. While this goes on, Roosevelt is on his way to South America where he will try to form a solid front of both Americas against European economic aggression. Will he succeed? Latin Americans are none too democratic. The Argentine Minister is Fascist in mentality.

November 22. Sunday. Yesterday the German Government announced that they were sending a general to Spain as Chargé d'Affaires to the insurgent leader Franco who has been attacking Madrid, without success, for three weeks. This Franco had announced the blockading of Barcelona and had received protests, not publicly, from England and France, their ships being in Spanish harbors. Today our Consul in Bremen who spent several years in Madrid called and reported from friends of his in Spain that Franco had become so unpopular that several towns he had taken in August have revolted and he is too weak to hold them. This confirms other stories I have heard about Spanish resentment at bringing the Moors into the country to help the insurgents. The weakening position of Franco seems, therefore, to have been the cause of the German-Italian announcement of their recognition a few days ago and of the Germans sending a general named Faupel to help Franco.

In the Embassy office last evening a cable came from Madrid, signed by Wendelin, our Chargé d'Affaires there. He quoted a well-known German business man in Madrid as saying that Germans could not communicate home by wire or telephone and that they were in grave danger of being killed by Spanish Government supporters. Wendelin asked me to give his telegram to the German Foreign Office which I did about 8 o'clock. We then wired Madrid that we had done so, but had no assurances as to any aid to Germans in Spain. Of course Germany could not do anything, having recognized Franco as the government.

This news from Madrid was quite troublesome. It looked like a further German-Italian step toward war. Over the radio came the news a little later that England had sent a commission by airplane to Spain to see just what the situation is. France was reported yesterday to have allowed a regiment of troops to slip into Spain on the government's side. Mussolini is reported to have furnished Franco with war vessels under Spanish rebel flags to help blockade ports. How far can this go without actual conflict? Am I to be caught here in another European war? When such folly rules European governments, it is hard for me to venture to represent our government.

This noon we lunched with a wealthy American-German family. The husband said to me: "My foreign market has been sacrificed, but I am very busy making supplies for the German army. When arming is completed I shall have to close my plant and dismiss my workers." I said: That is going to be embarrassing. He said, "Yes, but our system allows nothing else." He did not go further, but I was sure he was not really resentful of economic nationalism with war as its objective.

November 25. Wednesday. I was asked this morning to call at the German Foreign Office. I took Mr. Mayer with me as a witness to what might be said. We went into Von Neurath's office at 1 o'clock and I remarked sarcastically: I am glad you have time to see me (having in mind the way he and Schurman delayed my interview some two months ago). The Secretary clearly caught my meaning.

Before we took our seats, Von Neurath handed me a copy of a treaty between Germany and Japan which I had anticipated and had predicted to be in preparation about two years ago. I read a paragraph or two and said: I hope this is aimed to prevent war. He replied: "Yes, that is the meaning, but it is directed against the Russian Comintern." I said: You are trying to put an end to propaganda. He said: "Yes." More than once he and Dr. Schacht have said to me that they greatly disliked propaganda. Of course they dislike any but their own.

We left the Secretary in five minutes and met other ambassadors as we came away from the office. All the world is to be notified through the press this afternoon of the agreement between Germany, Italy and Japan (the Anti-Comintern Pact) designed to check Communist activity outside Russia and also to frighten England and France once more. But my guess is that this treaty, which surely has secret clauses, contains also a military alliance of these powers against any other power that may deny them the right to annex other areas or countries, especially a promise to attack Russia in case Russia and Japan go to war in the Far East.

November 27. Friday. The German press has called upon the people to rejoice at the treaty published yesterday. It is curious that Von Ribbentrop, German Ambassador to London and not very welcome there, came by air to Berlin to sign this treaty and that Von Neurath, the Secretary of State, did not sign it, nor did Hitler. I suspect the Secretary did not wish to sign it, also that Von Ribbentrop had worked on the matter long before he was sent to London. It is Hitler's way of popularizing Von Ribbentrop who is not liked or respected very much here.

The Italian press announces today that Italy will enter the German-Japanese pact against Communism. The English and the French press attack this so-called "cultural pact between great intellectual peoples." Having preached for years against all races except Aryans, the Germans now accept the yellow race of the Far East as their equals. What would the old Kaiser, now at Doorn, say if he were free to speak? For so many years, he warned all Western peoples to have nothing to do with yellow or black races, in spite of the fact that he had an alliance with the Turks when the World War began.

November 29. Sunday. Miss Sigrid Schultz of the Chicago *Tribune* said today she had talked with the German press people yesterday and they were angered at Roosevelt's Rio de Janeiro speech because he talked about democracies and peace so frankly. I had read his address as reported in our radio bulletin. It did not attack dictatorships but it made very clear statements against the methods of such powers. He implied that all democratic peoples must unite against aggressors who take other people's territory. That is what irritated the German journalists. Not one newspaper yesterday or today referred to the President's address.

December 4. Friday. Today I received a report of a teachers' convention held near Frankfurt. The government speaker was quoted as saying: "Only one religion is fit for the German people and this is the *Deutsche Christen*. It is time for us to take care that a Jew bastard out of the House of David is not forced upon the German people as God. Any teacher who still talks to his pupils about a life in heaven is not fit to educate German youth."

The quotation above shows the drift of Nazi superstition. This is only another repetition of Von Schirach's former speeches and it is practically the same thing as Rosenberg's famous book on the *Myth of the Twentieth Century*, which has sold 500,000 copies in Germany. Rosenberg, curious as his reasoning is, stands closer to Hitler than ever.

December 5. Saturday. Today I saw Dr. Dieckhoff in the Foreign Office. I indicated to him the general fear of war on the part of foreign correspondents as well as many Germans. Dieckhoff pretended at first that there was really no fear of this in Germany. I could not agree. He then gave me a chance to ask for the truth of English newspaper reports that 5,000 German soldiers had been seen landing in Cadiz to help the Fascist Franco take Madrid. He acknowledged the truth of this but said they were volunteers to help defeat the Russian Communists fighting for the Spanish Government. He agreed that the Italians were doing even more and that a general European war was quite possible if the struggle went on. My guess is that next spring will be the dangerous moment.

When I asked Dieckhoff if Germany would like to see Mussolini repeat Julius Caesar's performances in Spain and France, he indicated a dislike of Mussolini, saying that Ciano had pressed for recognition of Franco some weeks ago and that Hitler had agreed. I asked whether Germany were really satisfied with this. He did not say no, but he at once reminded me of the German suggestion of last August that no volunteers of any country should be allowed to go into Spain on either side. If this had been agreed to by the various powers represented in the London Non-Intervention Commission, then armies and airplanes might have been kept out. I knew neither Italy nor Germany would keep any such agreement. He said Russia would not have kept the agreement. I replied that Russia would have kept out if the others had made perfectly clear they would do so. However, I said, Fascist propaganda had been going on in Spain a long time. He did not deny it.

Then he told me that the French and English Ambassadors here had been with Von Neurath this morning to say that France and England repeated their demand, made after the Friday conference in London, to Germany and Italy that these countries agree to send no more troops into Spain if Russia and France did the same. I asked him if Germany would accept. He said the Foreign Office agreed to the proposition, but he could not guess what Hitler would do. I remarked: You know Mussolini has taken the islands in the Mediterranean that belonged to Spain and that he intends to control Spain. He will not accept the French-English demand. Will Germany support Italy in this? He did not answer, but I could not avoid the feeling that the Foreign Office officials were somewhat nervous about Hitler's intervention in Spain.

I then asked Dieckhoff what Germany would say if the Pan-American Conference, now in session in Buenos Aires, asked for a world peace conference. He indicated his approval and even thought Hitler might agree in case President Roosevelt called such a conference. The press here has shown opposition to the Buenos Aires conference, especially to the President's speeches there and at Rio de Janeiro, in both of which he pointed to the dangerous results of unwise dictatorships assuming the right to conquer other nations. As I have heard Dieckhoff say more than once that Germany must control the whole Danube zone, I felt that Roosevelt's peace addresses must have bothered him a bit. But he insisted that Roosevelt's appeals for peace, if they turned into a call for a world conference, would interest Germany and perhaps bring Hitler into co-operation. My thought was that Hitler will listen only if all democratic countries including Russia were united against him, and if Japan agreed also. This I fear is impossible and so the United States, England and France will be the only hope of saving the world from another war. Even that will not succeed if Germany and Italy do not go bankrupt and have serious shortages of foodstuffs.

December 9. Wednesday. Yesterday a Foreign Office official, talking to Counselor Mayer, indicated more uneasiness about war than Dieckhoff showed when I saw him on the 5th. He reported confidentially, however, that Germany had complied with the British-French demand (in my mind deceptively). Germany will keep all troops and airplanes out of Spain, if Russia and France will do the same. He made no comment as to Italy's aid to Franco. I do not believe Mussolini will ever agree to the demand of the Non-Intervention Commission in London. The German official said further, "Germany was not willing to leave the decision to the Spanish people." That is the Mussolini-Hitler dictator idea. They will control Spain.

I have official reports from different parts of Germany on the subject of general education. All teachers, with one or two exceptions in the Catholic states, must serve several weeks each year in camps where Party leaders tell them what to teach. German school children once or twice each week through the year must meet political leaders to learn the great and sacred duty of Germany and to imitate and follow the Fuehrer. The young folk everywhere must heil Hitler and show great enthusiasm about the German empire and their duty to die for it at any time.

Boys of ten to fourteen years are organized as *Deutsche Jungvolk*. They wear small knives at their side. The girls of the same age are organized, and even march in military formation, as *die Jungmädel*. They wear uniforms according to instructions. The boys from fourteen to eighteen are called *Hitler Jugend* and wear daggers ready for stabbing an enemy. They drill and march in the streets and enter the army when called up at seventeen or eighteen. The girls of the same age are called *Bund Deutsche Mädel* and are urged to marry early, bear many children and ask no questions.

All these youths are taught "true interpretations of heroic German history." Nobody is allowed to teach the facts about critical periods when leaders made blunders. All professors in high schools and universities under fifty years of age must be in labor camps for four weeks each year to learn political, race and religious theory as interpreted by true prophets like Dr. Alfred Rosenberg. Sometimes men with families are excused and sometimes professors actually refuse to conform. They are left alone for a while to ponder their misdemeanors. If they do not submit, gradually they are sent to less desirable positions or dismissed. In all the universities on which we have reports, great changes in history, philosophy, social and political science have been made. Leipzig is perhaps the most completely reorganized to meet Nazi purposes.

The reports show some resistance in different regions. It seems not to be successful. A professor at Berlin has recently been ordered to Jena because he had not surrendered. Strangely enough, his students insist on going there too. This is a picture of intellectual Germany.

December 13. Sunday. A great highway system is now being constructed and extended all over Germany in the hope of being able in the shortest possible time to carry German armies to her frontiers. Dr. Todt, whom I know well and who I think is not a convinced Nazi, is supervising this expensive building.

No cross roads are permitted on these great *autobahns*, or through highways. Dr. Todt says cars and trucks can travel just as fast as rubber tires will permit, perhaps 100 miles an hour. The roads all begin in Berlin and go directly to frontiers. One I have seen in East Prussia, another in Hanover leading toward the Dutch border. They do not go through any big towns or cities, but go close enough for regiments to get to them in a few minutes.

Yesterday I saw a clipping from the front page of a Washington paper attacking me violently as a complete failure here and pretending that the President is of the same opinion. This is news to me. The man who wrote the article on the foreign service situation pretends that the Department has given him the information. His name is Drew Pearson. I have never met him when in Washington.

The story asserts that the President and the Department are planning to have Ambassador Bullitt sent here to deal with the Nazis because he favors their policies. Bullitt has a curious history. He went to Russia for Wilson in 1919. He made certain recommendations on his return to Paris during the Peace Conference. Wilson could not get consideration of his Russian propositions, mostly because the English had forbidden Lloyd George to agree. Clemenceau would not think of allowing the Russian delegates to come to Paris. This led Bullitt to think Wilson had refused to consider his scheme, and in August or September, 1919, Bullitt attacked Wilson before the Senate Committee on Foreign Relations in a way unprecedented in American history.

He was sent to Russia early in 1934 as Ambassador, on the assumption that the Communists had agreed to pay certain post-war debts and that they would then leave off their propaganda in the United States. Bullitt took a large staff and many consuls, in spite of the fact that little real work could be done in Russia until commercial treaties were negotiated. He also spent huge sums building an Embassy palace and offices, said to be about $1,000,000, not too much if carefully applied. Not having succeeded very well at the end of his first year, he became angry. Coming through Berlin in the spring or summer of 1935, he reported to me that he was sure Japan would attack eastern Russia within six months and he expected that Japan would take all the Far Eastern end of Russia.

At luncheon with the French Ambassador, he repeated his hostile attitude and argued at length with the French for the defeat of the Franco-Soviet peace pact then being negotiated, which the English Ambassador reported to me was the best possible guarantee of European peace. This attitude of Mr. Bullitt seemed to me to be out of his range because France and England might think the President was speaking through him. I felt compelled to report the account as given me by the French Ambassador. Later, or about the same time, when the new Italian Ambassador came here directly from Moscow, we were told that Bullitt had become attracted to Fascism before leaving Moscow. I understood how disappointed he must have been at the failure of the Russians to keep their promises made in Washington in 1934, but I could not see how an intelligent American could become a Fascist. Perhaps he was not.

Last September, Mr. Bullitt was appointed Ambassador to Paris. He has made a good beginning there. But the story goes that he is on the reactionary side. The Washington newspaper story says he is in full sympathy with Nazi ideas. This is hard to believe. However, yesterday Monsieur Marcel Knecht, editor and owner of Le Matin in Paris, came to see me, reporting that Bullitt, working for an alliance between France and Germany, had requested him to see me and ask me to advise the President to lend a hand in this. Knecht convinced me that he is an able but very conservative man, perhaps a Fascist in France.

A little while after Knecht left, a telegram from Bullitt urged me to see and talk with Knecht. Does this mean that the United States is intermeddling, or that Bullitt is moving, as in 1935, without official instructions? Now, one may really ask, is the newspaper story true or half true? My position is difficult, but under such criticism I cannot resign, as I planned, next spring. To give up my work here under these circumstances would put me in a defensive and positively false position at home.

December 16. Wednesday. The information we have had, official and otherwise, reporting that Germany is willing to cease sending troops to Spain, is of course untrue. Wherever I see a German official and the Italian Ambassador they are in earnest, confidential conversation. Today at the Argentine Legation it was especially noticeable. When I meet the Italian now he speaks laconically and shows a positive hostility toward the United States. Before the Buenos Aires conference, he made several efforts to sound me out and pretended friendship. Now that Argentina is about to defeat Roosevelt's general American peace plan under pressure from Britain, he resumes his former indifferent attitude. While German officials show a more friendly attitude, I notice evidence that Germany and Italy are committed to the defeat of the English proposition to have all countries keep their soldiers out of Spain.

December 18. Friday. We lunched with Dr. Schacht. Ambassador Luther from Washington was present. Schacht pulled me to one side and stressed the German folly of arming to the last man. But in public he continues to refer to colonies as absolutely necessary for Germany, even at the cost of war. Nothing else was said of any significance, Luther saying nothing at all though he had been reported to have almost denounced Roosevelt and his speeches in Brazil and Argentina. He had also spoken most bitterly about American limitation of credits to Germany. How he can complain when Germany has refused so long to pay her debts to American bankers and bond holders, I can hardly understand. However, Luther said nothing unfriendly to me. He is due back in Washington before Roosevelt's second inauguration on January 20.

December 25. Friday. The German situation continues most critical. Foodstuffs are being regulated as in World War times and the poor people are being warned daily that cannon are more important now than butter. They are scared, or supposed to be, so that all possible sacrifices can be made for armaments. Even I, as a diplomat, have to sign a document in order to get meat from a local grocer. Stores are not allowed to sell to anybody not listed, and then only limited amounts daily or weekly.

Although we import most of our supplies through Hamburg, we cannot always be sure we will be supplied, so we must register like the natives.

What the German people think of all this one cannot be sure but there are frequent signs of impatience, even anger. The real trouble with Hitler is that he has not yet got his vast armies into a condition which would guarantee success in case he undertook to do what the army officers coaxed the Kaiser into trying in 1914-1918.

Hitler agreed with Mussolini in October to recognize the Franco Fascists as the government of Spain. Both of them have been sending troops, war planes and arms to Franco since early August, although both of them entered the British neutrality agreement about the same time, saying they would not send men and arms to Spain. But, as already noted, they recognized Franco when he was thought to be taking Madrid in early October. Hitler sent General Faupel, who had been a military propagandist in South America for several years, as his representative to Spain. He was to direct military affairs for the Fascists and Nazis. The people in Germany have not been permitted to know that 20,000 soldiers and technicians have been sent to Spain.

However, this week Faupel returns to Berlin to tell the Fuehrer that Franco says he must have 60,000 German soldiers if he is to overthrow the government there. The reports from the English press say that Italian troops are not being sent, according to promises, and that England and Italy are getting together. Does that mean a lone German conquest of Spain? If so, France will be in a dangerous position. In view of this danger France lets the English know that they plan to send 100,000 soldiers into Spain to defeat the Germans.

This is the present danger of 1936. What will Hitler do? If he is defeated in Spain his prestige will fall tremendously. Our reports continue that some German troops have deserted to the Government side when they were ordered to attack Madrid. Hitler's financial condition does not seem equal to his plan. The shortage of food makes his people uneasy. Any loss of prestige, according to all his boasts, would be contrary to God's will. Now he must decide what to do. If he withdraws from Spain the world will know it, but his own people will only know about his recognition of Franco. That would leave him another year to execute another stroke. What can that be? I wait and watch until my time to retire.

XI

December 29, 1936 to June 4, 1937

December 29. Tuesday. I talked tonight with Dr. Schacht. He joked about a reported shipment of great Douglas bombing planes to the Spanish Government from the United States. I had received information that $2,770,000 worth of these planes were on the way and that the State Department had announced this was no violation of the neutrality act. When I replied to Schacht: Yes, but a hundred bombing planes were sold to Germany in the autumn of 1935 for delivery to Italy from the same American plane factories against the President's order, he was silenced. His conversational tone indicated that he knew about the deal for Italy. He added: "Well, that was to aid Italy to extend her colonial realm."

I asked Schacht then about Germany's reply to the French-English demand to agree to keep arms and soldiers out of Spain. He said: "Germany is not sending soldiers there and the Fuehrer will soon give a favorable answer. He is as ready as anybody for peace. The only obstacle to a real settlement is the English refusal so far to restore our colonies." Then he added, "France is ready to restore our colonies any time. I was assured of this when in Paris representing the Fuehrer last August. Why does England refuse? We can never have a disarmament agreement until we get our colonies."

He went on to say all Germany's pre-war colonies were not enough and a third time reiterated, "New Guinea must be given

376

us." I said: The Netherlands owns part of that great island. He replied: "The Dutch will agree to give us their part. Why should not England agree?" I told him I had learned from Minister Gie of South Africa that great difficulties would follow English cession of colonies and that the populations were much opposed to a change of ownership. Schacht acknowledged also having talked with Gie, but insisted he was wrong. I wonder what lies behind Schacht's saying that Holland would not object to Germany's taking New Guinea. Several times the Dutch Minister, now on his way to the Far East, has indicated great opposition to this move.

I then asked Schacht what he thought of Secretary Hull's call for world peace in his last speech at Buenos Aires and whether he thought Germany would enter a new world peace conference. He replied: "I am sure world peace is the first condition to real recovery and I am sure Hitler will agree to such a peace, but Germany must have her colonies first."

I could not help remembering that Hitler had forbidden the Pope's peace appeal of Christmas Day to be broadcast over the radio in Germany. However, I asked Schacht to let me know if the Fuehrer indicated his approval of the Hull proposition so that I might wire to Washington about the time of the Secretary's arrival there. He said he would ask the Fuehrer in case he could see him. I doubt if there will be any reply, for I am sure Hitler will denounce the Hull move as soon as he gets around to it. I did not say the President himself had asked me to sound out the German Government, for that was in strictest confidence.

January 5, 1937. Tuesday. Public opinion, as revealed by the few people who get information from the outside world, is certainly troubled. The British-French demand that Germany, Italy and Russia cease sending arms and "volunteers" to Spain was not answered when Hitler came back to attend the funeral of General von Seeckt. General von Blomberg and other officers of the army were with the Fuehrer at the funeral. The generals are reported to have offered serious objection to sending more soldiers to Spain. Hitler is said to have rebuked them.

In the last days of December, 150 airplane officers and 2,000 S.A. and S.S. soldiers were being sent through Italy to Spain. This came to me confidentially from Munich. Yesterday, over the radio from London, we heard that Italy has sent 4,000 troops to Lisbon whence they will go to Franco's front near Madrid. Germany must have sent 2,000 more from the Stettin region. Naturally not a word of this appears in any German paper.

The American airplane sale, which the State Department could not prevent under the 1935 neutrality law, involved $2,700,000 worth of airplanes. As these planes were to be sold by a private business firm to one of the parties in a civil war, there was nothing to do. But Germany made loud protests until leaders here learned that Congress, now gathering in Washington, was almost sure to stop the shipments. Then the press rejoiced in this indication that American neutrality means German-Italian domination of Spain. That is apt to be the case unless France sends scores of thousands of soldiers and hundreds of planes to Madrid. If France does that, will Germany go to war with France? If so, what will Italy do? Hitler will meet all the diplomats on January 11 and we may expect to hear sharp challenging language about all democracies.

January 11. Monday. At 11:45 I was in the old Reichspalast where Von Hindenburg lived. All the diplomats were there. The Frenchman, much troubled about the position of his country, was busy talking. He showed serious concern. We waited and talked fifteen minutes before Hitler appeared. The Italian seemed the least sought after by others. He was as aloof to me as in August when I returned to my post, and I reciprocated. Sir Eric Phipps was as discreet as ever, but he revealed more sympathy for the Fascist crowd in Spain than I had noted before. I believe now he is almost a Fascist, as I think are Baldwin and Eden. The Russian Ambassador was as calm and undisturbed as if his country had not been denounced here every day since last September. No Ambassador or Minister said anything revealing, although I twitted the Englishman a bit about their treaty with the greatest Machiavelli of modern decades. He smiled but would say nothing.

At 12 o'clock the Fuehrer came into the great hall where forty or more of us stood in a line around the walls. Since the Papal Nuncio was reported to be ill, the French Ambassador stood at the head of the line. I was next, the British third, the Turk fourth and the Russian fifth, according to our length of service here. The Fuehrer looked somewhat embarrassed as he came in, red in the face. The Frenchman stepped forward to read the address of welcome, which the Nuncio had prepared, and Hitler faced him. Nothing serious was said or suggested. When this was concluded, the Fuehrer read his reply, also saying nothing, which rather surprised me since the international situation is so dangerous. I had expected hints to the British and French. Not a word. The first paper was written and read in French; Hitler replied in German. I understood little of the French statement, but grasped most of the German, difficult as Hitler's German is.

After these greetings were finished, Hitler shook hands with the Frenchman and the two talked in German in low tones so that others might not hear them, Hitler speaking a little the louder of the two. I imagine the Frenchman complained at the German attacks on France today in all papers because Hitler alluded to the French press in a slightly critical tone.

He next turned to me and pretended to be very cordial. I alluded to the unfortunate commercial relations between our two countries. He turned to complimenting President Roosevelt on his vast majority and on his constructive measures. I agreed and said: I am glad you read the President's addresses. He said he had done so, but I doubt it. Then I said: I have recently read Dr. Schacht's article in *Foreign Affairs* which I thought very able; in the main I agree with all he said. The conversation closed after a few more words and he turned to the English representative. I understood nothing that they said. Hitler went the whole round, even chatting cordially with the Russian. After the Fuehrer, Secretary von Neurath passed, giving his greetings and indulging in a bit of conversation.

January 27. Wednesday. Today I received news from Ambassador Davies at Moscow that he had told the President that Dr. Schacht was now even more enthusiastically in favor of world peace than he was in December when I talked with him. I had been skeptical in my report to the President, because I remembered how Schacht had attacked the President and Hull when I saw him in August.

Ambassador Davies had an important interview with Schacht just before he left Berlin on January 16. Schacht captivated him. The essence of the interview was that Schacht urged upon Davies the hope that President Roosevelt would call a peace conference in Washington. Schacht proposed that such an international gathering ought to agree beforehand upon the subjects and the major problems and their solution. Davies had some doubts about the willingness of Roosevelt to take the lead.

Schacht said that he was authorized by his government to offer definite terms to France and England based upon the following points: stabilization of the present frontiers of European countries; establishment of perpetual peace in Europe; discontinuation of the present arms race; abolition of sanctions, to be replaced by some administrative machinery which would permit the members of this proposed alliance to enforce their decisions; substitution of a workable agreement between powers for the present League of Nations.

However, the first German stipulation before any such agreement can be discussed or arrived at must provide Germany with colonies, access to raw materials, and regions open to settlement and migration. Schacht was certain of the support, at least in principle of the French nation, through conversations he had had with Premier Léon Blum. However, he said the French Premier had been flatly rebuffed when he approached the English Foreign Office.

In addition to the interview Davies had with Schacht, he saw a number of his old friends in the German Foreign Office. He was impressed with the unanimous opinion among these men that the question of civil war in Spain was no longer a threat to world peace. He further gathered the impression that Hitler was planning a recall of his "volunteers" and technical experts from Spain. Davies agreed with his friends that the internal affairs of Spain were questions which should be settled by Spaniards themselves without pressure from abroad. I have had so many similar assurances from officials in the Foreign Office that I am a bit skeptical of the sincerity of these professions.

I had received a message from Hull about January 25, intimating that Ilgner, of the I. G. Farben trust, also president of the Carl Schurz Foundation, a propaganda organization in the United States, had been active in Latin America against the conference at Buenos Aires, and especially against Hull's commercial treaties. Ilgner announced in Chile, I believe, that he was Schacht's representative there. All this made me think Davies had fallen for the Nazi proposals for commerce and loans. At any rate, I decided to wire my own interpretation of Schacht's attitude. He is a liberal in some respects, but he has no such power in international matters as Davies thinks.

Recently reports have come to me that American banks are contemplating large new credits and loans to Italy and Germany whose war machines are already large enough to threaten the peace of the world. I have even heard, but it seems unbelievable to me, that Mr. Bullitt is lending encouragement to these schemes.

January 29. Friday. I received a telegram from the Chemical National Bank and Trust Company in New York saying that Arnold Bernstein, a Hamburg Jew and president of the Red Star Steamship Line, and four of his assistants had been imprisoned. The telegram said that their bank had loaned the Red Star Line $1,000,000 and that the Erie Railroad had loaned $4,000,000. If Bernstein and his fellows remained in prison many days, the New York creditors would take possession of the Red Star ships on which they had a mortgage. Bank business must go on.

I referred the matter to Consul General Jenkins and asked him to call up the consulate at Hamburg and get what information he could. The case was not one for our government to take up because the imprisoned persons are all Germans and because the Red Star Line is a German company flying the swastika flag. Yet the arrest interrupted large American business interests, even throwing men out of employment.

January 30. Saturday. The Fuehrer spoke two and a half hours today before what he calls the Reichstag. Troubled with lumbago the last month, I decided not to attend but asked two of our staff to go and report what was said.

I did go to a tea given by the Crown Prince who had not invited diplomats to his house in a long time, rarely I believe since 1934. The party was rather interesting. A large number of diplomats were there, also German business and professional people. I spoke with the unhappy Crown Prince a few minutes, also with his clever son, Louis Ferdinand. They seemed greatly pleased to think that Americans were friendly toward the dethroned Hohenzollerns. There has been repeated talk that there is to come in a year or two an uprising which will put the aged, exiled Kaiser back upon the imperial throne. I heard a few days ago that the movement is advancing too fast and may defeat the Hohenzollern interest. In any case, there was evidence of much friendliness at the big tea party at Potsdam.

This is the day when Europeans are all looking toward Berlin to see if a move is made that signifies war. But the Fuehrer, according to reports of our people who heard him speak, was more conciliatory than he has been since 1933. He said Germany has regained her equality with other nations, her people are again contented, and they now only await the return of their colonies. He knows the other powers will do this but only on condition that Germany agrees to limit armaments and return to the League of Nations. He therefore said nobody has a right to say how many soldiers and bombing planes Germany shall have. So no agreement as to colonies is likely to be made, in my opinion.

February 2. Tuesday. We attended a musicale and dinner given by the Crown Prince at the Esplanade Hotel. There were perhaps 1,500 people who listened to the music and 200 who sat down to dine with the ex-Crown Prince. I was at his table;

my wife was at the Crown Princess' table. The Crown Prince told me of his five-year exile on an island in the North Sea. I had not known he was there so long. He talked of German history, showing more knowledge than I had expected from former royalty. He agreed with me that historical writing in Germany in the next generation is almost certain to deteriorate. He did not say Party domination was the cause, but he made that idea plain.

It seemed a little curious to see Madame Schacht bow so low before the Crown Prince when he greeted her, especially since the little Nazi cross is so conspicuous around her neck. The same courtly attitude was revealed by several other government people and their wives. Schacht was not there. We could not get away before 12 o'clock. I noticed the French Ambassador and other representatives of countries all over the world. The Russian, the Pole, and the Turk were not present.

February 3. Wednesday. We attended the first dinner the Fuehrer has ever given to the whole diplomatic corps. Many officers of his government, Goering, Schacht, Goebbels, and others were there. It was held in the Fuehrer's new palace, more elaborate than anything I have ever seen and finished only a few weeks ago. There were close to seventy-five servants marching in and halting in military fashion before the tables. Hitler certainly does not save his people's money, though he ate no meat and drank no wine. There were no champagne toasts, the rule here at big dinners. Personally, I was not in a position to talk to the Fuehrer, which would have been embarrassing to me. I did talk a little across the table to Goering whose fame in the world, or ill-fame, dates especially from the firing of the Reichstag building in 1933 and the killings in June, 1934. Of course I could not talk freely with him, being unable to forget these things. However, I must not imply that Hitler was not equally guilty.

The great party adjourned from the tables into a large reception room where Hitler and Goering stood at one end to receive greetings and thanks. I noticed the French and British Ambassadors were most unrestrained in their apparent happiness. But

Schacht and Goebbels did not hang about the Fuehrer at all, and Von Neurath only a moment or two. At eleven o'clock the French Ambassador and his wife departed and the others all quickly followed. I had expected the party would last until two o'clock, but I would not have stayed so long.

I have been out every night for about a week and must continue to do so for another week. This dining until late at night and getting home at 12 o'clock is very tiresome to me, having to be in the office rather early every morning and remaining, except for lunch time, until 7. My wife must go out almost every day she does not give a luncheon or tea. She takes much of the burden from me.

February 12. Friday. I have heard from our Consul in Frankfurt am Main that the government has forbidden all Jews who fought in the World War to hold any assemblies, although they have hitherto held veterans' meetings.

Business firms in that district are to reduce the wages of all workers in *Ersatz* plants, making substitute raw materials, by 10 per cent. Perhaps this is to cheapen prices of such goods. In Frankfurt, three workers have been in prison a year because they were thought to be associated in some way with Communists. They have just been tried and sentenced to four, six, and eight years, respectively, in prison.

A few weeks ago Dr. Schacht made a long address on his sixtieth birthday at a great Reichsbank celebration. I learn today that Dr. Goebbels censored it sharply. Schacht had said the 11,000,000,000 mark debt must be paid. That was not allowed to be printed. But the debt is certainly four times that amount, including 3,000,000,000 to United States banks and bond holders. He also said German circulation of marks has increased 50 per cent since 1933 and he added that the *Ersatz* industry must not go on increasing, as it costs about four times as much as what imports would cost.

February 20. Saturday. This is the first evening in a week I have not been somewhere to dine. Last Tuesday, the 16th, Dr. Sering sat next to my wife at a luncheon we gave for American bankers trying to settle German debt problems. He started to criticize severely Hitler's treatment of universities. My wife said: "I did not think you could speak so freely." He replied: "I say what I think. They can shoot me any time they want to. This system is ruining German intellectual life." This same old gentleman is well acquainted in the United States. He said quite as much to me two years ago, and nothing has been done to him.

Last night we attended a musicale of a Nazi official at the Bristol Hotel. There were perhaps 150 people present. The concert was not bad. At the dinner table, my wife sat next to the Duke of Coburg. I sat near Dr. Schacht who said loud enough for German officials to hear him: "Mussolini is annexing Spain; his next move will be to annex Egypt." I said: I learn that Mussolini has built a great road from the Red Sea to the Egyptian border. How did he get the money? Schacht replied: "Money does not have to be gotten now, we only issue paper and keep it circulating rapidly, thereby maintaining people at work. That is all." It surprised some people to hear this from the ablest finance official in the world, but no one added any remarks. I think the Nazi officials resented this, but they dared not say anything in his presence.

February 21. Sunday. I went to the old Kaiser Opera House at 12 o'clock today. Hitler and his chiefs sat where the royal family sat when I was here in 1899. It was a memorial service in honor of the two million Germans killed in the World War. There was no prayer or religious note. About fifty flags of all nations were held by soldiers on the stage. After a beautiful piece of classical music, General von Blomberg, chief of the new Nazi army, went to the stage and delivered an address which could not have been delivered in any democratic country.

He did not speak of the war as a calamity due to some leaders' blunders. He did say Germany's plight at the end of the war was the worst in history, which is not true, though conditions were bad enough. His main objective was to say Hitler had saved the German people as no other leader had ever done, to thank him for arming the whole nation, and to bow before him for his immense wisdom and patriotism. The "Heil Hitler" ceremony followed, with everybody but myself and a few other diplomats extending their right hands while the orchestra played the Horst Wessel song. This is modern Germany!

February 23. Tuesday. Today I talked for about an hour with Dr. Dieckhoff. I wished to let him know what an unfortunate effect the failure of Germany to answer the State Department's invitation to participate in an economic conference in Washington would produce. In three whole weeks, no answer has been received to the invitation presented in January. I also wanted to mention the effect of the government's issuing decrees to all business men not to answer any questions of our Commerce or Treasury Department officials here about American investments in Germany. One other object was to learn, if possible, what German officials really think about the international agreement to keep all troops and war supplies out of Spain. Finally, I wanted to know what Von Neurath was doing in Austria.

Dieckhoff has seemed to me to be the most democratic of the men in the Foreign Office, even more so than my deceased friend, Von Bülow, who passed away last June. Dieckhoff is reported not to be liked by Von Neurath, his chief, but I am not sure this rumor is correct. He has always seemed to recognize the brutal mistakes made here by the Hitler regime. So I felt that we might possibly have a real conversation.

He agreed at once that it was a mistake not to answer the American invitation to participate in the conference set for the first week in April. The delay, he said, was not due to Von Neurath's feeling. It was perhaps due to Dr. Schacht's attitude, which he said was not always what Schacht professed it was. The real objection to acceptance, he thought, was due to the indifference or hostility of the Labor and Economics Ministries —that is, Hitler's men. As to the refusal to give any information about American investments in Germany, he frankly agreed with me that it was a mistake. I gave him the dates of the two almost offensive letters the government had sent, one to me, the other to our Consul in Hamburg.

As to German-Italian relations, he really said nothing although he talked plenty. He would not agree that Mussolini intends to dominate Spain, though he had once before frankly said Germany would not protest if Mussolini annexed Egypt. His conversation revealed indirectly the doubtful wisdom of Germany's alliance with Italy.

As to Von Neurath's visit, it was only a return formality for the Austrian Foreign Secretary's visit here. I was sure it was more and asked about the reported rioting of the Viennese people when Von Neurath appeared. He insisted that there had been only wild Nazi demonstrations and that some of the uncontrollable fellows had to be arrested to keep them from doing too much. In my judgment it was all arranged here for propaganda purposes and the Austrians were expressing their hostility to the Nazis. Hence the arrests. It is contrary to law for an Austrian to heil Hitler.

Dieckhoff did say that a four-power agreement was Germany's object, also that Germany wanted control of Austria and Hungary, but that this would be defeated if a Hapsburg heir were to be put upon the ancient Austrian throne. Von Neurath was really trying to advance Germany's aggressive attitude toward domination of the Balkan states. This is in part aimed at smoking out Mussolini into a revelation of his real attitude towards the Austrian restoration. Nobody seems to think the poor Austrian people are free to have the kind of government they wish. Dieckhoff, liberal as he has always seemed to be, showed again his view that the Danube region belongs to Germany. It is the old Kaiser's policy, only far more urgent with Hitler than with the pre-war regime. Europe never recognizes the natural rights of different nations. Power is the only real thing.

February 28. Sunday. Another week of dinners and luncheons is past. We were out nearly every night, once with the Russian Ambassador, where he had forty guests at the table, ambassadors, ministers, and representatives of German officialdom but no high German official. The dining hall, heated by old-fashioned German stoves, was quite cold for me, even for the British Ambassador, although Englishmen at home never have warm houses. At least, I have never seen any there except hotels where Americans stay.

March 4. Thursday. Today I talked again with Dr. Schacht. He complained at first rather sharply about the American newspaper report that Germany's selling of $69,000,000 worth of bonds in America, to meet certain interest payments due creditors, had increased German debts, two billion dollars of which were kept secret. Schacht said this false story would hurt Germany's credit.

When he emphasized the point, I told him about reports I had from our Consuls in Latin America to the effect that German representatives in Chile, Brazil, and Argentina had done what they could to defeat Secretary Hull's peace efforts at the Buenos Aires conference and that one of the men there had claimed he represented Dr. Schacht. He asked who it was. I declined to give his name at that time since the information to me from Washington was confidential. What Schacht said made it clear he was thinking of Ilgner's work there, as I was, and he did not deny it.

I then asked Schacht about the possibility of a world peace conference. He favored the idea and spoke with much emotion, it seemed, about the danger of war which he said he always opposed, even the vast appropriations here for armament. He said Hitler was against war and had urged peace or armament reductions. I did not mention the many times Hitler had said such things and then proceeded in the opposite direction. Schacht then said arms manufacturers were the people who had defeated peace efforts since Wilson's attempts in 1918, and who had also defeated the League of Nations negotiations on the subject every time they were undertaken.

He repeated his hope that Washington might have a preliminary conference looking towards world peace and practically asked me if Hull would like to have him over there for discussion. In case he were invited to go, he would persuade Hitler to agree to having a peace conference, get him to accept his idea of substituting freer world trade for war preparations, and obtain a real peace agreement among the four important nations: Germany, France, England, and the United States. I consented to speak of this in a telegram to Washington. What he said about Hitler's recent speech on seizing business men's property and one by Von Ribbentrop in Leipzig relative to German demands for colonies, surprised me a little. He said both speeches were bunk, intended for local consumption, but both harmful abroad.

Then I went to Secretary von Neurath. He said: "No war is likely." I answered that arming to the last degree by all nations was most dangerous. He admitted as much but laid the blame on England. I reminded him that England was the last of all the nations to arm. He could not deny this, and then said munitions manufacturers had really been responsible for the dangerous armaments of European countries.

When I asked about the Spanish situation, he bluntly said: "We shall never allow the present government of Spain to win the civil war. It is Communism and we shall never allow that in any European state." That contradicted the peace idea with which he began. I said: Do you feel that no other nation has a right to govern itself, even foolishly? He said: "No, not when it involves Communism. If that happened in Spain, France would turn Communist and then attack us." I had not forgotten Dieckhoff's statement about Von Neurath's visit to Vienna where he protested against Austrian restoration of the Hapsburg monarch. That was not a Communist move, yet the Nazis insisted it must not happen. These Germans, even those who are considered liberal, seem to me never to think about the rights of smaller nations.

When I raised the question of a possible world peace conference, he at once said: "No, it cannot be successful." This was the opposite of Schacht's idea. His plan was to make nations more prosperous by gradual disarmament and spending of money in other directions. But when I repeated the danger of continued rearmament for all nations, Von Neurath agreed again. I left him, convinced that his former half-liberal attitudes had been practically abandoned.

These conversations, especially that with Von Neurath, revealed more clearly than formerly that the German Government is now determined to control, and actually annex, neighboring countries. The Balkan states are theirs, the Mediterranean states are Mussolini's. Official pronouncements over the radio from Rome give strong evidence of an agreement to these ends, although the German and Italian peoples dislike each other almost as much as the French and Germans.

March 6. Saturday. Yesterday the German press attacked and denounced Mayor La Guardia of New York for a remark he made about an exhibit in the World's Fair building next year, in which a bust of the brown-shirted Hitler should be erected, the exhibit to be called the Chamber of Horrors. The *Völkischer Beobachter* and the *Angriff*, official papers, went the limit in denouncing La Guardia as a terrible Communist, racketeer, and whoremonger, Jewish they said. They even attacked the United States Government for allowing such a speech, unaware, it seems, that free speech is the law of the American land.

I telegraphed a summary of what was said, but have made no protest until I receive instructions. Unhappily for Dr. Schacht, this comes at the time Secretary Hull authorized Ambassador Luther to telegraph Berlin that he hoped soon to be able to arrange a treaty with Germany for better commercial terms. This is the third time this sort of thing has happened here just as some negotiations were under discussion in Washington. In 1934 Hitler published a statement that nobody was to be arrested and imprisoned—Jews especially—except upon due process of law. On March 6 of that year he loudly declared to me that any German who started propaganda in the United States would be pitched into the North Sea. Before I returned on May 16, 1934, both these promises had been violated, Goebbels making a terrific speech against the Jews while I was on the Atlantic. On June 30, 1934, hundreds of opponents and many actual supporters were murdered upon Hitler's order without trial or evidence of anyone's guilt. How could Secretary Hull urge a treaty to be adopted by the Senate that year?

In June, 1935, when a deal was being negotiated in New York for bank credits so that Germany could buy $35,000,000 worth of cotton, Goering made a violent denunciation of Catholics. At once it caused the banks to refuse credit, and cotton could not be had. Goebbels followed a few days later with another denunciation of the Jews. So another Nazi defeat in trade resulted.

On March 4, Schacht asked me to telegraph the government how glad he would be to go to Washington in the hope of negotiating a trade arrangement and told me he expected to carry Hitler's approval of a world peace conference. The next day these violent newspaper scandals broke, La Guardia being popular in America. So another blunder!

March 9. Tuesday. Two priests from a monastery in Bavaria, built by American Catholics, came to see me this morning. The German district leader had forbidden them to speak or read the Bible in their monastery or church rooms. They could not understand this when their salaries were paid from the United States, but they feared that, if they should speak or read the Bible, they would be ordered out of the country. If they went away, their monastery which cost American contributors 300,000 marks would be taken over by the Nazi Party.

I could do nothing for them but advise caution and a visit to our Consul General who might possibly help them. This is the second case of this kind brought to my personal attention. Consul Jenkins reported to me that all he could do would be to give the facts to the Secret Police chief and persuade him that such a move would be harmful to German interests. However, the ownership of property by foreigners in Germany is entirely under the control of the Nazi Party.

March 12. Friday. Max Jordan, N.B.C. representative in Europe, called and reported that the opinion of press people and radio managers at home favors Roosevelt's judicial reform which is now being so hotly discussed. In spite of editorial control and big business influence, both reporters and workers all favor Roosevelt's plan. He said the Senate strongly opposed him, but the majority would vote for the measure. I hope so. If they defeat the President, his second term will be like Theodore Roosevelt's second term—argument and pressure for reform, without success. Only Franklin Roosevelt's defeat would be much worse and more dangerous because his majorities have been overwhelming in three Congressional elections, surpassing anything since Jefferson, who was also defeated in his major purposes except for the purchase of Louisiana.

Jordan then talked of German popular attitudes as revealed to him by a journalist whose name he dared not give. He said many airplane accidents and deaths had occurred this winter but not a word of them was allowed in the press. Only one case was reported: the accident a month ago in Berlin which could not be kept secret because it occurred in a busy section of the city, five people being killed. The reason for keeping all such accidents secret is to prevent young people from being discouraged, as so many thousands are ordered regularly into air service. I had known this was a rule of the government for more than two years.

He then said he was informed that some fifty soldiers were ordered to go on an unknown mission from Hamburg. They were forbidden to tell their parents they were going out of the country, to Spain, but some of them spoke of it. A meeting of parents was held in the town near where the soldiers received orders. The Nazi local officials arrested and imprisoned all the parents, for how long Jordan did not know. He added that a number of the soldiers committed suicide rather than go on the secret journey. If this is correct, it means something serious for Hitler and Goering to think about.

This afternoon at 5:30 I went to the German Foreign Office, Mr. Lee with me, to make the protest Secretary Hull cabled me from Washington against the shameful German press attacks on February 4, 5 and 6 against the women, the people and the government of the United States. Knowing the motives of the Nazi officials, Goebbels and Rosenberg, also Hitler himself, I could not expect any real regrets even from Secretary von Neurath.

I told Von Neurath, who showed himself a little embarrassed, what a blunder the Germans had made. He acknowledged this, but said he had stopped the extreme vituperation of the *Angriff* articles from being published in other German papers. I then had Mr. Lee read Secretary Hull's protest and showed Von Neurath several other German papers which had reprinted what the *Angriff* had said. He could not deny what had happened and he agreed with me it was very stupid, though he pled in excuse that some American papers had attacked Germany violently during the last four years. He could not justify present-day German folly. The conversation ended. I was sure Von Neurath, even if he had wanted to, did not dare apologize as Hull had done for La Guardia's ridicule of Hitler, and that he would really not say anything to the Fuehrer or Goebbels. They are incorrigible.

March 15. Monday. This afternoon I learned that Ernst Hanfstaengl, long a close supporter of Hitler and chief of the Nazi foreign press office, was ordered about February 20 to close his office and go to Valencia, Spain, on some mission. I was to have had lunch with Hanfstaengl on February 22 and he informed me he had to leave Berlin. A close friend told me today that Hanfstaengl went to Munich, his home, did not go to Spain, and has since disappeared. I hear he is in a concentration camp and in danger of losing his life. He has not been seen by Hitler in two years or more and I have noted at the Carl Schurz luncheons that he was rather free in criticizing Goebbels and others in the regime. I never ventured frank talk with him after the summer of 1934. Since he gave much money to Hitler in 1923, helped him write *Mein Kampf,* and was in every way familiar with Hitler's motives, he would be an unreliable man out of Germany. What a book he could write!

A report today reveals that the Germans and the Czechoslovaks have negotiated a treaty for mutual good relations, Beneš having agreed to treat all Germans in his country as well as the Czechs themselves, but that now Hitler denounces the agreement. He can allow no treaty with any people who have an understanding with the Russians. In view of this, I put no faith in the recent German offers to negotiate a new Western four-power pact. His first demand will be to forbid French relations with Russia. The basic point of these moves is that Germany will have her own way as to the boundaries and status of the Balkan states and the right to annex them when she thinks the time ripe. That is the *Mein Kampf* doctrine.

I wrote Messersmith, our Minister in Austria, a few days ago that the best and perhaps the only guarantee of world peace is for all the Balkan states to form a co-operative confederation ready always to help one another. That would be a union of

80,000,000 people. Germany would have to think twice before she moved against such a union. I suggested he talk this over with Schuschnigg. European nations have practiced war since the fall of the Roman Empire; what might not civilization have become if peoples could have learned the basic principles of Christianity which all Western peoples have professed superficially for a thousand years!

March 17. Wednesday. Today Dr. Dieckhoff asked me to see him at 6 P.M. I went. The Secretary seemed troubled as we shook hands. He began at once to talk about another La Guardia speech made in New York. He seemed to have been instructed to insist that I tell President Roosevelt or Secretary Hull to stop the New York Mayor from criticizing Hitler. Since Dieckhoff had been Counselor to the German Embassy in Washington from 1922 to 1926, I could not see how he could ask such a thing seriously. Of course I replied, No, that can't be done; you know that freedom of speech and the press are guaranteed to all our people. He knew that, he said, but hoped something could be done anyway.

When he had talked a little further about our press criticism, I said: You know our people were friendly to the German people after the World War ended, far more than to France because the French Government refused to disarm. He said that such an attitude was very clear to him when he was in Washington, but why were Americans so hostile now? After some discussion we parted company, both quite aware nothing can be done in the United States or in Nazi Germany to better relations.

March 30. Tuesday. It's a long time since I made my last notes. I have attended dinners and lunches often enough. Two of them were a little revealing. On March 18, we were at the home of the former Foreign Secretary, Von Kühlmann. He had served under the Kaiser in 1918 and supported the Kaiser's attitude toward the Brest-Litovsk negotiations, but he was defeated by the generals of the army who demanded vast annexations. Since we have been here we have seen him occasionally.

At his dinner were twelve or fourteen guests. The British

Ambassador talked to Von Kühlmann about Spain as if he were a sincere supporter of the cruel Franco, although he formerly talked to me as if he were staunchly opposed to Franco. The latter, I suppose, was a diplomatic attitude for my benefit. Dr. Dieckhoff was present and talked like an opponent of his Fuehrer. Other people spoke equally freely. One eminent man said to my wife: "There is no use of our always talking about conquering territory on our eastern frontier; eastern France must be annexed to Germany, especially as the French population is declining." This reminded me of the French Ambassador's statement to me in 1933: "We must annex German territory to the Rhine. Wilson defeated us in this."

From the Von Kühlmann dinner I went to the eighty-fifth birthday dinner of Dr. Sering. There were some hundred guests present, including Dr. Schacht and other officials whom I had met frequently. I was late and so did not hear the speeches made by Sering and Schacht, but I was told they had done what is most dangerous here—criticized the Nazi policy and German military activity. I knew both of them thought that way, but was surprised to hear they had felt free enough to talk before a large group of people. Schacht said to me: "My position is very critical; I do not know what is to happen."

There was a Cabinet meeting on March 19 and Schacht is reported to have challenged Hitler's Four-Year Plan in some of its items. But nothing has happened and Cabinet decisions are reported all in favor of Hitler and Goering.

The Catholic priests or bishops read an encyclical from the Pope, on March 21, in all their German churches. It was a warning to the Catholics to keep their faith, a protest against Hitler's efforts to destroy the Catholic Church, and an appeal for religious liberty. Religious liberty proclaimed by Catholic leaders upon the order of the Pope! Not a word of this papal message was mentioned in the press, but copies were published in England and other countries, many people here learning in this way what had happened.

Today I visited the Papal Nuncio, hearing that he was well again after a long illness. I congratulated him on what the Pope had done in proclaiming religious liberty in a Europe where religious liberty is absolutely denied, and especially because the aged and half-ill Pope seems to me to show real courage even under the nose of Mussolini. The Nuncio was most delighted and insisted that the great Catholic Church is really struggling for religious freedom now everywhere, even in Mexico. I spent a half hour with him and he told me that thousands of copies of the Pope's message were distributed by hand all over Germany; he did not know if anybody had been arrested.

April 3. Saturday. The Czechoslovak Minister came to the office this morning and talked more than half an hour. I had asked to see him at his house, but he insisted on coming to see me. I asked him about Balkan relations, a subject about which I wrote our Minister in Vienna a month ago. He said that Yugoslavia's treaty of recent date with Italy was a strong move in the direction of peace, that it was designed by Italy as a means of food relief in case of a possible war with England. And, he added, Yugoslavia is now much closer to Austria, but she will not think of consenting to the restoration of Otto, the Hapsburg heir, to the throne.

He then said a similar treaty between Rumania and Russia has just been agreed to, which means recognition of boundaries and co-operation between these countries for peace. Of course I had heard about the treaty but was not quite sure what it meant. He said the two arrangements, the Yugoslav-Italian and the Rumanian-Russian, were important steps toward co-operation and peace among all the Balkan states. Now Czechoslovakia and Germany must come to a similar agreement as to boundaries and national minorities. Then the Balkan states would be reasonably safe and mutually helpful, Austria and Bulgaria and Hungary each being pressed to co-operate with the so-called Little Entente. His only anxiety was on his last point, an understanding between Czechoslovakia and Germany. Propaganda was going on, emanating from Germany, every day against the one democracy in this part of Europe. He showed also some anxiety about a possible Hapsburg restoration, unwilling to allow this although Austria seems to ask it as a right.

April 7. Wednesday. Yesterday evening the Czechoslovak Minister at our dinner told me he had information that Ludendorff has an organization of young Germans who hate Hitler, also that considerable groups of the German army are co-operating quietly with the Ludendorff youth movement, Ludendorff's bi-weekly magazine going to them regularly. General von Blomberg, Commander-in-Chief and War Minister, learned of these facts and managed to get Hitler and Ludendorff to meet and talk in Munich, the excuse being Ludendorff's seventy-second birthday on April 9. The Minister wondered what this really meant. Perhaps we shall learn more two days from now. Today I heard that Ludendorff's magazine has been confiscated.

Secretary Lee of our staff today reported that Ambassador Luther, who has been recalled from Washington, was reporting two years ago to the German Foreign Office about Huey Long, the would-be American dictator. Herr K., now retired from the Foreign Office, had read the reports which Luther had been ordered to make. He did not reveal the contents but he did say to Lee that Luther had visited Louisiana and Huey Long more than once. I wonder whether our government in Washington has ever heard about this. I hope to learn just what was said about Huey Long, also about his death.

The twenty or more guests of yesterday were disposed to talk more freely than diplomats and German officials generally do. Some distinguished Germans criticized the Hitler regime most severely—a habit that is getting to be quite common again. What does this mean? Or do they think a democrat likes to hear this?

April 10. Saturday. On Thursday I talked a half hour with the Russian Ambassador. He spoke of having dined on March 20 with the nephew of General Goering, who is an official in the Reichsbank. Others present, Prince Louis Ferdinand told me, were the French Ambassador, Dr. Schacht and Prince Louis. The Soviet Ambassador did not admit that there are negotiations now going on for a secret treaty between Germany and Russia. I had heard this from our Minister in Norway this week. The Russian Ambassador announced that he had just returned from Moscow and that he goes on April 20 as Ambassador to France.

On Friday night, I heard from Walter Duranty, New York *Times* correspondent in Moscow since 1921, that secret negotiations are on between Germany and Russia. Another rumor. I think something is on, but feel it is merely a commercial arrangement. How could Hitler make a political treaty with the Communists?

This morning at 12 o'clock, the British Ambassador came to say farewell. He is leaving April 16 for Paris where he is to serve the next few years as Ambassador. When I told him of the three stories I had heard about German-Russian negotiations, he showed a good deal of concern. I told him I was not convinced, but that it seemed that something was on. I had the feeling he wanted to telegraph what I had said to Downing Street at once.

April 11. Sunday. A confidential report from Frankfurt reveals some other aspects of German life to me, but not a word on these subjects appears in the German papers. Great crowds of church people met in their churches between March 31 and April 4. At the city of Darmstadt, the Nazi Black Shirts and Brown Shirts, opposed to religious activity except in the Party churches (*i.e.*, Rosenberg's semi-barbaric religious cult), gathered in great crowds about the principal church and arrested five pastors on account of their sermons. In the Frankfurt district, thirty-seven persons were imprisoned for Bible study meetings and thirty are still in jail. No charges were made. The Nazi district leaders ordered this and imprisoned people without trial. These victims were simply Protestant worshippers who perhaps made it plain that they will not change their religious beliefs.

In the Catholic Saar area, a crucifix on the wall of a denominational school was ordered to be taken down at Easter time. A picture of Hitler was put in the place of the crucifix. The parents whose children attend this school objected strongly and some of them kept their children at home. The parents were fined and some fathers were dismissed from their positions. When the people were called on to vote whether all denominational schools should be closed, they voted 97 per cent in favor of abolishing them. But the general feeling all over Germany is that the people must all vote one way when any election takes place. If they vote their own convictions, imprisonment is expected.

At Stuttgart, a former liberal city, an American traveler who took photographs of an ancient village near by was arrested March 30. No one may take photographs without government permission. When the local authorities found they had arrested an American spending money in Germany and utterly unaware of this stringent law, they released him, after two hours in prison.

A report last Friday from Panama says 500 German Christians passed through the great canal on their way to tracts of land which the Columbian Government had given them. Were these emigrants escaping their country to seek religious freedom? Some people here say 10,000,000 would go if they could.

Yesterday afternoon, April 10, there was real sunshine, so promising that my wife, daughter and I went for a two-hour drive into the famous Spreewald region south of Berlin. Halfway out there was a vast military field with elaborate barracks running nearly a mile along the left side of the road. The forests all the way showed immense cuttings, done under the Four-Year Plan about which Goering speaks so often. The wheat and barley fields seemed in better condition than I had expected after so much bad weather. It has rained almost every day since October 1. The old town of Spreewald reminded one of the late Middle Ages, but the people appeared healthy and were better clad than some people I used to see in large sections of Chicago where wages were always twice as high as here.

April 13. Tuesday. Yesterday Mrs. Peters, author of a book, *Roosevelt and the Kaiser,* called and told me about an Iowa man here who pretends to be an advanced student. He is an agent of the Nazi-American organization headed in Detroit by a certain Fritz Kuhn who raises money and helps the man here by giving him contacts with the Propaganda Ministry and with

Hitler. She said he attacked me freely for not being a Nazi co-worker. I asked her to see the man again and learn just what he does.

April 15. Thursday. American churches are beginning to show movies revealing what Germany does to Catholics and Protestants who contend for religious rights. The German papers have begun again their hostile articles criticizing the freedom of church people in the United States, but they are not so vitriolic as early in March when the La Guardia attack on Hitler was made. They affect not to understand such freedom and wonder how a people for whom Von Steuben fought during their Revolution can be so critical of the country from which Von Steuben came. They do not seem to know that Von Steuben was sent to America by revolutionary France.

The press also speaks similarly of Carl Schurz, never intimating that Carl Schurz was imprisoned here for his love of freedom and escaped through France to the United States where he fought the rest of his life for democracy, so denounced in present-day Germany. Their persecutions are quite as severe as those of the sixteenth century, except as to actual deaths. Hundreds of preachers have been imprisoned for teaching Christianity.

April 17. Saturday. The German Official Gazette of April 14 came to my attention today. It lists ninety-one Germans who have been deprived of their nationality. Ludwig Renn, author of a famous book against war, is the most prominent denationalized person on the list. Many others are children of opponents of the Nazi Party. One of these children is only two years old.

At the same time, information comes that members of the old German aristocracy have been arrested because they are reported to be monarchists, active for restoration of the royalist regime. Stricter observation and punishment of Jews is evident. They cannot hold meetings of any sort, except church service. They cannot play tennis, football, enjoy river sports, canoeing or swimming. This ancient realm of religious liberty is becoming a terrible autocracy. Perhaps one-third of the masses are enthusiastic for a system which denies every man his personal liberty.

April 20. Tuesday. Yesterday afternoon George Lansbury, English Labor leader and peace agitator, spent two hours with Hitler. I think the visit was maneuvered by Von Ribbentrop to encourage pacifist and peace sentiment in England, thereby weakening the pressure for increased armaments, perhaps also to confuse French-English relations.

We had given a luncheon to the Russian Ambassador who is leaving soon for Paris and I was not at the Embassy promptly. The I.N.S. representative, the very able William Shirer, called me as I was about to leave for Potsdam to visit the old Frederick II mansion, and told me that Lansbury said to him that Hitler spoke highly of President Roosevelt and argued that if Roosevelt called a world conference for peace, he, Hitler, would co-operate. I was skeptical because Schacht and Von Neurath had both said on March 4 that no conference should be called until economic agreements among the greater world powers were made. I called the Embassy and asked that a telegram be sent to Washington. I had mailed Hull a careful letter that day in which I analyzed the situation here, indicating especially the anxiety about war. The defeats of Franco in Spain have done much to check Hitler's belligerency temporarily.

Today I had the disagreeable duty of sitting in the cold, outdoor air on a platform in the Berlinerstrasse, opposite the famous Technical College, and watching along with the rest of the diplomats the great military parade in honor of Hitler's forty-eighth birthday. In spite of the peace avowals which had been made yesterday and all the lessons of the terrible Spanish conflict, Hitler stood on a platform for two hours watching 15,-000 soldiers go by and reviewing millions of dollars worth of war machines of all kinds. I have never seen such a huge military demonstration in my life.

The whole of Germany was allowed a holiday and in Berlin hundreds of thousands of people were marching the streets to pay tribute. Children were everywhere conspicuous. Although many distinguished people seem very much opposed to the Nazi regime, there seemed to be nothing but enthusiasm today.

The diplomats were not all of approving frames of mind. The French Ambassador, whose country did most to start Ger-

many on its military course, seemed miserable, although a part
of his fortune had come to him from huge sales of arms during
the early Hitler regime. The Turkish Ambassador, in spite of
the dictatorship in his country, was depressed to see what vast
equipments Hitler chose to show us. Some Latin American representatives showed disgust. It was, of course, most depressing
to me to be reminded for two hours how all European powers
had abandoned Wilson's urgent recommendations of 1918-1919.
The League of Nations, which promised so much, is ruined. As
I looked at Von Neurath, who sat near me, I thought his face
revealed distress, and when we were leaving and shook hands
with Dr. Schacht, he revealed much unhappiness. It was to him
about the same as it was to me. I shall not attend another Hitler
birthday celebration if I am in Berlin next year.

April 22. Thursday. On Tuesday evening General Goering,
reported to be ill, hurried off to Rome where he is to see Mussolini on his way to southern Italy for a supposed rest cure.
Hitler went by flying machine to Munich where another military demonstration was given him on the 20th. There was also
an exaggerated Party speech by Hess who said that the Fuehrer
is the modern Jesus.

Talking with the Czechoslovak Minister, I learned that
Goering told him some days ago that several attempts to murder Hitler had been thwarted this year. I received a telegram
this morning from Washington announcing that the young Jew,
Helmut Hirsch, who had been condemned to be executed because he was accused of trying to murder the famous, or rather
infamous, Streicher of Nürnberg, is an American citizen. That
makes it necessary for me to visit the Foreign Office and insist
that justice be done and that real evidence of the crime must be
produced, with punishment meted out according to law.

April 25. Sunday. The German papers feature the meeting of
Mussolini with Schuschnigg, the Chancellor of Austria, on Fri-
day, April 23, in Venice. There is to be no growth of the Little
Entente in the Balkan zone except under the supervision of
Mussolini and Hitler. This reopens the severe problem about
which Ministers from Austria and Czechoslovakia have talked

hopefully of late. Mussolini will not allow these two countries to make a defensive alliance. He will not now permit a Hapsburg restoration although he had for three years promised to invade South Germany if Hitler tried to invade Austria to stop the Hapsburg movement. Now Germany and Italy are forming a solid front against the East as well as the West. The Hapsburg claim is the easiest excuse for Mussolini; the Balkan countries are sharply divided on this issue.

Tomorrow Goering, who went to Italy on the 20th for his health, sees Mussolini, I think to counteract any influence Schuschnigg may have had. On May 3, Von Neurath goes to Rome. There is some bargaining about Spain, too. Italy wishes to annex Spain, or at least control it, but for the last month things have not been favorable there. What will Von Neurath say for Hitler? My guess: If you guarantee us Austria, we will guarantee your influence in Spain if England continues her two-faced policy. The idea of Italy and Germany is to extend their power by threats of war, to hasten this business before England is fully ready and also before Poland, now uneasier than ever, unites with Rumania and the Little Entente. The Foreign Minister of Poland is now in Belgrade to negotiate, they say, with Rumania. If Hitler and Mussolini go to war there will be insurrections of their peoples. If the Balkan states form a union for self, and mutual, defense, Hitler and Mussolini will have to stay at home. In case the Spanish Republicans win the struggle there, the spread of dictatorships in Europe will cease, and Hitler and Mussolini will fall.

April 27. Tuesday. An official of the German Foreign Office, with us at luncheon today, said to my daughter: Helmut Hirsch, the American Jew who aimed at killing Hitler, cannot be let off with life imprisonment. He must be executed though he did not actually try to commit the crime.

There has been no proof shown us and no word about the case printed. The American press has been very restrained in its accounts thus far. The Germans do not seem to recognize the likelihood of violent reaction in the United States in case this twenty-year-old boy is executed without evidence of his guilt.

I think he may have been used in a plan of revenge by the group of Germans in Prague whose brothers and close friends were executed by Hitler June 30, 1934, but I think if proof cannot be found and published, this fellow should not be executed. I have said this to the Foreign Office officials more than once. The Germans came back with the statement: "The American, Simpson, pardoned by us last December, is now making addresses in the United States against the Nazi system and for the Communists whose propaganda he tried to distribute here." Therefore, they say, "We must execute Hirsch." I reply: That will mean violent press attacks because evidence is being withheld from us officially, and from everyone.

April 30. Friday. Aware that Hitler was holding on May 1 a great propaganda assembly, as he did on April 20, his birthday, I chose this time for a few days' relaxation from my work. A week ago the Propaganda Ministry sent me a formal invitation. I had attended his birthday show which I felt was a reflection on Hitler rather than an honor to him. That seemed to me enough even for a diplomat, so I wrote that I was to be away and indicated that the Counselor and staff would attend instead.

This morning at 11 o'clock, my wife, daughter and myself, with our good chauffeur, took to our car. The weather was more beautiful than it has been since last September. We drove over the great *autobahn* to Hanover. From there we went to ancient Marburg, through Göttingen, a beautiful country with peasants in their fields, men and women, hard at work. We spent the night in the city where the questionable Von Papen made the only free speech that has been delivered in Germany since our arrival here.

May 1. Saturday. As we started on our journey toward Verdun, the wonderful ancient palace on the top of a high hill was so appealing that Martha and I climbed the stairways and looked at the marvelous medieval structure. A thousand Nazis were shouting and singing in honor of their Fuehrer on one side of the hill. Nazi flags were waving, though very few projected from the windows of residences. We crossed the Rhine at Coblenz, drove across the lower end of Luxemburg, went to the city of the same name in the afternoon, and then visited Verdun, where we looked at the graveyards full of dead soldiers and at the houses wrecked by the Germans during the World War. It was a sad view, every field and forest showing what great bombs had done. 500,000 soldiers are reported to have been killed in the struggle here between French and German armies. I have never seen anything more condemning of war as a method of solving any kind of problem than I saw at Verdun and in the miles of land around it.

May 3. Monday. We visited the famous League of Nations building in Geneva this morning. The American representative, Arthur Sweetser, relative of some of our internationalist friends in Chicago, was most kind but discouraged about the future of the Wilson scheme which he and I had advocated in 1918-20 in Chicago and the Middle West. He told me much about the defeats of League efforts for world peace, and agreed entirely with my official reports on the British-French blunders and the crime of the Hoare-Laval betrayal of Ethiopia in November-December, 1935. He said he was sure at the time that if sanctions had been applied that autumn Mussolini would have been compelled to submit to League decisions.

May 4. Tuesday. We set out for Berlin at 10 A.M. over the route via Basle, Heidelberg and Frankfurt. It was a beautiful section of Europe. Between Basle and Heidelberg, in Baden, I counted forty-five women working in the fields in ten minutes just looking to my right. There were perhaps a few more men, though not many young ones. Germany has her young men in arms. She has always had her women at work on farms: plowing, digging weeds out of wheat fields and planting potatoes. That is what they were doing today, sturdy, big-handed women as active and able as men. Americans would be surprised to see this, and their women, if in the fields, would look far less vigorous or able.

We reached Heidelberg about 8 o'clock and there took the *autobahn* towards Frankfurt where we wished to spend the night. It was a wonderful road like the one between Potsdam and Hanover. Being late, we allowed our chauffeur to drive about 90 miles an hour. It was dangerous because tires might get hot and explode; however, nothing happened and we found ourselves well located in a good hotel.

May 6. Thursday. On Monday, Lord Lothian, Lloyd George's wartime secretary, the former Philip Kerr, came to Berlin at Hitler's request and he is reported to have had two hours with the dictator. He is to be with us for luncheon today. On May 3, Von Neurath was in Rome to talk with Mussolini. The same day Goering was in Yugoslavia to talk with their government chief. I shall probably learn a little of what this is all about within the next few days. I believe, though, Hitler and his intimates are uneasy about what is happening in Spain and equally anxious about the possibility of a general co-operative arrangement among the Danube-Balkan states. Germany thinks she must control if not annex them, but Italy wants to do the same thing, especially if Spain recovers its independence.

We had Ambassador Dieckhoff, leaving tonight for Washington, as honor guest. I welcomed him in a brief speech in which I mentioned humorously the low tariff policy of the Roosevelt Administration and the freedom of the Philippines. The guests laughed except Lord Lothian who pretended afterward that he had never heard of our low tariff negotiations. Dieckhoff replied without referring to these difficult points, perhaps afraid of being quoted by German guests.

When we retired from the dining room, I was able to talk a little with Lothian whom I had met in London in 1928. He was then in private life in London and still quite enthusiastic about his former chief, Lloyd George. Now he ridiculed him and especially his recent speeches against the Tory British regime. He praised Hitler for saving Germany in 1933 and referred to his long talk of May 3 with the Fuehrer, saying it was mostly about Mussolini and British-German relations, now quite critical. Further he was not wiling to go, referring more than once to my letter to him in 1935 about the dangerous European situation. His hatred of France was revealed twice, as well as his dislike of Woodrow Wilson's efforts in 1918-20. I could hardly make out just where he belonged in European alignments. He seemed to be more a Fascist than any other Englishman I have met. Recent English criticism of Italy and especially Germany with reference to their barbarism in Spain bothered him.

May 12. Wednesday. After a week of quiet, I learn today from the press people that my careful letter to Senator Bulkley of March 1 has been violently discussed in the United States Senate. My object was twofold: (1) to show how the Supreme Court, under Marshall, rendered its decisions claiming the right to veto acts of Congress; (2) to reveal once more how victorious parties defeated Presidents Cleveland, Theodore Roosevelt, and Woodrow Wilson, their own chiefs elected by overwhelming votes, when they tried to do what they had been elected to do. My conclusion was that democracy in the United States is in more danger than at any time since Lincoln.

Strange to say, Senators focused on a single sentence at the end of my letter in which I said a near-billionaire had been reported to me as favoring a dictatorship, not unlike those in Russia, Germany and Italy. There was no reference at all to the major facts of our past history. Fearing something like this might happen, I had sent a copy of my letter to Judge Moore, asking him to send it to the Richmond *Times-Dispatch* for publication. And about the time the Senate discussion started, perhaps the second day, it was printed. As yet I have not learned what the press in general did. I fear its reporters simply followed the senators' attacks.

May 15. Saturday. Clippings came to me revealing what has been published about my letter—misrepresentations of a shameful kind. Senators Borah and King are my main attackers. Their aim was to make it appear absolutely necessary for me to resign my post in Berlin and then testify as to the millionaires who were being manipulated from European capitals. The State Department refused to co-operate with the Senators and I believe warned them of their folly. I sent a telegram to the President today calling attention to the fact that no notice was taken of the real argument of my letter. I also sent one yesterday to Judge Moore, asking him to remind Senator King how the one sentence had been magnified and to add that I could not give names of people who had talked to me confidentially in the United States about possible dictatorships. I gave the American press people here careful summary statements of what I had said and why my information as to plans for the dictatorship could not be given out. They say full reports of this explanation were published. If so, some corrections may come.

Not a word has come to me from the German Foreign Office. I do not think anything has been said in the German papers, though I am sure telegrams have come from the German Embassy in Washington. The Germans, in my opinion, think I might publish a book on my sad four years here if they start attacks on me. I am sure the Foreign Office people are half in sympathy with me, also that its officials are wise as to what is best to do and say in such situations. I am ready to resign, as Washington officials know. To do nothing here is not appealing to me.

May 19. Wednesday. Today I received a cordial letter from President Roosevelt in which he said he agreed with me about the Supreme Court problem and added that this year is the best time to have truthful, frank, national discussion. The letter was written just before he left for his Gulf of Mexico vacation trip. So he was not in the United States to see how the Senators attacked me for the letter I had written. The President also asked me for my personal opinion of the new Ambassador, Dieckhoff, soon to arrive in Washington.

Judge Moore wrote me also and stated that the President has promised the Berlin post to Davies, at present in Moscow, or rather on the way via London where he probably spent large sums to see the Coronation ceremony on May 12. Moore was so sure of this that he did not deliver my last letter to the President. From my point of view this type of appointment seems so improper and unbecoming to our democratic country that I am greatly disposed to decline to resign as I had offered to do. The idea of having a man here who speaks no German, is insufficiently versed in European history or the background of the present situation, and is preparing to spend $100,000 a year!

At any rate, I shall postpone my return to the United States and also give the President my judgment of such a man in so important a position.

May 20. Thursday. Today a poor seventy-year-old German came to see me. He lost everything he had during the inflation period and is on the pension list. But he had made an invention for preserving wood against fire and thought he could borrow some money and begin a business which would give him some property again. He had applied for his patent, he said, but the government would not allow him to register it. I was not sure, but he showed me an announcement which indicated that all inventions and discoveries belong to the government. At any rate, he was afraid, expecting to be arrested if it were known that he saw me, especially as he wished to get a passport to the United States where he hoped he could sell his invention and make a living. I could not encourage him because he has no means at all to start with.

This is only one of many such cases that come to my attention. I received a few days ago the Rockefeller Foundation report for 1936. It shows that 1,639 German professors and teachers have been dismissed since 1933 and that the Rockefeller Foundation has given $532,181 to help these poor people. The German system prohibits all opposition and criticism; it controls all teaching from the low grade schools through the universities; it will have only one church—based on certain ancient superstitions before the dawn of German history. The system has been operating only about three years but the people seem to have surrendered to an amazing extent. Their government has a propaganda chief in the Foreign Office who spends millions of dollars a year trying to spread their system over the world.

The German papers this morning carried violent attacks upon Cardinal Mundelein of Chicago because he criticized the cruel German system before a great audience of priests. Apparently American Catholics are joining the Jewish and other church people in attacking the German religious autocracy.

I had an appointment with Dr. Schacht this morning at 12

o'clock. I asked him if the new Ambassador, Dieckhoff, had real authority to negotiate a commercial treaty with the United States. He did not say yes or no, but he insisted that he agreed with Secretary Hull as to lowering tariffs and thus moving towards world peace. However, he quickly said Hull had prevented Brazil from giving Germany a bilateral treaty and a credit arrangement. I did not believe this, but he insisted that he knew that Hull threatened Brazil with refusal to take coffee if she made concessions to Germany.

When Schacht went a step further and said Germany would make no other treaties except bilateral agreements like those with Italy, Belgium, and others, I saw he did not agree with Hull, and he then complained of American opposition. I asked him if he had read the German attack on Cardinal Mundelein of Chicago. He said, "Yes." I then handed him the Rockefeller report on the dismissal of 1,639 professors and teachers and called his attention to the Rockefeller Institute's gift of $532,181. He did not deny the truth of the account, but at once said: "Yes, Catholics, Jews, and teachers suffer in Germany. It is the effect of the revolution like that of France in 1789." I questioned this. He said it could not be stopped for years and seemed reconciled to the arbitrary system which he formerly condemned when talking with me. I was somewhat surprised. The conversation came to an end and I felt I must telegraph the gist of his comment to Washington. There is no prospect of improving German-American relations, no chance at all. Schacht talked as if the Hitler system were permanent.

May 29. Saturday. As I returned this afternoon from Magdeburg, I found a letter marked "confidential" on the desk as I entered the house. It was from Meissner, Hitler's Private Secretary. It was Hitler's reply to my letter to him of April 30. I had requested commutation of sentence for poor Hirsch's crime, an "attempt to kill Streicher," they say. My points were that he had not done the deed, nor been caught trying to do it, and that he was an American citizen who would not under American law be executed for planning a thing that had not been done.

Hitler's reply was that no leniency was possible. Some time after reading the letter, I called Meissner on the telephone for a brief talk. His housekeeper reported that he was out for the evening. I hoped the execution might be delayed, as I was more convinced than ever that the young boy was at worst a dupe in the affair and should not be killed.

This morning I had another curious case brought to my attention. A German woman came to me with the hope of finding a way to emigrate from Germany with a man to whom she had been engaged since 1933. The man was an engineer in high public position before Hitler came to power. He was a half-Jew. She was an assistant in the French Embassy. But the man was dismissed from his position in 1933. He tried to find employment but failed. People were forbidden to employ him. So the marriage was postponed because it was forbidden in Germany.

The woman some time ago lost her position and could not find another. The *Stürmer* attacked the couple because of their continued devotion to each other. She managed to see Hitler himself to ask his tolerance, that is, the right to marry. Hitler refused, and the Secret Police took her fiancé's passport to leave Germany away from him. Letters to both of them were seized, especially all from outside Germany. The Fraülein hoped the American Consulate here might help her and her fiancé to go to the United States where they had kinspeople, but could not hear from them because letters were always stopped.

It seemed to me a sad case, but I could hardly see how anything could be done. She said if nothing could be done they were going to slip across the French border and the French Ambassador had promised to help them if they were arrested for want of passports.

Another illustrative fact of a day or two ago was the way the dead bodies of the *Hindenburg* disaster were buried at Frankfurt on May 22. The Hitler district leader there had charge. The people who accompanied the bodies to the cemetery were uniformed Storm Troopers, Black Shirt companies, and the *Hitler Jugend*, tens of thousands of them. The civilians were crowded off the streets or stood in the rear when services were conducted. Although Catholic and Protestant priests and people were present, the leader, Sprenger, made no reference to God or any possible salvation of souls except that contained in the ancient pagan belief: "They had gone to their Valhalla." This seems to indicate that Rosenberg's religious system is being accepted. No complaints were reported in Frankfurt at this new-old religious service. When the burial was finished, a great volley of guns was fired and military planes flew over the crowd.

May 31. Monday. As usual after some months here, I have a persistent headache. Yesterday was a busy day, although it was Sunday. I spoke at the American Church on Decoration Day, my subject being "Do unto others as you would have them do unto you,"—from St. Matthew VII. My idea was to show how men nearly always lose a war, even those who win the last battles. To avoid being misquoted by the press people in the United States, I gave a brief outline to the American press in Berlin. I spoke half an hour to a perfectly still audience. I fear no German paper will print a word this week, as it was about peace.

Having received a note Saturday afternoon that Hirsch was to be executed, I went to Von Neurath today to see if he could not influence Hitler to respect American law. Von Neurath indicated sympathy with my attitude and said he would see Hitler tomorrow morning and present the case, at least to ask delay.

Since everybody was excited about the bombarding of a German war vessel off the eastern coast of Spain and the killing of more than twenty Germans, I asked Von Neurath how it had happened. He declared he did not know, but he said he had opposed the German bombing of a Spanish city in return. He insisted that he had urged once more that Germany agree to the withdrawal of all troops that were fighting in Spain, but he was doubtful whether the Non-Intervention Commission in London could do anything, Germany and Italy having withdrawn. He indicated that the situation was dangerous.

June 2. Wednesday. I went this afternoon to see Meissner, Hitler's secretary, and stressed again the injustice of executing Hirsch with no evidence given to us or to our government. I also told him Secretary Hull had telegraphed me again to ask delay or, if proof was conclusive, a life sentence. He said it was proved that Hirsch was to have bombed and destroyed the Nazi Party building in Nürnberg and to have killed Streicher, the notorious Jew hater, editor of the *Stürmer,* but Meissner agreed that consideration should be given to American law since Hirsch was an American citizen. He promised to see Hitler Wednesday morning and present my appeal. But he indicated that executions were done in secret in Germany and that he feared the Fuehrer would not even delay it.

The Spanish situation looks a little easier, but reports come that airplanes, submarines, ships and German soldiers are already on the way to Spain. The new English Ambassador here is reported to be in full sympathy with the German-Italian aggression in Spain. His name is Henderson, and he was in Argentina several years before coming here. He had already revealed his complete pro-Franco attitude, seemingly unaware of the dangers to England. He is also reported to have informed the German Government that England would make no objections if Hitler seized Austria and Czechoslovakia.

Miss Schultz, correspondent of the Chicago *Tribune,* reported this afternoon that Von Neurath is leaving Berlin on June 7 to visit the governments of Yugoslavia, Hungary, and Bulgaria. My guess is that his mission is to defeat the efforts of Austria, Czechoslovakia and Rumania to enlarge the Little Entente for mutual protection. This visit seems also the logical outcome of the plan to help Italy conquer Spain. Germany will then advance its thousand-year aim to annex or at least subordinate all the Balkan countries. Italy is to be the master of the Mediterranean area except for France, and Germany the master of the 80,000,000 people all the way to Greece. Information today is sad.

June 3. Thursday. I made two revealing if ineffective visits this afternoon. I saw the French Ambassador at 5 P.M. He agrees as to the imminent dangers of today, Italy taking Spain, and Germany, later, taking the Balkan states. He said Von Neurath had told him Tuesday that he had prevented or at least argued successfully in a Cabinet session Monday against Germany's continuing her bombing in Spain. This is stronger than what I had learned Monday.

When I indicated our troubles about Hirsch, he said he knew about the case but was not surprised at Hitler's attitude. Then he added: "I know that Mussolini ordered the killing of the King of Yugoslavia when he landed in Marseilles two years ago. That is the dictator's way of doing things."

From the French Embassy I went directly to the German Foreign Office, where Von Mackensen, son-in-law of Von Neurath, told me that his father-in-law had argued with Hitler Tuesday morning, as he had promised to do, against the execution of Hirsch. He then said Meissner had seen Hitler this morning and again at 2 this afternoon to warn him about the international repercussions of the case, but, he added, "Hitler would not even postpone the execution and Hirsch is to be beheaded tomorrow morning at sunrise." There is no way to stop it. I reminded him of previous German blunders in relations with the United States. He agreed, but gave no indication of a better understanding of things.

June 4. Friday. The poor Hirsch had his head chopped off this morning at sunrise. When the press representatives came to me I felt compelled to give the facts about the execution and all our efforts to save his life, though we never claimed complete innocence on his part. This young Jew, not unnaturally, may have listened to the advice of persecuted Germans outside the country and may have wished to kill Streicher whose one profession for five years has been to persecute Jews and drive them out of the country.

With all the troubles people have in Europe, the United States also shows rather sad evidence of abuses there which may, after a while, lead to troubles for the democracy which all of us hoped to achieve, and which we actually believed in though it has not been really practiced on a national scale.

Governments which claim to be democratic, that is, claim to be acting always for the good of their peoples, often abuse their opportunities. But this is only a mild criticism of what has taken place in all greater countries since the end of the World War. I can't forget the published reports that American and British arms manufacturers defeated the League of Nations' peace efforts more than once. Soon after coming here, I learned the French munitions makers had helped Hitler to power. Is it possible for mankind to be just and fair? Is it possible for governments and powerful corporations to act in the interests of the masses of men?

XII

June 5, 1937 to September 28, 1938

June 5. Saturday. This has been a hard week, with the German bombing of helpless people in Almeria, Spain, early Monday morning, and the refusal to grant Hirsch any consideration at all, though our government repeatedly asked for actual proof and consideration of our law since the man had not actually been caught trying to murder Streicher. But treatment of peoples is more arbitrary than it has been since the Middle Ages. What is to come of all this one cannot say: German domination of all Europe or another war?

June 14. Monday. We had a luncheon party yesterday for Colonel Knox, candidate last year for the Vice Presidency of the United States. We had Dr. Von Kühlmann, a former German Foreign Secretary, and Captain Wiedemann, a personal adviser and companion to Hitler. The Ambassador from Argentina sat on my right, trying hard to speak English. Some leading newspaper correspondents were present too: Lochner; Ebbutt of the London *Times;* Shirer of the Hearst press; and Deuel of the Chicago *Daily News,* Knox's paper for the last six years.

Knox surprised me, he having been a sturdy Republican all his life, by talking in a friendly way about John L. Lewis, the powerful C.I.O. labor organizer who has caused so many sit-down strikes all over the United States. Knox said he had known Lewis a long time (he was a Republican labor chief until 1932) and had seen him just before he left the United States. He thinks Lewis will be a candidate for the Democratic nomination in 1940, and having practically all labor organizations behind him, he will bolt the Democratic convention if not nominated and then run as a labor independent. This, Knox said, would give the Republicans their chance to regain control of the country, but, he added, his party must be liberal if it wants to win. From his talk I inferred that he and leading Republicans are already encouraging Lewis. Knox talked as though he agreed with most of what Roosevelt has done or is trying to do, and I inferred further that he is beginning his own moves for the Republican nomination. He has spent a month in Europe, has had talks with Mussolini and others in Italy, but will not see Hitler or Goering while here.

Saturday Stalin executed eight Russian Red Army generals. They were supposed to be intriguing with Germany, even with Fascists in France, for the overthrow of the Soviet Government. It has been charged that the Russian generals had promised to give Germany the Ukraine and break off the treaty with France and Czechoslovakia. What was really behind it all I can hardly judge, but Wiedemann, who sat next to me at the table yesterday, said that he had to get all possible information he could Saturday and Sunday and telephone it to Hitler, then at Berchtesgaden near the Austrian border. That made one wonder if some of Hitler's chiefs had not been doing something in Russia.

However, the German papers treat the matter as one of the barbaric crimes of modern history, never intimating that Hitler and Goering killed hundreds of their German opponents in June and early July, 1934. High officers of the German army held a meeting in Berlin and compelled Hitler to confess some of his crimes. Nor was there any published evidence of the guilt of any of Hitler's opponents. Curious now to find that Goebbels, who had a big share in the German murders of 1934, is in control of all the German papers denouncing Russia's executions.

June 17. Thursday. Hitler has made a speech to young Italians just at the time when the papers are boasting of the peace talk with England which Von Neurath is going to London to negotiate. Hitler talked of his readiness for war. People in the United States seem determined to stay neutral even facing a Europe under the control of a single dictatorship.

The preoccupation of European powers with the events in Spain the last two weeks, and with happenings in Russia, seems to have given Hitler, Goering and their fellows the first opportunity they have had since they came to power to annex parts, if not all, of Czechoslovakia. Austria they would like to have too, but they can't be sure what Mussolini would do. The German dictators crave annexation without war, as they are bankrupt and foodstuffs are very scarce. The drought of the last three weeks seems to have cut wheat and other foodstuff crops by about 30 per cent over one-half of Germany.

Last Monday, when peace talks with England began, five Protestant preachers were arrested, Jacobi of the Kaiser Wilhelm I Memorial Church, who has talked over his religious freedom problems with me, being the most prominent. At the same time arrests in Munich and searches of the Catholic bishop of Cologne were made. The London *Times* correspondent says his paper refuses to print more than half his stories now, but the *Manchester Guardian* publishes accounts which seem to reach it through secret channels via the Foreign Office in London.

June 20. Sunday. My wife and I had dinner yesterday evening with the Latvian Minister. Nearly all the guests were of independent minds in conversation, which is unusual for Berlin. The Minister is not a rich man and his house and dining room showed modest but entirely adequate conveniences. He made it plain to me in the very beginning that he is opposed to the Nazi dictatorship, also that he is uneasy about the outcome of the London conference between Germany, England, France, and Italy. The French Ambassador, François-Poncet, sat opposite me at the table and was free to speak even before guests about the dangers ahead, but he never acknowledges the blunder his country made in January, 1935, in promising Ethiopia to Italy and forcing the League of Nations into its last great defeat.

The Latvian Military Attaché, who sat on my right, spoke freely of the dangerous probable consequences of Russia's weakening position. The Czech Minister was more concerned about the threats to his little country. He acknowledged the drift of things revealed in the *Manchester Guardian*, wondering whether Beneš could make friendly approaches to Hitler after the daily press attacks in Germany against his government. He reported that he had made a formal protest to the German Foreign Office about falsehoods as to his government's encouraging maltreatment of Germans in Czechoslovakia. His wife said to my wife: "If Germany attacks our country, Russia will come at once to our defense." I doubt this, unless France attacks Germany in the Rhine zone.

Sitting with the Latvian Minister and the French Ambassador after dinner, I raised the Spanish problem. The Frenchman was hopeless and said Blum would be overthrown in two days. I doubt this, but I know the situation is dangerous in Paris. François-Poncet then said England is going to yield to the German demands in the Near East. Will that mean war? I asked. He said: "No, perhaps not at once, because France is so pacifist." He said, however, that he had rented his summer house here, near Potsdam, on the condition that he may give it up in a month. He is really afraid war will break out about the end of July.

I do not believe this because Germany's foodstuffs are limited and Hitler intends to take Austria or Czechoslovakia without war. Russia is the only really uncertain power. The French Ambassador also said to me that he knew the Germans had been dealing with Russian generals to overthrow the Stalin government, perhaps to procure for Hitler the coveted Ukraine.

June 23. Wednesday. Thus far we have had an anxious week. On Monday, the papers described the fall of the Blum government in Paris. With Russia in its supposed weakened position and the Popular Front in France (30 per cent Communist) fallen, Hitler apparently thought the time was approaching for him to dictate to Europe. So he told Von Neurath he was not to go to London. The English had apparently made liberal promises to Germany, but Hitler, it seems, demanded more, either in Spain or in the Czechoslovak-Austrian region, perhaps in both. England had indicated it could not go farther and Hitler stood on his sensational demands and so refused to allow Von Neurath to attend the London conference.

Tuesday the Propaganda Minister, Goebbels, made a violent speech against Russia, Czechoslovakia, France and England, and the papers loudly denounced Foreign Minister Eden for having said he could not make further concessions. We had reports from the Foreign Office, as also from the British Embassy, that Henderson, the British Ambassador, had practically delivered a lecture to Von Neurath, aimed at Hitler. He had done his best for two months to help Germany and England settle Spanish difficulties, perhaps even Germany's claims toward the east. Just as success seemed about to be won, Hitler had broken off negotiations. Henderson called it pure folly and showed his own anger.

When I saw Von Neurath at his annual charity reception, he showed a disposition to talk. I said: I am sorry you are not going to London to settle that long-drawn-out Spanish war. He at once replied that he too was sorry and otherwise indicated his realization of Hitler's arbitrary blunder. There were 1,000 guests on Von Neurath's lawn. Several diplomats showed their sympathy with Von Neurath, even the Frenchman, the Latin Americans, and especially the Ministers from the Danube-Balkan states.

Today it is reported that Mussolini is displeased with Hitler's decision, that the German army officers are equally dissatisfied because they hoped to get their forces out of Spain, and that Hitler himself is for once embarrassed. I doubt this last. Anyway, we telegraphed the violent press attacks on England and the reported restiveness here, in spite of press behavior. My opinion is that Hitler hoped to get what he wanted because France and Russia were so upset, and hoped to alienate England from France.

Concerned about the British attitude, I went to see Ambassador Henderson. The first point discussed was my two-year advocacy of British-American commercial co-operation and lower tariffs. The Ambassador said he agreed entirely. But when I asked him about his government's attitude toward Germany he said: "My government has been unwise in its relations with Germany. I told Von Neurath that, and also told him Hitler's decision to keep Von Neurath at home was equally unwise."

He turned to a general discussion of things: "Germany under Hitler is renewing the Bismarck policy of annexing all European peoples of German descent, Austria, Czechoslovakia, and other countries." Although I had suspected Henderson was inclined to favor German annexations, I did not think he would go so far in his statements. He then added: "Germany must dominate the Danube-Balkan zone, which means that she is to dominate Europe. England and her Empire is to dominate the seas along with the United States. England and Germany must come into close relations, economic and political, and control the world." He said: "France is a back number and unworthy of support. Franco is to control Spain." He seemed not to be aware of British-American opposition to the ruthless Nazi treatment of Catholics, Protestants and Jews. I wonder if Ambassador Henderson really represents his government? What would happen to Britain if Germany annexed all the peoples all the way to the Black Sea?

June 30. Wednesday. I heard from a friend today distressing news about the new Under-Secretary of State, Sumner Welles. According to the story as I hear it, six Senators secured his appointment by threatening quietly to vote against Roosevelt's Supreme Court reform if he did not name Welles to the post. He was Ambassador to Cuba early in the Roosevelt regime. His conduct there was most embarrassing, I have heard.

He has one of the greatest houses in Washington, with fifteen servants, and another house for summer use in Maryland. He prides himself on spending twice as much as Secretary Hull and gives parties hardly matched by any of the Ambassadors in Washington. I was a little surprised to read a day or two ago in the press that Roosevelt had spent a Sunday with Welles at his Maryland mansion. Politics is a strange game, even with a real man like Roosevelt.

July 6. Tuesday. President Quezon of the Philippines came to call and to indicate his objective: to see what Germany is like, to talk with Hitler, and also to discuss possible trade agreements. I had met Quezon about 1912 when he was lecturing in Chicago for Philippine independence. He seems quite able and thoughtful. The independence of his country is his basic ideal in life and it seems about to be realized, but he showed some uneasiness about Japan and expressed the hope that Germany might recover her colonial possessions in the Far East. I thought he preferred this because it might prevent Japan from annexing his country. He also dreaded the time when American tariffs would be applied in the Philippines.

July 12. Monday. George S. Messersmith, American Minister to Austria, called. He is soon to succeed Under-Secretary Carr in our State Department, Carr having been in the position for forty years.

I reported to Messersmith that the Austrian Minister in Berlin had shown much anxiety to me about the fate of his country as we were walking together privately in the Tiergarten. Messersmith said the concern was due to conversations between the British Ambassador here, Henderson, and an important official from Vienna. The British Ambassador said Austria, being Nazi, must be annexed to Germany. This was at once reported to Schuschnigg, the Chancellor of Austria, and that led to immediate telegraphic inquiries in London.

Schuschnigg was satisfied by denials from Minister Eden, but Messersmith added that he was still expecting trouble when he left Vienna, especially about the Hitler conferences in Berchtesgaden, Von Papen having made demands which could not be accepted. Messersmith said Austria would go to war if Hitler sent an army into the country. Something like this is always happening.

Karl von Wiegand called this afternoon, having been in Austria recovering from an illness contracted in Spain. He said that

Austria is still in great anxiety, but that he talked an hour in Munich with General von Reichenau, one of the foremost officers in the army, and the general was most impatient with the Fuehrer who is committed to open intervention in Spanish affairs. Von Reichenau said the army in general is by no means in sympathy with the Hitler system, but that Hitler has greatly increased the S.S. forces, taken the best young officers from the army and built up the S.S. for personal purposes. Five thousand S.S. troops are kept in Munich all the time, with other units scattered over Germany. The idea seems to be to guard against any internal or army revolt. All policemen are also taken from the S.S. and are exceedingly well trained.

July 13. Tuesday. The Chinese Ambassador called this morning to express his appreciation of American sympathy at the moment the Japanese attacks were beginning in North China again. He added: "Japan chose this moment to attack China because Russia is in such a domestic difficulty that she cannot give us any aid. The Japanese military people are also pressing for war at this moment because they think a victory in China would restore the government's popularity with the people who have voted twice in recent elections overwhelmingly against the present regime." While I do not know enough of the situation in the Far East to be too certain of his statement, I think his analysis is reasonably logical and seems to be correct. The Ambassador showed great concern, but said his government would fight desperately against Japan.

July 14. Wednesday. In view of the international difficulties and dangers I called on Secretary von Neurath of the Foreign Office this morning at 12 o'clock. As I entered the Foreign Office, the Japanese Ambassador was leaving. Von Neurath said to me that Russia is provoking the Chinese to fight the Japanese. When I told him what the Chinese Ambassador had said yesterday, Von Neurath insisted that Russia was the instigator, but he added Germany is willing to support the United States and England if they negotiate a peace in the Far East. When I asked about the Spanish situation, he replied that Mussolini is no longer insisting that Germany send more men and ammunition to Spain. What specific conclusions one may draw is not quite clear, but all statements as to the Spanish war seem to indicate that a solution favorable to Germany and Italy is being arrived at.

I am more inclined to accept the Chinaman's conversation as true than I am that of any high German official. Von Neurath is personally opposed to much that Hitler does, but he always surrenders.

July 20. Tuesday. Upon the request of Secretary Hull I called on Von Mackensen, Under-Secretary here, this afternoon. For half an hour I tried to learn what Germany really thinks of the United States protests against war in the Far East. All I could get from him was: "Russia secretly helps both Japan and China in the hope of weakening both powers." Germany, he said, was equally friendly to both Japan and China and not disposed to help either side. When I inquired about his attitude toward the Hull memorandum which I had been asked to present, he said he could not give me a written reply as Von Neurath is away until September 1, and he was leaving tomorrow; but he insisted that Germany approved the British and American protests against the war in the Far East, except that no official support could be given. I had some doubts.

Then he entered into a discussion of American-Brazilian trade relations as operating to defeat German trade there. When I said the cause of the American attitude was simply its opposition to German export subsidies when they sent goods to Brazil, he acknowledged that these subsidies were being granted whereas a month ago when he protested to me about our trade arrangement he had said Germany gave no subsidies. When I insisted he had said there were no subsidies, he replied, "No, I did not say so." However, I know he did say so and I reported to Washington his denial.

Not satisfied with the Foreign Office statements about the Far East, I went to see the French Ambassador. He said Russia had nothing to do with the Far Eastern outbreak, but added that if Russia does enter the war on the Chinese side there will be a European war. When I asked about Germany and Spain, he said Hitler talked to him last Sunday as if he were fairly certain the war there is soon to end. Then François-Poncet added: "Italy's internal troubles and opposition are so great that Mussolini will not send more troops to Spain." I had my doubts though I can believe the Italian people are opposed to continued participation in the Spanish war.

The French Ambassador spoke of the propaganda mass meeting for fine arts last weekend in Munich. He said Hitler's speech was almost childish. When I asked him about his attendance at the Nürnberg Party Congress next September, he said: "All other diplomats have indicated that they will attend. I have asked my government whether I should go. They do not answer, so I told Bülow-Schwante, in charge of protocol, that I could attend only one day and not listen to the propaganda speeches." This will be the first time ambassadors from democratic countries have attended. I told him I could not attend such Party propaganda meetings. I have not done so and cannot do so unless ordered by my government, which would lead to my resignation. I do not care to sit by quietly and listen to Hitler and Goebbels denounce democracies. He agreed, but added, "We may all have to attend to avoid trouble."

July 24. Saturday. My wife and I left our home at 10:45 A.M. and drove to Hamburg by 5:30, having stopped a half hour on the way for luncheon. I got my room on the *City of Baltimore* promptly and the ship sailed slowly down the Elbe at 7 P.M.

July 26. Monday. Yesterday there was what they call a choppy sea and nearly everybody was seasick. I got on shipboard worn out with a headache from which I had suffered two months, also a nervous indigestion which troubled me so that I ate nothing for thirty hours.

Reports from Berlin say that many more Protestant preachers have been arrested, fifty-seven in jail, Niemoeller's brother among them. Two Germans who lived near the Polish boundary were executed Friday because they were reported to have told Poles what the German army plans were. The same arbitrary treatment of all opponents, Catholics, Protestants, Jews and, of course, indiscreet talkers, continues. The totalitarian state idea goes on without moderation. I have hoped to leave Germany permanently for more than two years. What the President will say this time I can't guess. but I can hardly stand such an atmosphere.

August 4. Wednesday. We arrived early this morning at Norfolk. We drove to Round Hill before 5 o'clock in the afternoon. The farms all the way looked very prosperous, the ancient region of Virginia far more so than I had expected. From Leesburg to Round Hill, crops looked still better.

August 11. Wednesday. After a week of light work on my farm, repairing damaged roads and moving the old smoke house to a better location, I was with President Roosevelt for luncheon. A score of men were waiting to see him when I came away. The President is greatly troubled about the danger of war and also the continued depression in the United States. He talked most frankly for an hour.

He said: "I wish you to return to Berlin for two or three months. When you retire I have promised Ambassador Davies, now in Russia, to appoint him your successor."

Mr. Roosevelt had heard that I had been announced as one of the speakers at the Williamstown Institute of Human Relations early in September. He urged me to go and "speak the truth about things." I told him I had been asked to speak before some Virginia and North Carolina universities, but I added that I was not quite well and needed a real vacation. He urged me to accept all the invitations I could. It was plain that he wished me to interpret and discuss American and international problems as best I could.

After the conference in the White House, I saw Secretary Hull, who surprised me by reporting that Ambassador Dieckhoff had protested to him on August 6 against an interview published on the 5th, on my arrival. I had not mentioned Germany or events there, though I referred to Martin Luther, and I could not see how any fault could be found in what I said. Mr. Hull had said at once to Dieckhoff: "I agree entirely with what our Ambassador said and cannot see how a protest can be made." The Secretary and I talked nearly an hour, and we were as much in agreement about European affairs as we have been from the beginning. He made it plain that he did not wish Davies to be Ambassador to Berlin and he seemed glad to know I had been urged to return even for three months.

My good friend Judge R. Walton Moore, now Counselor to the Department, advised me to call on the new Under-Secretary, Sumner Welles. I have long believed Welles was opposed to me and everything I recommended. However, I sent my card to Mr. Welles' office and offered to call, but he was engaged and I did not care to wait and so returned, driving my own car, to the farm.

Washington was more crowded with automobiles than I had ever before noticed. It was difficult to travel or even walk in the city. It took me nearly an hour to get to a store where I bought a box for filing letters, the store being only three blocks from the State Department. On the way home, hundreds and hundreds of cars were on the road. The man on Pennsylvania Avenue from whom I bought some gas said: "Washington has 700,000 automobiles though her population is hardly 600,000." I was glad to get out of the city.

September 4. Saturday. This morning I read in the New York *Herald Tribune* a paragraph of a confidential letter I had sent to Secretary Hull advising against attendance at the Nürnberg party show by Prentiss Gilbert, now our Chargé d'Affaires in Berlin. There was also reference to a telegram I had sent him from Williamstown, also protesting strongly against this violation of our 150-year-old diplomatic custom of not attending official party celebrations in foreign countries.

The letter had been sent ten days before I left for Williamstown, for Judge Moore to hand to Secretary Hull without letting anyone else see it. Now it has been published in the press as if I had said it publicly at Williamstown, only a few days after Gilbert had upset the precedent I set for four years, by attending Hitler's great Nazi propaganda spectacle.

September 30. Thursday. I went to Washington to attend the funeral of my distinguished and almost life-long friend, Dr. J. F. Jameson, long-time editor of the *American Historical Review* and at the time of his sudden death assistant national librarian. It was a sad occasion, many of my former historical friends and associates there. He was the most learned historian I had ever seen. Now he is gone, about seventy-eight years old.

October 18. Monday. After arranging some work to be done by Tom Reed, a good tenant in one of my houses, I set out for New York again to begin my journey once more to Berlin. The State Department had arranged for me to go on October 20 and Secretary Hull had said to me the preceding Friday, I believe, that the President at his home, Hyde Park, New York, wished to talk with me again. I had talked with him a second time about the middle of September. So I asked my son to meet me again at New Brunswick, N. J. It was a long drive. I reached my destination at 5 P.M. and William was at the door of the Wilson Hotel. He drove for me then and we were in his apartment early in the evening, a quiet place to rest even in New York City. When I was just going to sleep, the President's secretary called me and said I was expected there at 11 o'clock tomorrow, which means another early start.

October 19. Tuesday. Driving over the wonderful New York parkways, we reached the President's house—a marvelous place —at 11:30.

The President revealed his anxiety about foreign affairs, discussed the Japanese-Chinese situation, and talked of the possibilities of the Brussels peace conference which Norman Davis is to attend for him. One thing troubled him: Could the United States, England, France and Russia actually co-operate? If so, the Japanese could be halted and the dictators of Europe finally be brought to some more peaceful position. I could see little chance of real co-operation when England had refused so long to make a treaty with the United States even on trade matters.

Before we finished I urged again that he appoint Professor Shotwell of Columbia as my successor in Berlin. He said he would appoint either Shotwell or a service man, Hugh Wilson, now in the State Department. I told him a second time he ought, if possible, to appoint Shotwell because of his university connections as well as his national reputation as a scholar. He agreed with me on this, but did not commit himself.

After the conversation was over, William and I were asked to lunch with the President, his mother, and the Delanos of Washington. It was a delightful occasion. As I left the President, he said again: "Write me personally about things in Europe. I can read your handwriting very well." I promised to write him such confidential letters, but how shall I get them to him unread by spies?

Last night I attended a meeting of some of William's friends who are with the peace organization for which he works and lectures. Some twenty peace advocates all approved Roosevelt's recent speech in Chicago in which he almost advocated war to stop the Japanese in China and the Italians in Spain. This surprised me a little. The spokesman of one vast American peace organization said American neutrality would not assure peace. He thought a boycott of Japan should be applied and wished my son to lecture on the meaning of boycott to the country. Columbia professors, business men, and journalists were the people present, and one very active woman. That was last night; the same ideas were discussed vigorously this evening.

October 20. Wednesday. George P. Brett, Jr., president of the Macmillan Company, called to leave a copy of my book, *The Old South: Struggles for Democracy,* which is to be published on October 26. He also urged the preparation of my second volume, *The Old South: Our First American Social Order,* but did not say I should resign my position which I had expected to do September 1. I could not promise how soon my work would be ready. Not a line is written yet. He said that the volume just out was considered very interesting by his critical workers and proofreaders. I thanked him for the illustrations which had not been easy to get.

When he departed other people came, so that I was engaged until the ship was about to start. I had spent two and a half months in the United States, but I had the same sort of nervous headaches which plagued me when I sailed from Hamburg on July 24.

October 29. Friday. In Berlin once more. What can I do?

November 3. Wednesday. I have had three busy days reading documents and recent newspapers to get the drift of things. It has been decided that I am to leave Berlin for good about March 1, 1938. The President indicated that date though I had asked to be relieved September 1, 1937. He seemed to me to wish I would stay a few months longer on account of the embarrassing pressure of men like Davies, now at Moscow, and Thomas Watson who also wishes to be here. I feel I must go because of the unbearable tension of Nazi Germany, my increasing years, and the difficulty of writing the other volumes of my *Old South* if I wait much longer.

In the Embassy office, engagements to see people are as frequent as formerly. On Monday, Senator James Lewis of Chicago spent an hour talking confidentially about the President, American economic conditions, and foreign dangers. Much as he has traveled about Europe, he showed ignorance of real American policies.

Tuesday Dr. Cheng, the Chinese Ambassador, spent half an hour explaining his government's position and its hopes that the United States and England may unite to support China against Japan's cruel and amazing imperialism. He said he was going to Brussels to see how the nine-power conference feels about things. Dr. Cheng was a student at the University of Chicago while I was there and had reported some time ago that he knew me there as a professor.

Today the Swiss Minister spent an hour reviewing European conditions and the Nürnberg Party Congress which he attended for three days. In spite of certain indications which I have noted before at big parties, I think he is still anti-Nazi and afraid his little country may be annexed to Hitler's Germany. He did not tell me about the Nazi Party in Switzerland which has been granted privileges there. Fear of Hitler is the cause of this, the Swiss Government feeling that to do otherwise might cause aggressive German action.

Tonight I went to a dinner party at the Kaiser Wilhelm Institute, the new president taking his place, my friend, the former president, Planck, retiring. This organization is not Nazi and some outstanding business men who were present made their attitudes plain. They had no Hitler decorations on their coats and they did not say "Heil Hitler" when others came up to them and shook hands.

November 13. Saturday. Tonight we went to the annual ball of Dr. Frank, head of the bar association and member of the Hitler Cabinet. An enormous crowd, nearly all diplomats, was present. Everybody was expected to contribute to the *Winter-hilfe* (annual Nazi charity drive) by purchasing tickets which might give them a prize. Nobody won any prize that I heard of, though everybody gave 10 to 20 marks. At Frank's table were the French Ambassador and his wife, the Italian and Polish Ambassadors, with others. A quite interesting Judge of the People's Court sat on my right. We talked German history, since present conditions cannot easily be discussed.

November 16. Tuesday. Douglas Miller reports to the government at home that the director of the Deutsche Bank, Herr Weigelt, told him that Germany now is flying airplanes to China. The Chinese Ambassador, a second visitor this morning, said that Germany is shipping all kinds of war supplies over Russian railroads both to China and Japan. I notice reports that Japan sends millions of dollars worth of gold each week to New York to pay for war materials.

The story of German-Italian propaganda in Brazil which has been coming to me for a year now emerges into an account of the rise of a Fascist state there. The new dictator, Vargas, has now announced that he will not pay interest on American loans or repay the capital. All treaties may now be declared void when the dictator wishes to do so. The State Department which arranged a trade treaty a little over a year ago is now helpless and Secretary Hull has shown his disapproval.

November 18. Thursday. After a busy day we went to a dinner at the French Embassy given in honor of Ambassador Bullitt of Paris. There were forty guests present. After dinner Bullitt, the French Ambassador, Dr. Frank, Dr. Rosenberg, myself, and one or two others sat together and listened to Rosenberg present to Bullitt the Nazi social philosophy. I could not see exactly whether Bullitt approved it or not, but Rosenberg and Frank argued their Nazi ideas. The Frenchman seemed to be amused. I said nothing.

Bullitt had been three days in Warsaw and he reported to me this morning that Foreign Minister Beck of Poland had assured him again and again that the Poles would do everything possible for peace, not ally themselves with any nation, except on commercial matters, and not intervene if Germany annexed Czechoslovakia or if Russia seized Finland.

No German seems ever to think seizure of other people's territory is wrong. It is the result of hundreds of years of teaching. Recently, Von Papen pressed the query in Paris: "What will France do if we take over Austria?" Now the Poles, who are in as tight a place as any people in Europe, are said to be joining the German-Italian-Japanese combination against Russia. I think they will be compelled to come into the so-called anti-Comintern pact. A journalist who has been long in Russia said to me today that many German and Italian secret workers have been in Russia two years with the object of overthrowing Stalin and setting up a Fascist system. Certainly there have been Italian-German propagandists in Latin America doing their utmost to upset our treaties and to set up dictatorships in alliance with those of Europe. We have heard here about their work in Brazil for nearly a year, and recently a Chile man reported a Nazi Party in that country of 35,000 men, adding that the Chilean Government expects to be a German colony in a year or two. The Colombian Minister came to see me two days ago and said that the activity all over Latin America was so great that he wished me to report it.

With so many efforts to make a solid Fascist front from Rome to Tokyo and similar efforts to swing Latin America into alliances with these Berlin-Rome dictators, and especially to defeat all easier trade relations, it seems to me that real co-operation between the United States, England, France and Russia is the only way to maintain world peace. One thing seems to me certain: there will come a complete totalitarian domination of Europe and Asia if democratic countries continue their popular isolation policies. All peoples are so afraid of another war that Hitler and Mussolini think they can keep everybody scared and seize what areas they want. I am afraid they are right in their appraisals. If things go on in this way, England and the United States are going to find their economic conditions worse than ever. Although one cannot agree that Communism is any better than Fascism, it would be a great thing for the United States, England, and France to unite with Russia and simply say that certain things must cease to be done.

November 19. Friday. We entertained Bullitt at luncheon today, twenty-four guests present. Dr. Schacht said to me as he came in: "I have not attended a Cabinet meeting since September 5." This looks as if he were definitely out of the regime. I asked him, confidentially, if he would accept an American bank presidency. He said: "Yes, and I would be delighted to see the President often." I wondered what he was going to do with the Hitler statue in his parlor or with the painting of Goering which I saw in his house the last time I was there. Poor man—the ablest financier in Europe but utterly helpless and in grave danger in case he were known to be considering migration to the United States. Of course he will lose his property in the event that he is able to slip out some way.

November 23. Tuesday. I had a message today from Secretary Hull which surprised me a great deal. I had agreed last August in a conversation with the President to return for three months, after spending my vacation at home. The last time I was with the President, October 19, he frankly said he had given up his earlier plan and would appoint Shotwell or Hugh Wilson. He said he was glad I was going back for some months. I told him March 1 was the best time for my retirement partly because of the weather conditions and partly because I did not wish to have the German extremists think their complaints of

August 6, a protest by Dieckhoff against my statement on arrival in America, and September 5, in connection with my advice to the State Department not to send a representative to Nürnberg, had operated too effectively. They had no real reason to complain at anything I had done or said.

Now comes a telegram indicating that I must retire between December 15 and 31. Ambassador Hugh Gibson of Belgium is to be appointed, and I was asked to present his name to the Foreign Office at once. The President was reported to have asked all this to be done.

The reason for this violation of my understanding with the President is the opposition to me of Under-Secretary Welles. I have recently seen signs of opposition to everything I have recommended, except my refusal to go to Nürnberg. Since last spring, Welles has had a controlling influence inside the Department of State. It is well known to me that he is violently opposed to my policies in regard to public service.

November 29. Monday. Having been in bed nearly all the time since last Tuesday, when I had to beg Von Neurath to excuse me from sitting with him at dinner, I managed to go to my office. Von Neurath had invited all diplomats to attend an opera Tuesday night in honor of the Hungarian Prime Minister and others who were here for a week. I felt I must accept, but after the opera ended, I was unequal to the continued strain and was excused from dinner. The object of all this reception and hospitality was to press the Hungarians for union with Hitler Germany. I noticed that the Hungarians did not heil Hitler or raise their hands in salute when all Germans did.

In my office I learned from the consulate in Hamburg that scores of importers of coffee have been imprisoned there because they had left some of their profits in the exporting countries, and had not reported them to Goering's economic office. One of the most eminent of the prisoners committed suicide. A report came from Munich that Julius Streicher has made an address in which he declared that the Jews govern the United States, La Guardia being their chief. Other evidence was brought from Munich and Stuttgart that Hitler's government is doing its utmost in South America to bring those countries into alliance with Germany and Italy. This has been going on at least three years at enormous expenditure.

November 30. Tuesday. We received notice from Washington that Gibson has declined the appointment to Berlin. I was requested to inform the Foreign Office that Hugh Wilson of the State Department was to be appointed. While evidence is wanting, I believe the German Foreign Office refused to receive Gibson. He had been an official in Belgium during the World War and had also written a valuable book about Germany and certain German leaders. I do not think the present regime could endure more than was said in my book on Woodrow Wilson. I notified the Foreign Office at once and they replied that their answer would be sent us in three or four days.

David Lloyd George, Britain's war-time Prime Minister, warned his government today against entering into a "thieves' bargain with the dictators" and suggested it would be better for Britain to go to war now rather than make an abject surrender to the Fascists. This Lloyd George address is very different from his statements of 1934. But he seems to me to be right now. How can England do anything after allowing Mussolini to master the Mediterranean, Ethiopia, and half of Spain?

December 3. Friday. Not a word from the Foreign Office about the new nominee to succeed me. I can think of no reason for this delay. Wilson was ten years in Switzerland but this should be no excuse for a German objection. Yet I would not be surprised if Hitler refused the United States representation for quite a while. He and Goering are the most conceited men I have ever seen, and both of them are angry, even uneasy, about the slowly changing attitude of the United States.

Today the *Völkischer Beobachter*, Nazi official organ, carried a great headline saying the United States approved Russia's sending 300 war planes to poor China. Yesterday our Secretary of State was attacked because he agreed with a New York *Times* editorial advocating American-English co-operation in world affairs and especially a boycott of Japan. Hitler sells war supplies to both China and Japan, even furnishing German officers to China. The object is, however, to have Japan control China so that both may be ready to fight Russia if war ever comes in Europe.

A report today from Warsaw says the Danzig League of Nations official, Burckhardt, saw Hitler when he passed through Berlin on his return from Geneva. Hitler said to him: "Whenever I choose to do so I can annex all sections of European countries where there are large German elements." He simply meant that Europe is so afraid of him that he can take Danzig, Austria, and Czechoslovakia with no real resistance. I doubt this except one at a time and not too near each other in sequence. Is this not a strange Europe after all that happened in the World War?

December 9. Thursday. Last Monday, December 6, I had a long talk with Dr. Schacht. He spoke freely, insisting that what we said was not registered in the Secret Police office. I was not so sure as he seemed to be. I told him we are retiring about January 1. He said he hoped to have us at his house before we go.

I showed him a copy of the interview I gave the Associated Press in Norfolk last August 4 and told him about Ambassador Dieckhoff's protest against this to Secretary Hull. Schacht read all I had said and then added: "There was no reason for a protest, none at all." I told him that I thought Von Mackensen, the Under-Secretary in the German Foreign Office, had done this, not Von Neurath. He made no reply. Hitherto he has always seemed to be in agreement with Von Neurath, not his son-in-law Von Mackensen.

I then told Schacht about my confidential letter to Hull being published in the New York papers on September 4, appearing as if I had spoken it at Williamstown, Massachusetts, against the Nürnberg Congress. Schacht was not surprised though he seemed not to have heard of the Foreign Office attitude in protesting to Washington either in August or September. But he then went on to say I was very popular with the German people, especially among the educated and professional people. I have seen considerable evidence of this, particularly in the invitations from German universities to deliver lectures, but Schacht had not given such facts before, though we have generally agreed on nearly all matters of international concern. Schacht later talked of his position as being uncertain. If he had to give up his bank presidency, he said he would go to the United States. As yet, he said, that was not to be definitely considered, and he was not sure what he would do. He said: "I am, as you know, no longer Economics Minister. That is General Goering's job now, and he knows little about the problems before him." I inferred from what Schacht said about the people's opposition to the Nazis, especially business people, that he thinks the Nazi regime will be overthrown.

December 11. Saturday. I had a conversation this morning with Baron von Neurath. There was nothing new but we reviewed existing conditions. I asked him about the colonial question, so much discussed during the last month. He said Germany cannot produce more than 80 per cent of her necessary foodstuffs and Germany has a population increase of 500,000 a year. Then he stressed the subject of land shortage. He added: "We shall not get our colonies back in several years, but we must have them."

I said to him: You know modern populations will not emigrate. Nearly all people wish to live in big cities where unemployment is great. People simply will not leave great cities and you know that the city populations constitute nearly three-fourths of the people in England, Germany and the United States. How will colonies help solve your economic problem? He insisted: "We would get raw materials from colonies." I replied: Yes, but the cost of raw materials from colonies is always greater than their cost through international trade. I gave illustrations.

He insisted on the colony demand. I know Germany is entitled to some colonies and conceded her right to their restoration through negotiation. But my reference to trade relations led Von Neurath to state again that he supported Secretary Hull on the subject of international trade. But, he added,

"Germany will not change her policy," which is one of extreme barriers against imports.

When I asked him about the possibility of a four-power pact (England, Germany, France and Italy), he promptly said it could not be arranged. He did not give the reasons, but I inferred that he meant that no reduction of armaments would be agreed to.

When I asked him if he knew I had not referred to Germany in any address I had made in the United States, he said: "Yes, Dieckhoff, our Ambassador in Washington, informed me that the newspaper stories of September 4 were taken from a confidential letter you had sent to Secretary Hull." I reminded him of what I had more than once said to him about my not attending Nürnberg Party shows. He said he understood my position. It was rather curious in view of the protests which were made in Washington.

When I was about to leave he asked my wife and me to dine with him if we could. I told him I was afraid we could not do so, it being about Christmas time and the date of our departure still uncertain.

December 14. Tuesday. How our modern civilization drifts backward towards medievalism! Today the Czechoslovak Minister called, tremendously concerned about the fate of his country because democratic countries do nothing and thus give Mussolini, Hitler and Japan increasing sway over the world. He said Russia, though an ally of his country and France, is helpless.

Yesterday the Russian Chargé d'Affaires came to see me and insisted that democratic countries, England, France and the United States, wish his country to save China without their assistance. Russia, said he, will not do that, but she would cooperate with those countries if they would help China.

After the Czechoslovak Minister left this morning, the Chinese Ambassador came to talk again about his country's dangerous condition. He repeated information I had received from Washington over the radio: that the Japanese had destroyed American and English vessels in Chinese rivers, even killing

Americans, and that our President had demanded complete restoration and apologies from the Emperor of Japan. He wanted to know whether the United States would really do anything. I could not give any assurance though I agreed with him that democracies must save China or themselves soon come into grave danger. We parted sadly, he saying his country might have to be subjugated and I acknowledging that modern civilization seemed to be on the verge of disaster.

At noon I sent a message to Roosevelt summarizing what had been said and giving my opinion that if the United States and England did not stop Japan, our people would come to realize in a year or two what their position was. I advised a boycott. If that did not succeed, I said, our navy and part of the British fleet should join and appear in Chinese waters. The Italian and German peoples are not yet willing to go to war against China, or even against England. I hope my opinions do not reach Hitler as some other confidential messages of mine have done. Anyway, it seemed my duty to send such a warning.

December 19. Sunday. The last few days of luncheons and dinners have been almost unbearable to me, being busy all the time in the Embassy office. And we have declined more than we could accept. High officials like Von Neurath have said they hoped to have us to dinner and now their invitations have failed to be sent. But German university and business men have crowded us with their invitations. Today we were with the Giebels, two days ago the Alberts, a day or two before a prominent bank president. In all these cases, fifteen to twenty guests were present, all very frankly revealing their opposition to the Hitler regime, none giving the "Heil Hitler" greeting or wearing the Party decorations, even when some wore uniforms.

On Thursday, December 16, I went to Leipzig, my old university, to deliver a lecture on George Washington. I had been asked so many times since I have been in Berlin that I finally accepted, but I asked a personal friend there to see that no Party demonstrations were made. Pictures of men in Hitler uniforms, a flag behind me as I spoke, or an audience shouting "Heil Hitler" would have been reported to the United States in a way to ridicule both me and the university where I got my Ph.D. in 1900. Therefore I made my tactful request a week before.

When I arrived a large reception was given by Professor Wartburg. A score of professors were present. Conversations, as in Berlin, criticized the Hitler regime. When I appeared in the famous old university lecture room where Wundt, the distinguished philosopher, used to lecture, there was a vast crowd, students, professors, and persons whom I had seen years ago. Mrs. Arnold Liebisch, wife of the deceased book dealer whom I knew so well when a student in Leipzig, sat just in front of me. And Miss Gray, the English woman who used to entertain students, was beside her. Miss Gray looked little older than in 1899. She had been visiting ancient Leipzig and remained a few days longer to hear what I might say.

I noticed a number of uniforms as I entered the reception room and a few people greeted each other in the Hitler manner, but none did that for me. It was a university crowd and the conversations were most cordial and liberal. It took me an hour to read my Washington address as I had to make each sentence as clear as possible, the university having insisted on an English delivery. To my surprise, the audience understood well enough to applaud statements and laugh at jokes I made. More people in Germany speak and understand English than anywhere else I have ever been where English is not the native language.

After the address a dinner was given and once more people talked freely to me and even to one another. Leipzig University professors are not satisfied with their situation, even less satisfied than Berlin professors seem to be. I was glad to see once more the old university where I first learned history in a critical manner. The old part of the city was much as it used to be when I was there.

December 20. Monday. We called on the French Ambassador and Madame François-Poncet this afternoon at 5 o'clock. Madame François-Poncet reported that, in her opinion, the

Hohenzollerns and the conservatives in general are restless and more bitter than ever. She said she had heard much talk of that sort. But, she added, the leaders of the opposition are so indiscreet that their attitude and plans will be fully revealed to the Nazis and there may be another killing like that of June 30, 1934.

I have heard, and already recorded, much opposition talk, but I do not think a revolt or effort to overthrow Hitler will come in the near future. Everybody knows here how cruelly Hitler-Goering-Goebbels would act if any more opposition is made and consequently nothing will be done, unless the army offers a solid front for a change. But so far as one can judge, the army is under such control that its opposition chiefs can do nothing.

A little later the French Ambassador said: "You are going away at a good time. In my opinion there will be war next spring. One main reason is that Mussolini's situation in Italy is so bad that he will resort to war to save himself. He wants control of the Mediterranean and all the French and Spanish possessions in North Africa. In order to get these, Germany will be called on to help him, and Germany will be given Austria and Czechoslovakia. But all the Danube peoples are more nervous than ever and closer to France than ever before. If Italy and Germany go to war for these areas, we shall have to attack them and England will support us. This is the reason England cannot lend naval assistance to China, nor can we."

I then said: But if France and England would co-operate with the United States in a boycott of Japan, the war on China would be stopped in two months. Can't you do something for this co-operation before it is too late? He agreed that a real boycott would have the effect I indicated, but he said that business people in democratic countries would delay and resist so much that nothing would be done; and, therefore, next spring would be the Mussolini-Hitler time to begin war.

I asked him whether he thought the German masses would support a war. He said: "Yes, they have nothing else to do, if ordered to go to war, but after a few battles they might refuse to fight." My opinion is somewhat the same, except I do not think Hitler is quite ready and so will hold Mussolini back another year.

December 21. Tuesday. At a luncheon given us today as a farewell by Dr. Schacht, conversations were as free and critical as I have ever heard in Germany. Dr. Schacht's removal from his directorship of the Economics Ministry may be taken as one cause. But the head of the International General Electric Company here as well as others from banks and industrial plants were even more outspoken. They were most fearful of the Hitler regime. One thing which worried the electric company chief was the order by Hitler to give up his great administrative building which represents a 10,000,000 mark investment for the company. The company is to be allowed only 6,000,000 marks. He said he told Hitler's official spokesman: "Then I will leave Germany and settle in eastern France." What Hitler said when told this was not stated, but it is clear enough that the electric man would be imprisoned if he tried to leave Germany.

Schacht spoke of the defeat of Germany in 1918 as wholly due to Woodrow Wilson's bringing America into the World War. But I said: Wilson's Fourteen Points were the one great promise of international peace and co-operation and every country on both sides had helped to defeat his purpose. Don't you think Wilson, fifty years from now, will be regarded as one of the greatest Presidents the United States has ever had? He evaded an answer but turned his attention to the Japanese-Chinese war and opposed Germany's alliance with Japan. Then he showed the true German attitude: "If the United States would stop the Japanese war and leave Germany to have her way in Europe, we would have world peace."

I did not comment and others also failed to make remarks. Schacht meant what the army chiefs of 1914 meant when they invaded Belgium, expecting to conquer France in six weeks: *i.e.,* domination and annexation of neighboring little countries, especially north and east. Much as he dislikes Hitler's dictatorship, he, as most other eminent Germans, wishes annexation— without war if possible; with war, if the United States will keep hands off. Much as I admire Schacht for some of his courageous acts, I am now afraid he would not make a good American if he migrated.

December 23. Thursday. Yesterday a most responsible official here from the old regime and still in office came to see me. He is in a position to know a great deal about the drift of things in Hitler's autocracy. He said close friends reported to him that Dr. Schacht is apt to be killed any time, especially next spring. I heard this rumor yesterday. It has been repeated since by another visitor. I wonder if I should send a confidential note warning Schacht before I leave.

Today the Minister from Switzerland came to say farewell. He talked of his country and its dangerous position: "Propaganda for Nazi annexation to Germany goes on there all the time and my government does not dare to try to stop it. The Germans plan to annex Austria peaceably or even by war, ultimately, if necessary, and I see no way to avoid another great war unless the United States, England and France co-operate without further delay."

A letter from the President today says he understood my position here and my need to remain until March 1 as I had explained to him at his Hyde Park home, but the German Foreign Office had compelled him to recall me by January 1. This was not wholly surprising, except for my talk two weeks ago with Von Neurath, who is very clever and who practically denied any such intervention. I may be wrong, but I believe that Under-Secretary Welles may have used his influence with the President. I wrote the President as much today. While I know Hitler-Goering-Goebbels might wish my recall, I am sure the chiefs of the Foreign Office realize how free I would be in the United States to describe the system here in case I were asked to leave. Anyway I am planning to learn the truth of things when I go to Washington. I have been told that Welles has been a definite irritation to the State Department ever since last May.

The Chinese Ambassador and his wife called this afternoon. He still hopes and pleads that the United States and England will put a stop to the Japanese murder of his people. He said he was leaving tonight for Paris. While he did not say so, I believe he is going to protest against French concessions to Japan in French zones of influence in China. I told him to repeat in Paris what he had told me.

December 26. Sunday. I went to Dr. Schacht's house in Dahlem. I wished especially to see Schacht whose life is said to be in danger, but he and his wife were away at their country home about fifty miles from Berlin. I left my card with a few words, carefully written, designed to suggest a possible conversation. More I did not dare say lest it endanger him more. As we came away from Schacht's home, Herbert Goering, nephew of the general who has taken Schacht's place as economic dictator, passed us looking at our car. I am afraid he reported my visit to the government.

In the afternoon we gave a reception to all our staff people, the consular service people, Military and Naval Attachés, and the journalists. There were some seventy guests. It was a delightful meeting.

I forgot to note that my wife and I went to the old Reichstag building on our way home from Schacht's house. There we saw the so-called anti-Communist pictures about which we had heard. It was the most shameful exhibit I have ever seen. No really intellectual person would ever put up such pictures as the thousands we saw, especially not in this famous old legislative hall. The pictures showed Communist contrivances in all countries in the world, and the Communists were all Jews. The pictures showed murders, rapes, thefts, revolutions and seizures of governments. Not a crime one could think of but Jews and Communists were performing it. There were two or three thousand visitors present. I cannot see how any intelligent government official would allow such a show, which concluded with Mussolini and Hitler saving all mankind.

September 20, 1938. Tuesday. Having kept no daily account of things since I left Berlin, I must now review briefly what happened.

We left Berlin on December 29, driving to Hamburg to get

on the *Manhattan,* an American ship. When we walked about the boat, we found that more than half of the second-class passengers were Germans hoping to locate in the United States. More than half of these were Jews. But at our table in the dining room there were several Nazis or Nazi sympathizers. one a West Virginia woman, the wife of the Yugoslav Minister to London. She described to us the London situation where there are apparently many aristocratic Fascists or Nazis now.

There were some interesting newspaper correspondents from Spain on board. They were going home to the United States hoping to tell the real truth about Mussolini's and Hitler's performances in that historic country. They are absolute opponents of Italian-German interference in Spain. I expressed my doubts that the American press would allow them to report just what was going on in that country.

On the last night of the year 1937, our ship set sail from Southampton for New York, where we arrived without serious storms on January 8. Before we reached the harbor, more than a score of journalists had managed to get on the ship and were urging all kinds of interviews. I could not give the facts about my resignation, or recall, or even about what I thought was being planned by Hitler, until my arrival in Washington and my interviews with the President and Secretary Hull.

When I saw the President and told him a little of what I thought of Under-Secretary Welles and his methods, no reply was made. When I talked with Secretary Hull, he confirmed in part what I thought had been done to recall me when it had been understood that I was to retire in March, 1938. For me to have gone back to Berlin on November 1, and for my wife to have spent over $1,000 for furniture, became a disgrace when I received notice on November 23 to return in January. There were and are still officials in the State Department who do not like me or the things I tried to stand for.

Invitations to lecture piled up on my desk from all parts of the country. I spoke in Baltimore twice, in New York several times, and in many other places, being paid liberally for my efforts. When these appointments were ended, in the spring, my wife and I returned to our farm near Round Hill, Virginia.

On May 28, my wife failed to join me, as usual, at breakfast, and I discovered that she had died from a heart attack during the night in her room. It was the greatest shock that ever came to me. Nobody had dreamed that she had any serious illness, although our physician in Berlin had warned her to climb steps slowly. She had a moderate heart trouble, and she had exerted herself socially more than I had. She was only sixty-two years old, and I was sixty-eight. But there she lay, stone dead, and there was no help for it; and I was so surprised and sad I could hardly decide what to do.

I have been four and a half years in Europe with the hope of serving my country. How much one could do is an open question. The present-day world has learned nothing from the World War. Instead of keeping the treaties of 1919-23, nearly all peoples have violated them. Twice as much money is being spent now each year in preparation for another war as was spent in 1913, in spite of the fact that nearly all peoples are bearing the greatest debts known to history. Shall we be confronted by another world war? And would isolation be possible for any great industrial country?

With war preparations and the raising of trade barriers beyond anything known to modern history, another method of government has been adopted in Rome, Berlin and Tokyo. Over that vast area freedom of religion has ceased to exist and universities no longer govern themselves. In a single country 1,600 professors and teachers in high schools have been dismissed. Leaders in several countries have undertaken to dismiss, expel, imprison or kill Jews. There is no doubt that they have at times profiteered, but what other class or people has been free of such members? Anyone who knows the facts of 1914-20 cannot forget that Jews fought bravely on both sides of the terrible war, and some outstanding members of this people gave millions of dollars to save the helpless, even starving, Germans in 1918-20.

In a vast region where religious freedom is denied, where intellectual initiative and discovery are not allowed, and where race hatreds are cultivated daily, what can a representative of the United States do? Democratic peoples must maintain their faiths at home; their representatives must try to improve international co-operation; and on proper occasions they must remind men of the importance of world peace, easier commercial relations, and the significance of democratic civilization for which peoples have struggled since the sixteenth century. With these ideals in mind, I felt that I must represent my country the best I could while dwelling among the Germans, who are by nature more democratic than any other great race in Europe.

Could one be successful? I made addresses on suitable occasions and described our international difficulties, never criticizing the government to which I had been sent. When invitations to partisan affairs were sent to me, I maintained the attitude which our country has maintained since the Presidency of George Washington. Was it the duty of representatives of democratic countries to attend conferences where democracy was ridiculed and attacked? I cannot think so.

The logical outcome of vast war preparations is another war, and what would another war leave of modern civilization? There are curious misunderstandings. Great business and industrial groups failed to recognize the necessity of international co-operation after 1920. Some of their chiefs defeated world peace efforts at Geneva more than once because they thought the sale of arms and war materials more important than world peace. Other groups insisted in 1923 and 1930 on trade barriers which made debt payments impossible. So many influential men have failed to see that inventions, industrial revolution, and financial relations have brought mankind to a point where co-operation and peace are the first conditions of prosperity for the masses of men everywhere.

Principal Persons of the Diary

ATTOLICO, BERNARDO: Italian Ambassador to Germany 1935-1940.

BALUGDZIC, ZIVOJIN: Yugoslav Minister to Germany 1933-1934.

BARTHOU, LOUIS: Foreign Minister of France and initiator of Franco-Soviet alliance; killed October 9, 1934, with King Alexander I of Yugoslavia, in Marseilles.

BASSEWITZ, RUDOLF VON: Chief of Protocol in German Foreign Office.

BENES, EDUARD: President of Czechoslovakia 1933-1938.

BINGHAM, ROBERT WORTH: U. S. Ambassador to Great Britain 1933-1937; died December 18, 1937.

BLOMBERG, WERNER VON: Field Marshal; German Minister of Defense 1933-1938; retired.

BOHLE, E. WILHELM: Leader of Foreign Department of Political Organization of the Nazi Party.

BRUENING, HEINRICH: German Chancellor 1930-1932; now living in the United States.

BULLITT, WILLIAM C.: Special assistant to Secretary of State 1933; U. S. Ambassador to Soviet Union 1933-1936, to France since 1936.

BÜLOW, BERNHARD WILHELM VON: Secretary of State in German Foreign Office; died June 21, 1936.

CERRUTI, VITTORIO: Italian Ambassador to Germany 1932-1935.

CHENG TIEN-FANG: Chinese Ambassador to Germany 1936-1938.

CIANO, COUNT GALEAZZO: Son-in-law of Mussolini; Italian Foreign Minister since June, 1936.

CINCAR-MARKOVIC, ALEKSANDER: Yugoslav Minister to Germany 1935-1937.

CRANE, CHARLES R.: Former U. S. Minister to China; died February 15, 1939.

CUDAHY, JOHN: U. S. Ambassador to Poland 1933-1937; now Ambassador to Belgium.

DARRE, WALTHER: German Minister of Agriculture since 1933.

DAVIS, NORMAN H.: U. S. Ambassador-at-Large 1933-1938; now chairman of American Red Cross.

DIECKHOFF, HANS HEINRICH: Secretary of State in German Foreign Office; German Ambassador to United States since 1937; absent from his post since November, 1938.

DIELS, ROLF: Chief of Prussian secret police under Goering 1932-1934; now provincial governor in the Rhineland.

DIMITROV, GEORGI: Bulgarian Communist tried and acquitted on charge of burning the Reichstag in 1933; now general secretary of the Executive Committee of the III (Communist) International.

DINICHERT, PAUL: Swiss Minister to Germany 1933-1937.

DOLLFUSS, ENGELBERT: Chancellor of Austria from May, 1932, until his assassination by Nazis in July, 1934.

EARLE, GEORGE H.: U. S. Minister to Austria 1933-1934; now Minister to Bulgaria.

EDEN, ANTHONY: British Under-Secretary of State for Foreign Affairs 1931-1933; Lord Privy Seal 1934-1935; Secretary for League of Nations Affairs June-December, 1935; Secretary of State for Foreign Affairs December, 1935-1938; now Secretary for War.

FRANÇOIS-PONCET, ANDRE: French Ambassador to Germany 1930-1939, to Italy 1939-1940.

FRANK, HANS: German Commissioner for Justice 1933-1935; president of the Academy for German Law; Minister without Portfolio in the German government since December, 1934.

FRITSCH, WERNER VON: Colonel General; Baron; head of Reichswehr until 1938; killed outside Warsaw September 22, 1939.

GIBSON, HUGH: U. S. Ambassador to Belgium 1927-1933 and 1937-1938; Ambassador to Brazil 1933-1937.

GILBERT, PRENTISS B.: U. S. Consul at Geneva 1930-1937; Consul-General and Counsellor of Embassy at Berlin 1937-1939; died February 24, 1939.

GOEBBELS, JOSEPH PAUL: Propaganda chief of Nazi party since 1929; German Minister for Propaganda and Public Enlightenment since 1933; president of Reich Culture Chamber and editor of *Der Angriff*.

GOERING, HERMANN WILHELM: Commander-in-Chief of German Air Force; Reich Marshal; president of Reichstag since 1932; Commissioner for the Four-Year Plan; Minister President and Minister of the Interior of Prussia.

HANFSTAENGL, ERNST: Former friend of Hitler and chief of German Foreign Press Bureau; now interned in Canada.

HENDERSON, SIR NEVILE: British Ambassador to Germany 1937-1939.

HERRIOT, EDOUARD: French Minister of State in Doumergue and Flandin Cabinets 1934-1936; president of Chamber of Deputies 1936-1940.

HESS, RUDOLF: Chief of the Central Political Commission of the Nazi party since 1932; Deputy Leader of the party since 1933; German Minister without Portfolio and member of the Cabinet Council.

HINDENBURG, PAUL VON: President of Germany 1925-1934; died August 2, 1934.

HITLER, ADOLF: Leader of the Nazi party; Chancellor of Germany since 1933; Leader and President of Germany since 1934; Commander-in-Chief of German armed forces since 1938.

HOARE, SIR SAMUEL: Secretary of State for India 1931-1935; Secretary of State for Foreign Affairs June-December, 1935; First Lord of the Admiralty 1936-1937; Home Secretary 1937-1940; now British Ambassador to Spain.

HOETZSCH, OTTO: Professor of History at University of Berlin until his dismissal in May, 1935.

HOUSE, COLONEL EDWARD M.: Personal representative of President Wilson in Europe during and after the World War; died March 28, 1938.

HULL, CORDELL: U. S. Secretary of State since 1933.

HUTCHINS, ROBERT M.: President of the University of Chicago since 1929.

ILGNER, MAX: Head of the I. G. Farben (chemical) trust in Germany.

KHERCHOVE DE DEUTERGHEM, COUNT ANDRE DE: Belgian Minister to Germany 1931-1935.

KHINCHUK, LEV MIKHAILOVITCH: Soviet Ambassador to Germany 1930-1934.

LaBOUGLE, EDUARDO: Argentine Minister to Germany 1933-1938.

LAVAL, PIERRE: French Foreign Minister 1934-1936; now Vice-Premier of France under Marshal Petain.

LEE, IVY: Public relations counsel at one time employed by Max Ilgner for advice on German publicity; died November 9, 1934.

LEY, ROBERT: Leader of German Labor Front since 1933; Reich Organization Leader of Nazi party.

LIMBURG-STIRUM, JOHAN PAUL VAN: Dutch Minister to Germany 1927-1937.

LIPSKI, JOSEF: Polish Ambassador to Germany 1934-1939.

LITVINOV, MAXIM: Soviet Commissar of Foreign Affairs 1931-1939; now retired.

LONG, BRECKINRIDGE: U. S. Ambassador to Italy 1933-1936; now Assistant Secretary of State.

LOTHIAN, MARQUESS OF, PHILIP HENRY KERR: Former Liberal party leader in England specializing on foreign affairs; now British Ambassador to the United States.

LOUIS FERDINAND, PRINCE OF HOHENZOLLERN: Second son of former Crown Prince Wilhelm of Germany.

LUDENDORFF, ERICH: German general in World War; associated with Hitler in 1923; died December 20, 1937.

LUTHER, HANS: German Ambassador to Washington April, 1933-March, 1937.

MacDONALD, J. RAMSAY: British Prime Minister 1929-1935; Lord President of the Council 1935-1937; died November 9, 1937.

MacMURRAY, JOHN V. A.: U. S. Minister to Baltic nations 1933-1936; now Ambassador to Turkey.

MARCKS, ERICH C.: Professor of History at University of Berlin.

MASTNY, VOJTECH: Czechoslovak Minister to Germany 1933-1939.

McDONALD, JAMES G.: League of Nations High Commissioner for German Refugees 1933-1935; now president of Brooklyn Institute of Arts and Sciences.

MEISSNER, OTTO: Secretary of State in the office of Reich President.

MESSERSMITH, GEORGE S.: U. S. Consul General in Berlin 1930-1934; now Ambassador to Cuba.

MOFFAT, JAY PIERREPONT: Chief of Division of Western European Affairs in State Department 1932-1935; chief of Division of European Affairs 1937-1940; now U. S. Minister to Canada.

MOORE, R. WALTON: Assistant Secretary of State 1933-1937; Counsellor of State Department since 1937.

MOREHEAD, JOHN M.: U. S. Minister to Sweden 1930-1933.

MUSSOLINI, BENITO: Head of the government and Prime Minister of Italy since 1922; First Marshal of Italian Empire since 1938.

NEURATH, KONSTANTIN VON: German Minister for Foreign Affairs 1932-1938; now Protector of Bohemia and Moravia.

OBERLAENDER, GUSTAV: Founder of the Oberlaender Trust administered by the Carl Schurz Foundation; died November 30, 1936.

ORSENIGO, CESARE: Papal Nuncio in Germany since 1930.

PAPEN, FRANZ VON: German Chancellor 1932; Vice-Chancellor 1933-1934; Ambassador to Austria 1934-1938; now Ambassador to Turkey.

PHILLIPS, WILLIAM: Under-Secretary of State 1933-1936; U. S. Ambassador to Italy since 1936.

PHIPPS, SIR ERIC: British Ambassador to Germany 1933-1937, to France 1937-1939.

PILSUDSKI, JOSEF: Dictator of Poland until his death May 12, 1935.

REICHENAU, WALTHER VON: German Field Marshal.

RIBBENTROP, JOACHIM VON: German Ambassador-at-Large 1935, to Great Britain 1936-1938; German Foreign Minister since 1938.

RITTER, KARL: Chief of Economic Section of German Foreign Office; German Ambassador to Brazil 1937-1938.

ROEHM, ERNST: Chief of staff of German S.A. (Brownshirts); collaborator with Hitler until his killing, at Hitler's order, June 30, 1934.

ROOSEVELT, FRANKLIN D.: President of the United States since 1933.

ROPER, DANIEL C.: Secretary of Commerce 1933-1938.

ROSENBERG, ALFRED: Director of Foreign Office of Nazi party; editor and authority on Russia and the Baltic.

RUST, BERNHARD: German Minister of Science, Education and Popular Instruction since 1934.

SACKETT, FREDERIC M., JR.: U. S. Ambassador to Germany 1930-1933.

SAHM, HEINRICH: Mayor of Berlin 1931-1935; Minister to Norway 1936.

SCHACHT, HJALMAR HORACE GREELEY: Former German Minister of Economics and president of the Reichsbank.

SCHEFFER, PAUL: Editor of the *Berliner Tageblatt* 1933-1936; U. S. correspondent for German newspapers.

SCHLEICHER, KURT VON: German general; Chancellor 1932-1933; killed by Nazis June 30, 1934.

SCHURMAN, JACOB GOULD: U. S. Ambassador to Germany, 1925-1930.

SCHUSCHNIGG, KURT VON: Chancellor of Austria 1934-1938; imprisoned by Nazis since occupation of Austria in March, 1938.

SCHWERIN VON KROSIGK, LUTZ VON: German Minister of Finance since 1932.

SEECKT, HANS VON: German general; creator of the Reichswehr; died December 27, 1936.

SHOTWELL, JAMES T.: Professor of History at Columbia University.

SIMON, SIR JOHN: Secretary of State for Foreign Affairs in British Cabinet 1931-1935; Home Secretary 1935-1937; Chancellor of the Exchequer 1937-1940.

STREICHER, JULIUS: Editor since 1923 of *Der Stuermer*; Nazi party chief of Franconia since 1933.

SURITZ, JACOB: Soviet Ambassador to Germany 1934-1937, to Paris 1937-1939.

TAUSCHITZ, STEPHAN: Austrian Minister to Germany 1933-1938.

THYSSEN, FRITZ: German industrialist; heavy contributor to Hitler's campaign funds; in 1939 a fugitive from Germany.

TOGO, SHIGENORI: Japanese Ambassador to Germany 1937-1938.

TUGWELL, REXFORD G.: Assistant Secretary of Agriculture 1933; Under-Secretary of Agriculture 1934.

VIERECK, GEORGE SYLVESTER: German-born publicist in United States.

WELLES, SUMNER: Assistant Secretary of State since April 6, 1933; Ambassador to Cuba April-December, 1933.

WHITE, FRANCIS: Assistant Secretary of State 1927-1933; U. S. Minister to Czechoslovakia July-December, 1933.

WIEDEMANN, CAPTAIN FRITZ: Hitler's commanding officer in World War; personal adjutant to Hitler from 1934; since 1938 German Consul General in San Francisco.

WILSON, HUGH: U. S. Minister to Switzerland 1927-1937; Ambassador to Germany since 1938; absent from his post since November, 1938.

Index

Czechoslovakia, foreign policy, 230, 234. *See also* Annexation and Germany, relations with Czechoslovakia

Czechoslovak Minister, *see* Mastny

Daniels, Josephus, 97, 178
Danish Minister, 80
Danzig, 361, 363
Darre, Walther, 113, 190, 199, 259, 263, 314
Davidson, 46, 108, 203-04
Davies, Joseph E., 380-81, 408-09, 426
Davignon, Jacques, 349
Davis, John W., 280
Davis, Norman H., 6, 8, 12, 37, 48, 107, 115, 428
Davis, Richard J., 243
Debts, German, 4-6, 8-9, 13-14, 16, 21-22, 49, 62, 69-70, 73-75, 80-82, 104, 109, 111-12, 114, 119-20, 122, 126-27, 129-30, 136-37, 173-74, 176, 196, 219, 255, 302-03, 344, 384, 388
Deeds, Edward A., 200-01, 283
Dern, George Henry, 97
Deterding, Sir Henri, 186-87
Deuel, Wallace R., 162
Deutsche Christen, see Religion, Nazi
Dickstein, Samuel, 52, 131
Dieckhoff, Hans Heinrich, 25, 26, 32, 76, 101, 102, 155-56, 157-58, 184, 203-05, 233, 269, 282, 298, 311, 312, 318, 346, 351-53, 367-69, 386-87, 394, 395, 406, 408, 410, 426-28, 434, 436, 438
Diehn, August, 55, 60, 130
Diels, Rudolf, 20, 26, 29, 65, 67
Dietrich, Hermann R., 284
Dimitrov, Georgi, 65-67
Dinichert, Paul, 230, 259, 281-82, 361, 430-31, 443
Disarmament, *see* Armaments, limitation of
Dodd, John D., 8, 97, 207
Dodd, Martha, 7, 13, 22, 32, 64, 80, 118, 147, 172, 186, 188, 239, 265, 280, 333, 357, 404

Dodd, Mrs. Martha J., 3, 7-8, 11, 22, 32, 57-58, 71, 73, 77, 82, 87, 108, 116, 119, 130-31, 141, 164, 186, 207-09, 262, 273, 280, 325, 333, 384, 404, 418-19, 425, 446
Dodd, William E., interviews with Hitler, 48-49, 88-89; on conduct of Ger.-U. S. relations, 390-91; on democracy, 414-15; on economic nationalism, 6, 46-47; on European situation, 331-32, 341, 347, 446; on Hitler, Goering and Goebbels, 90-91, 123, 171, 231, 236-37, 276, 322, 323, 393; on Nazi system and opposition to it, 179-80, 260, 321; on Roosevelt, 84-85; on U. S. diplomatic service, *see* Foreign Service, U. S.; on University of Chicago, 96, 335-36, 337; on war and peace, 34-35, 46, 51, 64, 198, 208, 252, 446-47; refusal to attend Nazi Party Day, 24-26, 28, 29, 32, 44, 48, 267, 269, 349, 356, 425, 427, 434, 438; speeches and press statements, 13, 30, 43, 46-47, 50, 51, 55, 56, 60, 62, 95-96, 159, 161, 171-72, 207, 209, 225, 252, 253, 255-56, 202, 336, 342, 406, 412, 426, 439-40, 445; talks with President Roosevelt, 4-6, 7-8, 97-98, 207-08, 213-14, 426, 428-29, 445; travels in Germany and Europe, 22-23, 60-62, 142-44, 147-48, 153-54, 160-61, 181, 260, 265-66, 325-26; 350-51, 404-06; trips to U. S., 92-100, 205-16, 333-38, 425-30; writings, xi, 3, 4, 28, 128, 135, 207, 238, 429
Dodd, William E., Jr., 7, 11, 22, 64, 67, 80, 117, 131, 181, 348-49, 428-29
Dollfuss, Englebert, 29, 72, 82, 132, 133
Doriot, Jacques, 348
Douglas, Lewis W., 181
Drexler, 34
Dufour von Feronce, Albert, 320-21
Duggan, Stephen, 92
Duke, James B., 60